# Additional Praise for *Drawing Fire*

'While many label Israel "an apartheid state", Benjamin Pogrund actually experienced apartheid, from Sharpeville to Mandela's liberation. He is therefore well placed to dissect the easy analogy between Zionist Israel and apartheid South Africa. This critical and detailed account of the complexity of Israel's situation will not please some, but it will be an eye-opener for many who have hitherto accepted the conventional wisdom. For those who do not think in monochrome, this is an important book.'

—**Colin Shindler**, Pears Senior Research Fellow in Israel Studies,
SOAS, University of London

# Drawing Fire

## BY THE SAME AUTHOR

*Robert Sobukwe: How Can Man Die Better*

*Nelson Mandela*

*War of Words: Memoir of a South African Journalist*

*Shared Histories: A Palestinian-Israeli Dialogue* (coeditor)

# Drawing Fire

## *Investigating the Accusations of Apartheid in Israel*

Benjamin Pogrund

ROWMAN & LITTLEFIELD
Lanham • Boulder • New York • London

Published by Rowman & Littlefield
4501 Forbes Boulevard, Suite 200, Lanham, Maryland 20706
www.rowman.com

16 Carlisle Street, London W1D 3BT, United Kingdom

British Library Cataloguing in Publication Information Available

**Library of Congress Cataloging-in-Publication Data**

Pogrund, Benjamin, author.
Drawing fire : investigating the accusations of apartheid in Israel / Benjamin Pogrund.
pages cm
Includes bibliographical references and index.
1. National characteristics, Israeli—Political aspects. 2. Israel—Social conditions—21st century. 3.
Israel—Politics and government—1993– 4. Israel—Ethnic relations. 5. Zionism. 6. Apartheid. 7.
Human rights—Israel. 8. Human rights—South Africa. 9. Palestinian Arabs—Government policy—
Israel. 10. Arab-Israeli conflict—Influence. I. Title.
DS119.76.P64 2014
956.9405'4--dc23
2014006848

ISBN 978-1-4422-2683-8 (cloth : alk. paper)
ISBN 978-1-4422-7575-1 (pbk. : alk. paper)
ISBN 978-1-4422-2684-5 (electronic)

Printed in the United States of America

For my parents, Bertha and Nathan Pogrund, who gave me life, and for Anne, who shares it with me

ISRAEL & THE PALESTINIAN TERRITORIES TODAY

- - - - 1949 Armistice Line

LEBANON

SYRIA

Golan

Haifa

Nablus

WEST BANK

Tel Aviv

Ramallah

Jerusalem

Ashkelon

Gaza

Hebron

JORDAN

Beer Sheba

ISRAEL

EGYPT

Negev

# Contents

Foreword     ix

Preface     xiii

Acknowledgements     xxi

1   The Beginning     1

2   Freedom and War     29

3   Inside the Green Line     53

4   The Occupation     89

5   What Was Apartheid?     115

6   Are They the Same?     133

7   Comparing Israel and Apartheid South Africa     139

8   The Critics (1)     153

9   The Critics (2)     183

10   Boycotts     221

11   The Big Issues     245

12   The Way Forward     269

Appendix 1     281

Appendix 2     283

Appendix 3     285

Appendix 4     287

| | |
|---|---|
| Notes | 289 |
| Selected Bibliography | 305 |
| Index | 307 |
| About the Author | 323 |

# Foreword

Is Israel an apartheid state? There is nobody to trust more for a dispassionate, informed answer than Benjamin Pogrund. He has unique experience. He has lived the question as a victim of apartheid for twenty-six years of valiant reporting in South Africa and more than fifteen years as an Israeli citizen in Jerusalem, deeply sympathetic to Palestinians under occupation. In Israel, he founded the Yakar Centre for Social Concern in 1997, which was dedicated to fostering dialogue between Jews and Jews, Jews and Muslims, Jews and Christians, and Palestinians and Israelis.

In South Africa, he was jailed and persecuted as an enemy of the state and for five years denied a passport. His crime was to recognise and objectively report the lives of blacks under apartheid, the cruelties inflicted on the leaders, and the seeds of the political aspirations that finally led to freedom. The mainstream press was not doing that. The townships were off limits. His brave newspaper, the *Rand Daily Mail*, was critical of the policies of apartheid, and its owners yielded to government pressure and shut it down in 1985. But it was the scrupulously accurate reporting by Pogrund, of torture in the prisons among much else, that most enraged the Afrikaner government (and eventually stirred world opinion), and it was the honest competence of this straight journalism that impressed the nascent black leadership. Here was a white Jewish reporter prepared to risk his neck to find and reveal what was happening – favourable or not to their movement – and whatever the pressure never reveal his sources. It was a stand for which the government put him in prison, and persecuted and investigated him as a threat to national security. It was also a stand that won Pogrund the trust of the African resistance, in particular, Nelson Mandela and Robert Sobukwe. Pogrund was the first non-family guest in twenty years welcomed in prison by Nelson Mandela. He became a biographer of both Mandela and Sobukwe, and in the later years continued speaking for them.

He found it hard to write this book. It had to be hard because when you know both scenes so well, and don't come loaded with preconceptions, you have to think and find the right words. That's an exercise in cognition and judgment unknown to the grandiose ideologues and unthinking boycotters prominent on the Left in Europe, and fringe academics and credulous students whose vehemence in indicting Israel as an apartheid state is matched only by the depths of their ignorance of both societies. Far easier for the glib to purloin the odium of 'apartheid' than painstakingly to assemble evidence for the indictment and assess it judiciously, sparing no one. Look how Pogrund sets the scene:

> Each of the two main competing groups, Jews and Arabs, has right on its side, through history, land, religion, geography and tradition. The dilemma is how to satisfy their separate demands and aspirations to a tiny piece of land. The problem is bedevilled because in the long struggle between them, neither side has always behaved well, inflicting death and destruction on the other.

He empathises with Jewish fears about annihilation, and he empathizes with Palestinian cries for freedom. He believes in Israel's right to exist but thinks occupation is wrong. I know the anguish of his ambivalence, but also the determination he brings to resolving the dilemmas. He tracks the history of Israel since its founding, the displacement of Palestinians, the Arab invasions, the intifada, the incursions of the settlers, the attempts to achieve the two-state solution he supports, and the war of extermination by Hamas, who pledged never to recognise Israel. He has compiled an incisive comparative tabulation of all the civil society discriminations against Arabs in Israel and whites against blacks in apartheid South Africa. There is no comparison. The apartheid propagandists stand as vainly naked as the fairy tale emperor admiring his gorgeous raiment. This is not because Israel is without sin, but because the anti-Semitic mob never lets a certainty stand in the way of a slogan. Forget the democratic practices of Israel, its elections and higher education open to all, its free and highly critical press, its independent judiciary, its equal welfare benefits and medical treatments caring for Jew and Arab. Close an eye to all the oppressions of the Arab states surrounding Israel, the suicide bombings by the jihadists glorified by the Palestinian Authority, which poisons the minds of children in its schools and viewers of its television programs. Why do the apartheid propagandists ignore, and thereby implicitly condone, the human rights abuses of others? Why do the United States and Europe continue to finance the odious 'education' programs of the Palestinian Authority that expunge Israel from the map? One hears Yeats again: 'The best lack all conviction while the worst are full of passionate intensity'.

Pogrund is gentle in his assessment of the most credible of the campaigners for a boycott of Israel, Archbishop Tutu. How is it, one may ask, that this good man became associated with apartheid defamers? The sad answer is that while he was an inspiring leader in South Africa, he knows too little about Israel. Pogrund has conversed with Tutu. He corrects his factual errors on discrimination in Israel. The archbishop means well, but he is close to selective sanctimony when he says he supports Israel's right to exist while lending his good name to people who would like to see every Jew dead.

Pogrund, by contrast, roundly exposes the liars and hypocrites among the committed enemies of Israel – but he is unflinching in his criticisms of Israel. He condemns the occupation of the West Bank 'with all the consequent injustice, harshness and cruelty together with the creeping settlement of Jews in the territory and East Jerusalem, plus its siege of the Gaza Strip'. The blindly arrogant settlers and their right-wing supporters are 'guilty of colonialism, a crime in international law'. They must be checked in discrimination against Palestinians, he says, or they will deserve the apartheid label with consequences grave beyond measure for Israel.

The boycott of Israel called for by the apartheid campaigners provides a cheap moral thrill, but it intensifies the fears of Israelis, driving them to the Right, and it does nothing for the Palestinians whose livelihoods are tied to the innovative Israel. The Left's case for boycotts is that sanctions freed South Africa. It is questionable. The opposite has been argued – that industrial sanctions increased the society's reliance on the conservative agricultural sector, the core of what became the Afrikaner Volksfront of extremist separatist groups.

Pogrund's view is that apartheid collapsed in South Africa 'when it became clear to those whites in power that it was not in their own self-interest to perpetuate by force what was clearly an unjust system of oppression, and when black leaders extended the hand of reconciliation to their former oppressors'. He is too modest to underline his part in that. Pogrund's years and years of reporting of the human rights abuses were surely central to the gradual disaffection with apartheid among decent South African whites and governments worldwide, but especially the US Congress. An opinion formed into a conviction: apartheid could not be tolerated any longer.

I have known Pogrund and his work for forty years. As, successively, editor of the *Sunday Times* of London and the *Times*, and editorial director of *US News and World Report*, I came to admire more and more his courage and judgment in reporting for us from South Africa, as I now applaud him for the intellectual integrity that has enabled him to distil what he learned in both the incipient black nation of South Africa and the embattled nation state of Israel.

Everyone who cares about how Palestinians and Israelis may live together in the same neighbourhood in freedom and without fear should read this compelling book, but especially the genuine idealists worldwide among the apartheid campaigners. Amid the detritus of the propagandists, the dedication to truth of Benjamin Pogrund, reporter, is morally exhilarating.

Sir Harold Evans
former editor of the *Sunday Times* and the *Times*
author of *The American Century* and *My Paper Chase*

# Preface

Living in apartheid South Africa was easy in moral terms. Living in Israel is difficult.

In apartheid South Africa the choice was clear and beyond escape: it was good versus evil. *Apartheid* was the Afrikaans word for apartness, which meant racial segregation and discrimination enforced by the white minority on the country's black, coloured and Asian peoples. It was wrong and inhuman, denying freedom and stunting and destroying lives. The problem for concerned people was not merely to do the obvious thing and reject apartheid, but to decide what to do about it. That is, how far to go in opposing it against an increasingly tyrannous government: from being a passive bystander to imperilling your liberty, even your life.

In Israel, the moral choices are many and complex and are a daily challenge. Each of the two main competing groups, Jews and Arabs, has right on its side, through history, land, religion, geography and tradition. The dilemma is how to satisfy their separate demands and aspirations to a tiny piece of land. The problem is bedevilled because in the long struggle between them, neither side has always behaved well, inflicting death and destruction on the other. Each side believes that it is in the right, and each side fears and rejects the other. Jews and Arabs are a mirror image of each other: each believes that force is the only language that the other understands; each believes that the other is trying to wipe it out. That there is some truth in these beliefs on both sides adds to the complexities.

I straddle both apartheid South Africa and today's Israel – not merely by having lived in both countries, but because I have been immersed in the problems and conflicts of each and in search for solutions.

I was born in Cape Town and before the age of ten was taking part in *Habonim* (The Builders), a Jewish socialist youth movement. As a teenager I held leadership positions. In May 1948, as a fifteen-year-old, I was in the Habonim group which performed folk dances at the Jewish celebration in Cape Town of the creation of the State of Israel. I grew up steeped in belief in Zionism as a beautiful and pure creed of Jewish emancipation after centuries of persecution. I was emotionally filled with awareness of my Jewishness: with the knowledge that the aunts and uncles and cousins whom my parents had left behind in Lithuania in the villages of Abel and Dusadt when they emigrated to South Africa in the 1920s had been murdered by the Nazis on 25 August 1941. The report of the SS Einsatzgruppen – Action Groups – signed by Jager, SS-Standartenfuhrer, on 1 December 1941, recorded the killing of '112 Jews, 627 Jewesses, 421 Jewish children' in Obeliai (Abel). It said: 'In Lithuania there are no more Jews, apart from Jewish workers and their families. The distance between from [*sic*] the assembly point to the graves was on average 4 to 5km'.

Also in May 1948, I was politically interested enough as a high school pupil to go and watch South Africa's general election results shown on a giant board outside the *Cape Times* newspaper in the city and to share in the shock of the unexpected victory of the National Party, the vehicle of an exclusive white Afrikaner nationalism with its programme of apartheid. I had my first political experiences – and made my first friendships across colour lines – in the student leadership at the University of Cape Town and in the National Union of South African Students in fighting the government as it imposed apartheid on what were called the 'open' universities because they admitted students of all colours (but maintained social segregation on campus). Then in the Liberal Party, canvassing for support in black townships and learning about nonracism; that was continued after moving to Johannesburg and working in the party's branch in the black ghetto of Sophiatown, which was soon to be demolished and its black residents, evicted at gunpoint, replaced by whites; it was renamed Triomf, Afrikaans for Triumph.

Involvement with South Africa superseded interest in Zionism and was put into practice during twenty-six years as a journalist with the *Rand Daily Mail* in Johannesburg, pioneering the reporting and analysing of black politics and black existence, from housing, education and health in urban ghettoes and rural areas to resistance to apartheid and torture and abusive conditions in prisons. It meant having friends, and links with people, who were visionary and brave beyond description in opposing apartheid and in defying the government's intolerance of dissent. Reporting on apartheid also led to a short spell in prison, a host of court cases with two criminal prosecutions – one went on for four years – denial of a passport for more than five years and security police harassment.

So I wasn't only a South African, or a white South African journalist, but I was totally steeped in what apartheid was and what it was inflicting on people.

The *Rand Daily Mail* was the leading voice against apartheid and paid for it through unremitting hostility from the government and its own management. It was closed down in 1985 by its owners under government pressure. I emigrated to Britain and worked in Fleet Street. In 1997, there was *aliyah* (emigration) to Israel at the invitation of Rabbi Michael Rosen, head of Yakar, an Orthodox Jewish synagogue and learning community in North London. He moved Yakar to Jerusalem and asked me to come and open a Centre for Social Concern to bring together Israelis and Palestinians, Jews and Muslims, and Jews and Christians, and to tackle the discord among Jews caused by differences in practising Judaism.

It was a good time to start a dialogue centre. Peace in the Middle East was in sight. The promise of the Oslo Accords, which had been agreed between Israelis and Palestinians four years earlier, was strong: Palestinians had accepted the reality of Israel's existence and Israel had accepted the reality of a Palestinian state-to-come. Many problems had to be resolved for a two-state solution: the borders, Jerusalem as a capital for both peoples, refugees, settlements, security and access to holy sites. But everything was possible, so it seemed. However, Oslo failed to bring peace because each side undermined it: Palestinians resorted to violence and Israel continued to build settlements on the West Bank. Suspicion, fear, hatred and rejection became dominant. It's been a roller coaster ride with hope rising and falling from year to year and sometimes from week to week.

Sometimes, tracking and trying to understand the changing scene has been a throwback to the South Africa of the late 1980s and early 1990s in what proved to be the dying years of apartheid: day after day, the bits and pieces of information, the statements by leaders, the accusations and mutual recriminations, the hints and lots and lots of disinformation. Living in London, I was one of the three or four people who were mainstays on television and radio and in newspapers, called on to explain and analyse events. The number of TV and radio commentaries that I did was a rough barometer of what was happening in South Africa. Hardly a week went by without at least one or more commentaries. Some days there were up to eight, from Channel 4 News at 6 a.m. until the BBC World Service late at night. I always kept in mind what the late Donald Woods, who left South Africa and lived in exile in Britain, told people who were always asking how long apartheid would last: 'It will last five years – and I've been saying that for the past 20 years'.

In Israel, South African experience has been crucial in drawing two particular lessons from the anti-apartheid struggle:

- Make contact, create trust: Despite the best apartheid efforts to keep whites and blacks separate, people climbed over the barriers and made friends. Those relationships were all-important when circumstances changed and negotiations began.

- Nonviolence: In 1961 the African National Congress turned to armed resistance. But it decided not to kill white civilians, out of belief in Mahatma Gandhi's nonviolence philosophy and for strategic reasons. The policy was basically adhered to. As a result, when circumstances changed and negotiations began, it was a significant factor in ensuring that whites did not fear being swept into the sea by the black majority and were willing to yield power. In contrast, Palestinian suicide bombings and drive-by shootings – unknown in South Africa – confirmed Jewish insecurities and fears and pushed most of them to the right. The violence has been counterproductive for achieving peace. So too is the Israeli violence through occupation of the West Bank.

   For twelve and a half years, until early 2010, the Centre for Social Concern tried to make a modest contribution to bringing about peace. It organised hundreds of public and private meetings in Jerusalem and elsewhere in Israel. Speakers from across the spectrum debated and argued every conceivable subject. Nothing was beyond scrutiny. Emotions often ran high; the only rule was that personal abuse was barred. This is a tiny sampling of meetings: Facing fundamentalism in Islam and Judaism; The Palestinian state: Do good fences make good neighbours?; Is Israel's Army losing its way?; Zionism: Hope and reality; Must journalists be loyal to the government?; Business ethics as a challenge to Judaism; Reflections on Jonah; Yiddish in Russia; Why has my child left Judaism?; How top foreign reporters view Israel; Is apartheid relevant for us?

   Many on both sides were eager to know about each other. We ran seminars, which were held overnight alternately in Palestine and Israel, in cooperation with a Palestinian organisation, such as on an issue much argued over between Jews and Arabs: 'Who got here first?' But we added a subtext which took the argument to another level: 'And does it matter?' We hired buses and took groups of Israelis to tour Palestinian areas, including the Gaza Strip – with a Palestinian guide and explanatory meetings included – and bussed Palestinians to Israeli areas with an Israeli guide.

   The second Palestinian *intifada* (uprising) of October 2000 ended these close encounters. After that it became difficult – even more so than under apartheid – to maintain personal contact. There has been too much killing and threat. Security is the reason and the excuse. Israel does not let its citizens cross into Palestinian territory without permission and severely restricts Palestinians entering Israel. Scheduling meetings in Jerusalem with Palestinian speakers became difficult because it was usually uncertain until late whether Israeli authorities – the Civil Administration for the West Bank, which means the army – would give permission.

   Despite these problems, a project with a Palestinian organisation shared Jewish and Arab experiences from their different perspectives and led to publication of a book, *Shared Histories: A Palestinian-Israeli Dialogue*, containing fourteen academic papers and discussions. Even during the tense times and a growing gulf, with Palestinians increasingly saying no to 'normalisation', a follow-up project was carried out with publication of *Shared Narratives: A Palestinian-Israeli Dialogue* in 2013.

\* \* \*

Of course I have constantly looked for comparisons between the apartheid to which I was witness in South Africa and what I see happening between Israelis and Palestinians. There are many times when I feel deep anguish when I see the fear and suffering of Jews, and many times when I feel deep anguish when I see the deprivation and suffering of Palestinians. I have benefited from the soul-searching debate in Israel – the information, reappraisals and analyses of the past that began to emerge in the 1980s, attributable to a maturing society and the opening to public scrutiny of government files covering the 1948 period in which the state came into being.[1]

I have had to struggle to relate the image of the pure and beautiful Zionism with which I grew up to the reality of Jewish behaviour, which at times is inhumane and beyond toleration and which has grown worse with Israel's occupation of the West Bank/Judea and Samaria and the spread of settlements. The ugly reality must not be denied, as some do from the standpoint that Israel can do no wrong or that it must be defended at all costs against its enemies. Anti-Semitism is certainly a factor behind some of the attacks on Israel, but it must not be overstated, as some do, as a means of counterattacking. The Holocaust is inextricably bound up with Israel's existence, but it must not be misused, as some do, as an emotional weapon to silence genuine critics. At the other extreme, Israel's failings and mistakes must not be used, as some do, as an excuse – even more, a cover – for condemning Israel to the extent of denying its very right to exist.

Israel's accomplishments are wondrous; but it is not a perfect society and its people sometimes behave badly and violate their moral standards, like people anywhere in the world. They must be judged and treated the same as other people and countries. None of it has lessened my belief in Zionism or the imperative of Israel as a home and sanctuary for Jews.

So I haven't merely been a Jew who came on aliyah, but I have been steeped in trying to understand the conflict between Jews and Arabs and in looking for answers.

The United Nations World Conference Against Racism held in Durban in 2001 was a turning point. Until then I had in a general way equated the pain of the oppressed in South Africa with the pain of oppressed Palestinians. With the UN conference coming up, Tova Herzl, Israel's ambassador in Pretoria, asked me to join the Israeli government delegation because of my

South African background. I hesitated: I was a journalist and it wasn't my role to be involved with government. Then she sent me the draft resolutions for the conference prepared at the third regional preparatory conference held in Tehran in February 2001. In the English phrase, I was gobsmacked. I knew apartheid and had already learned enough about Israel to know that the draft was a concoction of lies and distortions. To make it worse, the Iranian government had excluded Israeli and Jewish NGOs from around the world from the conference – a strange way to prepare for an international meeting which was to consider issues crucial to everyone.

The actual text accused Israel of 'a new kind of apartheid, a crime against humanity'; it singled out Israel for alleged 'ethnic cleansing of the Arab population of historic Palestine'; it said Zionism was 'based on racial superiority'. The fourth and last regional conference, in Geneva in May, was supposed to finalise the text. The UN secretariat omitted the Tehran gross wording. But the Arab and Muslim states rejected this and secured inclusion inside brackets – which meant proposed but not agreed – of the Tehran language.

Surprised and angry, I recognised that the calumnies and the dishonesties were organised and orchestrated. I joined the Israeli delegation and was in Durban for the tail end of the conference of NGOs. The spirit of the draft resolution was fully in the open, in a hatefest against Israel and Jews, denouncing what was called Israel's 'brand of racism and apartheid and other racist crimes against humanity' and urging its 'total isolation'. Copies of the infamous tsarist police forgery 'Protocols of Zion' were on sale. But the NGOs overreached themselves. They were so malevolently extreme that their resolutions were almost entirely rejected by the conference of governments which followed immediately after. The 9/11 Twin Towers attack three days later pushed Durban to the backburner. It took a few years for those who had pushed their extremism at Durban to get going again in earnest and to seek to link today's Israel with apartheid South Africa.

Now Israel is accused of being 'like apartheid South Africa' or it is the 'new apartheid' or it is 'reminiscent of apartheid' or it 'resembles apartheid' or it is 'tantamount' to apartheid or it has 'elements' of apartheid or it perpetrates the 'principle' of apartheid, or it is even 'worse than apartheid'. These phrases are used mainly in regard to Israel's occupation of the West Bank, but some critics also apply them to Israel itself. They are more than mere words: the obvious aim is to have Israel declared as illegitimate a state as was South Africa and hence open to international sanctions. And even more, at least for some, to deny the validity of its existence.

If the apartheid accusation is correct, then Israel merits harsh condemnation. For it to be an apartheid state would be a betrayal of the Jewish ethics which underpins its existence, of the dreams of its founders and of the words of the Declaration of Independence of 14 May 1948:

The State of Israel . . . will promote the development of the country for the benefit of all its inhabitants; will be based on the precepts of liberty, justice and peace taught by the Hebrew Prophets; will uphold the full social and political equality of all its citizens, without distinction of race, creed or sex; will guarantee full freedom of conscience, worship, education and culture; will safeguard the sanctity and inviolability of the shrines and Holy Places of all religions; and will dedicate itself to the principles of the Charter of the United Nations.

Use of the word *apartheid* in the world has broadened and softened, referring to just about anything that means separation. In Cuba, the ban on tourists staying at swank hotels was labelled as 'tourism apartheid' before it ended in 2008. A ban on some bathing costumes on Brazil's beaches was described as 'bikini apartheid'. In Britain, bans on same-sex marriages were described as 'a form of sexual apartheid'. The fact that racial minorities, especially blacks, are the majority in US prisons is called the 'New American apartheid'.

However, even with all this, the word remains powerful and continues to convey the evil that it was in South Africa. It's a grave charge to level against Israel. If Israel is an apartheid state, it would deserve to be shunned and cast out by the civilised nations of the world. International sanctions would be justified to punish it and to pressure it to change.

But is Israel the new apartheid state? Merely saying so doesn't make it so. Repeating the phrase over and over doesn't make it true, but is merely primitive propaganda used either out of ignorance or malevolence.

\* \* \*

Religion is at the heart of Israel's existence and is at the same time the reason for threats to its survival: the Muslim world rejected the founding of a Jewish state, and many have continued to seek its destruction despite peace treaties signed by Egypt and Jordan. Iran in particular has continued as an implacable enemy, with direct threats of annihilation and also working indirectly through Hamas and Hezbollah.

The Israel-Palestine conflict has wide consequences, affecting the neighbouring countries of Egypt, Jordan, Syria and Lebanon, plus the Middle East as a whole and stretching also to the West's relations with the Arab-Muslim world. The extent to which the conflict actually does affect the West's relations is itself a matter for debate. Is it correct, as some claim, that Israel is the root cause of the Middle East's tensions and instability? It certainly is a significant factor. However, that deep forces going far beyond Israel are primary factors was evident from early in 2011, with popular protests and uprisings in Tunisia, Egypt, Yemen, Jordan, Syria and elsewhere. Resentment of dictatorships and gaps between corrupt elites and the deprived masses of people were endemic for many decades and were bound to burst into the open sooner or later, with unknown consequences for Arab relations with Israel and the world at large.

\* \* \*

For more than forty years apartheid was a focus for international attention, with extensive reporting and analyses in newspapers, radio and television and many books. The considerable output is vastly overtaken by the reporting and study of Israel/Palestine. It's a never-ending torrent, attesting to the broader interests at stake and greater complexities. Dealing with the colossal mass of scholarly and non-scholarly material is a formidable task. What follows here is not a comprehensive history of Israel-Palestine but a selection, distillation and interpretation of events through the eyes and senses of this observer. The information and reflections will deal with aspects of the two countries, including similarities and differences, exploring long-held myths, claims, counterclaims, proposed actions against Israel and, finally, looking for the way forward.

In telling the story I have set out to bring together what I have learnt in South Africa and Israel. It will no doubt evoke both agreement and disagreement, hopefully more of the former than the latter.

# Acknowledgements

I have been fortunate to have had the help and guidance of many friends and colleagues in writing this book.

Professor Milton Shain has been friend and mentor, always willing to share his knowledge and ideas. He read my early and later drafts and was continually encouraging. As director of the Isaac and Jessie Kaplan Centre for Jewish Studies and Research at the University of Cape Town, he invited me as a visiting fellow for two years in succession; I am deeply grateful to him and the trustees. Janine Blumberg, the centre's administrator, made the visits possible, and I thank her and other members of staff for making me feel so welcome; Veronica Belling was of sterling support in the library.

Professor Gideon Shimoni generously read the manuscript and offered invaluable criticisms and suggestions. I am indebted to Tova Herzl, former Israeli ambassador to South Africa, who awakened my interest in the issues in this book by persuading me to join the Israeli government delegation to the Durban anti-racism conference in 2001. Out of that has come a good friendship.

Charisse Zeifert in Johannesburg has been a friend throughout, always responding immediately to my many requests for information.

Dr David Harman was unstinting in giving authoritative information on complex educational issues and on much else in Israel, too. Professor David Kretzmer helped me work through the thicket of land issues. Dr Frances Raday, with her knowledge and wisdom, has guided me through the law.

Sherman Teichman, director of the Institute for Global Leadership at Tufts University, was an early and continuing supporter and invited me to the university as an INSPIRE Fellow (Institute Scholar/Practitioner in Residence). His students, Jonathan Wolff and Amit Paz, ably researched the accuracy of quotations ascribed to Israeli leaders.

I am grateful to Dr Colin Shindler for allowing me to draw from his books on Jewish and Zionist history and to Dr Moshe Amirav for sharing his love and knowledge of Jerusalem.

Bassem Eid was a never-ending source of information about the West Bank and Palestinian life. Danny Rubinstein was always willing to answer my questions. Paul Scham was an invaluable sounding board for ideas. Dr Ervin Staub shared his thinking and research about the psychology of human behaviour.

I thank Michelle Leon who gave me access to the Times Media Group library in Johannesburg and helped me to choose photographs to illustrate the apartheid era; and I thank the Times Media Group for granting me permission to reproduce them. I also thank Uri Avnery for granting me permission to publish his article about the 1948 war; Dr Ali Qleibo for permission to quote his description of Jerusalem's Arab community; Ziad Abu-Zayyad and Hillel Schenker for permission to draw material from the *Palestine-Israel Journal*; and Raphaela Meli for her photograph of a West Bank checkpoint.

I am grateful to Palestinian friends for engaging in debate, and to Sue Melmed, Ruth and Zeev Abraham, and Judy and Bob Goldman for many hours of discussion – and argument – over the years, which helped to illuminate Israeli issues.

Dorothy Harman, friend and literary agent, warmly supported the need for this book and put much effort into securing a publisher. The result has been the pleasure of working with Marie-Claire Antoine, my editor at Rowman & Littlefield in New York.

A special thank-you to Sir Harold Evans for his thoughtful and generous foreword.

Anne endured, and our marriage thankfully survived, the emotional and intellectual roller coaster entailed in the research and writing of this book.

My thanks to everyone but, of course, responsibility for the text is entirely mine.

*Chapter One*

# The Beginning

*Jewish history explains today's Israel: the people who gave the world belief in One God and who clung to their faith over centuries of exile and persecution, returned home. Their Zionist dream succeeded.*

\* \* \*

Zionism is the national liberation movement of the Jewish people. It sprang out of the fiery ideas of freedom during the French Revolution of 1789. It grew during the nineteenth century with the rise of nationalism in Europe and advanced in response to the rise of modern anti-Semitism. It flourished during the twentieth century alongside liberation movements in Africa and Asia. It triumphed in 1948 with the creation of the State of Israel in the era that saw dozens of countries achieve independence.

Zionism has never been monolithic. From the start, it meant different things to different people who competed fiercely with each other. The one shared determination was to fundamentally change the nature of Jewish existence, to bring Jews out of the persecution and degradation which had by and large been their lot for two thousand years after defeat by the Roman Empire. But exactly what to do and how to do it set off ferocious disagreements. The dividing lines were often blurred: ideologists contradicted each other yet also fed each other with ideas. Idealists sought a perfect society based on socialist theory merged with social justice and the biblical teachings of the prophets. Others ridiculed this as utopian and pushed for a modern capitalist, technological state. Among religious Jews, many rejected creating a state, arguing that it could not happen before the coming of the Messiah; other religious Jews, however, supported the formation of a state because they saw it as the start of a process which would lead to the messianic age.

1

Whatever the differences in approach, the bedrock was certain and was expressed with steely determination by an early Zionist thinker, A. D. Gordon (1856–1922): 'We shake off the old life which has grown rancid on us, and start from the beginning. We don't want to change and we don't want to improve, we want to begin from the beginning'.

The old life, and the beginning, originated perhaps four thousand years ago with Abraham, his son Isaac and grandson Jacob – the patriarchs revered alike by Jews, Christians and Muslims. The Book of Genesis tells the story of God summoning Abraham from Ur to Canaan – today's Israel/Palestine – to form a people with belief in the One God. That is the start of the Jewish narrative. When famine struck, Jacob and his twelve sons moved south to Egypt; their descendants were enslaved (see timeline in appendix 1).

After four hundred years, Moses led his Israelite people back to Canaan. But first they spent forty years wandering in the Sinai desert: there they were forged into a nation and received the Torah, which included the Ten Commandments.

The ancient history, with its often-sparse information and shrouded in the mists of time, is subject to interpretation, conflicting claims and political spin. It records one conquest after the other, with wholesale massacres and expulsions. In the Israeli village of Tzippori, for example, excavations have revealed fourteen layers of civilisation over the centuries, each one built atop the previous one.

The 70 CE expulsion of Jews from Jerusalem and destruction of the Temple culminated four years of savage warfare. The Roman historian Tacitus reported 660,000 dead during the siege of Jerusalem. Some of the Jews who survived were sold into slavery in marketplaces throughout the Roman Empire or laboured in its mines and as galley slaves in its fleet. Sixty years after Jerusalem was razed to the ground, Emperor Hadrian rebuilt it as a Roman colony and renamed it *Aelia Capitolina*. Later, in an angry response to the Jewish Simeon Bar Kochba revolt, he set out to erase Judaism from Judea province, renaming the area *Syria Palaestina*; he forbade circumcision and Jews were barred from the city on pain of death.

Jews went on living in the Holy Land outside Jerusalem and exile began only after the seventh-century arrival of Muslim conquerors. Jerusalem, however, remained the focus of Jewish existence and small numbers of Jews always lived there and in other towns in a religious context, dreaming of messianic redemption. They were mostly 'Sephardim', the term for Jews who settled in Portugal and Spain, but over time it came to be more broadly used for Jews of the Middle East and North Africa. Jews who made their way into Europe were called 'Ashkenazim'.

Jewish communities in Muslim countries were substantially better off than in Christian lands in Europe.[1] But they were still subject to humiliation and persecution – and even worse from time to time. As 'People of the

Book', Jews (Christians and others of revealed faiths, too) are viewed as *dhimmi*, protected persons, under Muslim rule and can practise their faith. But that has not always guaranteed good treatment. Instead, Jews (and Christians) must openly acknowledge the superiority of the 'true believers', Muslims. Regulations enacted over the years have barred dhimmis, on pain of death, from criticising the Koran, Islam or Mohammed.

Dhimmis have been excluded from public office and armed service and barred from carrying arms. They have been prohibited from riding horses or camels, only asses, and only side saddle, not astride; their synagogues and churches cannot be taller than mosques; their houses cannot be higher than those of Muslims; and they cannot drink wine in public. They have had to show public deference to Muslims, always yielding them the centre of the road. They are not allowed to give evidence in court against a Muslim and their oath is not accepted in a Muslim court. They must wear distinctive clothing.

Despite these restrictions, Jews generally lived in peace for long periods in Muslim societies. But they were never totally secure. Some of the notable outbursts against them were in Granada, Spain, in 1066, when the Jewish quarter of the city was razed and its five thousand people were murdered; in Fez, in 1465, thousands were slaughtered after a Jew was accused of treating a Muslim woman in an 'offensive manner'. Violent anti-Jewish feeling swept through the Muslim world before and after the creation of Israel in 1948 and nearly all Jews left.

Whatever Sephardic Jews suffered, the lot of their Ashkenazi brethren in Europe was crueller: the centuries are a never-ending saga of crimes against them on a scale beyond any other people in history. The sustained hatred has stemmed from the accusation that Jews killed Jesus Christ. This was carried down the ages. Although the Roman Catholic Church late in the twentieth century formally removed blame from Jews, the stigma still remains among those who want to believe it.

The eleventh to thirteenth centuries were among the worst when Crusaders went on expeditions to evict Muslims from the Holy Land, killing Jews en route. 'The ignorant mobs were incited by the leaders of the Crusades to pillage and massacre whole Jewish communities. Thousands of Jews perished, and entire communities were wiped out'.[2] A passage from a medieval Hebrew account in Northern Europe during the First Crusade describes an Ashkenazi response to Christian attempts to force them to convert: 'The women girded their loins . . . and slew their own sons and daughters, and then themselves. Many men also . . . slaughtered their wives and children and infants. The most gentle and tender of women slaughtered the child of her delight'.[3]

Accusations have included the blood libel – that Jews murder non-Jews, especially children, to use their blood for Passover, which celebrates the release from Egyptian bondage, and other religious festivals. Another myth has been that Jews secretly stab the consecrated host – the wafers used in Christian masses for transubstantiation into the body of Christ. Jews have suffered punishment for this down the ages, such as in Belitz, near Berlin, where men and women were burnt at the stake in 1243. The last known accusation of desecration was in Romania in 1836.

The Black Death – plague – which afflicted Europe at various times, was blamed on Jews who were said to have poisoned wells. Lepers and others with skin diseases were also blamed. If not wholesale murder, then mass expulsions, such as from England in 1290, with Jews readmitted 360 years later; and from France in 1306, with official readmission coming 483 years later with the Revolution. Jews were evicted from Prague in 1794 and from Moscow in 1891.

The paintings of medieval times sustained the fear and hatred: Jews were regularly depicted with horns, a tail, an evil face and a twisted body, and in the company of supposed images of devils and monsters.

Christians also tried to get rid of Jews by enforced baptism. In Spain, the Inquisition, from 1480 onwards, targeted Conversos, Jews who had converted to Christianity but who were still viewed with suspicion (Muslims were also targeted): exact numbers are uncertain but over a period of ten years, perhaps thirteen thousand Jews were killed. In 1492 forty thousand out of a total of eighty thousand Jews were expelled from the country, although the community had lived there for more than one thousand years, holding professions from bankers and traders to physicians and astronomers. The other forty thousand are said to have accepted conversion. The Inquisition was abolished in 1834.

At the end of the eighteenth century in Frankfurt, a major European trading centre, Jews were still prevented from leaving the ghetto after dark or on Sundays and Christian holidays.[4] The ghetto consisted of

> a single dark lane, the Judengasse, foul-smelling and dank, sunless because of its narrowness and its tall, overcrowded houses. . . . By 1743, some 3,000 Jews crowded into a space originally intended for 300 in conditions of squalor and congestion unknown elsewhere in the city. . . . Inside the Christian quarters no more than two Jews were allowed to walk abreast and for some reason they were not allowed to carry walking sticks.

The murderous hatred was carried into the twentieth century with the Holocaust and other outbursts of rejection and violence. It is imprinted on the Jewish soul, shaping the outlook, fears and hopes of many in Israel and elsewhere.

Change, for Jews as much as for Europeans, began with the French Revolution in 1789 and its Jacobinism, 'that full-hearted fraternalism which rushed through France with truly Messianic fervour, and which swept before it all ancient cruelties and anachronisms'.[5] The vision of the new France was a nation of free people, summed up in the slogan, 'Liberty, Equality, Fraternity'. It had particular relevance for Jews: 'the condition of a reviled and despised people, walled up in their ghettos, became a potent symbol of a stultifying, repressive past – and their liberation a signpost on the way to change'.[6]

The ideas of freedom spread through Europe as ancient empires went into decline. The rise of nationalism dominated the continent in the nineteenth century. Many Jews rejoiced and saw their future opening up, in absorption into the emerging nation-states. It was called Emancipation. Liberation from ghettos set off a torrent of thinking and self-examination in which the traditional absolute authority of rabbis was challenged. A modernised Judaism was demanded in tune with the changed status of Jews in society. In Hebrew, it was *haskalah* (the Enlightenment). Out of it came the Reform movement and later also Conservative and Modern Orthodox. Reform, today the biggest stream of Judaism in the United States, sought to reconcile criticism of the Bible with Judaism and religious practice with modern life. Its actions included ending gender separation in synagogue prayer, instead allowing men and women to sit together, accepting female rabbis and using local language alongside Hebrew in religious services.

But emancipation did not totally free Jews: by the middle of the nineteenth century, the new nation-states were losing their shining purpose and becoming chauvinistic and imperialist. Many Jews found they were despised as outsiders who did not belong in the national fold. With this, a virulent anti-Semitism, an extension of the age-old condemnation of Jews, came to the fore. The phrase, 'anti-Semitic', was coined in 1881 by a real anti-Semite, a German journalist, Wilhelm Marr, to express *Judenhass*, Jew-hatred.

Jews in Russia, meanwhile, were under the whip. They had a long history: seven hundred years earlier, in 1241, the Mongol invasion caused Polish princes to want a loyal population on the border. They invited Jews and thus the then-mighty Polish-Lithuanian commonwealth – at its height the second biggest state in Europe – blossomed for Jewish settlement.

Poland was gradually seized and divided by its neighbours, Russia, Prussia and Austria. It ceased to exist. Hence, before the eighteenth century ended, nearly one million Polish Jews had become Russian, with a further two hundred thousand early in the nineteenth century. The Jews who willy-nilly now found themselves in a hostile Russia were, from 1772 onwards, during the rule of Catherine the Great, penned within the 'Pale of Settlement'. The word 'Pale' derived from a stake, as used to build a fence. It covered one million square kilometres, from the Baltic Sea in the north to the Black Sea in the south. By the end of the nineteenth century, nearly five million Jews lived there, a minority among Christian Russians; two hundred thousand Jews lived in other parts of Russia.

More than six hundred laws, enacted from 1649, even before Catherine, and which were to remain until the 1917 Revolution, pressed down on Jews, ranging from prohibiting them from taking Russian first names to the banning, and sometimes public burning, of books and journals that offended officials, as well as quotas for universities and professions, and mass expulsions and pogroms from time to time. Outright massacres were the ultimate, as with Bogdan Chmielnicky, whom Ukrainians to this day revere as a hero for fighting against Polish domination in the mid-seventeenth century, who had more than one hundred thousand Jews murdered.

In 1827 Russia compelled all able-bodied men to do military service for twenty-five years. It bore down especially on Jews: ten males were conscripted each year for every one thousand Jews in the population; for non-Jews, it was seven for every one thousand, every two years. Apart from staffing the army, a declared purpose was to get Jews away from their communities; many were compelled to undergo instruction in Christianity. There was also specific discrimination because, unlike others, Jews were conscripted for tax arrears. If a community did not have enough able-bodied men – and this problem began to grow after emigration en masse got going in the mid-nineteenth century – it had to supply two conscripts for each missing person. To make up shortfalls, community committees chose men previously exempt: cripples, invalids, old men, only sons, the oldest sons and the sole supporters of families. Children as young as eight were sent to the army: they were usually taken far away from their families and kept until the legal conscription age of twelve when they were inducted into the army; in between, records speak of the children being marched long distances, suffering death tolls up to 50 percent. During World War I, some four hundred thousand Jewish conscripts fought in the tsar's army.

The assassination of Tsar Alexander II in 1881 by a revolutionary (non-Jewish) movement, *Narodnaya Volia* (The People's Will), had dire consequences for Jews. Tsar Alexander III took over on a wave of Slavophilism and reaction: Russia moved to the nationalist right and Jews were labelled liberals, revolutionaries and subversives – as well as Christ-killers. A succession of pogroms was stoked up in Ukraine with deaths and gutting and looting of homes and shops. 'A shudder of fear passed through the Jewish community of the Pale'[7] and was soon proved to be justified: 'a paralysing grillwork of legal disabilities was dropped on the Jews. . . . Russian Jewry was at last about to be placed under slow sentence of death'.

The 'May Laws' enacted by Alexander III on 3 May 1882 included barring Jews from settling 'anew' in any rural area, including the Pale – thus blocking them from moving to villages from crowded cities. A Jew was not allowed to take in his widowed mother from another village, or inherit his father's business in another village, or go to hospital in another village. Anyone who did any of this faced expulsion.

Many managed to cling on through bribery, but most were forced out of their homes: 'Jews by the hundreds of thousands began to pour from the countryside into the congestion of the cities. Ultimately the rural Jewish community was all but obliterated'.[8] Jewish quotas for universities and gymnasia were slashed and for the Russian Bar were cut from 22 percent to 9 percent. With rural Jews driven into evermore wretchedness in cities and towns, even a high-ranking Russian official – Ussarov, governor of Bessarabia – was moved to note that workers 'toil hard for a living so scanty that a rusty herring and slice of onion is considered the tip-top of luxury and prosperity'.[9]

At the climax, most of Moscow's Jewish community – twenty thousand people – was expelled overnight. The police put a cordon around the city, carried out searches through the night and marched men, women and children in manacles to railway stations. Mass expulsions were repeated in St Petersburg and Kharkov.

\* \* \*

The events of 1881 and 1882 shocked Jewish intellectuals. They had believed that the solution to Jewish problems lay in the liberalisation of Russian society; many believed in outright Russification. But the new tsar's policies made clear that they would not be allowed to assimilate or absorb into the Russian people and that they were not wanted.

'The recent pogroms have violently awaked the complacent Jews from their sweet slumbers', wrote Chaim Hisin.[10] 'Until now I was uninterested in my origin. I saw myself as a faithful son of Russia which was to me my raison d'être and the very air that I breathed'.

Jewish members of revolutionary movements felt a special sense of betrayal as their Gentile comrades turned against them: The People's Will, responsible for the tsar's assassination which had triggered the pogroms, urged peasants to join in the violence against Jews: 'Wherever you look, whatever you touch, everywhere the kikes. The kike curses the peasant, cheats him, drinks his blood. The kikes make life unbearable'.[11] Yet faced by this statement of crude hatred and incitement, most Jewish and non-Jewish intellectuals kept silent, explaining they did not want to alienate the Russian masses.

Leon Pinsker was among the deeply shaken Jewish intellectuals. He had served as a doctor in Russia's army in the Crimean War and had even been decorated by the tsar, an unusual distinction for a Jew. Out of his disillusionment and despair came a pamphlet which reverberated among Jews: 'Auto-Emancipation'. Published in 1882, he argued that emancipation by others, as hoped for through the French Revolution, Emancipation and the Enlightenment, was a pipe-dream. Jews had to emancipate themselves through creation of a Jewish national home:

> The great ideas of the 18th and 19th centuries have not passed us by without leaving a trace. We feel not only as Jews; we feel as men. As men, we, too, wish to live and be a nation as the others. And if we seriously desire that, we must first of all extricate ourselves from the old yoke, and rise manfully to our full height. We must first of all desire to help ourselves and then the help of others is sure to follow. . . . The lack of national self-respect and self-confidence of political initiative and of unity are the enemies of our national renaissance. . . . Help yourselves, and God will help you!

This seminal document opened entirely new ways to overcome the centuries of Jewish compliant acceptance of oppression. Its concept was as excitingly relevant then as it was to be in the mid-twentieth century – and into the present time – for black people in the world, and especially in the segregated United States, apartheid South Africa and colonised Africa.

It is known by other names – Black Power, African Nationalism, Black Consciousness – but Auto-Emancipation is the starting point for blacks, as much as it has proved itself for Jews, in urging self-regard: to believe in yourself, to have confidence in yourself as a human being and thus to overcome the humiliation and debasement inflicted by others. It was enunciated for blacks by W. E. B. Du Bois in the United States and by Anton Lembede, Robert Mangaliso Sobukwe and Steve Bantu Biko in South Africa as the way to achieve mental, and then physical, freedom.

However, for large numbers of nineteenth-century Russian Jews living in dire peril, salvation meant getting out immediately. Emigration grew to the United States, Britain, Canada and South Africa. In the violent years of 1881–1882, emigration jumped to 76,414 and was driven further by the hateful start to the twentieth century: on 6 April 1903 a Christian boy was found murdered in a town near Kishinev in Russia's Bessarabia province, now the capital of Moldova. A relative had killed him and was later found. But two newspapers placed the blame on the Jews, and one of them used the blood libel, that the boy had been killed for his blood to be used in baking matzo. Three days of rioting erupted, with 120 dead and babies 'literally torn to pieces by the frenzied and bloodthirsty mob'.[12]

By 1914 around three million Jews had emigrated from the Russian Empire. From this emerged much of the cosmic burst of Jewish talent in the West during the twentieth century in every field of human endeavour: business, banking, medicine, science, politics, composing and playing popular and classical music, theatre and movies, architecture, journalism, books and magazines and art. They extraordinarily helped to transform their new countries and the world.

Those who remained had the option of seeking comfort in religion, or trying to assimilate, or overthrowing the regime through revolutionary action, or fostering liberal democracy. Jews went for all of them. But the notion of a Jewish home also gained popularity, albeit with disputes about where it should be. At one time or another, more than thirty areas in various parts of the world were proposed as host countries, including Uganda, Madagascar, Argentina, Alaska, Angola, Ecuador, French Guyana and Tasmania.

Palestine won. It was inevitable. In addition to the continuous Jewish presence, however small at times, wherever Jews were in the world they looked at Palestine and Jerusalem as the geographical location of the spiritual and emotional core of their existence. It was central to Judaism and to the teachings of the rabbis. 'Next year in Jerusalem' was a mantra in the soul of the people.

While the religiously pious were the ones who actually lived in Palestine, the nature of the people began to change, in a tiny way, in 1882 when Jewish students in Russia founded an organisation, *Bilu* (an acronym from the Hebrew for 'O House of Jacob, let us go'). The first group of fourteen pioneers reached Jaffa that year. Among them was Chaim Hisin, who had written so poignantly about his feelings.

They were a manifestation of the thinking and daily behaviour which were giving rise to a new Jewishness. A Zionist intelligentsia was evolving: 'In the closing years of the 19th century a transitional generation of Jewish intellectuals emerged who were educated in the *yeshiva*, religious seminary, but drawn towards the world of modern thought and rational action. They could neither renounce past understanding of Judaism nor accept it'.[13] It was this period that saw the rise of Jews as a nation, rather than as dispersed, isolated and marginalised People of the Book.

There emerged now one of those singular individuals who from time to time exerts a direct and dramatic bearing on the course of events: Theodor Herzl. He, above all others, is the father of modern Zionism.

Herzl was born on 2 May 1860 in Budapest, Hungary, to a German-speaking assimilated Jewish family from Austria. The family moved to Vienna and Herzl studied law and then turned to journalism and literature. He worked as the Paris correspondent of the leading Viennese newspaper, *Neue Freie Presse* (New Free Press). He had only little adherence to religion or Judaism, and as a young man he was involved with a group striving for German unity under the motto of 'Honour, Freedom, Fatherland'. But consciousness of anti-Semitism was growing in him, not only because of the barbarity in tsarist Russia but in the rising tide of rejection of Jews in France and elsewhere in Europe. Later, that was to be added to by the notorious Dreyfus Trial in France, in which a Jewish army captain, Alfred Dreyfus, was falsely jailed for treason but after public outrage was later exonerated and freed.

Herzl saw the solution in conversion to Christianity and intermarriage. In January 1893 he proposed a mass baptism in Vienna's St Stephen's Cathedral. Yet he was sharing the feelings of betrayal among Jewish liberals that so many of their Christian colleagues were not standing up against the surge of anti-Semitism in Western Europe. By 1894 his views had changed so rapidly that he wrote a play about the flaws of assimilation as a solution for what was widely termed the 'Jewish problem'.

Herzl wrote a short book in German entitled *Die Judenstaat*, translated as 'The Jewish State' or 'The State of the Jews', and subtitled 'Proposal of a Modern Solution for the Jewish Question'. He said that anti-Semitism would not fade away, and assimilation gave no protection to Jews. They would continue to be viewed as aliens in the countries in which they lived, no matter how much they contributed. The solution was mass emigration to a new land where a Jewish state could be established.

Herzl later admitted that he had been unaware of the same ideas developing among Jewish intellectuals. Moshe Leib Lilienblum, a Russian Jew, was a leader among them: in 1881 he had written that the reestablishment of Jews in Palestine was the only solution to the Jewish problem. His statement led to the formation two years later of a committee in Odessa for the settlement of Palestine. Representatives of European Jewry discussed the first concerted plans for settlement in Palestine. This was the foundation stone for what became Zionism.

The word itself came shortly after from Nathan Birnbaum, an Austrian journalist. It derived from Zion, pronounced '*Tzyion*' in Hebrew, a hill in Jerusalem, and means a marker or commemoration. He coined the terms 'Zionistic', 'Zionist' and 'Zionism' in 1890.

But it was Herzl, through *The Jewish State* and its publication in English in April 1896, who catapulted Zionism onto the Jewish and world stages. Herzl's genius was as a visionary who simultaneously fired people's imaginations and gave them hope of escape from perpetual repression and yet was also a practical organiser and an inspired publicist. He did not impress everyone. Many Jews dismissed him as a crank; as did Baron Maurice de Hirsch, a Jewish philanthropist in Paris whom Herzl went to see to solicit support for mass migration to a Jewish state: 'De Hirsch stared at his guest incredulously for a moment, and within a matter of minutes succeeded in closing the interview'.[14]

Herzl was undaunted. The First Zionist Congress was held in Basel, Switzerland, from 29 to 31 August 1897. He was elected president of the World Zionist Organisation, which came into being with a declared programme: 'Zionism aims to establish a publicly assured, legally secured home for the Jewish people in Palestine'.

Herzl travelled the world to propagate Zionism, meeting leaders from the sultan of Turkey to the German kaiser. In 1903 the British government made him an offer: a large Jewish settlement could be created in Uganda in Africa. It would be under British control but would have self-government. The 6th Zionist Congress in Basel that year voted to consider the offer. Acrimonious debate followed. Two years later, the Congress turned down the offer and committed itself to a Jewish state in the historic land of Israel. That, unswervingly, became and remained the goal.

Herzl did not live to know of the rejection. He died of a heart attack in July 1904, aged forty-four. In his will, he asked to be buried in the vault in Vienna alongside his father 'and to lie there till the Jewish people shall take my remains to Palestine'.[15] In August 1949, a year after Israel's creation, his remains, and those of his parents, were taken for reburial in Jerusalem – on Mount Herzl, named after him. A phrase on the frontispiece of Herzl's novel *Altneuland* (Old New Land), published in 1902, came to be the lodestar for Zionist dreams: 'If you will it, it is not a legend'. In tsarist Russia, Zionism was illegal, but *Hovevei Zion* (lovers of Zion) groups had been formed since the start of the 1880s to collect money for Jewish settlement in Palestine, to study Hebrew and run classes in gymnastics and self-defence. They met secretly, often in the guise of wedding parties, and went to Germany for their annual convention in 1884.[16] Groups mushroomed in Russia and around the world to support the new Herzl-driven movement.

Yet most Jews in the world remained at best uncaring and at worst hostile to the Zionist dream. Religious leaders generally saw it as a challenge to their authority and standing in communities. The ultra-Orthodox rejected, as many still do, return to the historic homeland before the coming of the Messiah as forcing God's hand; human intervention could not be justified. The Reform and Liberal movements also condemned Zionism.[17]

In 1913 only about 1 percent of the world's Jews had signified their adherence to Zionism.[18] Most Jews thought the idea was either unrealistic or feared that creating a Jewish state would expose them to charges of dual loyalty in the countries where they lived. In the United States, which grew to be the home of more than 50 percent of the world's Jews – a balance which changed only in 2009 in favour of Israel – Zionist groups were very much a minority: in 1914, in a Jewish population of three million, only about twelve thousand worked together loosely in the Zionist Federation; New York had five hundred members and the biggest single donation at that point was $200.

In Britain, in 1915, Edwin Montagu, a Jewish member of the cabinet, vehemently opposed Zionism. In a letter to Prime Minister Herbert Asquith, he said, '[I]t would require nothing short of a miracle to produce a Jewish State in Palestine'.[19] He did not believe a Jewish state could ever become a viable entity. Jews tending olive trees or herding sheep could not be imagined. In Palestine, Jews would have no common tongue: Hebrew was of little use in practice.

* * *

However, some of the initial Zionist supporters, those who did believe in Herzl and the dream of a state, did so with full heart and total passion. They were invested with strength beyond their numbers as they rode three tides in human events which fortuitously came at that time.

First, people and land. Especially large numbers of settlers went to Palestine during distinct periods starting, according to Zionist chronology, with the First *Aliyah* (Hebrew, literally, 'going up') from Russia, from 1862 to 1903, in the first expression of enthusiasm for land settlement. It brought immigrants, nearly all from Eastern Europe, with the limited aim to renew Jewish identity in the Holy Land; they saw themselves as part of the Ottoman Empire. They bought land and at worst clashed with neighbouring Arab farmers and Bedouin nomads over local issues such as different approaches to land cultivation and grazing.

The Second Aliyah, from 1904 to 1914, also had Jews getting away from Russian oppression, many of them refugees from the failed revolution of 1905. Among them was David Ben-Gurion, who was to play a dominant role in the eventual creation of the State of Israel.

These were the new Jews inspired by Pinsker's Auto-Emancipation. They gave expression to what was called a new 'muscular Judaism'. They believed in *halutziut*, the ardour of pioneering. The *kibbutz* and *moshav* – agricultural settlements – grew out of their utopian determination that the socialist Jewish state was to be built by the workers who would shape the new society in their image.

They were the means for getting Jewish title to land; their settlements, situated wherever land could be bought, were targets for attack by hostile Arabs: the first vital structures of a new kibbutz, built on day one, were a watchtower and a protective fence. They projected the image to the world of Zionism's new rugged, fighting, self-confident Jew. They were radically different from the subservient Jews whom Arabs had dealt with for centuries. There could no longer be any contemptuous spitting at them, literally or figuratively. The two waves of immigration trebled the size of the Jewish population: it reached 86,000 in 1914.[20] The immigrants did not invade with weapons but came with hoes and ploughs to develop the land. They were colonisers – but not colonialists in the nineteenth-century use of the term to describe the land theft, dispossession and racial arrogance of European nations which conquered and divided up Africa and Asia among themselves. The Zionist settlers were not the settler freebooters of Britain, Germany, France, Spain, Belgium, Portugal and the Netherlands, who were the conquerors in Africa, Asia and the Americas. A crucial distinction which sets them apart from colonialism was that they did not have a mother country from which they had come to exploit a weaker country's resources and to ship the resources to the metropole.

Land was purchased from Arab owners, whether the local *fedayeen*, the peasants, or often from absentee owners, the *effendis*, who lived in Beirut or Damascus or Paris. If the latter, it meant that the fedayeen were displaced, and suffered. Money for buying land was donated by both wealthy and poor Jews throughout the world. A brilliant strategy was the Blue Box – a small metal collection box in blue and white colours which became an everyday fixture in vast numbers of Jewish homes in which to put money 'to redeem the land'.

The Jewish National Fund (JNF), created in 1901, administered the money, the big donations and the small change, not only to buy land but to improve it through modern agriculture and planting trees. Forests had been natural to the biblical landscape, but the countryside was largely denuded by the start of the twentieth century: peasants cut down trees for firewood and vast areas were used to fuel the new steam locomotives. The JNF has since planted more than 240 million trees. Imaginative marketing has helped: it became part of Jewish life in the world to give money to plant trees in Palestine/Israel to honour a person or group, or to commemorate a birth, bar mitzvah, or wedding or anniversary.

For many, the use only of Jewish labour, however menial the work, was a primary principle. It was part of creating the new Jew. David Ben-Gurion described the ethos: 'A nation that does not do its own dirty work commits suicide. Do you think we would have recreated the Jewish world if we had consented to the Arabs doing our dirty work?'[21] In line with this outlook, there was, at first, also a ban on hiring labour from outside the kibbutz. That, however, is long past, and many thousands of workers are now imported from countries like Thailand and the Philippines to harvest kibbutz crops. They have replaced the Palestinian workers who have been turned away because of political violence.

Given the significance and achievements of the kibbutzim, surprisingly small numbers have been involved: in 1922, 700 people lived on kibbutzim; in 1939 there were 24,105 people on 79 kibbutzim – 5 percent of the Jewish population – and the number rose to 65,000 by 1950. The peak was 129,000 in 1989. In 2010 the numbers had dropped to about 100,000 on 270 kibbutzim.

Most of the European immigrants settled in towns, and in 1909 a new step was taken with the purchase of sand dunes to the north of the Arab port of Jaffa for the first Jewish town in two thousand years: Tel Aviv. A quarter-century later, during the 1930s, the city had an influx of Jews fleeing Germany's growing Nazi malevolence: they brought with them intellectual and technological quality; the architects among them transplanted the Bauhaus design and their many buildings are an admired feature of today's Tel Aviv, the White City, Israel's largest city.

Land settlement continued with the Third Aliyah, from 1919 to 1923, a post-war continuation of the Second Aliyah. About thirty-five thousand came from Eastern Europe, motivated by Jewish nationalism, the harshness of their lives and the prospect of British rule. The overthrow of the Russian tsar was a particular factor. The first revolution in February 1917 freed Jews from their marginal lives and, with all other Russians, from tsarist tyranny. But after the Bolsheviks seized power in October 1917, they gradually suppressed Zionism. They banned Hebrew in 1919 and condemned Zionism as the work of the bourgeoisie who were hoodwinking the proletariat with its ideology of the 'dead' Hebrew language which they said was nothing but the heritage of clericalism. In September 1924 mass arrests and deportations of Zionists began.[22]

The United States put restrictive quotas in place in 1924 so Jews wanting sanctuary had to look elsewhere. The Fourth Aliyah, from 1924 to 1928, brought more than sixty-seven thousand Jews to Palestine from Poland, Russia, Romania and Lithuania, with others also from Yemen and Iraq. Palestine experienced severe economic problems from the mid-1920s and many recent immigrants left.[23]

*  *  *

The second major element in transforming Zionism into statehood was language. The Bible was written in Hebrew and Jews have used it for prayer and study for millennia. But it faded as a spoken language when Jews were dispersed through the world. As the centuries passed, Jews spoke the local language of wherever they were living. In about the thirteenth century, a dialect based on German grew among Ashkenazi Jews. Written in Hebrew script, it grew with borrowings from Hebrew, Aramaic and other languages. By the eighteenth century, it was called Yiddish and was the everyday language of Jews. Criminals in Germany – non-Jews – used it during the nineteenth century as a secret language; police detectives had to learn it to penetrate the criminal underworld. Yiddish was popularly known as *mame-loshn* (mother tongue) in contrast with Hebrew which was *loshn-koydesh* (holy tongue).

Hebrew began to revive during the nineteenth-century Enlightenment. But the real boost came in 1881 when Eliezer Ben-Yehuda, a lexicographer and newspaper editor, left Russia to settle in Jerusalem. He brought Hebrew to life as a modern spoken language. It gradually replaced the babel of languages of immigrants from many countries. Ben-Yehuda, a dedicated Zionist, argued that the revival of Hebrew in the land of Israel could unite all

Jews worldwide. Modern Hebrew became an official language in 1921, during the British mandate period, alongside Arabic and English.

The third major element in the growth of Zionism was political. Events one hundred years ago combined with Jewish commitment to further the Zionist goal. The window of opportunity opened with World War I in 1914–1918: the map of Europe and the Middle East changed dramatically from the start to the end of the war; both before and afterwards it was a vastly different set of countries from what exists today. When the war began, the Ottoman Empire was in decline after four centuries, many years of which had seen it dominant in the Middle East and Western Asia.

Scholars disagree about details of the history of Palestine. But what is clear is that it has taken on different geographic and political connotations over time. The boundaries were never consistent but always included at least the land between the Mediterranean Sea in the west and the Jordan River in the east, or beyond. Canaan was part of it. Jews came in the second millennium, led by Moses out of Egypt. The word 'Palestine' is said to have derived from 'Land of the Philistines', the Sea Peoples who invaded the southern coastland in 1200 BCE and created a powerful empire. Following on the Jewish kingdoms, the Romans in the second century CE changed the name of *Provincia Judea* to *Syria Palaestina*.[24]

Today's Middle East countries did not exist except as administrative units in the Ottoman Empire – *vilayets* (provinces) and *sanjaks* (districts) – after an internal reorganisation in 1864. Syria and Iraq were the sites of ancient civilisations but for many centuries did not have separate existences. So, too, was the case with Lebanon, home of the Phoenicians who had flourished for some 2,500 years, from 3000 to 539 BCE. There wasn't a Palestine: the area was not a separate entity but was spread over various Ottoman provinces.

The name changed over the centuries. Most of Christian Europe referred to it as the 'Holy Land'. 'Palestine' disappeared from official use during Ottoman rule but remained in popular and unofficial usage. The Arabic word for it is usually transcribed as *Filisti*, *Filastin* or *Falastin*.

Britain revived the name 'Palestine' in 1917 to describe its mandate territory. Palestine now acquired fixed boundaries, its own government and a political identity separate from the surrounding countries which also emerged out of the Ottoman Empire. Its residents – Arabs and Jews, Muslims and Christians – were known as 'Palestinians'. Its separate identity was given international recognition when the League of Nations gave Britain the mandate in 1922.

\* \* \*

The weakened Ottoman Empire made its final mistake of siding with Germany and Austria-Hungary against the Allies in 1914. Its future was decided by foreign officials even before the war was over: in 1916 François Georges-Picot, for France, and Mark Sykes, for Britain, secretly agreed to split the Ottoman Empire into several zones of influence. The area of Palestine was shared between Britain and France. The next year, more negotiation with France led to Britain being given sole sway over Palestine, satisfying its anxiety to protect the Suez Canal and its links with India and its empire in the east.

While World War I was fought chiefly on the blood-stained ground of Europe, Britain wanted to stoke up opposition to Ottoman rule, so it promised to support Arab demands for post-war independence in return for an uprising. In 1916 Arabs led by T. E. Lawrence rose up. The size of the revolt has been overblown and romanticised in writings and in the movie *Lawrence of Arabia*. But, small in numbers as it was, it was part of the British military drive to evict the Turkish army, and it helped to achieve that: Britain's General Edmund Allenby entered Jerusalem through the Jaffa Gate – on foot out of respect for the Holy City – on 11 December 1917, the latest in history's long line of conquerors but, unlike most who came before him, benign and promising security for all.

British rule did not begin happily. The first military governor for Jerusalem, General William Borton, collapsed under the burden and resigned after two weeks, saying that 'the only tolerable places in Jerusalem were bath and bed'.[25] His successor, Sir Ronald Storrs, proved of hardier stock and not only lasted until 1926, first as military governor and then as governor, but left his colossal imprint on the city. He had much to do: the city has been described as 'neglected, trampled and hungry. The war years had left Jerusalem devoid of vital infrastructure and its inhabitants devoid of any source of income – the pilgrims as well as the wheat granaries in Transjordan. Hunger and cold were the fate of the residents.'[26]

Storrs modernised sanitation, the water supply, street design and building laws. His most visible legacy was his order that every building be faced with local stone; with only some exceptions this continues to the present, so that Jerusalem is a harmonious vista of grey, brown and pale pink buildings large and small. Storrs tried to bring together Jews and Arabs but admitted: 'Being neither Jew (British or foreign) nor Arab, but English, I am not wholly for either, but for both. Two hours of Arab grievances drive me into the Synagogue, while after an intensive course of Zionist propaganda I am prepared to embrace Islam'.

\* \* \*

Intricate manoeuvring followed World War I, with Britain, France, Arabs and Jews jockeying for influence and control. An international treaty formally stripped the Ottoman Empire of all its Arab provinces, leaving Turkey as the rump. The League of Nations, the world body set up to ensure peace forever, sanctified the arrangements: modern Syria and Lebanon were created as mandates of France; this lasted until 1943 for Lebanon, when it became independent, and 1946 for Syria.

Britain was given the mandate over Palestine, but it was a complex story.[27] The purpose of the mandate was as set out in the Balfour Declaration – to create a Jewish national home while also protecting the rights of non-Jews. But Winston Churchill, then colonial secretary, was negotiating with regional Arab leaders about their demands for land, while inside the new Palestine, Arab rioting against the Declaration and Zionist settlement erupted in 1919 and was not quelled until 1921. The British government restated its policy: on 30 June 1922 a White Paper affirmed commitment to Zionism and a Jewish national home, but this was tempered by the assurance that 'the disappearance or the subordination of the Arab population, language or culture in Palestine' was not contemplated, and the Balfour Declaration did 'not contemplate that Palestine as a whole should be converted into a Jewish National Home, but that such a Home should be founded in Palestine'.

The White Paper also hived off Transjordan, the land east of the Jordan River, thus excising 75 percent of Mandatory Palestine, to provide a haven for Abdullah, one of the Arabian princes at war with one another. Britain also surrendered land in the north of Palestine, handing it to France for inclusion in the Lebanon mandate. The League of Nations endorsed the mandate details. The Zionist leader, Dr Chaim Weizmann, protested, writing to Churchill to note that '"the fields of Gilead, Moab and Edom, with the rivers Arnon and Jabbok . . . are historically and geographically and economically linked to Palestine, and it is upon these fields, now that the rich plains of the north have been taken from Palestine and given to France, that the success of the Jewish National Home must largely rest . . ." Yet the Zionist leaders did not campaign strongly against the administrative separation of Transjordan; they regarded it – not without reason – as a merely provisional measure. So did the Colonial Office . . . [which had] decided not to allow Zionism in Transjordan for the present but also not to bar the door against it for all time'.[28]

It was not to be. The people of Palestine, both Jewish and Arab, were excluded from Transjordan, which went its own separate way under British tutelage. In 1946 Britain asked the new United Nations organisation to end its mandate, and the territory became today's Hashemite Kingdom of Jordan.

These twists and turns of decades ago are forgotten today, but for many years they underlay the claims of right-wing Israeli political parties to extend Israel's boundaries far to the east, up to Iraq. The remaining 25 percent of Palestine remained under British mandate rule, until 1948. This land is what is today Israel, the West Bank and the Gaza Strip.

Arabs were angered by Britain's agreement to give Syria to France, its denial that it had promised them the western Palestinian area and again when

Britain issued the Balfour Declaration promising a Jewish homeland in Palestine.

The declaration, which proved to be one of the century's most far-reaching documents, was preceded by intense intrigue and argument. It finally came about through a combination of factors starting with pressure by influential Jews in Britain: a mere twenty years after Theodor Herzl, they were driving for the Zionist goal he had set. They were aided by fortuitous circumstances: Chaim Weizmann was not only an eminent Russian-born scientist at Manchester University who had given inestimable help to Britain's war effort by developing chemicals for munitions, but he was also president of the World Zionist Organisation and a mighty advocate for Jewish aspirations. A man of striking ability and charismatic personality, he was a friend and trusted confidant of the elite in Britain, ranging from C. P. Scott, editor of the *Manchester Guardian* (now the *Guardian*) who backed Zionist aspirations, to David Lloyd George, who was to become prime minister in December 1916, and Lord Balfour, who became foreign secretary.

Across the channel, the French Foreign Ministry was dismissive of Zionism. But officials thought Jews were influential in Russia, in the collapsing tsarist regime, and also wanted Jewish support for a post-war French presence in Palestine. On 4 June 1917 the Foreign Ministry issued a cautiously worded statement saying that it approved a text presented to it by Zionists that 'circumstances permitting, and the independence of the Holy Places being safeguarded . . . it would be a deed of justice and of reparation to assist, by the protection of the Allied Powers, in the renaissance of the Jewish nationality in the land from which the people of Israel were exiled so many centuries ago'. It went on to say, 'The French government cannot but feel sympathy for your cause, the triumph of which is bound up that of the Allies'.[29]

The French, it seems, meant the statement to be mere words without any action. But the fact of it opened the way to Britain issuing its own statement of support for Zionism, especially as Lloyd George, with British imperialist interests at heart and determined to protect the Suez Canal area, wanted to keep out the French. Palestine under British control or protection was desirable. He and other colleagues were also devout Christians who had fundamental beliefs derived from the Old Testament about the justice of the Jewish cause. Lord Balfour later explained that he and Lloyd George had been influenced 'by the desire to give Jews their rightful place in the world; a great nation without a home is not right'.[30]

Not everyone agreed: at a cabinet meeting, Lord Curzon stated that Palestine was mostly 'barren and desolate [and] . . . a less propitious seat for the future Jewish race could not be imagined'. He did not seem to have said this out of concern for Jews, for, as he also said, Zionism was 'sentimental idealism, which would never be realised' and anyway 'how could the Jews ever overcome the far more and stronger Arabs'.[31]

In an astonishing irony in history, British leaders were worried that Germany was about to issue a statement supporting a Jewish state in Palestine. This, they feared, could push German-born Jews in the United States, who had no allegiance to the Allied Powers, to influence the United States not to enter the war (this factor disappeared on 7 April 1917 when the United States entered the war on the side of the Allies). They were also alarmed that Germany might gain a foothold in the Middle East area so vital to British interests.

Out of this medley of factors came the Balfour Declaration – in fact, it was a brief letter. It was first submitted to President Woodrow Wilson of the United States, who did not object to it. Written by the foreign secretary, Lord Balfour, it was sent on 2 November 1917 to Lord Rothschild, the head of Britain's Zionist Federation:

> His Majesty's Government view with favour the establishment in Palestine of a national home for the Jewish people and will use their best endeavours to facilitate the achievement of this object, it being clearly understood that nothing shall be done which may prejudice the civil and religious rights of existing non-Jewish communities in Palestine or the rights and political status enjoyed by Jews in any other country.

Immediately, this became the charter of the Zionist movement. From that moment, transforming the words of promise into the reality of a Jewish state was the Jewish goal.

But exactly how was the declaration to be implemented? Jews had no doubt that 'national home' meant a Jewish state. But it was not so clear to Britain: the declaration also committed it to uphold the rights of the 'existing non-Jewish communities' and its regional interests were at stake with the wider Arab population.

Britain began with a White Paper in 1922 which tried to ride two horses: it gave the assurance that developing a Jewish national home did not mean imposing Jewish nationality on everyone; it also accepted that Jews had a right to be in Palestine, which should grow into a centre for them. Britain's first high commissioner, Sir Herbert Samuel, worked to bring Jews and Arabs together. A Jew and a Zionist, he believed in an integrated political community to lead to a unitary state. His first proposal, also in 1922, was for a legislative council with elected Muslim, Jewish and Christian members, plus nominated members. Arab leaders refused to take part, demanding that the Balfour Declaration first be annulled. Samuel then proposed an advisory council of ten Arabs and two Jews nominated by him, but the Arabs were pressured to refuse to serve. Thus the pattern was set for Palestine for the years to come: continuing Arab rejection meant that the territory was run by the high commissioner and his officials; it never had a constitution, a parliament or country-wide elections.

* * *

The arrival of Jews in Palestine in the late nineteenth century did not alarm local Arabs. There was no Palestinian national identity to be challenged and no politics were involved.[32] The shift in Arab-Jewish relations came after 1908 when Young Turks seized control of the sinking Ottoman Empire and set about modernisation. As in Europe the previous century, release from the stultifying past gave life to ideas of freedom and nationalism, and these swept through the far-flung lands of the empire. That included the area now known as Palestine, spurring the emergence of a national identity among the Arabs there.

Palestinian nationalism is a developing area of research interest among scholars. Until recent years, even the existence of Palestinians as a coherent group of people was denied by many Israelis, and this view continues to be heard. The notion of a Palestinian nationalism with a beginning very soon after the rise of modern Zionism is probably beyond comprehension for many Israelis. Yet it's a fact of history that the rise of Jewish nationalism in the form of modern Zionism contributed to the growth of a Palestinian consciousness.

Early notice of developing Arab cohesion and alarm about unfolding events came as soon as December 1908 with the launch of *al-Karmil*, a weekly Arabic-language newspaper that 'became the primary vehicle of an extensive campaign against Zionist settlement in Palestine'.[33] Another newspaper, *Filastin*, was started in Jaffa in 1911: an editorial in 1914 warned: 'We are a nation threatened with disappearance in the face of the Zionist tide in this Palestinian land'.[34]

The Balfour Declaration confirmed Arab fears, not only because of its promise of 'a national home for the Jews' but also because the text referred to them not as Arabs or Palestinians but only in a non-way, as 'existing non-Jewish communities'. The post-war boundaries creating new states and also defining Palestine were the work of faraway colonial masters in London and Paris. Knowledge of being brushed aside was deepened in July 1922 when the League of Nations gave Britain the mandate over Palestine – 'an internationally recognized document representing the consensus of the great powers of the day as to the disposition of the former Ottoman territory of Palestine'.[35]

Arab resentment showed itself tangibly in 1920: at Passover/Easter, a religious Muslim parade which began in East Jerusalem turned violent and led to the death and wounding of several Jews. In November the next year, the fourth anniversary of the Balfour Declaration was marked by Arab violence. Arab opposition to Zionism and Jewish settlement was centred in the elite in the community – the landowners and the professional people. But it was seriously weakened by factionalism: the elite were cleft by division, especially between the two leading notable Muslim families of Jerusalem, the Nashashibis and Husseinis. Their struggle for power, going back to the nineteenth century, grew fiercer by the day. In 1920 a Nashashibi replaced a Husseini as mayor of Jerusalem; the next year, the British administration balanced the scale – and played one against the other – by ensuring the selection of Hajj Amin al-Husseini as Mufti of Jerusalem. He became the primary leader of Palestinian Arabs.

\* \* \*

In Jewish eyes, Jews and Arabs were at best in much the same situation under British rule, with both sides enjoying advantages and disadvantages; at worst, Jews accused Britain of failing to deliver on the Balfour Declaration: it did not create the Jewish homeland and finally betrayed Jews by withdrawing support for the homeland in its White Paper in 1939. Even more, it restricted immigration from Europe in the 1930s and thus condemned untold numbers of Jews to the gas chambers and compounded this cruelty still further by denying entry to survivors after World War II. Jews agreed that Britain had to quit; to the extremist Irgun (*Irgun Zvai Leumi*, the National Military Organisation), and its breakaway Lehi (*Lohamei Herut Yisrael*, Freedom Fighters of Israel, also known as the Stern Gang or Group, depending on who said it, after its founder, Abraham Stern), British perfidy justified murder of its soldiers and officials.

However, the Palestinian historian Rashid Khalidi derides the belief that Britain was even-handed. And he says that claiming that it actually favoured the Arabs through most of the mandate era is 'an even more myopic and partisan view'.[36] He notes that Palestinians pressed Britain for self-determination. But Britain always said they had to accept the terms of the mandate as a precondition for any change in their constitutional position. The Palestinian dilemma was that these terms denied them any rights of self-determination, and even if they did accept, they would subordinate themselves to the rights of the Jews.

In the early years, there were a few, even strong, friendly connections between Jews and Arabs. But they did not last. The lead was taken by Emir Feisal, who with T. E. Lawrence took part in driving out the Ottoman army in 1917. Britain made him king of its mandate territory, Iraq. Before that, he led the Arab world at the post-war Paris Peace Conference and on 3 January 1919 signed an agreement for Arab-Jewish cooperation with Dr Chaim Weizmann, president of the World Zionist Organisation. It said they were 'mindful of the racial kinship and ancient bonds existing between the Arabs and the Jewish people' and realised 'that the surest means of working out the consummation of their national aspirations is through the closest possible collaboration in the development of the Arab State and Palestine'.

They agreed to work together to encourage the migration of Jews into Palestine on a large scale while protecting the rights of the Arab peasants and tenant farmers, and to safeguard the free practice of religious observances. The Muslim holy places were to be under Muslim control. The Zionist movement undertook to assist the Arab residents of Palestine and the future Arab state to develop their natural resources and establish a growing economy. The boundaries between an Arab state and Palestine should be determined by a commission after the Paris Peace Conference.

However, Feisal grew disillusioned and in July 1933 he asked Britain to limit Jewish migration and land sales, for fear that 'otherwise in the near future the Arabs would either be squeezed out of Palestine or reduced to economic and social servitude'.

That indeed was already the Arabs' attitude: overwhelmingly, they did not want Jews to return to Palestine. On the Jewish side, early Zionist thinkers discussed in idealistic terms making friends with the Arabs and sharing the land with them. But as Jewish numbers mounted and Arab opposition hardened, for Zionists it was no longer the Arab question but the Arab problem. Arab resistance towards a Jewish state was implacable; among Jews, the Zionist movement moved ahead determinedly to achieve a state.

\* \* \*

The 1920s were uneasy years, especially late in the decade because of drought, poor harvests and economic depression. But 1929 was the turning point, trouble stemming, as it has so often done, over competing religious claims: above the Wailing Wall in Jerusalem is the large plateau of *Haram el-Sharif*, the Noble Sanctuary, also known as the Temple Mount, the third holiest site in Islam. Jews had access to the wall but were not allowed to put chairs there; nor could they erect screens to separate men and women in prayer as required by Orthodox Jewish practices. In taking up the mandate, Britain's policy was to maintain the status quo in religion so these restrictions were enforced. But now, Jewish activists protested and late in 1928 they put up screens at the wall; the police removed them. Muslims reacted angrily to the Jewish action, fuelled, too, by anger about Zionism and Jewish immigration. By August 1929, Arabs and Jews were attacking and killing each other. Britain could do little: its parsimony had reduced the Palestinian police force to a mere 1,576, only 173 of whom were British.[37] The Royal Air Force had the job of garrisoning Palestine but had an armoured car detachment of only eighty-five men.

On Friday, 23 August, thousands of Arabs poured out of the Noble Sanctuary after prayers and attacked the nearby Jewish Montefiore district with stones, guns and grenades. The next morning, in Hebron, thirty kilometres away, home to a Jewish community of 650, Arabs from villages set out to slaughter Jews: 69 were murdered. Some Jews were saved by Arabs who took them into their homes. A total of 133 Jews and 116 Arabs died before the violence was quelled. The riots probably ended most Jews' dream of a united state.

Britain sent an investigatory commission: its head, Sir Walter Shaw, blamed Arab fear of a Jewish-dominated Palestine and Jewish immigration, together with the creation of a landless class of Arabs. The next year, Britain sent another committee of inquiry – the Hope-Simpson Commission which led to a new White Paper. It recommended that state land be set aside for landless Arab peasants; it also said that Palestine had limited ability to absorb immigrants and proposed that Jewish immigration be restricted. The recommendation fell away after strong Jewish pressure against it.

The economic depression that the world suffered in the 1930s coincided with the Fifth Aliyah – an inpouring of Jewish immigrants because of the rise of Nazism in Germany and virulent anti-Semitism in other European countries. The Yishuv was enriched by educated, skilled Jews, but unemployment was high among both Jews and Arabs. Anger built up among Arabs. It needed but a trigger event to open the gates to upheaval. That happened on 15 April 1936 when an Arab gang robbed a bus and killed a Jewish passenger; the Haganah, the Jewish defence force formed in 1920, hit back by killing two Arab farmers. An Arab general strike began on 19 April, and mob violence swept through the land. On 25 April, in a belated move to overcome the paralysing factionalism, an across-the-board Arab Higher Committee was formed. By the end of October, when it called off the strike, one thousand Arabs and eighty Jews had died. The violent unrest went on.

Britain set up another inquiry under Lord Peel. It reported in July 1937 that the mandate could not be implemented until the antagonism between Arabs and Jews was ended – but that it was the mandate which created the antagonism and kept it alive. Peel recommended that the mandate be ended and Palestine partitioned into separate Jewish and Arab states.

Neither Arabs nor Jews agreed. The Arab Higher Committee said it violated Arab rights; Jews favoured partition but objected that the amount of land allocated to them was inadequate.

In January 1938 Britain appointed yet another commission, headed by Sir John Woodhead. The majority of this commission backed a three-way partition: a Jewish state of less than 5 percent of Palestine – a coastal strip about twenty kilometres wide; an Arab state in most of the remaining territory of central Palestine; and the rest, including Jerusalem, to remain a British mandate. Arabs rejected this, fearing that many Jews would cross into their designated land; Jews rejected it outright because it gave them so little.

So Britain organised a conference in London. The Arab delegation refused to meet the Jewish delegation, or to recognise their authority, or even to use the same entrances to the building. The British government submitted its own proposals. Both sides said no. The conference ended in failure on 17 March 1939.

But its end coincided with Britain's success, after bringing in seventy thousand troops, in finally crushing the Arab rebellion that had been ongoing since 1936. More than three thousand Arabs died, as well as two thousand Jews and six hundred Britons. Arab leaders were in exile or in prison. The Mufti had fled the country. The economy was in chaos.

With war approaching in Europe, Britain was alarmed about access to oil fields and air fields in the Middle East. It acted to mollify the region's Arabs. It went into reverse: a new White Paper said there could never have been any intention for Palestine to become a Jewish state against the will of the Arab population. Instead, with more than 450,000 Jews having now settled in Palestine, it said the Balfour Declaration regarding a 'national home for the Jewish people' had been met. The goal now was for an independent Palestine within ten years, ruled jointly by Arabs and Jews in such a way as to ensure that 'the essential interests of each community are safeguarded'. Jewish immigration must be limited to seventy-five thousand over the next five years, after which it would end unless the Arab community agreed to it continuing; transfers of land must be restricted to specified areas.

The Mufti, in exile in Baghdad, spurned the White Paper because it did not provide for immediate independence; however, general Arab reaction was to view it as a victory. For Jews, it was a grave setback, the end of the Zionist dream. Then World War II began, on 1 September 1939. David Ben-Gurion articulated the dilemma of opposing Britain in Palestine and supporting it in the war: 'We shall fight with Great Britain in this war as if there was no White Paper, and we shall fight the White Paper as if there was no war'.[38]

Mufti al-Husseini campaigned against Britain and then fled to Berlin. Confirming the worst Jewish beliefs about him, he fostered ideological and working links between radical Islam and Nazism. He met Hitler on 28 November 1941. It was a meeting of 'hearts and minds', and the Nazis made full propaganda use of it by distributing a photograph and broadcasting details on the shortwave radio service beamed to the Arab world.[39] Husseini told Hitler that he was 'admired by the entire Arab world' and that 'the Arabs were Germany's natural friends because they had the same enemies as had Germany, namely, the English, the Jews and the Communists'. He said Arabs were prepared to cooperate with Germany 'with all their hearts and stood ready to participate in the war'.[40] Hitler responded that Germany stood for uncompromising war against the Jews, and this naturally included active opposition to the Jewish national home in Palestine.[41]

Husseini spent the war years broadcasting anti-Allied propaganda to the Arab world for the Nazi Foreign Ministry and helped to enlist Bosnian Muslims to join Germany in fighting against the Soviet Union on the Eastern front. He fled Berlin as the war ended and ended up in Egypt where he was hailed as the 'Arab hero and symbol of al-Jihad and patience and struggle'. His influence waned.[42]

The Jewish response to Nazism was totally different. Thousands volunteered for the British forces: a Jewish brigade was formed, which fought as a unit in Italy. That had the result, by the end of the war, of producing a cadre of twenty thousand to twenty-five thousand trained Palestinian Jews who went into the Haganah to fight against Britain, and Arabs.

Zionists held back for much of the war. But as the Nazi genocide attempt became known, Britain's enforcement of quotas on immigration caused outrage. The saga of illegal immigration began, with boatloads of survivors from Europe running the British naval blockade in rusted old vessels. Some got through, others were intercepted and the would-be immigrants interned on nearby Cyprus – fifty thousand of them between 1946 and 1948. On occasion they were shipped back: sending a boatload to Germany caused especial anger among Jews and non-Jews. The drama in the struggle was portrayed in the well-known book and movie *Exodus*, with a beautiful, blonde, non-Jewish woman in love with a handsome Jewish freedom fighter.

The war and Holocaust ended, and Jewish leaders met again in Basel, Switzerland, on 9 December 1946 for the 22nd Zionist Congress. Chaim Weizmann looked at the gaps in the audience since the last congress held before the war, and said sombrely:

> Now in the light of past and present events the bitter truth must be spoken. We feared too little and we hoped too much. We underestimated the bestiality of the enemy; we overestimated the humanity, the wisdom, the sense of justice of our friends.[43]

As details of the Holocaust horrors emerged, belief grew in the West that settling Europe's remaining Jews in Palestine was a necessity. The murder of six million transformed the outlook of Jews worldwide: 'Zionists, anti-Zionists, atheists, ultra-Orthodox, socialists, capitalists, rich, poor – the Nazis made no exception. All Jews automatically became survivors'. A major shift occurred among Jews in the United States with enthusiastic support for Zionism. So much so—and given America's emergence as a superpower at the end of the war—that the United States became the centre of international Zionist effort.

Division was still intense among Jews about what to do. David Ben-Gurion led the mainstream Jewish Agency which served as a government-in-waiting for the Jews. He believed in awaiting total Allied victory over Germany before attacking Britain. But Menachem Begin, the Irgun leader since 1943, pressed for the end of self-restraint. In 1944 the war was won, he argued, yet Jews were being driven into the gas chambers. He declared war on Britain. [44]

Irgun embarked on terrorist bombing and shooting against British soldiers and Arabs, which were supplemented by Lehi which assassinated Lord Moyne, Britain's minister of state for the Middle East, while he was visiting Cairo in 1944. When the British forces captured, tried and executed Jewish terrorists, Irgun retaliated by kidnapping two British soldiers and hanging them.

Britain had had enough, and in February 1947 Foreign Secretary Ernest Bevin threw the Palestine problem to the United Nations. The General Assembly set up a UN Special Committee on Palestine (UNSCOP) made up of representatives of eleven nations. They went to Palestine in June 1947, spent five weeks there and issued a report: even while noting that Jews formed only half the population and owned 6 percent of the land, they unanimously recommended ending the British mandate and granting independence to Palestine (see appendix 2).

They were divided on its shape. A minority of three called for a federal state. The majority recommended partition into two states: Arab and Jewish, with Jerusalem as an international zone, saying: 'The basic premise underlying the partition proposal is that the claims to Palestine of the Arabs and Jews, both possessing validity, are irreconcilable'. They recommended economic union between the two states-to-be. Zionist leaders were not happy with the planned allocation of land but accepted; Arabs rejected it.

The report needed a two-thirds majority in the UN General Assembly. A tense vote on 29 November 1947 saw thirty-three votes in favour, thirteen against, and ten abstentions. Jews in Palestine and the world listened avidly via radio to the one-by-one roll call of nations. They were ecstatic: the two-thousand-year-old dream was in sight, a mere fifty years after Theodor Herzl and the launch of the Zionist movement. The vote:

- In favour (59 percent): Belgium, Belorussian SSR, Bolivia, Brazil, Canada, Costa Rica, Czechoslovakia, Denmark, Dominican Republic, Ecuador, France, Guatemala, Haiti, Iceland, Liberia, Luxembourg, Netherlands, New Zealand, Nicaragua, Norway, Panama, Paraguay, Peru, Philippines, Poland, South Africa, Soviet Union, Sweden, Ukrainian SSR, United States of America, Uruguay, Venezuela.
- Against (23 percent): Afghanistan, Cuba, Egypt, Greece, India, Iran, Iraq, Lebanon, Pakistan, Saudi Arabia, Syria, Turkey, Yemen.

- Abstentions (18 percent): Argentina, Chile, Republic of China, Colombia, El Salvador, Ethiopia, Honduras, Mexico, United Kingdom, Yugoslavia.
- Absent: Thailand.

It's a myth – propounded by critics of Israel – that the resolution was passed because Western nations dominated the General Assembly; they did not have a majority and could not muster a two-thirds majority on their own. The US State Department opposed partition out of concern for damaging relations with Arab countries, but President Harry Truman ordered a yes vote.

Not only did Eastern European countries vote for partition, but some were enthusiastic about the Jewish cause to the extent that, late in 1947, the Polish, Czechoslovakian and Hungarian governments opened training camps for the Haganah. The Hungarian army and secret police (their country was not then a UN member) trained about 1,500 local Jews, and 7,000 Polish Jews were trained by Red Army and Polish army soldiers.[45] There was little coherent Arab leadership in Palestine, but Arab and Muslim states, in totally opposing partition, ominously promised they would use military means to prevent it from happening.

The United Nations was now committed to partition. Britain refused to help. It didn't even wait for the General Assembly vote but, already in September 1947, announced that the mandate would end on 15 May 1948. Britain did not set up any institutions of government to facilitate a handover of power. It sulked. Speculation has stretched to the thought that Britain shared the widespread view that the Jews did not stand a chance against the Arab masses, and when they lost the door would open for Britain to reenter Palestine to restore order and retain a hold. Whatever it was, Britain left a vacuum. Jews and Arabs were left to slug it out.

*Chapter Two*

# Freedom and War

*Violence and terror spread on both sides after Jews accepted and Arabs rejected UN partition. The Zionist dream became reality: the State of Israel was created. But only three years after the Holocaust, Jews fought for survival.*

\* \* \*

At 8:20 a.m. the day after the United Nations 29 November vote for partition, eight Arabs from Jaffa attacked a bus on the coastal plain, killing five Jews. A half-hour later, they went for another bus, killing two. Arab snipers also fired at Tel Aviv from Jaffa, killing one person. This is widely viewed as the start of the civil war between Jews and Arabs. However, the historian Benny Morris questions whether these were immediate responses to the United Nations. Their primary motivation might rather have been retaliation for an Irgun attack ten days earlier on an Arab family near Ra'anana when five men were seized and shot – which was, in turn, retaliation because it was believed, perhaps wrongly, that the family had informed the British about Irgun members training nearby, and this had led to a British attack and the death of five Jewish youngsters. [1]

The official Arab response to the partition decision was a call by the Arab Higher Committee for mass protest through a three-day general strike to start on 2 December. On that day, an Arab mob carrying clubs and knives surged out of the Old City in Jerusalem and fell on Jews in the adjacent Mamilla district and then went on a rampage into the city centre's Jaffa Street, assaulting Jews and looting shops. British soldiers and police did little to halt them, but Haganah members opened fire.

Whichever the true first episode, Arab anger burst out in violence through the country. The uncompromising rejection by Palestine's Arabs of partition and their own state was to drive them, encouraged and aided by the seven nations of the Arab League and in defiance of the wishes of the majority in the United Nations, into a disastrous course of action against Zionism and Jews. Within months, it was to result in the devastation of Arab society and everyday living, the stunting of Palestinian self-identity and national aspiration, which had been developing, and to the dispersal of the bulk of Palestinians through the world. Hundreds of thousands in successive generations were doomed to lives of deprivation, misery and hopelessness. Nor has this yet ended. Whereas for Jews the year 1948 is joyously celebrated as *milhemet ha'atzma'ut*, the War of Independence, to Arabs it is the *Nakba*, the catastrophe.

The Arab fate wasn't anticipated at the end of 1947. Instead, it was thought that the Jews would soon be overrun and evicted, or more. That is what Britain's military head, the chief of the imperial general staff, believed: 'In the long run the Jews would not be able to cope . . . and would be thrown out of Palestine unless they came to terms with [the Arabs]'.[2]

An Arab militia of several thousand was quickly formed and became the Arab Liberation Army. Armed soldiers, some well-equipped with heavy armament, poured across the borders under its umbrella. Some were Palestinian Arabs and others were from Lebanon, Jordan, Egypt, Syria, Iraq and even distant Libya, as well as elsewhere in North Africa. Britain's army and police and officials were intent on getting out, with as few casualties as possible. They were less and less concerned, and increasingly less able, to keep the two opposing sides apart and to halt the violence. Attacks and counterattacks and reprisals became the gruesome everyday way of life.

The Etzion Bloc to the south of Jerusalem was kept under siege, and the first kibbutz finally surrendered on 13 May to a mixed force of Arab militia and Jordan's Arab Legion. The defenders gathered and put down their arms. They were shot down – 127 of them, including 21 women – with confused reports of whether the killers were the irregulars or legion soldiers, or both. Some defenders escaped into a cellar, but hand grenades were thrown in and the building was collapsed over them. A total of 157 Jews died, including the massacre victims. Five survived, saved by legion officers. The other three kibbutzim surrendered. Survivors were imprisoned. The settlements were razed.

These and other attacks imprinted on the Jewish psyche the certainty that the Arabs were determined to do nothing less than wipe them out, and that this was a war with few boundaries on behaviour. Any lingering doubts were dispelled when, on 6 February, the Arab Higher Committee told the UN secretary-general:

The Palestinian Arabs consider any attempt by Jewish people or by whatever power or group of power [*sic*] to establish a Jewish state in an Arab territory to be an act of aggression that will be resisted by force. . . . The Palestinian Arabs make a grave declaration before the UN, before God and before history that they will never submit to any power that comes to Palestine to impose a partition.[3]

Irgun and Lehi, usually acting separately, were by then well into terrorism with the frank aim of instilling fear in both Arabs and Britons. Irgun and its mother Revisionist body had argued the issue internally after the Peel Commission in July 1937 recommended partition: the Revisionists rejected it, as did the Arabs, but the Zionist Organisation accepted it in principle. Faced by the resurgence of violent attacks by Arabs, the Jewish Agency and its Haganah underground armed wing had adopted a policy of *havlaga* (restraint). The Irgun derided this and opted for retaliation. The tipping point for them had come on 9 November 1937, when Arabs murdered five Jewish workers in the field of a kibbutz near Jerusalem. Kibbutz *Maaleh HaHamisha*, the Hill of the Five, was named after them and is today a successful hotel and conference centre. Retaliation was delivered five days later: Irgun history marks 14 November 1937 as 'Black Sunday', with 'transition from "passive" to "active" defence'.[4]

From then on, Irgun, and the smaller Lehi, on the one hand, and Arabs, on the other, threw bombs into the marketplaces of each other's communities, sometimes also killing their own, set off a mine in a cinema, planted mines on roads and shot at people in cafés and on streets. Hundreds died.

Roads linking towns and kibbutzim and moshavim were a focus for Arab attack. Ben-Gurion had decreed that none of the 250 settlements, however isolated, was to be abandoned. In a few cases, women and children were sent to safety, but otherwise the Haganah fought unremittingly to keep open the links. Only in the most extreme instances was there withdrawal or surrender. The road from Tel Aviv to Jerusalem was a particular target for Arabs. It was vital and vulnerable: rising from the plain, the road went through narrow gorges starting at Bab-al-Wad, now called Sha'are Hagai, and was open to attack from the surrounding hills. Metal sheeting was bolted onto trucks which drove in convoy carrying food, fuel and ammunition to the one hundred thousand Jews in Jerusalem. The trucks were decimated.

In the last ten days of March, only 41 supply trucks (out of 136) from Tel Aviv got through.[5] Convoys were suspended for a time after 22 March when an entire convoy of thirty vehicles was destroyed. A few dozen bare chassis lie at the sides of today's highway as mute memorials to the many who died during those desperate days.

By the end of March, the death toll reached two thousand, with four thousand injured, more or less divided between Jews and Arabs. That was in a population of less than two million.

The UN's Special Committee on Palestine, alarmed, had already reported on 12 March that 'present indications point to the inescapable conclusion that when the mandate is terminated, Palestine is likely to suffer severely from administrative chaos and widespread strife and bloodshed'. Reflecting the deep worry, on 25 March President Harry Truman withdrew support for partition, at least at that time. He called on the United Nations to take on temporary trusteeship without delay: unless 'emergency action' was taken, he said, there would be no public authority in Palestine capable of preserving law and order. He urged a truce.

Both Jews and Arabs rejected him: the Jews because they insisted on going ahead with partition and the Arabs because they wanted partition dropped. A few days later, Chaim Weizmann powerfully conveyed the Jewish position in a letter to Truman: 'The choice for our people, Mr President, is between statehood and extermination'.[6]

\* \* \*

Now there was a shift in tactics which was to fundamentally alter both the immediate and the far future: the Haganah, after fighting defensively in accordance with its policy of restraint, went on the offensive. That followed the new approach in *Tochnit Dalet* (Plan D), so named because it was the fourth strategic plan prepared by the Haganah since 1941. It was formulated in early March under the direction of Yigael Yadin, the Haganah's chief of operations, and was sent to brigade commanders on 10 March.[7] It was meant to be implemented in the first half of May when British troops moved to leave and Arab armies mustered on the borders for invasion. It ordered the Haganah to defend the state against invasion and ensure free Jewish movement. The Haganah was to secure connections in response to the Arab attacks on the roads. Land was to be seized and consolidated. Brigade commanders were given the power to decide whether villages were destroyed or occupied. Resisting villages were to be destroyed and their people expelled. Villages and towns had to be cleared so that Arab residents would not be there to aid the invaders. The Arab armies would be impeded because roads would be choked with fleeing refugees. Significantly, nowhere did Plan Dalet 'speak of a policy or desire to expel "the Arab inhabitants" of Palestine'.[8]

There was no formal launch of Plan Dalet: 'The massive Haganah documentation from the first half of April contains no reference to an implementation of Plan D, and only rarely do such references appear in the Haganah's paperwork during the following weeks'.[9] It came into effect piecemeal as needs developed. And the needs were indeed critical, and the United Nations and the United States were right to be anxious. 'In late March, the Haganah endured a series of major disasters on the roads', Morris notes.[10] 'They appeared to portend defeat in the war – and demonstrated the imperative for a basic change in strategy that would shift the initiative to the Yishuv and allow a diversion of energies from protecting convoys to smashing the Arab militias in their home bases. In less than a fortnight, the Haganah lost most of its armored vehicles and dozens of its best troops'.

The first action under the plan was Operation Nachshon, early in April, to reopen the Tel Aviv–Jerusalem road and to neutralise the Arab villages from which attacks were mounted. On Friday 9 April the Haganah was in the last stages of a see-saw battle with large forces of Syrians, Iraqis and Palestinians for the village of Kastel, overlooking the road. The Arabs were defeated. Villagers fled or were rounded up and expelled, with or without their possessions. Their houses were blown up. Jerusalem was relieved, at least for the time being.

* * *

Also on that day, 4.8 kilometres (3 miles) away, on the edge of Jerusalem, a combined armed force of Irgun Zvai Leumi and Lehi attacked the Arab village of Deir Yassin and its six hundred people. The mass killings they perpetrated had far-reaching effects, which still reverberate today. To Arabs it became a lesson in what the Jews were capable of doing and would do to them; it generated fear and drove untold numbers to flee their homes, never to return.

More than sixty years later, Deir Yassin remains a potent political event: early in 2013, Google carried 343,000 references. Yet the facts about Deir Yassin continue to be hotly argued with widely different claims about what did or did not happen.

For enemies of Israel, Deir Yassin conveys the evil of Jews and the Zionism which brought about the Jewish state; they describe it as part of a carefully conceived plot to drive out Palestinians. A 'Deir Yassin Remembered' organisation ensures anniversary ceremonies are held each year.

What critics overlook, whether by design or ignorance, is that Deir Yassin was a maverick operation, way outside the Jewish mainstream. Irgun and Lehi were dissident extremist right-wing groups. They bitterly opposed the Jewish Agency, which was the representative body for Palestine's Jews, and also the Haganah, the agency's underground military arm which later became the State of Israel's army. The Haganah's Jerusalem head, David Shaltiel, knew that the dissidents planned to attack Deir Yassin and gave written, cautious, approval. He evidently did so because he believed he had no choice; clearly, he did not have the slightest suspicion of a massacre.

When the Deir Yassin killings became known, Irgun and Lehi faced wholesale and vehement Jewish condemnation. The Jewish Agency expressed its 'horror and disgust' and the two chief rabbis, Ashkenazi and Sephardic, said they were horrified at 'behaviour which casts a slur upon the Jews' struggle for survival'.[11] To the Jewish right wing, however, it was and remains simply a battle in which some innocent villagers died, and massacre accusations are lies meant to besmirch the impeccable Irgun and Lehi fighting forces.

The number of deaths – '254' or 'more than 200' – was reported by newspapers and on radio at the time because it was stated authoritatively by the Irgun's Jerusalem commander, Mordechai Ra'anan. He later recalled his press conference: 'I told the reporters that 254 were killed so that a big figure would be published and so that the Arabs would panic not only in Jerusalem but across the country, and this goal was accomplished'.[12]

As Ra'anan said, '254' was successfully used by Jews to scare and stampede Palestinians; Palestinians also used it successfully to prove that the Jews had murderous intentions. 'Nobody counted the bodies, nor those that were buried, and everybody exaggerated their numbers', according to a later statement by Shimon Monita, a Lehi participant who was actually a Haganah spy inside the organisation:

> The dissidents were interested in boasting and scaring the Arabs; the Haganah and the Jewish Agency were interested in making dissidents look bad and scaring the Arabs; the Arabs were interested in making the Jews look bad; the British were interested in making the Jewish terrorists look bad. Everyone grasped at the number that Ra'anan had made up.[13]

But the Arab exaggeration backfired calamitously for them because it accelerated Palestinian flight in many parts of the country, thus clearing land for Jews to take over and forever enlarging the refugee problem.

The claimed death toll was eventually shown to be wrong. This came thirty-nine years later from the Research and Documentation Centre at the Palestinian Bir Zeit University on the West Bank as part of its documentation of destroyed Arab villages. In 1987 the centre reported that it had checked through the names of Deir Yassin villagers and was 'absolutely convinced' that the number killed did not exceed 120 'and that the groups which carried out the massacre exaggerated the numbers in order to frighten Palestinian residents into leaving their villages and cities without resistance'. It listed the names of 107 who died and 12 wounded.[14]

Exaggeration has also been perpetuated by mindless journalism, such as the *Guardian* in London in 2001: a report about the Sabra and Shatila murders in Lebanon dragged in a reference to Deir Yassin as 'the Palestinian village where 254 villagers were massacred in April 1948, in the most spectacular single attack in the conquest of Palestine'.[15] That was three errors in one sentence: the number who died was wrong, the reference to 'conquest of Palestine' was simplistic and there was ignorance of the greater number of deaths – Jewish – in the Etzion Bloc a short while before.

Deir Yassin has a sad postscript. At the time, in condemning the massacre, the Haganah announced: 'We will maintain the graves and the remaining property . . . and return it to the owners when the time comes'.[16] That has not happened. Instead, where the village once stood there is now the Givat Shaul mental hospital. Old stone buildings that were once part of the village are in use inside the hospital compound.

\* \* \*

The war intensified. The day after Deir Yassin, artillery manned by 250 Syrians fired about forty large-calibre shells into Jerusalem's Jewish western suburbs, killing three Jews and injuring seven. 'It was the first time so far as is known that heavy calibre shells have ever been fired into Jerusalem', reported the *New York Times*.

Yet another low point came the next Tuesday: a regular weekly convoy of Jewish doctors, nurses and guards in buses escorted by armoured vehicles set off for Jerusalem's Hadassah hospital on Mount Scopus. The area was under Arab control. The convoy had British assurance of safe passage but was ambushed by Arabs in Sheikh Jarrah: seventy-eight people died during more than five hours of withering gunfire and firebombs. British soldiers a kilometre away did not intervene, except for one early brave attempt. Perhaps Arabs were retaliating for Deir Yassin, or perhaps because they accused the Haganah of using the hospital as a base for attacks.

But although not apparent on the surface, the Jewish situation was no longer as bleak and life-threatening as it seemed. The balance of strength was changing: in November 1947 one out of three Jewish combatants had weapons; the Haganah, built up as an underground defensive force, had only light weapons and not enough of them; it had no artillery, tanks, military aircraft, anti-tank or anti-aircraft guns. Weapons began to come from abroad. The first shipment of many arrived by air from Czechoslovakia on the night of 31 March 1948 at Beit Daras, a former RAF airfield: four kilometres of light bulbs rolled out on the ground provided illumination for a Douglas Skymaster cargo plane chartered from an American company; once the aircraft landed, the landing lights were switched off, and in an hour and a half the weapons were unloaded, the landing lights switched on and the plane flew back to Prague – all under the noses of a British military unit and Arab villages in the vicinity. The two hundred rifles, forty machine guns and one hundred sixty thousand bullets were rushed to Haganah units. Czechoslovakia was by then inside the Soviet empire and could only have supplied Israel with the approval of Joseph Stalin in Moscow. So although anti-Zionist, indeed anti-Semitic, he was supportive of the Jewish state.

From April onwards, the Haganah was better armed than its Arab opponents. In May, after the invasion by Arab armies, the balance was to swing in favour of the Arabs. But it returned to the Jews in June and stayed like that.

As part of the change, the pattern of attack in Plan Dalet was put into wider effect to clear roads as well as towns with large Arab populations. The front-page headlines on Tuesday, 7 May in the *Palestine Post* (later renamed the *Jerusalem Post*) conveyed the events:

*Haganah wrests Safad from Iraqis and Syrians in bitter fighting*
*Gangs flee to hills in West*

*Red Cross plan for Holy City*
*To be a 'hospital' respected by armies*

*Jaffa capitulates: An 'open' city*

*Jerusalem road cleared by Jews*

*Jerusalem still without water*

*Ibn Saud promises to intervene 'at time agreed upon'*

*Road truce in Western Galilee*

*Britons leave as 'E-Day' looms*

*Russia to open consulates*

An estimated three hundred thousand Arabs fled their homes, many on foot in long lines on the roads. But by then, about one hundred thousand Arabs had already fled. They included the elite of the Palestinian community, the urban educated and those who had money. Their departure created a great void inside Palestinian society. Jaffa was a striking example: when the town surrendered, only four thousand of the seventy thousand Arab residents were still there; the municipal council could no longer muster a quorum; the mayor had gone and only one person was left of the three-man caretaker committee he had appointed when he left.

Within months, the Arab exodus was to total 700,000–750,000. The obvious triggers were fear of conflict and fear of the Jews, and especially after the story of Deir Yassin did its rounds, complete with its exaggerated death toll. Additionally, there was the sharply declining economic situation: jobs were lost; fields were not harvested and food supplies dried up; markets closed and supplies from Jewish merchants ended; electricity, water and fuel were scarce or nonexistent; public transportation ceased; all the Arab banks closed. The Arab population did not have the capacity and organisational ability of the Yishuv to keep going.

The initial Jewish belief, which still persists, was that many Arabs fled at the urging of leaders who told them in radio broadcasts that they would soon return home once the Jews had been defeated and evicted; the creation of the Palestinian refugee problem is thus held to be the fault of the Arabs themselves.

This version of events was challenged by a new generation of Israeli historians whose work began to appear in the late 1980s. The radio story has little support. The 'New Historians' emerged with new information and insights after accessing declassified Israel Defense Forces (IDF) files and other documentary sources. This results in Benny Morris, a leading New Historian, noting that Arab leaders had no consistent policy about people moving out of battle areas or potential battle areas, whether out of the country or to other parts of Palestine: 'This ambivalence was to characterize their thinking and behaviour down to mid-May 1948. Advice and orders changed from month to month and place to place'.[17]

The radio allegation is rejected in a particular study by the Palestinian historian Walid Khalidi: 'I can find no significant trace of this allegation in Zionist sources in 1948, although one would expect it to be made then'.[18] He reports that he could not find any trace of such broadcasts in minutes of the Arab League General Assembly, or in leading Arab newspapers in the region, or in the day-by-day broadcasts from Arab capitals and secret Arab stations as recorded by the BBC's Caversham Park monitoring station in Britain. What exists instead is overwhelming contrary evidence, as Morris finds, of repeated orders to Arabs not to flee.

In any event, Plan Dalet obviously contributed hugely to the exodus: that was its declared aim. But here, too, there was inconsistency and confusion. More than four hundred villages were cleared and destroyed; many, many thousands of villagers were driven into exile at gunpoint. But it did not always happen. Many villages were left untouched, including those which made their peace with the Jews, such as Abu Gosh outside Jerusalem. In Haifa, which began with the second highest number of Arab residents in the country, local Jewish leaders implored Arabs to remain and to live with them in peace, but most chose to flee. Arabs who remained in the country became Israeli citizens.

War raged in a small geographical space, and the tempo was building up during April and early May. The Haganah feared far worse was to come after the British left on 15 May, and armies of the surrounding Arab countries invaded. It was vital to clear the land as much as possible beforehand and to continue after the invasion, so as to link Jewish towns and settlements, to destroy shelter for the enemy and to get rid of potential attackers and saboteurs in the rear.

Clearing the land of Arabs opened the way to murder, rape and looting of the civilian population. The combatants were not spared:

> Until April, neither side generally took prisoners, partly because they had no
> adequate facilities to hold them. . . . In practice neither side, after capturing
> enemy positions, houses, or traffic, kept prisoners. Captured combatants were
> usually shot out of hand. . . . During the first stage of the civil war, Jews
> probably killed more POWs than vice versa simply because Jews overran
> more Arab positions.[19]

After May, however, both sides generally observed the Geneva Conventions
in taking prisoners.

Atrocities can be found in any war over the centuries. But to ascribe
barbaric behaviour to Jews in 1948 runs counter to Jewish self-image and
self-belief. Many Israelis refuse to accept that such things happened, and
Morris is strongly criticised by 'Old Zionists' for his revelations.

The essential fact about 1948 is that it was not a static situation, and the
Jewish leadership's attitudes changed as events unfolded. They ended up
with policies about expulsion which had not been on the agenda at the start
(even though some leaders had spoken in favour of 'transfer'). Initially, the
elementary aim was to survive: to weather the successive onslaughts by
Palestinian Arabs and Arab states.[20] At first, the desire was to incorporate
clusters of settlements in the state; West Jerusalem, with its large Jewish
population and its emotional significance, featured large.

> But as the war progressed, a more general expansionist aim took hold: to add
> more territory to the miniscule state and to arm it with defensible borders. By
> September, some spoke of expanding as far eastward as the Jordan River, seen
> as a 'natural' frontier (both the UN partition borders and the new lines created
> by the May–July 1948 hostilities were a strategist's nightmare), while incorpo-
> rating the historic heartland of the Jewish people, Judea and Samaria, in the
> new state.

After four or five months of fighting, a third aim emerged: 'to reduce the size
of Israel's prospective large and hostile Arab minority, seen as a potential
powerful fifth column, by belligerency and expulsion'.

* * *

Some Arabs see that period differently. A populist view is that Plan Dalet
wasn't simply a response to events but that getting rid of Arabs from the
mandate territory of Palestine was secretly and carefully preplanned. The fact
that Deir Yassin was an Irgun/Lehi activity is brushed aside, and some say it
was an organised starting point: 'It stands as the starkest early warning of a
calculated depopulation of over 400 Palestinian villages and cities and the
expulsion of 70 percent of the Palestinian population', according to a Palestinian website.[21]

Ilan Pappe, a UK-based former Israeli academic, takes this even further by saying that the Deir Yassin village

> was doomed to be wiped out because it was within the areas designated in Plan Dalet to be cleansed. Because of the prior [peace] agreement they had signed with the village, the Haganah decided to send the Irgun and Stern Gang troops, so as to absolve themselves from any official accountability. [22]

This seems to be an important statement. However, Pappe does not offer any supporting source, let alone any evidence, so it's difficult to say whether it really means anything. [23]

* * *

With Britain's departure imminent, ruinous war raging up and down the country and the frightening prospect of invasion by Arab states, the thirteen-member Jewish ruling council, the *Minhelet Ha'am* (People's Administration), met on Wednesday, 12 May to decide what to do. They argued fiercely whether to accede to the wishes of US president Truman and other international friends and hold back on creating a state. Ben-Gurion was the driving force in rejecting delay. The leap to independence was agreed by a majority of one vote.

'State of Israel Is Born' was the banner headline in the *Palestine Post* on Sunday, 16 May: 'The first independent Jewish state in 19 centuries was born in Tel Aviv as the British Mandate over Palestine came to an end at midnight on Friday, and it was immediately subjected to the test of fire', it declared.

The state should have been declared on 15 May, when the mandate ended, but that was the Sabbath so the momentous event was celebrated the day before. Nor could newspapers report it until Sunday.

What to call it? Judea and Zion were suggested, but Ben-Gurion's 'Israel' was accepted. New postage stamps were already being printed so the first issue did not bear the country's name but said 'Hebrew Post' in Hebrew and Arabic. The Tel Aviv Museum of Art on Rothschild Boulevard was the launch venue. An official found a dusty portrait of Theodor Herzl for the occasion, and he also found two large Zionist flags – but they were dirty and had to be rushed to a laundry. British interference to block the independence declaration was feared, so the venue was kept secret. But as a radio station broadcasted what was going to happen, it didn't matter, and indeed there was no problem.

At 4 p.m. on Friday, 14 May, David Ben-Gurion read to more than two hundred leaders packed into the hall a Declaration of Independence that proclaimed the existence of a Jewish state called Israel at midnight that night. It took sixteen minutes to read. The council members signed the proclamation, and it was quickly put into a bank vault for safety, in case proof would be needed to show that a Jewish state had indeed come into being. A rabbi recited *Shehecheyanu* (Who has given us life), the two-thousand-year-old Talmudic prayer of thanks to celebrate special events. The gathering closed at 4:38 p.m. with emotional singing of the Zionist anthem, *Hatikvah* (The Hope), which now became the state's official anthem and remains so. Ben-Gurion ended the event with the words 'The State of Israel is established! This meeting is adjourned!'

Earlier, at 8 a.m. that Friday, Britain's high commissioner, Sir Alan Cunningham, had walked out of Government House in Jerusalem. Dressed in general's uniform, he inspected an honour guard of the Highland Light Infantry, flew to Haifa and boarded the Royal Navy's HMS *Euryalus*. With him were other British top officials. They left after midnight, to the crash of a seventeen-gun salute. That was the formal end of the mandate, even though five thousand soldiers stayed in Haifa until the end of June to mop up. During this time, Britain played hardball and debarred a Panamanian ship carrying Jewish immigrants from using the port; they were instead brought ashore by tugs and lighters.[24] The night before the rearguard finally left, explosions lit the port area as equipment and records were destroyed. In the harbour, depth charges exploded every half-hour to ward off any frogmen who might have tried to fix limpet mines to the British ships. In the early afternoon of 30 June, the Union Jack was lowered to the mournful sound of the 'Last Post'. The Israeli flag was promptly raised.[25]

On the morning of 15 May, at six minutes after midnight Israeli time, 6:11 p.m. in Washington, DC, the United States was the first country to give recognition – de facto, but still recognition – to the new state. It was done at Truman's insistence; he was still at odds with his senior officials. He had, in fact, invited a request for recognition: but as the state had not yet been declared and was nameless, the written request by the Washington representative of the Jewish Agency for Palestine asked for recognition of 'the Jewish state'. A host of countries followed, and the Soviet Union gave de jure recognition on 17 May. De jure recognition by the United States was to follow in January the next year, and Britain within the month after.

At a minute after midnight on 15 May, Transjordan's King Abdullah, standing on the eastern side of the Allenby Bridge on the Jordan River, fired a shot from his revolver into the air and shouted 'Forward!' Jordan's Arab Legion soldiers rolled into the West Bank. Arab armies in the south and north entered at dawn, crossing over the UN-sanctioned borders.

Their declared purpose was to eliminate the new state. As the Arab League told UN secretary-general Trygve Lie, they aimed to create a 'United States of Palestine', a single democratic state. They proclaimed Palestine as an Arab country. Egypt said they were entering 'by invitation and with the unequivocal consent of the Palestinian people'. Lie condemned their actions as 'the first armed aggression which the world had seen since the [Second World] War'. But the United Nations failed to rush in a military peacekeeping force to repel the aggressors and protect its own partition decision – the first of many acts of omission and commission over the years to come which caused Israel to lack faith in the world body.

Arab leaders stoked up popular belief that it would be a swift and easy victory. Thus the Arab League's secretary-general, Abdul Pazek Azzam Pasha, said: 'This will be a war of extermination and a momentous massacre, which will be spoken of like the Mongolian massacres and the Crusades'. Ahmed Shukairy, the spokesman of the Mufti of Jerusalem, announced that the Arabs' goal was 'the elimination of the Jewish state'.[26]

Once more, though, the story was more complex than it seemed, chiefly because of King Abdullah of Jordan. He had been speaking to Zionist leaders for years trying, unsuccessfully, to persuade them to accept Jordanian sovereignty over the entire Palestine area; he said Jews would get a small autonomous area which he called a 'republic'. Now, still in secret contact, he pragmatically recognized Jewish strength and Arab weakness. His aim was to seize the West Bank, assigned by the United Nations as a Palestinian state, and to take Jerusalem, too – which is what he proceeded to do. In the south, Egypt crossed the border intent not only on aborting the new Israeli state but also to seize land for itself.

Studies in recent years have shown that much of the blood-curdling threats and promises, however sincerely meant as expressions of hatred against Jews, were empty boasting, and many of the invaders were poorly armed and badly led while the Haganah was relatively strong. But as contemporary records of the time show, this was not known then. Walter Laqueur, a war correspondent in Jerusalem through the fighting, noted: 'For a while this war went very badly for the Jews of Palestine: there was not much optimism in Jerusalem during March 1948. But then the tide turned, resulting in the Arab exodus'.[27] Jews believed they faced an existential threat and they fought to live. As Laqueur put it, '[T]he Palestinian Jews, unlike the Arabs, had nowhere to go: they were fighting with their backs to the wall'. With the British gone, survivors were rushed in from the displaced persons camps in Europe and, despite minimum training, were sent into battle.

\* \* \*

Sixty-one years later, in an article in *Haaretz*, Uri Avnery, father of Israel's peace movement, powerfully recalled the Jewish mood and attitudes of that fraught period, with the added perspective of current knowledge.[28] The background was what had appeared in the newspaper on Friday, 14 May 1948 with the front-page headline: 'State of Israel will be declared today'. The editorial described Britain's White Paper of 1939 as a 'shameful' betrayal of the historical right of the Jewish people to return to their homeland. It spoke of the 'unprecedented enslavement and suffering' of Jews. It referred to the 'increased danger' and 'desperate struggle' with neighbouring Arab nations who refused to accept the return of Jews to their land. It said that if Jews withstood the test and succeeded, then this will be 'the day that we will lay the foundation for a life of security and liberty for ourselves and for our children'.

*I didn't read the* Haaretz *editorial of May 14, 1948, on the day it appeared. In fact, I saw no newspapers at all then.*

*My unit – B Company of the 54th Battalion of the Givati infantry brigade, later to become the "Samson's Foxes" company – was stationed at Kibbutz Hulda, near the dining hall, which was off-limits to us. On that Friday, the ban was lifted for a few hours so we could listen to David Ben-Gurion's speech declaring the establishment of the state.*

*The truth is that we, the soldiers on the front, couldn't have cared less. To us it seemed an insignificant event. The state had existed in practice for some time and existed everywhere we won. We knew that if we won the war, there would be a state and that if we were defeated there would be no state – and that we would not be around, either.*

*We were told we would be going into action that night. Our mission: to conquer the village of Al-Qubab, between Ramle and Latrun. It looked like a tough operation. We were immersed in preparations, such as cleaning our rifles.*

*Still, I went to the dining room. I was curious about one thing: the name of the new state. Judea? Hebrew State? State of Jerusalem? When Ben-Gurion reached the words "which is the State of Israel," I left. I knew the rest would be blah blah.*

*The truth is that the* Haaretz *editorial also now strikes me as blah blah. It's a collection of all the clichés of the time. Still, it's touching, because it reminds us of what we believed in then. For many of us, the article generates a so-called cognitive dissonance: on the one hand, what we felt then; on the other, the truth as we know it today.*

*For the combatants and the entire Yishuv, as the Jewish community in Palestine was known until 1948, it was an existential war, pure and simple. The slogan was "No alternative," and we all believed this without question. We fought with our backs to the wall. The enemy attacked us from all sides and our families' lives were in danger. We believed that we were few, very few, and poorly armed, facing a sea of Arabs.*

*Indeed, the Palestinians (who were called "the gangs") controlled all the roads in the first half of the war, and in the second half the Arab armies reached the Jewish population centers, encircled Jewish Jerusalem and approached Tel Aviv. The Yishuv lost 6,000 young people, out of a population of 635,000. Entire age groups were almost wiped out. Countless acts of heroism were performed.*

*We left no Arabs behind our front line, and the Arabs did likewise. In the circumstances of the time, that seemed an obvious military need. Soldiers in those days didn't think in terms of "ethnic cleansing," a term that didn't yet exist. We had no understanding about the true balance of forces between us and the other side. The Arabs seemed to be a vast force. We didn't know that the Palestinians were split internally, that they were incapable of uniting and creating a countrywide defense force, that they had no leadership and lacked serious arms. Afterward, when the Arab armies entered the war, we didn't know they were incapable of cooperating among themselves and that it was more important for them to beat one another to the punch than to strike at us.*

*More and more people now understand the full implications of the Nakba, the huge tragedy of the Palestinian people, and of all the individuals who lost their homes, land and most of their homeland. The war songs from the period evoke what we felt and thought as the events unfolded. A vast chasm stretches between the emotional reality of that time and the objective truth we know today.*

*There are people who see the war of 1948 as a diabolical scheme by the Zionist leadership, which intended all along to expel the Palestinians from the entire country and turn it into the Jewish state. Those who subscribe to this opinion compare it to the actions of the present-day settlers, who are dispossessing the Palestinians of the remainder of their land, and whose actions besmirch the pioneer past. Religious zealots and fascist hooligans, self-styled successors to the pioneers, are twisting the true intentions of that generation, and the actions of the Israeli army in the Gaza war besmirched the deeds of the 1948 fighters. As a member of the Givati Brigade of the time, I am unable to feel any sense of belonging to or identification with today's Givati.*

*How then is it possible to reconcile the contradiction between our intentions and feelings at the time, when we established the state and paid for it with our blood, pure and simple, and the historic injustice we inflicted on the other side? How is it possible to sing about the hopes and dreams of our youth, and at the same time recognize the terrible wrongs? How can we sing whole-heartedly the battle songs of that war without disavowing the cruel tragedy of the Palestinian people we fomented?*

*A few weeks ago, [US president] Barack Obama told the Turks they must come to terms with the massacre of the Armenians by their forebears, and in the same context noted that the Americans, too, must acknowledge the murder of the Indians by their ancestors.*

*I think the same is possible in regard to the disaster we brought on the Palestinians. It is necessary for our mental health as a nation and as human beings, and it is the first step toward future reconciliation. We must admit and recognize the consequences of our actions and repair what can be repaired, without disavowing our past and youthful innocence.*

*We have to live with the contradiction, because it is the truth of our lives.*[29]

\* \* \*

The United Nations brokered a truce on 29 May, to come into effect on 11 June. A succession of truces followed. They worked only partly. International arms embargoes were flouted and both sides fought for supremacy. In mid-

July, Egyptian planes were still bombing Tel Aviv: an air raid killed fourteen and wounded forty.[30] Irgun and Lehi agreed to disarm and to be integrated into the army. But it did not happen easily. The Irgun bought an American ship of 5,000 tonnes, named it *Altalena*, and sailed it from France with 1,600 immigrants and arms and ammunition. Ben-Gurion insisted that all the arms be handed to the IDF. The Irgun refused and Ben-Gurion ordered the army to shell the ship. It sank in full public gaze off Tel Aviv, with the loss of sixteen people and cargo. Ben-Gurion was abjured by the Irgun, but his action ensured that the country had a single national army.

Terrible consequences followed the drive to widen the corridor between Jerusalem and Tel Aviv by capturing Arab towns along the route – Lydda (now Lod) and Ramle – and expelling the residents. The towns were overrun and the Ramle people were bussed to the Arab front lines; the Lydda people were forced to walk seventeen kilometres (ten miles) in searing heat to the Arab Legion lines. There were deaths. The operations added another fifty thousand to seventy thousand to the refugee count. The residents' houses were handed to Jewish immigrants – both to block the expelled from reclaiming them and to give to the nearly 700,000 Jewish immigrants who poured in between May 1948 and December 1951: about 126,000 displaced Jews from Europe plus 270,000 from Eastern Europe plus the 300,000 who were the first wave of the 750,000 who fled from Arab lands.

By mid-October, Israel was fully on the offensive against the invading armies and to secure its borders. The Egyptian army was broken in the Negev and driven out. In battles at sea, naval commandos used boats with explosives to sink the Egyptian flagship *Emir Farouk*. The Arab Liberation Army attacked Jewish areas in the north and the IDF moved in: within two days it chased the ALA and the Lebanese army into Lebanon and ambushed and destroyed a Syrian battalion. The entire Upper Galilee was captured. Another fifty thousand local Arabs fled, some in advance of the fighting, others expelled. The battles ended only in May the next year when the IDF took Umm Rashrash in the south, at the head of the Red Sea. That became the Eilat holiday resort.

Even in defeat, the Arab states refused to recognise Israel. But armistice agreements were signed between Israel and Egypt in February 1949, followed by Lebanon and Jordan, and finally Syria in April. The agreed borders were called 'Green Lines' – that was the colour of the pens that marked them on maps; the thickness of the pens determined how much uncertainty arose later about exactly where the borders were.

The Arab Liberation Army had about 10,000 men, including 3,000–5,000 foreign volunteers. Egypt's combat forces rose to about 20,000, Iraq to 15,000–18,000, Saudi Arabia to 800–1,200 and Jordan to 8,000–12,000, plus Lebanon's 1,000 and Syria's 5,000. That was an estimated total of 50,800–63,200.

In contrast, the Haganah and Palmach had about 15,000 men and women under arms in March 1948. Using conscription and displaced people from Europe, in May this grew to 30,000–35,000. In June it was up to 60,000. By the end of the year, it was more than 108,000. The Jewish cause was boosted when the Druze – Arabs with a distinct religion separate from Islam and doughty fighters – broke with the Arab cause and made their peace with the Haganah.

By the end, there were 6,373 Jewish dead – about 4,000 soldiers and 2,400 civilians (in the Vietnam War context, it was akin to 2 million American dead). On the Arab side, 8,000 to 15,000 died. Israel ended up with 38 percent more territory than the UN partition had allocated to it, that is, 78 percent of the Palestine mandate territory apart from Jordan. No Palestinian state was created; instead, Jordan occupied the West Bank and East Jerusalem and Egypt took the Gaza Strip. The 700,000 to 750,000 Arabs who fled settled in the West Bank, the Gaza Strip, Syria, Jordan and Lebanon; about 156,000 remained in Israel.

\* \* \*

The state was created. Now began the nation-building.[31] There was need for haste. Within eleven months, the Jewish population soared by a third: nearly two hundred thousand immigrants poured in, survivors of the Holocaust in Europe and from Arab lands. A swift population census early in November was followed by the first elections for a parliament at the end of January 1949. A voter turnout of nearly 87 percent saw victory for David Ben-Gurion's party, *Mapai* (Labour). It stood for the socialism which had brought it through the mandate era. But it did not gain a majority; the proportional representation system brought in twelve parties, setting the pattern for coalition government for the future. Among the 156,000 Arabs remaining in the country, the voter turnout was 79 percent and they elected two Arabs – two from the Mapai-sponsored Democratic List of Nazareth and one from the communist Maki (which had endorsed partition).

By early March, Ben-Gurion had formed a coalition of Mapai and a religious bloc made up of two pro-Zionist and two anti-Zionist parties. The anti-Zionist parties did not view Israel as a truly Jewish state; in their view, this could only come about when the Messiah arrived. Meanwhile, they entered the cabinet to promote their interests. Again, thus was the scene set for the future, ensuring a high degree of influence for minority religious parties.

Jerusalem was a divided city. The Green Line, the armistice line, separated Jordan's Arab Legion in the Old City and East Jerusalem, and the Israeli-controlled West Jerusalem and the road to Tel Aviv. The only crossing between the concrete walls, barbed wire and mines was the Mandelbaum

Gate, named after a Jewish-owned house next to the Old City; it was used by diplomats, foreigners, Christian clergy and pilgrims, but Jordan did not allow anyone to cross whose passport contained an Israeli stamp. The border was overseen by thirty-one fortified surveillance points, nine Israeli and twenty-two Jordanian.

The enforced arrival of Jews from Arab lands added new complexity. Sephardim were 15 percent of the Jewish population and their numbers rose dramatically as Arab rage in the Middle East over the coming of the state of Israel was turned against local Jews. Anti-Semitism drove social and political persecution. There was also instability as colonialism ended.

In 1947 a pogrom and destruction of synagogues in Aleppo, Syria, caused half the city's Jews to leave. In Egypt, arrests, killings and confiscation of properties and businesses led to the flight of nearly 40 percent of the Jewish community by 1950. Kuwait expelled its tiny number of Jews. In Iraq, a pro-Nazi uprising in 1941 had set off mass killing of Jews, attacks on synagogues and looting of properties. In 1948 mass persecution was seen in large-scale arrests, expulsion from professions and universities and elimination of the business elite; 93 percent of Jews left in a forced exodus. Libya, Algeria and Morocco saw outbreaks of violence against Jews. In Yemen, a 'Magic Carpet' airlift took fifty thousand Jews to safety in Israel.

By the end of 1951, Sephardic Jews from Arab countries formed 56 percent of the total immigration, and they kept coming – thus effectively ending the close Jewish connection with Arab countries which stretched back to the Roman expulsion. Some Jews were able to sell their property when they left or smuggle valuables with them, but most had to abandon everything. Many were poor to start with.

Their arrival in such numbers overwhelmed the young state. They were housed in primitive conditions in tent cities and transit camps. Few had any training or skills to contribute to a modern society. The Ashkenazi religious and secular fought for control of their children, each wanting them in their separate schools. Payback time came twenty-five years later: resentment among Sephardim about the way the Ashkenazi leadership had treated them caused many to vote for the right-wing Likud, changing Israel's nature and direction.

\* \* \*

Equally demanding of attention were the Arab refugees who had fled or been chased out. Foreign Minister Moshe Sharett believed in diplomacy and compromise. However, Prime Minister Ben-Gurion believed that the state would not survive if the armistice lines of 1949 were allowed to stand. Army leaders, notably Moshe Dayan, a rising star and a Ben-Gurion supporter (he was appointed chief of staff in 1950), agreed that the borders had to be decided by military force rather than negotiations with Arabs. Dayan, born in Palestine, was the personification of the new Jew, the Israeli Sabra, named after the hardy bush – prickly on the outside and soft on the inside. With his black eye patch – he lost an eye while fighting in the British army against Vichy France troops in Lebanon during World War II – he became a famed and romanticised Israeli symbol for the world.

Policy was quickly decided, even while hostilities had not ended: it was immediate harsh action. This became the matrix for the future. Looking at the context makes the decision of the time more understandable in leading to Palestinian suffering and loss. Historian Colin Shindler describes what lay behind it. This was the heart of the Jewish Israeli case then and remains so decades later:

> The Israeli cabinet meeting of 16 June 1948 resolved not to allow any Palestinian Arab refugees to return. . . . In the aftermath of the bitterness of war, there was a deep fear that a returning Arab population would evolve into a fifth column, which would ultimately nullify the attainment of independence and turn military victory into national defeat. Many Israelis believed that the Arab world simply did not wish Israel to exist and were waiting to massacre and expel its Jewish population. The war therefore was no conventional conflict where there was an acceptance of victory and defeat, but instead the conflict was understood as a zero-sum game. This mindset also facilitated the destruction of Arab villages and their replacement with Jewish settlements to produce a territorial contiguity. [32]

The United Nations sought to end the plight of the refugees: the General Assembly's Resolution 194 in December 1948, which is often quoted by critics accusing Israel of failing to implement it, said that 'refugees wishing to return to their homes and live in peace with their neighbours should be permitted to do so' and that 'compensation should be paid for the property of those choosing not to return'.

Israel sat tight, relying on the 'and live in peace' phrase to argue that the refugees had no such intention and were dangerously hostile to the new state; additionally, the resolution said the refugees 'should' – not 'must' – be allowed to return home. Israel believed it had time on its side and the refugee problem would gradually disappear. But, of course, it didn't and is now critical in impeding progress towards peace.

Victory in war thus did not bring peace to Israel. Arab hostility remained. Israeli aircraft could not overfly Arab states. The country was under Arab League boycott. Egypt barred Israel-registered ships and other ships carrying Israeli cargo from using the Suez Canal, forcing a long, long voyage through the Mediterranean and around the west of Africa for trade with the East and Australasia. Arab governments provided bases in Gaza, Jordan, Lebanon and Syria for terrorist attacks across the borders. Dayan's tough attitude was applied in dealing with infiltrators, who became known as *fedayeen*, those who sacrifice, and in rounding up Arabs who came across the borders in the hope of returning to their homes or to smuggle goods; it was shoot to kill. Between the end of the war and 1956, 200 to 300 Israelis were killed and 500 to 1,000 injured. In turn, Israel killed 2,700 to 5,000 infiltrators.

Resurgent Palestinians also had to be reckoned with. After their loss in 1948, they counted for naught. It was 'the beginning of decades in the wilderness', as Rashid Khalidi puts it.[33] Those inside Israel were subject to military law and political activity was barred. Palestinians fared no better in the Arab countries in which they had taken shelter. Governments were nervous about the thousands of refugees suddenly in their midst and treated them with varying degrees of suspicion, sternness and cruelty. Jordan's government 'saw virtually any independent Palestinian organization as subversive and as a threat to the unity of the kingdom, and ruthlessly combated political activity of most kinds, making the West and East Banks of Jordan highly inhospitable for independent Palestinian political action'. In the Gaza Strip, the Egyptian army 'allowed only limited Palestinian activity, and none that could jeopardize Egypt's armistice agreement with Israel'.[34]

The failed elite leadership of the mandate era was swept away. In its place, leaders rose up among younger Palestinians dispersed in refugee camps and cities. Working from Cairo, Beirut and Kuwait, they revived Palestinian identity and a national movement. *Fatah*, the Palestinian Liberation Movement, began in 1959; there was also the rival Popular Front for the Liberation of Palestine (PFLP), and others. The Egyptian-dominated Arab League tried to control the growing activism and in 1964 founded the Palestine Liberation Organization (PLO). But Palestinians took it over as their own, and it became their representative national liberation organisation.

Fatah's aim to get rid of Israel was shared by the other militant groups. The Fatah constitution declared: 'Complete liberation of Palestine, and eradication of Zionist economic, political, military and cultural existence' (article 12). To achieve this, '[a]rmed public revolution is the inevitable method to liberating Palestine' (article 17). In the late 1960s and early 1970s, Fatah and others carried out attacks and plane hijackings, mainly directed at Israeli targets at home and abroad. They brought terror to international travel. In 1969 Yasser Arafat became the Fatah chairman – the year that 2,432 attacks on Israel were reported.

* * *

In a major policy shift, the Soviet Union entered the region and switched sides. Seven years after sending arms to Israel, Czechoslovakia now acted as a channel for Soviet weaponry: tanks, bombers, fighter planes, destroyers, torpedo boats and submarines gave Egypt superiority. By May 1956 Egypt had 45 bombers for Israel's 2, and 200 jet fighters for Israel's 114. France stepped in and supplied Israel with three hundred tanks, with fighters later on.

Dayan believed a second round of war was inevitable. Arab rhetoric and actions supported him. Egypt's minister of defence, Abdul Hakim Amer, said that his country's armed forces could now 'wipe Israel off the map'. Syria's prime minister told his parliament that his government's foreign policy was based on 'a war against imperialism, Zionism and Israel'. Iraqi troops moved into Jordan. By 1955 Israel had developed Eilat as a southern port at the head of the Red Sea so it no longer had to rely on the Suez Canal; but ships could not get there because Egypt blockaded the Straits of Tiran farther south.

War did come, in 1956, but in a roundabout way. Israel attacked Egypt, seizing the Gaza Strip and Sinai. It did so in secret collusion with Britain and France, intent on regaining control of the Suez Canal which Egypt had expropriated. An angry Washington and a threatening Moscow ended the adventure. Israel withdrew, but gained recognition of its right to passage through the international waters of the Straits of Tiran. A long-term change was that from now on Israel was firmly in the US camp in the Cold War struggle with communism.

On to yet another war, and this time it was to prove decisive for the future. The borders were fraught and vulnerable to terror attacks. In the north, Syria and Israel shelled each other's settlements. A joint military command was established between Egypt, Jordan and Syria. The Soviet Union, for its own ends, stirred the pot, supplying armaments to Egypt and Syria and claiming, wrongly, that Israel intended to attack Syria and seize its capital, Damascus.

In 1967 the Arab world was abuzz with bellicose statements; armies and military contingents were preparing for war. A Syrian general calculated that Syria/Egypt 'can destroy Israel in four days'. Iraq's president Aref declared: 'Our goal is clear – to wipe Israel off the face of the map. We shall, God willing, meet in Tel Aviv and Haifa'. Egypt's Gamal Abdel Nasser and his generals were telling their people that the shame of their 1956 defeat had been overcome, and it was now time to erase the humiliation of 1948. Nasser said he would regain Palestinian rights by force. 'We intend to open a general assault against Israel. This will be total war. Our basic aim will be to destroy Israel', he said on 26 May. On 2 June his commander in Sinai, General Mortagi, published his order of the day, calling on his troops to wage a war of destruction against Israel.

It is argued that Nasser's words were only that; he was huffing and puffing but had no real intention to attack. However, his actions said something else. He ordered the United Nations to remove its emergency force, which separated the armies of Egypt and Israel; secretary-general U Thant, only six months into the job, meekly obeyed. Nasser moved troops into the

Sinai and closed the Straits of Tiran to Israeli shipping. This in itself was a *casus belli*, a reason for war.

Israel believed Nasser and was certain he was going to attack. The apprehension was such that a government of national unity was formed in which the two bitter foes, the old-time leader David Ben-Gurion and his right-wing opponent Menachem Begin, came together in a broad coalition. Diplomacy failed. The world was not willing to enforce Israel's maritime right to the Straits of Tiran. The United States and France refused to supply arms. Israel's armed forces consisted of 275,000 men, 1,100 tanks and 200 combat aircraft. The combined Arab forces were 500,000 men, 5,000 tanks and 900 combat aircraft.

Israelis felt alone and abandoned. Their existence was again in peril: fourteen thousand hospital beds were prepared for the expected wounded, public parks were consecrated and graves dug for mass casualties, all amid 'a sense of helplessness derived from the inability to protect against the possible use of chemical warfare by the Arab states'.[35] Foreign correspondent Eric Silver reported in the *Guardian*: 'I have met no one in Israel in the past week who did not believe that the Arabs meant what they said; that they would annihilate the Jews'.[36]

Israel's generals urged a pre-emptive strike. They said the country would not be able to withstand a concerted Arab onslaught. Nor could it afford continued mobilisation of the reserves. On Sunday 4 June the cabinet voted twelve to two to attack.[37] Defence Minister Moshe Dayan and Chief of Staff Yitzhak Rabin set it for the next morning, between 7 and 7:30 a.m. That day, 5 June, Israel destroyed more than three hundred Egyptian planes on the ground. The Egyptian army of one hundred thousand in Sinai was no match for Israel's tanks, infantry and jets. Vast amounts of armaments were seized. An Israeli joke had Nasser phoning the Soviet leader, Alexei Kosygin, and asking for tanks, only to be told: 'If the Israelis want more tanks why don't they ask me directly?' In an epic battle, the IDF went up the Golan Heights and drove out the Syrians.

Israel sent a message, via three different channels, to Jordan's King Hussein, urging him to stay out of the conflict; there was no intention to attack him. But Hussein believed Egypt was winning – that's what Nasser was telling him – and he was also under huge popular pressure to attack. His artillery poured six thousand shells onto Jewish Jerusalem's city centre and suburbs. The IDF attacked and, to universal astonishment, swept aside Jordan's vaunted Arab Legion, albeit at a heavy price in lives, chasing them out of Jerusalem and over the Jordan River. It was an emotional, triumphant return for Jews to the Wailing Wall, the holiest shrine in Judaism, after being denied any access since 1948. Many saw it as a miracle given by God.

Many Palestinians fled to Jordan – Israel estimated 175,000 of them, Jordan, 250,000. For many it was a second tragedy after fleeing from Israel in 1948. This time, Israel did little to cause Palestinians to go; it also did nothing to persuade them not to leave or to return.[38] But the remaining Jews in Arab lands paid heavily for the war with attacks on them in Egypt, Yemen, Lebanon, Tunisia, Morocco, Syria and Iraq.

Israel was unprepared for occupation. There was experience of military rule in the Gaza Strip as a result of the Sinai campaign eleven years earlier and some contingency plans existed there. But the first controller of the West Bank, Shlomo Gazit, then colonel and later major-general, notes: 'There was no advance estimate, no concerted scenario regarding anticipated developments in the West Bank. The capture of the entire area and the institution of military government within it were possibilities that hadn't been foreseen'. The urgent aim was 'getting life back to normal'. A military bureaucracy was created.[39]

As early as 19 June, the Israeli cabinet met to decide what to do about the seized territories. By a majority of eleven to ten, the cabinet agreed to offer the return of Sinai and the Golan for peace with Egypt and Syria; Jerusalem was to remain Israeli and united; the Gaza Strip was to be retained; there was no agreement about the West Bank.

The Holy City was beyond argument. It was immediately declared the capital of Israel. East Jerusalem was annexed and the city's geographical area was stretched. Palestinians were offered Israeli citizenship; very few accepted, but they were given residential rights.

At the end of August, the Arab League met in Khartoum. Nasser, despite the disaster he had perpetrated, was lionised by the Arab masses. He argued against peace. The leaders agreed and declared: '[N]o recognition of Israel, no peace and no negotiations with her'. Instead, 'all steps necessary to consolidate military preparedness'.

Later, Sinai was returned to Egypt under the 1979 peace treaty and eighteen settlements were dismantled. The Gaza Strip was retained, but Israel withdrew in 2005, abandoning twenty-one settlements. In contrast, the Golan Heights were annexed in 1981, even though only seven hundred of the twenty thousand Golan Druze agreed to take Israeli citizenship.

The euphoria of victory in 1967 was soon tempered. During September, the country was hit by terror attacks: a bomb at a Jerusalem hotel, an explosive charge on a railway line, sabotage at a factory and then four soldiers killed by Egyptian artillery on the Suez Canal in what became a years-long war of attrition.

\* \* \*

The UN Security Council went into frantic discussion mode the moment details of Israel's June 1967 attack, and success, became known. Hostilities were ended through international mediation. Five unanimous resolutions followed, dealing with ceasefire violations, refugees and prisoners. On 22 November the council adopted Resolution 242, which became the basis for peace attempts into the future. It demanded:

1. The withdrawal of Israel armed forces from territories occupied in the recent conflict.
2. The termination of all claims or states of belligerency and respect for and acknowledgment of the sovereignty, territorial integrity and political independence of every State in the area and their right to live in peace within secure and recognized boundaries free from threats or acts of force.

Although 242 is so fundamental, it has been surrounded by argument: the English text, adopted by the Security Council, called on Israel to withdraw from 'territories'; the translated French text – both were the United Nation's official languages – called for withdrawal from 'the territories'. Dispute continues whether Israel is correct in arguing that the resolution acknowledges the indefensibility of its pre-1967 borders, and it can therefore adjust its borders; or whether, as Arab states and others maintain, 'the territories' means all the territories seized by Israel, which means the West Bank and the Golan Heights.

Much flowed from the Six-Day War, as Michael Oren explains:

> The War of Attrition, the Yom Kippur War, the Munich massacre and Black September, the Lebanon War, the controversy over Jewish settlements and the future of Jerusalem, the Camp David Accords, the Oslo Accords, the intifada – all were the result of six intense days in the Middle East in June 1967. Rarely in modern times has so short and localized a conflict had such prolonged, global consequences.[40]

Each event set off its own train of events among Israelis and Arabs. Increasingly, military occupation and Jewish settlement of the West Bank and East Jerusalem, and to a lesser extent the Gaza Strip, became the dominating factors.

# Chapter Three

# Inside the Green Line

*Israel cannot be given a simple label. It is complex and diverse with equality for all and discrimination against many. Little is straightforward: scratch the surface and find contradictions and surprises – in religion, the army, land, work, health, education and minority communities.*

\* \* \*

The state created on 14 May 1948 is Israel inside the Green Line. Borders with Egypt and Jordan have been agreed in peace treaties but not yet with Syria and Lebanon. A border with the West Bank awaits finalisation when a Palestinian state comes into being. 'Israel proper' is a democratic state with the usual hallmarks of democracies: universal franchise and an independent legislative arm of government, freedom of speech and of the press, freedom of movement, an independent judiciary, and the rule of law.

Yet Israeli democracy has limitations. The minority Arab community suffers discrimination. There is no unqualified separation between the state and religion. There are state of emergency laws which give the government power to do what it wants, to infringe civil liberties and to bypass normal legislative processes. They were taken over from the British mandate and promulgated by the new state four days after its creation at a time of deep crisis. Renewed by the Knesset from year to year, they are little known and the extent to which they are used is unclear; but they are there, a looming shadow. And (to be discussed in chapter 4) the country's democracy is undermined through its military occupation of the West Bank and control of the lives of 2.5 million Palestinians; another 1.4 million Palestinians are locked up in the Gaza Strip.

Civil liberties have been under pressure in recent years through growth of the right wing in the Knesset. That comes from deeper political developments: the move to the Right among Jews caused by factors including the impact of the suicide bombings during the second intifada and the rain of rockets from Hamas and others in Gaza and Hezbollah in Lebanon, the growth of religious fundamentalism, threats of annihilation by Iran's former president Mahmoud Ahmadinejad and his country's nuclear ambitions, changed worldviews brought by immigrants, Sephardic resentment against the Ashkenazi elite and the siege mentality fostered by world hostility.

*  *  *

Israeli Arabs/Palestinians (the name varies) make up 20.7 percent of the population of eight million – in 1948 they were 18 percent – and get the short end of the stick in education, municipal facilities, jobs and pay. The discrimination is unfair and wrong and reflects badly on Israel.

*But is it apartheid?* Answering this requires a review of the status of Arabs and Jews inside Israel proper. . . .

First, history has ensured that the people of Israel are deeply divided. During the Ottoman era, Jews were confined to pockets in the religious towns of Jerusalem, Hebron, Safed and Tiberias. The Jews who arrived from Europe in the late nineteenth century created their own agricultural settlements, fortified for protection against Arab neighbours. In 1909 the Jewish town of Tel Aviv was created, adjoining the ancient Arab port of Jaffa.

Separation was continued during the 1917–1948 years of British rule, except for some areas of Jewish-Arab coexistence, notably in Haifa. The British kept the separate Arab and Jewish schools they found; division was reinforced by the religious hostility between Judaism and Islam. As Zionism grew and more Jews arrived, Arab rejection also grew. Antipathy and fear became ingrained on both sides.

Israel after 1948 maintained what had gone before. Jews and Arabs coexisted in towns like Haifa, Lod and Ramle, but otherwise the two communities have lived apart, with some exceptions, with their own languages, social lives and businesses. More than 70 percent of Arabs live in majority-Arab communities. Separation is also found within each group: Muslims include also Druze and Bedouin. Among Jews, religion divides the ultra-Orthodox (with further splits between sects), Modern Orthodox and secular, with many living in their own residential areas, with their own schools and with little or no social contact across the lines.

Second, discrimination against Arabs is not cut and dry but is filled with nuances and ongoing change for the better. Defeated in war in 1948, and after about 700,000 to 750,000 fled, 156,000 Arabs remained. They have flourished, and by 2013 their numbers had grown to 1,670,000. They enjoy normal civic rights.

Improvements have come about in the Arab quality of life, some of them prodigious, as in health and education. At the individual level, it is seen in a multitude of achievements from judges on the highest court; a host of district and magistrate's courts judges; ambassadors to countries including Finland, Greece and Vietnam; high ranks in the army including heading the Border Police; holding cabinet positions (albeit junior) and serving as deputy speaker of the Knesset, which has led to a stint as acting president of Israel.

Landmarks are regularly notched up, such as the first Arab woman to be appointed a full professor (in education at Tel Aviv University in 2007), the head surgeon at a leading hospital and the head of a university politics department. In 2013, in the hypersensitive military sphere, for the first time a Druze was appointed to head the Golani infantry brigade, and a Bedouin became a tank commander.

Third, the most overriding fact of all: every Israeli adult, Jew and Arab, has the right to vote. Everyone is a full citizen and can vote for the Knesset and can stand for election. The vote provides the means to exercise power and influence.

The Knesset has had Arab members since the first elections in 1949. Arabs are as divided in their political support as are Jews: they vote for both Arab and Jewish parties. In the 2013 general elections, in the proportional representation system, three Arab parties (one of which has Jewish members) won 11 seats in the 120-member parliament; in addition, several Jewish parties have Arab MPs.

One group of Arabs does not have the national vote – those in East Jerusalem. They were offered citizenship after Israel conquered the eastern part of the city in 1967, but few accepted; they can vote for the Jerusalem city council, but few do, with most arguing that to vote would be to recognise Israeli occupation. Yet there is another side to the story: as residents of the city, East Jerusalem's Arabs have the same rights as Israelis to free movement around the country; they have national insurance protection, that is, equal access to medical care, hospitals, medicines and social welfare.

Fourth, there is no single Arab group: about 82 percent are Muslims. Christians make up 5 percent, but not all are Arabs and the number is down from the 20 percent of a century ago. Druze make up 8.4 percent, Bedouin 12 percent, and there are 3,000 Circassians. All are Muslims but each group has its own distinctive culture and interpretation of Islam. Each of the communities occupies a different place in the country's hierarchy.

Fifth, Israel is a hotbed of discrimination. Arabs are not the only victims. As the Arab advocacy organisation Adalah describes it: 'Inequality in Israel takes many forms. Some of the major fault lines that divide Israeli society, creating relatively privileged and deprived groups are: Western Jews (Ashkenazim) versus Eastern Jews (Mizrachim); men versus women; Israel-born Jews (Sabra) versus new immigrants (Olim); Orthodox versus secular Jews; rural versus urban dwellers; rich versus poor; left-wing versus right-wing supporters; and gay versus straight people'.[1] To which should be added the divisions between Jews and Arabs, plus those among Arabs mentioned earlier, as well as the gaps between Israeli Palestinians/Arabs and Palestinians on the West Bank and in Gaza and the religious divisions among Jews and the further divisions among ultra-Orthodox Jews.

It all makes for a country where a lot of people in all groups have sky-high chips on their shoulders with never-ending complaints and accusations about unfair treatment, whether real or perceived.

Sixth, Jews make up 75.1 percent of the population. The purpose of Israel is to provide sanctuary for them and to be their country. The Law of Return, enacted in July 1950, remains basic to Israel as a unique Jewish state: 'Every Jew has the right to come to this country', unless believed to be 'engaged in an activity directed against the Jewish people' or likely 'to endanger public health' or pose a threat to the security of the state. Citizenship is immediate upon arrival. The state helps immigrants, including air fare, tax breaks, subsidised housing and Hebrew lessons.

But who is a Jew? To the Nazis, one Jewish grandparent was enough for consignment to the gas chamber. A Knesset amendment in 1970 provided a definition in accordance with *Halacha* (Jewish law): '"Jew" means a person who was born of a Jewish mother or has become converted to Judaism and who is not a member of another religion'.

This seems simple enough, but it isn't because the Law of Return was considerably widened (also in 1970) to allow for immigration by the children and grandchildren of a Jew (whether male or female) and their spouses. Non-Jews can also become citizens through naturalisation, such as the parents of a citizen who has done military service, or residence or marrying an Israeli citizen.

They are admitted as Israeli citizens, but they are not Jewish unless they convert. In Israel, conversion and all matters of Jewish personal status are controlled by the Orthodox rabbinate. Judaism does not proselytise and rabbis are strict in allowing entry only to those who have studied intensively and who they believe will practise the faith at a high level (which only a minority of Jews actually do). Orthodox rabbis do not recognise conversions by the Reform and Conservative streams of Judaism – yet a Reform Jew living, say, in the United States can migrate to Israel and is accepted by the state as a Jew under the Law of Return. Rabbis also differ among themselves: some ultra-Orthodox rabbis reject conversions by some Orthodox rabbis.

Immigration has clouded the situation even more: 120,000 Ethiopian immigrants were accepted as Jews, which is why they were welcomed in the first place, but they were still compelled to undergo Orthodox conversion.

The million-plus immigrants from the former Soviet Union have dramatically changed the demographic picture: 40 to 70 percent are estimated not to be true Jews. Yuli Edelstein, as deputy absorption minister, estimated in 2002 that 70 percent were not Jewish and most were disconnected from Judaism and Israel.[2] They immigrated because they were married to a Jew, or related to one, or perhaps wanted to escape the rigours of life at home. What happens when they marry? They are not Jews in terms of Jewish law. They, and their children, will not be allowed to marry Jews, at least not inside Israel. And what about those Israelis, whether currently accepted or not as Jews, who refuse to have anything to do with the rabbis and go abroad for a civil marriage which is recognised by law when they return home? Their children will not be allowed to marry Jews whose parents were married by the rabbinate in Israel.

The Law of Return has also been extended to a spouse in a same-sex marriage. It was done for the first time in 2011 when a gay male couple, Jewish and Catholic, who had married in Canada four years before, came on aliyah. The Jew was promptly given citizenship, on 10 June. The Interior Ministry scratched its head about his husband but gave him citizenship on 10 August.[3]

These are all deep sociological factors whose effects on Israeli society, and its Jewishness, are still to be seen. The Law of Return and trying to define who is a Jew are fiercely argued. Some want to scrap the Law of Return; religious Jews, on the other hand, view the entry of large numbers of non-Jews as a mortal danger to Israel as the Jewish homeland.

While intrinsic for Jews, the Law of Return infringes the rights of Israeli Arabs. The immediate victims are Arabs born in Palestine/Israel who left in the 1948 and 1967 wars; they and their descendants do not have the right of return. A second level of deprivation applies to family reunification, which was provided for in the Oslo Accords; from 1994 to 2002 more than 137,000 Palestinians from the West Bank and Gaza who married Israeli Arabs moved into Israel.[4] The government responded to this as a security and demographic threat, charging that it was a disguised Palestinian effort to get into Israel and that many marriages were a sham or polygamous. Since 2002 Palestinian spouses have been barred from automatic Israeli residence and citizenship. A law the next year said that the interior minister could grant citizenship only if the applicant made a strong enough case that he/she identified with the State of Israel and that he or she or family members had cooperated with Israel or made a contribution to its security. Few qualify, with approval for only thirty-three out of three thousand applications.[5] In January 2012 the Supreme Court – by six votes to five – upheld the restriction, backing the security of the state: it recognised the right to marry but denied that this implied a right of residency. 'Human rights are not a prescription for national suicide', it said.[6]

Arabs deeply resent the restriction. The issue also plays to Jewish right-wing fears. The Shin Bet noted in 2007 that 14 percent of 272 suicide bombings which killed Israeli civilians had been carried out by Palestinian Authority Arabs who married Israeli citizens and came to live inside the pre-1967 boundaries; an official added that there had been a rise in the number of women joining the terrorist 'workforce' – married women as well as widows.[7] A less harsh view came from a later Shin Bet chief, Yoram Cohen, saying that during the previous year, 2011, there had been only three terror attacks in which Israeli Arabs were involved: 'They are not a fifth column and we don't relate to them as such'.[8]

To Hatam Iyat, an attorney from the village of Qara, the state had 'declared war on Israeli-Arabs'. He and Yasmin, his Palestinian wife of eleven years, had four children, and he protested: 'My wife's life in Israel has become temporary. The right has triumphed in its racist campaign'.

Yet however invidious Israel's restrictions on the entry of spouses, they are not unique. Denmark, the Netherlands, Germany and others impose conditions to do with age and/or income and language. Egypt applies discrimination similar to Israel in singling out a specific group: it strips citizenship from men who marry 'Israeli women', and also their children, if the marriage poses a threat to national security.[9] Saudi Arabia rarely grants citizenship to foreigners. The ExpatFocus website reports that for most people the only way to become a citizen is to marry a Saudi Arabian, 'but . . . is no guarantee that citizenship status can be granted, particularly if the foreign national is not a Muslim'.

\* \* \*

Now a closer look at Israeli complexities . . .

## THE ARMY

Military service is a crucial dividing line. In a country under unceasing attack or threat of attack since its founding, the military is a powerful presence. Service in the Israel Defense Forces is onerous with a compulsory three years for Jewish men and two years for women immediately after completing high school, followed for many by one month of annual call-ups for twenty years and more, plus emergency call-ups. Apart from loyalty to the country, army service confers benefits such as technology training in elite computer units, which can open up a later civilian career. After discharge, combat troops get a cash grant plus money for buying or renting an apartment, opening a business or studying. It's helpful but not a great deal for imperilling life for three years for little pay. Noncombat soldiers get about 70 percent of the assistance. Other benefits include university scholarships, tax breaks and discounted movie tickets.

Druze men (except those on the Golan Heights) and Circassians are conscripted in the same way as Jews and get the same benefits. Druze have attained the rank of major-general, commanding the Border Police and the Home Front. Bedouin are not conscripted, but 5–10 percent of those of draft age volunteer and hold officer ranks.

It's a major cleft in society that most Arabs are not conscripted, and only a tiny number volunteer. So they are spared dangerous duties and losing years of life – and do not get post-army benefits.

Since 2007 the government has offered an alternative – national service, as in hospital or community work, with monthly stipends and benefits similar to noncombat soldiers. Opposition has come from inside the Arab community: Jamal Zahalka, then a Balad Party MK, warned at the time that national service was a stepping stone towards imposing the army draft: 'They are trying to Israelise our youth', he said, threatening that 'anyone who volunteers for national service will be treated like a leper, and will be vomited out of Arab society'.[10] A former Shin Bet head, Ami Ayalon, rejected the 'Israelise' accusation, saying: 'We're not interested in a melting pot, but rather in an Israeli salad bowl'.[11] Despite continuing rough talk from Arab leaders, support for national service has slowly grown, reaching 2,400 in 2012 – but still only 6 percent of the 40,000 young people who reached age eighteen.[12]

Adalah has complained that 'granting benefits based on military service adds to the many obstacles faced by Arab youth in Israel today, limiting their access to higher education and employment in the civil service'.[13] As an example, it noted that the minimum age for admission to most medical schools is twenty to twenty-one years, and this prevents Arabs from applying upon graduating from high school at age eighteen. The age requirement is waived for Jewish and Druze students who delay their compulsory military service until after completing their medical education. Adalah also objected to special benefits given to discharged soldiers.

It's the argument of an outsider. For what Adalah is urging is that young people who do not serve the country – whether through army or national service – must be given an advantage over those who do. Better, surely, to argue instead for conscription to be widened so that it applies to everyone: that would be a massive contribution to reducing divisions and binding Israelis. True, Arabs would have difficulty serving in an army that is in occupation over fellow-Palestinians in the West Bank, but that is balanced by the difficulty which Orthodox Jewish soldiers have in carrying out army orders in destroying settler outposts on the West Bank.

Indeed, Jewish fury set off by action to end draft exemption of ultra-Orthodox men outdoes any Arab anger. In 1948 such numbers of Torah scholars had been wiped out in the Holocaust that Prime Minister David Ben-

Gurion is said to have decided to free scholars from military service, 'to keep the embers burning'. That was about four hundred men. Over the years the number has grown, and now an estimated forty thousand men are exempted; women do not even feature. The exempted ultra-Orthodox men are supposed to study full-time in a *yeshiva* (religious school), and they get monthly payments from the state so that they do not have to work. Neither Arabs nor secular Jews enjoy these benefits.

Successive governments, intent on coalitions to hold office, pandered to religious parties by excluding religious young men – and sought to dampen the anger of the wider public with a system of short-term voluntary enlistment for the religious; this failed because it drew only small numbers. Secular anger and army alarm have also risen because of increasing intrusion by rabbis who regard the West Bank as holy to Judaism and tell soldiers to defy orders to remove illegal settlements. The army insists that soldiers must obey their commander and not their rabbi. But rabbis have backed religious male soldiers who have walked out of army concerts because women soldiers were singing, as well as soldiers who refuse to take orders from women instructors.

An exacerbating factor is the denial and rejection of the state by some Jewish ultra-Orthodox religious parties and groups, such as the Satmar sect and the even more extreme Neturei Karta. To them, the army is a godless abomination. There is also a religious view that the army is not needed and that the safety of Israel and its people is in the hands of God. A variation of that peeped out with Eli Yishai, then interior minister and a leader in the Sephardic Shas Party, saying that the IDF had failed in the 2006 Lebanon war because soldiers did not 'turn their eyes to the Creator'. In the immediate row, Yishai hastily retreated and apologised for hurting bereaved families, saying he had been quoted 'tendentiously', although, as a newspaper noted, he had been recorded and broadcast on television.[14] It was not a new view for Shas. Its late spiritual head, Rabbi Ovadia Yosef, a revered Torah sage and former Sephardic chief rabbi, had previously said that IDF soldiers died in combat because they did not observe Jewish religious laws: 'They don't observe the Sabbath, they don't observe [the laws of] the Torah, they don't pray, they don't put on phylacteries every day. Is it any wonder that they're killed?'[15] Yishai defended him against the torrent of criticism: 'My rabbi does not err. Everything he says is the word of God'.[16]

Extending conscription to religious Jews – 'sharing the burden' is the phrase – was a major issue in the 2013 election campaign and propelled new parties, which demanded it, to prominence. The right-wing Yisrael Beiteinu Party tried to extend conscription to all Arabs, but the issue was left at the wayside in the intra-Jewish battle. The Knesset legislated to enforce conscription on religious young men, to be introduced over a period of years. With ultra-Orthodox groups threatening defiance, which would mean imprisonment, there is much scope for conflict, or for tempering the law. The depth of religious opposition was already being seen in harassment of the small number of Haredi young men already serving in the army or police: in one episode in Jerusalem's Mea Shearim suburb, dozens of ultra-Orthodox people cursed a soldier in uniform who entered the neighbourhood and chased him with clubs and sticks; police rushed in to rescue him under a shower of stones.[17]

## RELIGION

The Ottoman Empire allowed communities to control their domestic affairs, each applying its own laws to its own people in marriage, divorce, conversion and burial. Britain continued this during the mandate, and it is maintained in Israel today. The religious are in charge of marriages – intermarriage between Jews, Muslims and Christians is not the norm. The state does not make the rules.

In Judaism, descent is through the mother; in Islam, it is through the father. For Jews, marriage and divorce are in the hands of the Orthodox and ultra-Orthodox rabbis, and they will not marry a Jew to a non-Jew, or an Orthodox Jew to a Reform or Conservative Jew. Many will boggle at a nonobservant Jewish partner; they also apply stern rules to accepting a convert to Judaism.

In Islam, a non-Muslim man who wants to marry a Muslim woman must convert to Islam. Imams will marry a non-Muslim woman to a Muslim man, and she does not have to change her religion, provided she is Christian or Jew; her children will be brought up as Muslims.

Christians can marry in the churches, but some Orthodox churches will not marry a couple in which one partner is a Protestant.

There is a legal escape hatch: any couple, whoever they are, can go to any other country and enter into a civil marriage which is recognised by law when they return to Israel. Neighbouring Lebanon, with its mixture of religions, is the same; civil marriage is not allowed so couples go abroad. There are considerable problems if Sunni and Shi'ite Muslims want to marry each other. The West Bank is free of this. In 2011, while thirty-nine thousand Jewish couples married via the rabbinate in Israel, more than nine thousand wed abroad, some of them in civil ceremonies. Cyprus, a one-hour flight away, is a popular destination.

Freedom of religion is guaranteed by law, and equal rights are assured for all Israelis regardless of religion or ethnicity. But the principle is not always fully applied, particularly in regard to the West Bank. Israel controls entry to prayers on the Temple Mount/Noble Sanctuary in East Jerusalem: perhaps up to 150,000 are allowed on Fridays and holidays, but usually they must be married men above a specified age, forty or forty-five. Apart from concerns about smuggling bombs, the restrictions stem from occasional bursts of violence when Muslim worshippers atop the Mount throw rocks onto the heads of Jews praying at the Wailing Wall below.

Regarding Christians, Kairos Palestine says that Israel restricts the number of West Bank Palestinian Christians allowed to enter Jerusalem during the Easter holy period, and that the Holy Sepulchre Church in the Old City is rendered off limits 'through a complex network of walls, checkpoints, and security apparatuses' backed by the 'heavy presence' of Israeli police and military.[18] Israel's ambassador in Washington, Michael Oren, stirred up a hornet's nest in an article in the *Wall Street Journal*, saying that Muslims were harassing Christians and driving them to leave. Church leaders angrily responded that this was 'a shameful manipulation of the facts intended to mask the damage that Israel has done to our community'.[19]

## LAND

Mark Twain's quip 'Buy land, they're not making it anymore' could have served as the Zionist motto. Starting with the arrival in Palestine of Jews from Europe in the late nineteenth century and accelerating in the twentieth century, the drive was to acquire land: to make Jewish settlement possible, to transform Jewish existence from the ghettoes and cities into working the fields, and to fulfil the biblical promise of return to the Land of Israel. As David Kretzmer, a Hebrew University law professor, has described it: 'Jewish ownership and control of land was seen by the Zionist leaders of the pre-state era as the major component of success in the struggle for a Jewish state'.[20]

In 1901 the Zionist movement set up the Jewish National Fund (JNF) to buy land from Arab owners for Jewish settlement. The Rothschilds and other wealthy Jewish families made their own private purchases. Fighting restrictions imposed by the Ottoman rulers and then the British mandate government, each piece of land acquired was precious and the ownership of everything the JNF purchased was frozen to ensure that it would remain Jewish forever.

With all the effort, by 1948 only 5.7 percent of the land of then Palestine had been purchased. With independence, 'The government of Israel inherited the lands that had belonged to the British mandatory government, but most of these were uncultivable, waste lands or roads and forest areas that were at the disposal of the public. Most of the rest, especially the cultivable land, was owned by Arabs'.[21] This could mean that more than 80 percent of the land in Israel had belonged to the Arabs who became refugees.[22]

The 1948 war opened the way to far-reaching changes: the new state extended its UN partition land territory by 38 percent, from 14.92 million dunams to 20.6 million dunams (4 dunams = 1 acre = 0.4 hectare), and the state seized the lands of Arabs who had left their homes, whether they fled outside the borders or remained inside. The state ended up owning some 93 percent of the land, with the rest remaining as private property belonging to Arabs, Jews, Christian churches and the Muslim Waqf.

Israel the conqueror did not behave uniquely: in seizing properties, policies were evolved from what had been done elsewhere in the world. Regulations to eliminate all rights of former owners were 'inspired' by Britain's Trading with the Enemy Act of 1939, which dealt with Nazi Germany, and the actions of other countries where mass exchanges of population had taken place.[23]

In the government debates to decide what to do with the Arab 'abandoned property', the prime minister's special adviser on land and border demarcation, Zalman Lifshitz, argued for the permanent use of refugee property for the political and economic benefit of the new state.[24] He said that countries in similar situations, such as Turkey, Greece, Bulgaria and Czechoslovakia, had taken on vast powers to liquidate refugee property for state use and he urged the Israeli government 'to proceed in a similar manner' as 'there is no shortage of precedents'.

He focused on Pakistan, the Muslim state which had come into violent existence in 1947 in the partition of colonial India. There, too, as in Palestine, Britain had ended its rule, and the coming of independence set off intercommunal strife which led to the flight of large numbers of refugees hostile to the new state and the entry of large numbers of supporters. The difference was in the figures: the India-Pakistan conflict gave rise to 13 million refugees compared with Israel's 750,000.

It cannot be said if Lifshitz was aware of the irony of the new Jewish state using the legal techniques of a new Muslim state to deprive its own mainly Muslim refugees of their properties. However, he proposed 'a new law, similar to the . . . Pakistani regulations and based on the principles they contain'. Pakistani lawmakers, he noted, had drawn on Britain's Trading with the Enemy Act but had also introduced new elements to assist expropriation and transfer of ownership: they had created a mechanism for seizing Hindu and Sikh refugee property in Pakistan and its reallocation for the settlement of Muslim refugees from India.

Lifshitz presented his report on 30 March 1949, and the Knesset duly enacted laws later that year. The legal machinery to appropriate Palestinian refugee land, he noted, was 'based squarely' on the Pakistani legislation of 1948.

But unlike Pakistan and others, a state for Palestinians did not come into existence at that time. So Palestinian refugees did not have the benefit of state sponsorship, and they landed up in limbo in surrounding Arab states and inside Israel. Ever since, Palestinians, and the world, have paid dearly for that omission.

Having seized Arab properties, Israel recognised the need, for both legal and moral reasons, to pay compensation: it was the way to draw a line under its actions. Many Arab owners also recognised this, and hence refused to apply for compensation. By the end of March 1988, only 14,364 people had applied, and claims had been settled for 197,984 dunams.[25] The UN Conciliation Commission for Palestine, set up in 1949 charged with the mission of its title, had no success before fading away in 1966. But it did issue a 'Valuation of Abandoned Arab Land in Israel', which estimated seized Arab land at 16,323,971 dunams and assessed the value, on 29 November 1947, at US$281,074,511, with a further US$54 million for movable goods.[26] Arabs said the value was too low and Israel dismissed it as 'academic', noting that the land had been obtained through war and not as a business transfer.

* * *

In due course, the Israel Lands Administration was set up to control the state's holdings, called 'Israel lands'. The land cannot be sold, but is leased for periods of forty-nine or ninety-eight years. No legal restrictions apply in towns: lessees are chosen irrespective of religion, ethnic origin or anything else. In rural areas, in practice, Arab towns and villages have been consistently blocked from acquiring land they need for expansion, whether to build more houses or for industrial areas.

There is an exception. The state sold a large portion of the rural land expropriated from Arabs to the JNF, more than doubling its holdings so that they came to comprise about 13 percent of the state-owned 93 percent. It was a legal device to mask the fact that the state had seized Arab land. The land still formed part of 'Israel lands', but because of its specific JNF ownership, only Jews could lease it. Out of this came the establishment of hundreds of kibbutzim and moshavim, many on sites where Arab villages had stood. The JNF ceased to be a buyer but remained the guardian and supervisor of the land in its name and was also an agency acting for the state in afforestation and development. Over the years to come, it planted more than 240 million trees.

Expropriated land not sold to the JNF was transferred to the Custodian of Absentee Property and, in turn, passed to a Development Authority and leased to Jews, particularly the seven hundred thousand who poured in from Arab countries in the three years after independence. Later, some of the land that had been seized from the Muslim Waqf was returned to Arab communities.

In the JNF's original charter, the land it acquired was described as 'the perpetual property of the Jewish people', to be used for settlement of Jews. So leasing to non-Jews is barred. However, there is some flexibility, such as using a legal device whereby JNF land is exchanged with the Development Authority for other land; the JNF land is thus no longer JNF land and can be leased to non-Jews.

Israel does not have any laws restricting voluntary organisations that want to further the interests of one religious, ethnic or national group. Just as the JNF has applied its Jews-only restrictive policies, the same can be done by land-owning Christian churches and the Waqf.

* * *

The standing order was challenged in 1995. An Arab couple, Adel and Imam Ka'adan, applied to buy a property in Katzir, a Jewish communal settlement on land in the Galilee leased from the Jewish Agency. They were rejected, as Arabs, and appealed to the Supreme Court. In a 'path-breaking decision'[27] in 2000, the court ruled that the character of the State of Israel does not justify discrimination by the state between Jews and Arabs in regard to all public resources, including land, nor can the state get round this by placing the resources in the hands of a third party, such as the Jewish Agency. Conversely, the court accepted that the equality principle could be ignored in special circumstances, such as for affirmative action or state security.

Israel's highest court thus took what it said was 'a first step on a difficult and sensitive path', in which it did not overturn past discriminatory land policies but gave notice that they could no longer be automatically applied. As other Arabs followed the Ka'adan example, several Jewish rural communities amended their bylaws to demand that anyone who wanted to live there had to accept 'Zionist values and the values of the state as a Jewish and democratic state'. Adalah objected. Such demands, it said, were contrary to basic democratic principles; it noted that the Supreme Court had ruled that the state was obliged to treat Jewish and Arab citizens equally in the allocation of land.[28]

Arabs are not the only complainants: in 2002 *Hakeshet Hademokratit Hamizrahit*, a social movement formed to achieve equal rights for Mizrachi (Sephardic) Jews, went to court to complain that they were discriminated against in the allocation of rural land. A later report noted that the court forced the Israel Land Administration 'to walk on eggshells regarding the distribution of land among population groups' to avoid being sued again.[29]

And nothing is watertight. Haza and Nibal Tafesh, a Druze couple, were accepted as members of (Jewish) Kibbutz Elifaz in the south in March 2012.[30] They had been living there since 2007. Discussion over their membership application did not address their Druze background, said a kibbutz representative, but was concerned with their ages because they were older than others in the young community of twenty-nine Jewish families.

In 2010 the Knesset stepped in with a bill to allow small communities to reject candidates who did not meet specific selection criteria. It was obviously intended to exclude Arabs and ran into widespread opposition as being racist. None other than the Speaker, Reuven Rivlin – a veteran leader in the right-wing Likud Party – refused to bring the bill for further readings unless it was changed. An altered law applying only to the north and south of the country was enacted the next year. It bans discrimination against any individual but allows about seven hundred communities which have up to four hundred family units to reject would-be residents on grounds that they 'are unsuitable to the social life of the community . . . or the social and cultural fabric of the town', which, unless proved otherwise, seems very much like conferring the right to exclude anyone they do not like, whether Arabs, or Jews not considered religious enough, or too religious, or gays, or immigrants, or anyone.

The law was challenged within two years, with three petitions to the High Court.[31] Among them were Ofir and Danalee Kron Kalfa, both Jews. Ofir, thirty-two, headed a flagship project in the southern town of Sderot to create computer learning centres; his wife, twenty-seven, studied for a degree in administration and public policy. They applied, with their one-year-old daughter, for membership in a new community of 140 homes to be built on nearby kibbutz-owned land. The admissions committee rejected them as 'incompatible with the social life of the community'. They were later accepted.

Once more, none of this is uniquely Israeli but is like the 'gated communities' common in other countries. Britain, for example, has had them for more than a century, with walls – some two metres high, topped by glass or metal spikes – to keep 'working classes' out of middle- and upper-class housing estates. A study reported in 2003 that there were about one thousand gated communities in England.[32]

The land laws are not static. Fundamental change came in 2009 when the Knesset transformed the Israel Land Administration into the Land Authority with power to sell state land. It began with 800,000 dunams, 4 percent of the area of the state, most of it open spaces, with more intended to follow. It was claimed to be a means of bringing down house prices by reducing bureaucracy.[33]

The JNF is also moving: under pressure of demands for land for housing, it is reducing its forests to allow for development, especially of Arab villages in the north that are desperate for land.[34] If this goes far enough, it could end the land hunger which is probably the biggest source of Arab grievance. Their towns and villages are often locked into the same space as in 1948, yet the number of people has grown; there is no room for the children and grandchildren and no scope for creating industry. Tenders are invited for land for housing: during 2005–2009 the Arab community requested about 55,000 housing units and was given 21 percent of the needed land; Jews requested 217,000 housing units and were given 63 percent of the land needed.

Only a marginal amount of land was provided to Arabs for industry, commerce and tourism.[35] Siting factories is crucial for the financial health of municipalities because they bring jobs, local spending and *arnona* (property taxes). 'For our entire lives, we have accepted, as divine decree, that all factories in Israel are located in Jewish communities', notes Oudeh Basharat.[36] The sole arbiter of municipal jurisdiction is the minister of the interior. He decides 'where the rain of new factories will fall, and where drought will reign'. Until now, little sympathy has been shown for Arab needs.

Many Arabs have moved into 'Jewish' towns. They are estimated to constitute 15 percent of Upper Nazareth, and this is creating tension because some Jews do not want them there. This apart, Arabs are intensely resentful as they see government funds poured into creating and extending towns for Jewish residence. This has been a marked feature in recent years when the ultra-Orthodox Ariel Attias was minister of housing and construction and pushed to establish many new Haredi neighbourhoods.[37]

At the same time, the government acknowledges that Arab communities must be upgraded. More than $1 billion in funds is allocated for four years. But not all the money has been spent and several dozen villages are out of the loop. Thus the Mossawa Center reported early in 2012 that while government investment in Arab communities was rising, it was hardly sufficient to close the gaps between the Jewish and Arab populations.[38]

The development imperative was stressed at an unusual Knesset conference in June 2013 on the effects of the upcoming budget on Arabs.[39] It had been said that less than half of the $26 million allocated for 2010–2012 for Arab needs had actually been spent. This drove Welfare Minister Meir Cohen to say: 'The state's attitude towards the Arab and Bedouin sector is a disgrace'. Likud's Reuven Rivlin pointed to a crucial factor: 'If my dream came true and Arab parties were in the coalition, they would have political power and all these problems would be solved'.

The conference agreed that Knesset members and local authorities would meet regularly to examine how to remove barriers. Perhaps that was a turning point. Perhaps.

\* \* \*

But in 1948, with the bitter war over and Israeli Arabs subject to military rule, they were viewed as a potential fifth column. They were put under curfew, had to apply for permission from the military governor to travel more than a stated distance from their registered home and were subject to expulsions and detention without trial. As the domestic situation eased, the martial law restrictions were removed from the mainly Jewish cities and finally ended in 1966. Arabs were to enjoy the same citizen rights as Jews.

In 1976 came a transforming experience, triggered by a government announcement that it planned to expropriate thousands of dunams of land in the Galilee for 'security and settlement purposes'. For the first time since 1948, there was a national Arab response: a general strike and marches in towns on 30 March. It ended violently – the army and police killed six people, injured more than one hundred and arrested hundreds. The day is remembered every year as Land Day, both in Israel and on the West Bank.

During the early 1990s, hope swept through Israel as Prime Minister Yitzhak Rabin led negotiations with the Palestine Liberation Organization and signed the Oslo Accords. But the accords failed to bring Israeli-Palestinian peace, and a right-wing Jew assassinated Rabin. At the end of the decade, in the 1999 general elections, an estimated 94 percent of Arabs voted for Labour's Ehud Barak in the apparent belief that he would bring Rabin's pursuit of peace to fruition and that, domestically, an Arab party would, for the first time, be brought into a coalition government. Barak won, but ignored the Arabs. With an unwilling Yasser Arafat, he failed to win peace at the Camp David 2 talks in mid-2000. The disappointment and tensions helped to set the scene for the eruption of the second Palestinian intifada on 28 September.

The state's relations with its Arab citizens plummeted on 2 October. As the intifada on the West Bank gathered momentum, thousands of Israeli Arabs came out in support – and the worst domestic disturbances since 1948 ensued: thirteen Israeli Arabs died in clashes with the police. A commission of inquiry headed by former Supreme Court judge Theodor Or reported nearly three years later and began dramatically:

> The events of October 2000 shook the earth. . . . The intensity of the violence and aggression expressed in the events was extremely powerful . . . the consequence of deep-seated factors that created an explosive situation in the Israeli Arab population. . . . Government handling of the Arab sector has been primarily neglectful and discriminatory. . . . The establishment did not show sufficient sensitivity to the needs of the Arab population, and did not take enough action in order to allocate state resources in an equal manner. The state did not do enough or try hard enough to create equality for its Arab citizens or to uproot discriminatory or unjust phenomenon . . . serious distress prevailed in the Arab sector . . . poverty, unemployment, a shortage of land, serious problems in the education system and substantially defective infrastructure. [40]

Judge Or's clarion call could not have been more emphatic. Yet it's an unresolved grievance of the Arab community that no policemen have been prosecuted for their actions and policemen named in the report as culpable have received nothing more than a slap on the wrist.

\* \* \*

The Arab community is uncertain about its identity. Is it an integral part of Jewish Israel, enjoying civil rights yet subject to discrimination, or does its fate lie with fellow Palestinians on the West Bank and Gaza? Frustration has led to more insistent demands for change, moving past individual rights to communal rights. In December 2006 a group of prominent Arabs issued a document, *The Future Vision of the Palestinian Arabs in Israel*, telling Israel to stop defining itself as a Jewish state. They called for recognition of Israeli Arab citizens as an indigenous group with collective rights, saying Israel inherently discriminated against non-Jewish citizens in its symbols of state, some core laws, and budget and land allocations. They proposed a form of government, 'consensual democracy', similar to Belgium's system for Flemish and French speakers, with proportional representation and power-sharing in a central government and autonomy for the Arab community in areas like education, culture and religious affairs (not the best of suggestions, it must be said, in light of strains inside Belgium with Flemish speakers wanting to break away to create their own state; for months during 2010–2011, Belgians weren't able to agree on forming a government).

Jewish Israelis' reaction to the document ranged from some understanding to a more widespread indignation. Even among the centre-left, some condemned it as disturbing and harmful. On the Right, Israeli Arabs were accused of constituting a fifth column, a demographic and strategic threat to the survival of the state. Jewish critics argued that the Future Vision document 'negates Israel's legitimacy and raison d'être as the realization of Jewish self-determination' and undermines a two-state solution to the Israel-Palestinian conflict, since that implies the establishment of a Palestinian state alongside a Jewish one. Jews were especially surprised and affronted to find that many of those who prepared the document were staff members in the country's elite academic institutions.[41]

To what extent the demands reflect the community at large cannot be said for sure: according to Yoram Cohen, a Shin Bet chief, the ideological leadership of Arab Israelis 'is much more extreme than the public, and sometimes pulls in directions with which the public does not identify'.[42] However that may be, there cannot be any doubt that Jewish right-wingers speak and act in ways that dismay and alienate their Arab fellow citizens, such as calls by the Yisrael Beiteinu Party to transfer thousands of Arabs in the Galilee to the Palestinian Authority in exchange for Jewish settlements and settlers on the West Bank becoming part of Israel. It hasn't gone anywhere, but it worries Arabs; they want to be in Israel.

Restrictions have been introduced on commemoration of the *Nakba* (catastrophe), the Palestinian loss in 1948. To many Israelis, remembering the

Nakba is a Palestinian expression of their wish for the dismantling of the Israeli state. In March 2011 the Knesset voted to give the finance minister discretion to reduce government funding to any NGO that organises Nakba commemoration events. The education minister moved to excise the word from school textbooks; however, after the 2013 elections, with a right-wing government still in power, his successor reversed the ruling.

Orthodox rabbis have urged Jews not to rent or sell apartments to Arabs: by December 2010, three hundred signatories were reported for a decree to this effect, which claimed to be based on Jewish law. The right-wing Arutz Sheva news service's distasteful comment was that the decree came 'in the wake of years in which Arabs have flooded Jewish neighbourhoods and towns, changing the demographic status quo and often terrorizing the local Jews, while violently expelling any Jew who attempts to live in Arab villages'.[43] However, Arutz Sheva also recorded the shocked response of Israel's leaders: President Shimon Peres attacked the rabbis for bringing about 'a fundamental moral crisis in the State of Israel regarding the essence and content of the state as a Jewish and democratic one'. And Prime Minister Netanyahu said, 'How would we feel if they said not to sell apartments to Jews?'

The responses from leaders are significant in showing that there is another side to the coin, for time and again, the right-wingers, despite their noisy and best efforts, have failed to achieve what they want. Consequently, they have not thus far been able to get Knesset approval to disqualify various Arab parties and individuals in national elections. They also failed to revoke citizenship for 'disloyalty to the State'. They did not succeed in getting the restrictions on spouses from the West Bank gaining Israeli citizenship extended to Syria, Iraq, Lebanon and Iran.

Also contradicting the Right, advances to normalcy have been achieved by using the courts to ensure that discrimination gives way to legal rights. Thus, for example, in 2004 the Supreme Court ended four years of litigation by accepting a petition by Adalah that the Haifa municipality would publish all of its advertisements in Arabic as well as Hebrew newspapers. In 2009, following Supreme Court acceptance of Adalah petitions that Arabic was an official language, the Heritage Museum in the court building moved to label exhibits in Arabic, as well as Hebrew and English.

In 2012 Adalah struck at the core of Jewish preferential treatment by applying for an urgent injunction to prevent the Culture and Sports Ministry from staging free children's shows for *Pesach*, the Jewish Passover holiday.[44] The shows were to be performed in 110 predominantly Jewish cities and towns. Adalah won – four months later, the ministry allocated nearly $200,000 to provide free theatre tickets for Arab schoolchildren during the coming Eid al-Fitr Muslim holiday.[45]

In Jerusalem, a group of young Jewish men, mostly from the Yitzhar West Bank settlement, went round trying to determine which stalls in the famed Mahane Yehuda outdoor market employed Arabs and to discourage customers.[46] But this was a fringe group and the norm is that Arabs work as a matter of course in West Jerusalem, and in Tel Aviv and other cities, in stores and restaurants and throng the shopping malls. There is an occasional incident of intergroup violence, even murder, but nothing, at least thus far, compared to the scale of such urban violence in South Africa, Britain, France, Kenya and a myriad other countries.

Yet Adalah, while achieving so much, also seems to get confused about the meaning of rights. It has complained about barriers on travel and contacts between the Arab minority and the wider Arab and Muslim worlds, 'thus violating the rights of Arab citizens'.[47] It has also protested against an Israeli ban on importing books in Arabic from Syria and Lebanon, Egypt and Jordan (applied under the still-existent British Trading with the Enemy Act). Adalah condemned this as 'a clear violation of the rights to freedom of opinion and expression'.[48] It dismissed any justification as 'security pretexts'. Of course there is every reason for Adalah, as well as others, to be concerned about restrictions on travel and contacts and access to books. But Adalah shows itself to be insensitive about the state of war with Arab states, at best the state of hostility, suffered by Israel since its founding and security restrictions to do with this.

Adalah also lists discriminatory laws against Arabs.[49] Others pick up on the lists with claims of twenty, thirty or forty laws. It makes for anti-Israel sound bites but is misleading and meaningless because the lists do not only contain laws such as the Law of Return, which specifically discriminate against Arabs, but also laws which impinge on the liberty of both Arabs and Jews, plus right-wing-sponsored bills which might or might not end up as laws. So a false picture is presented.

There is also the case of Azmi Bishara, who was elected to the Knesset in 1966 to represent an Arab party. After he visited Syria in 2001, the Knesset decided, not unreasonably, that MKs wanting to visit 'enemy countries' must get permission from the minister of the interior. Bishara and other Arab MKs went on visiting without seeking permission. The police called them in for questioning, and the Arab Association of Human Rights, ignoring that Syria was a real and active enemy, objected that it was 'a pure political decision not a legal decision . . . part of the political policy by the State towards the Arab minority and their representatives'.

Bishara's visits led to press reports of his speeches expressing support for Hezbollah. In 2007 it was revealed that he was being charged with treason and espionage: he was accused of recommending long-range rocket attacks by Hezbollah and giving information on strategic locations in Israel that should be attacked with rockets during the 2006 Lebanon War; he had done this in exchange for huge amounts of money. Wiretaps had been authorised by the High Court of Justice. Bishara said he was leaving the country for a few days and would return for more police questioning. He did not return. From outside the country, he resigned from the Knesset and was later stripped of his parliamentary pension. His supporters attacked the Israeli government and claimed that no indictment was ever served on him – which is true because he made sure he wasn't around to receive one!

Hanin Zoabi, an Arab member of parliament, puts democratic tolerance to the test. Elected in 2009 for the three-member Balad Party, she rejects the idea of Israel as a 'Jewish state', which she says is 'inherently racist'. In May 2010 she was a passenger on the *Mavi Marmara*, the Turkish ship whose blockade-breaking attempt ended with Israeli soldiers coming down from helicopters, being attacked by passengers wielding iron bars, and killing nine of them. A video, publicly available, recorded the violent events. Zoabi, however, stated at a press conference in Israel, 'There was not a single passenger who raised a club'.[50]

Knesset members were incensed by her presence on the ship, and a committee voted to revoke her parliamentary immunity; however, Speaker Rivlin blocked that. Zoabi insisted she had taken part in 'legitimate political activity'.

Zoabi went to South Africa in November 2011 to condemn Israel in the 'Russell Tribunal' anti-Israel propaganda exercise. Later she was, again, loose with the truth in a newspaper article there. She said the Knesset had enacted 'a classic apartheid law' which 'prohibits Palestinian citizens from living in over 695 towns, effectively restricting them to Jews'.[51] The law does indeed exist. As noted earlier, it allows for 'gated communities', which are common in the world. But, unlike what she said, it does not apply only to Arabs but can be used against anyone.

Zoabi ran for mayor of the Arab city of Nazareth in municipal elections in 2013. She drew about 10 percent of the votes.

How is one to deal with Arab political parties which reject Israel's standing as a Jewish democratic state and even promote armed struggle against it? They evidently act in defiance of a 1985 amendment of the Basic Law for the Knesset, which says that a political party 'may not participate in the elections if there is in its goals or actions a denial of the existence of the state of Israel as the state of the Jewish people, a denial of the democratic nature of the state, or incitement to racism'.

To Arab members of parliament, threats by Jewish right-wingers to use this law to evict them shows rank discrimination and makes a mockery of Israel's claim to be a democracy. In fact, it was not enacted against Arab MKs. The target was a far-right *Jewish* party formed by Rabbi Meir Kahane, which propounded racist anti-Arab views. It gained entry to the Knesset in 1984, the amendment was enacted the next year, and it was barred from standing in the general elections in 1988. Kahane was assassinated in 1990 in New York by an Arab gunman and his party split, with a breakaway group calling itself *Kahane Chai* (Kahane Lives). The parties were barred from standing in the 1992 elections and were banned outright two years later.

\* \* \*

Jews of Ethiopian origin also complain of discrimination. In May 1991 Israeli army commandos, in Operation Solomon, carried out an extraordinary mission to transport about fifteen thousand Ethiopian Jews to Israel in less than thirty-six hours. The community now numbers 116,000 and on the twentieth anniversary of coming complained of discrimination to a parliamentary committee; they called on the government for affirmative action to help them.[52]

The discrimination periodically leads to outbursts of anger, as in January 2012 when five thousand demonstrated outside the Knesset with posters: 'Blacks and Whites – We're all Equal' and 'Our Blood Is Only Good for Wars'.[53] These were the children of the immigrants. The immediate trigger that time was the disclosure that 120 apartment owners in the town of Kiryat Malachi had signed a secret agreement not to sell or rent to Ethiopians.

Ethiopians suffer the same problems of immigrant families anywhere in the world – for example, the fear by veteran-established families of having too many immigrant children in school classes. Thus in the southern town of Arad, the municipality removed twenty-three immigrant children from religious kindergartens and transferred them to state kindergartens. The parents protested and kept their children at home for up to seven months; they later sued the municipality and the Education Ministry and won damages.[54]

The discrimination has been even more blatant – as with placing four Ethiopian girls in a separate class from their peers at a Petah Tikva grade school.[55] A single teacher was assigned to teach all their subjects, they had separate recess times and were driven to and from school separately. An official explained that the girls were not religiously observant enough, nor did their families belong to the national-religious movement upon which the school was founded. But one parent simply said: 'I don't understand why they are doing this to us . . . just because we are black'. The Education Ministry responded with outrage to the exclusion and promised swift action.

On the other hand, discrimination can lead to unfounded accusations: a blood donation stand set up in the Knesset was ordered to vacate after volunteers manning it told an Ethiopian woman member of Knesset, Pnina Tamnu-Shata, that her blood was not wanted. They were following Health Ministry guidelines but that did not halt the widespread protest; the Speaker, Yuli Edelstein, expressed shock and displeasure.[56] The fuss was needless: the ministry's guidelines say that people from Africa should not give blood because of the prevalence of AIDS; the same applies to people who were living in Britain during the mad cow disease scare in the 1980s. It has nothing to do with skin colour but where a would-be donor was living when.

Sephardic Jews also vent resentment, and not always with reason. One instance came after Shlomo Benizri, a former labour and welfare cabinet minister, was sentenced to four years' imprisonment for taking bribes. His leader in the Sephardic Shas Party, Eli Yishai, asked President Shimon Peres for amnesty, writing: 'I do not wish to mention the feelings of discrimination, the "second Israel", the sense of persecution and the bleeding social wound'.[57] His naked playing of the ethnic card and mentioning what he said he did not want to mention did not succeed, but it reflected continuing Sephardic claims that they are unjustly treated by the Ashkenazim. Yet this case was simply about a crook.

Moshe Katsav, the Iranian-born former president found guilty of rape and other sexual charges in December 2010, complained bitterly that he was the victim of an Ashkenazi establishment conspiracy because he was Sephardic. Some people actually believed him, despite the court's emphatic findings. Katsav was sentenced to seven years' imprisonment. Prime Minister Netanyahu rightly spoke of

> a day of sadness and shame, but it is also a day of deep appreciation and pride for the Israeli justice system. The court issued a sharp and unequivocal ruling on a simple principle, that of equality before the law; nobody is above the law, not even a former president, all are subject to the law.[58]

The Supreme Court rejected Katsav's appeal and he was jailed.

## WORK AND EARNINGS

The average monthly gross salary for Jews in 2007 was NIS7,885; for Arabs, NIS5,410. The more education a worker had, the greater the gap: salaried Jews with at least sixteen years of education earned NIS11,176; Arabs earned NIS7,729. Jewish men worked 51.8 hours a week compared to the 55.6-hour workweeks of Arabs.

In that year, 66.6 percent of Jewish women were working, compared to only 22 percent of Arab women (social factors keep many Arab women at home). Among men, employment was nearly the same: Jews 68.8 percent, Arabs 67 percent.[59]

But note that Arabs are not the worst off. Ethiopian immigrants have supplanted them as the lowest paid workers, according to a study based on 2010 statistics.[60] When Ethiopian immigrants first enter the workforce, they earn 30–40 percent less than Arabs with the same number of years of schooling.

Employers are reluctant to hire people with disabilities, or who are Arabs and Haredim, in that order, according to a study of employment trends at big companies.[61] But in 2012, a government-run campaign offering subsidies generated hundreds of requests by private businesses for Arab workers.[62] The government itself, however, lagged far behind its own target set in 2007 of having Arabs in 10 percent of public jobs by 2012: only 6.1 percent of workers in 2011 were Arabs and Druze. It ranged from 38.5 percent in the Interior Ministry and 10 percent in social affairs, to 1.5 percent in the Foreign Ministry and none in pensioner affairs.

Arabs are not always at the bottom of the scales because Jews can and do suffer worse discrimination. A Knesset Research and Information Center probe found that only 10 of the 4,623 people working for the Haifa municipality were Haredi, and only 5 percent of the Ashdod municipality workforce were new immigrants, even though 35 percent of the town's residents were new immigrants.[63]

Israel has the second highest poverty rate among OECD countries: 19.8 percent of families lived below the poverty line in 2010. Among Haredim, 56.9 percent of families were below the line; among Arabs, 53.5 percent; among children, 36.3 percent.[64] Among Ethiopians, 65 percent of the children were defined as poor, compared to 23 percent in the total population.[65]

## HEALTH

Two statistics provide a quick guide to a country's quality of life: infant mortality rate (IMR) – the number of deaths under one year of age per one thousand live births – and life expectancy – the average number of years to be lived by people born in the same year. Figures vary according to sources, but these are the overall patterns.[66] They show that Israel ranks high in the world.

*Infant Mortality*, a selection of world rankings, 2013 estimates:

*Life Expectancy*, a selection of world rankings, 2013 estimates:

| | |
|---|---|
| Afghanistan: 119.41 per 1,000 live births, ranked no. 1 (i.e., worst) | Monaco: 89.63 years, ranked no. 1 (i.e., best) |
| South Africa: 42.15 | Italy: 81.95 |
| Iran: 40.02 | Canada: 81.57 |
| Egypt: 23.30 | Sweden: 81.28 |
| Turkey: 22.23 | **ISRAEL: 81.17, ranked no 18** |
| Gaza Strip: 16.00 | Germany: 80.32 |
| Jordan: 15.26 | Jordan: 80.30 |
| China: 15.20 | United Kingdom: 80.29 |

Lebanon: 14.81

West Bank: 13.98

United Arab Emirates: 11.25

Kuwait: 7.68

Russia: 7.19

United States: 5.90

United Kingdom: 4.50

**ISRAEL: 4.03, ranked no. 199**

Germany: 3.48

Sweden: 2.73

Monaco: 1.81, ranked no. 222

United States: 78.62

Kuwait: 77.46

United Arab Emirates: 76.91

West Bank: 75.46

Lebanon: 75.46

China: 74.99

Saudi Arabia: 74.58

Gaza Strip: 74.40

Egypt: 73.19

Turkey: 73.03

Iran: 70.62

* * *

A closer look at Israel's infant mortality rate reveals remarkable improvement in the Arab community per one thousand live births: [67]

| | |
|---|---|
| 1955 | 62.5 |
| 1984 | 20.4 |
| 2009 | 7.1 |

And spectacular drops for all groups were recorded between 1970 and 2000, according to a study by J. Tarabei and others:

| | |
|---|---|
| Muslims | 78 percent |
| Druze | 82 percent |
| Christians | 88 percent |
| Jews | 79 percent |

The Tarabei study also reported two significant comparisons. Variations within the Arab community for the 1996–2000 period saw an IMR of 12.9 in the village of Kafr Kana, in the north, to 3.9 in Tamra village near Haifa. Among Jews, IMR ranged from 10.6 in the town of Or Akiva to 1.8 in Givatayim.

There were also variations between different Arab groups: the IMR for Arabs around the year 2000 was 8.6 but was:

| | |
|---|---|
| Muslims | 9.3 |
| Christians | 3.6 |

| Druze | 6.3 |
|---|---|
| Bedouin | 12.3 |

By 2012, the Muslim rate was down to 7.1, but in southern districts, where most Bedouin live, it was still above 12.0. IMR is affected by poverty and living conditions, hygiene and access to health services. In the case of the Bedouin, an additional specific factor is at work: intermarriage, said to occur among 60 percent compared to 32 percent among other Muslims, can cause congenital malformations in newborns. That, in 2000, accounted for 40 percent of infant deaths, compared to 23 percent among Jews living in the same southern area.

> The educational level of the Israeli Arab population and the organization of the medical services have improved considerably. Thirty years ago [in 1974] there were villages with minimal medical services, often lacking electricity and accessible roads. Today [in 2004], every village has one or more medical clinics with a permanent nursing staff and a resident physician, as well as infant welfare station services.[68]

National insurance and payments are compulsory for everyone, and all Israelis have equal access, free or with co-payments, to national health clinics, doctors and nurses, hospitals and drugs administered by *Kupat Cholim* (health maintenance organisations) and the state. While the basic principle of equality of access remains, wider benefits are available through private health insurance. As in other countries, the more you pay the more you can get. Gaps still exist, but are narrowing, as the tables below show.

**Table 3.1. Infant Mortality Rate, per 1,000 Live Births**

|  | Israel | Jewish | Arab | Arab gap |
|---|---|---|---|---|
| 1970–1974 | 21.9 | 18.6 | 32.1 | 13.5 |
| 1980–1984 | 14.4 | 11.8 | 22.6 | 10.8 |
| 2005–2008 | 4.0 | 3.0 | 7.0 | 4.0 |
| 2010–2012 | 3.6 | 2.7 | 6.6 | 3.9 |

*Source*: Israel Central Bureau of Statistics, Statistical Abstract, 2013, no. 64, 3.12.

**Table 3.2. Life Expectancy at Birth**

| All women | 1971 | 73.4 | 2012 | 83.6 |
|---|---|---|---|---|
| Jewish women | 1949 | 67.6 | 2012 | 84.0 |
| Arab women | 1996 | 77.2 | 2012 | 80.7 |
| All men | 1971 | 70.1 | 2012 | 79.9 |
| Jewish men | 1949 | 64.9 | 2012 | 80.6 |
| Arab Men | 1996 | 75.1 | 2012 | 76.9 |

*Source*: Israel Central Bureau of Statistics, Statistical Abstract, 2013, no. 64, 3.24.

While the health of all Israelis has been improving – and both Jews and Arabs rank in the top levels in the world – 'the disparity in health outcomes, particularly between Jewish and Arab Israelis, is still considerable, and this gap is one of the challenges that the [health] system faces going forward'.[69] Particular problems exist in regard to the large number of people who are outside the system or who fall between the cracks, such as foreign workers and the poor who cannot afford to buy drugs even at highly discounted prices; then there are Palestinians in East Jerusalem whose residency status and, therefore, eligibility is challenged by the National Insurance Institute – as a result, according to anecdotal information, unknown numbers transfer identities to get access to Israel's health system.

Another downside is that only 9.5 percent of medical personnel working in government institutions are Arabs, with a mere 0.25 percent in management posts, according to Ahmed Tibi, of the United Arab List-Ta'al, who headed a Knesset investigation.[70] Half of all state workers were in the health system, he said, but fewer than 10 percent were Arabs. On the other hand, there are exceptions: Dr Masad Barhoom, who is Arab, is director-general of the government hospital in Nahariya, a 'Jewish' city in the north.

Good intentions were expressed by then deputy health minister Ya'acov Litzman, who said: 'In health, there are no barriers. If something is good for the Arab population, it is also good for the Jewish population, and vice versa. The ministry is working to eliminate discrimination as much as possible'. Litzman's comment was all the more welcome because eighteen months earlier he had claimed that Barhoom 'doesn't allow his [Jewish] employees to pray' at the hospital and noted that he 'isn't a Jew'.[71] That sort of declared prejudice is, of course, not unique to Israel. Dr Leonid Eidelman, head of the Israel Medical Association, promptly thumped Litzman: the accusation was totally unfounded and his words 'raise the smell of racism'.

## EDUCATION

In Ottoman times, formal schooling was limited. Arabs studied in Turkish, with Arabic as the second language mainly for religious purposes. Illiteracy was up to 70 percent for men and 90 percent for women. Jews studied in Hebrew in their own religious schools, which existed in only a few towns.[72] They were cut off from the world, concerned only with prayer and study in *yeshiva* (religious school). Change began with the Jewish nonreligious settlers who came late in the nineteenth century and opened schools for their children.

Britain's mandate government created a department of education: the Ottoman state schools became the Arab public school system and were eligible for full government funding. The Jewish school system was sustained as 'voluntary schools' with grants-in-aid – but in practice little money was given. English, Arabic and Hebrew were made the official languages. Later, the Jewish public school system was recognised and subsidies were increased. Separate schools were set up for Arabs with teaching in Arabic: only about 40 percent of children, mostly boys, were at school.

Within the Jewish system, in addition to religious schools, three main types of schools developed: Mizrachi, focusing primarily on knowledge of Judaism; labour, in which physical work as a human and national value and the group were dominant; and general schools, with no articulated ideology except Jewish nationalism.

When Israel came into being, schooling was made compulsory and free for children aged between five and thirteen. The existing dual system was maintained and extended with a new education law: Jewish state schools were split into secular and religious. In the years since, it has all become much more complicated with different sets of schools in the Arab community and a proliferation of schools among Jews.

These days, Arab students can attend Jewish state schools, but only 1 percent do so. Almost no Jews attend Arab schools. Language and cultural barriers are too great.[73] There are exceptions: the small village of Neve Shalom-Wahat as-Salam ('Oasis of Peace' in Hebrew and Arabic), midway between Jerusalem and Tel Aviv, runs a kindergarten and primary school for Jews and Arabs. Inspired by this, a Jewish social worker and an Arab teacher founded Hand in Hand in 1997 – four bilingual and multicultural schools around the country have more than one thousand pupils.

In a new breakthrough, the Education Ministry in 2013 launched a five-year programme to integrate five hundred Israel-Arab teachers into Jewish schools to meet a shortage of teachers for core subjects – science, mathematics, English and Arabic.[74] While the obvious aim is to help Jewish schools this will open up jobs for eighteen thousand Arab university graduates and can help to break down barriers.

That Arab education has for years been underfunded and under-resourced is well known. The negative results are seen in the following statistics.[75]

**Table 3.3.  Average number of pupils per class**

| Elementary Schools | Secondary Schools |
| --- | --- |
| Arab 29 | Arab 30 |
| Jewish 24 | Jewish 27 |

*Source*: Israel Central Bureau of Statistics, Statistical Abstract, 2013.

Drop-out rate among ninth–twelfth graders:

Jews 4%              Arabs 7%


Median years of study, ages fifteen and above:

Jews 12.7            Arabs 11.1


Matriculation passes among twelfth graders:

Jews 56%            Arabs 49%


University entrance passes among twelfth graders:

Jews 48%            Arabs 32%

Once more, however, the story is more complicated. Noted educationist David Harman explains that the fundamental fact about the education system is that the state supports multiple parallel tracks. These tracks were born in the pre-state era, some Ottoman, most during the British mandate.[76]

> Compulsory education from five to sixteen has been in place since 1968. The Ministry of Education, in accordance with the law, gives every child a financial basic basket, the *sal chinuch*, basket of education. This is meant to cover X number of hours per week of schooling for a set core curriculum; it includes money for cultural activities. The basket is revised from time to time.

All public schools receive a 'basket' of hours based on student numbers regardless of religion, colour or anything else. Private schools and ultra-Orthodox schools receive grants which are calculated differently but are also based on student numbers and the extent to which schools adopt the government's set core curriculum – except with deviations in favour of ultra-Orthodox schools.

Harman explains,

> Say there are 80 children at grade level: they will get enough money for 36 hours of instruction; that translates into teachers' salaries and enables a school to hire, say, two teachers for two classes of 40 each. But in an area where parents want more teachers, they raise money for it, either from school fees or the local authority. If parents want piano lessons for their children, they must pay for it. The extra lessons are known as 'grey education' and this is where the gaps between schools start growing.
>
> The state also aims to extend extra activities to poorer areas. The private Charles Bronfman Foundation puts in money to pay for counselors and teachers in the afternoon; it administers the scheme and gives $1.5 million a year and the state puts in another $60 a child. There are 4,500 of these teachers and

counselors throughout the country – at all schools, Jewish and Arab, except ultra-Orthodox and private. There are also about 250 community centres around the country in Jewish and Arab areas. Established in the late 1960s they are wholly paid for by the government and do ballet, arts and crafts. Arabs share in this equally.

\* \* \*

Israeli Arabs, however, complain of 'systematic, institutionalized discrimination in the education system' and point to negative effects on their children in school results and in later life, denying them access to higher qualifications and better jobs and better pay.[77] They note that the Education Ministry controls the form and structure of Arab schools, but few Arabs have decision-making powers inside the ministry with, in 2006, only 126 officials out of 2,031 – 6.2 percent. They note that there is little teaching about Palestinian or Arab history, geography, literature and culture. They point to underrepresentation in universities: Arabs hold only 1.2 percent of all tenured and tenured-track posts. They note that discrimination is evident in the earliest years: because of the shortage of state-funded preschools in Arab towns, only 67.4 percent of two- to five-year-olds were in kindergartens in 2007–2008, compared to 84.9 percent among Jews.

In a cry that comes from the heart of a minority community, they say that while Arabic is an official language its status is vastly inferior to Hebrew: there is 'clear inequality' in opportunities for Arab speakers compared with Hebrew speakers to use their language in official and public forums.[78] They say, too, that the state education system 'ignores the rights, the needs, and the priorities of Arab students and thus denies them the opportunity to develop a positive cultural and national identity'.[79]

These bleak views are matched by Sikkuy: 'An analysis of government policy towards the school system in the Arab sector reveals a lower investment compared to the other educational streams which is reflected in relatively sparse resources in comparison with those invested in the Jewish school system'.[80] However, it also notes that many beneficial changes have taken place in Arab education: the number of students has increased and the quality of teaching and level of education have improved, but 'large gaps' remain between Arab and Jewish schools. The Higher Arab Monitoring Committee complains that only part of a joint plan it worked out with the Education Ministry in 2008 to overcome decades of neglect and discrimination has been implemented, resulting in a shortage of 6,100 classrooms and 4,000 teachers in Arab communities.[81]

Yet, while discrimination exists, the Jewish-Arab gap also stems from broader factors – nor, again, is it entirely one-sided in favour of Jews. Instead, Education Ministry statistics show that gaps in education – and they have been widening – are between wealthier and poorer communities.[82] The picture is seen in percentages of twelfth graders who wrote *bagrut* (matriculation) exams in 2010–2011.

The gap between well-off and poorer towns was seventeen percentage points. The average pass rate was 70.5 percent. The five highest scorers were wealthier Jewish towns, led by Shoham with 86.2 percent. At the bottom of the list were Jewish ultra-Orthodox and Arab communities, all economically poorer: the lowest were two Jewish towns, Betar Illit with 10.88 percent and Bnei Brak with 10.89 percent. The lowest Arab towns were Kafr Qasem, 26.82 percent, and Kalansua, 35.18 percent. Jerusalem achieved 41.68 percent, Tel Aviv 73.68 percent and the Druze town of Marar, 79.6 percent. Consistently good matriculation results are achieved by the private St George Christian School in Nazareth – where most pupils are Muslims.

The significance of socioeconomic factors was again shown in the results of the Meitzav exam, which, every four years, compares elementary school pupils across the country. Results for 2012–2013 showed widening achievement gaps of dozens of points in mathematics, science and technology between pupils from the poorest and richest populations. For all subjects and all levels, the gap between Jewish and Arab pupils was also dozens of points. An educational expert warned that the results were a 'red flag which brings the values and economic future of the country in[to] question'.[83]

* * *

A web of factors underlies disparities in education.[84] The immediate reason why Arab children receive so much less than Jewish children is the amount of money that cities put into their school systems. At the top is (Jewish) Herzliya with NIS5,000 (about $1,250) per pupil a year; at the bottom, the (Bedouin) city of Rahat with NIS58 ($14.50). Herzliya is both wealthier than Rahat and also prioritises education: it invests 14 percent of its independent budget in education while Rahat invests 2 percent. (Despite this, the town has thrown itself into improvement, and its matriculation pass rate rose from 42 percent to 54.96 percent in 2010–2011.) That is a general pattern, with most Arab municipalities devoting single-digit percentages of their budgets to education. The Circassian village of Kfar Kama is an exception, allocating 33 percent. It also goes beyond Jews and Arabs: the Jewish municipality in Tel Aviv spends about twice the amount on education as does the Jewish municipality of Jerusalem.

Priorities are influenced by the money available: Arab municipalities collect taxes from only 27.3 percent of their residents compared to 63.1 percent in Jewish municipalities of equivalent economic rankings. Poor management is a factor, as is the low incomes of many residents. Arab municipalities also collect virtually no business taxes: residential taxes are 66 percent of total revenues, compared to 43 percent in Jewish towns. The reason for the lack of business taxes takes the story back to the land problem: Arab municipalities do not have the space to establish industrial zones for tax-yielding businesses.

* * *

An especially dire situation exists in Jerusalem for Arab children. The shortage of classrooms for them has been critically scrutinised by the Supreme Court. A hearing in January 2011 was revealing both in the details of deficiencies and the behind-the-scenes complications arising from the city's disputed political and international status. The court heard a petition by the Association for Civil Rights in Israel, which called on the government to repay Arab families turned away from public schools for lack of space and who instead had to send their children to private schools or recognised but unofficial schools; in both cases, parents had to pay tuition fees. [85]

Chief Justice Dorit Beinisch assailed the state for failing to solve the severe shortage of classrooms; she said almost half the students in the city's Arab sector did not study in public schools. The state's lawyer said that the Education Ministry was aware of the problem in East Jerusalem – to which Beinisch responded tartly: 'It was only when we asked the director of the budget that the Finance Ministry agreed to allocate special funds. The state did not initiate anything'.

According to the Jerusalem municipality, 42,000 Arab pupils study in the Israeli public school system, 20,000 in the recognised but unofficial stream, 14,000 in private schools and 6,500 in Waqf Islamic trust schools. Estimates of the number of classrooms lacking in the public school system, never mind poor resources, ranged from 1,000 to 1,500. Since 2001, the city has built 296 classrooms. One reason why it was difficult to determine how many classrooms were lacking was because it was not known how many families would refuse to send their children to Israeli-administered schools, even if classrooms were available for them.

The government argued that the private schools did not have permits from the Ministry of Education, were illegal and the state therefore refused to pay for them; the state did subsidise up to 75 percent of the recognised but unofficial schools, and parents had to pay only a fraction of the fees. But the court pointed out that the state's position violated the compulsory education law that all children are entitled to free education.

This time, positive action came quickly: a month later, the Jerusalem municipality's budget included additional funds for education. That was 'welcomed' by the Association for Civil Rights in Israel but with the cautionary note that after many years of neglect not enough was being spent 'to bridge the gaps and to bring the living situation in East Jerusalem into the 21st century'.[86] The city's mayor, Nir Bakat, did drive ahead, with several hundred new and renovated classrooms reported ready late in the year and more being built, plus programmes for gifted pupils and sports facilities. But the shortage of classrooms must still be overcome, and in September 2012 Acri and Ir Amin, in a joint report, protested a shortage of 1,200 classrooms in East Jerusalem, noting that even when current planning and building was completed there would still be a 750-classroom shortage.[87] The average number of pupils per class was thirty-two compared to twenty-five in the western part of the city, and, unlike Jewish children, Palestinian children did not enjoy reduced-cost public transportation. There was also an alarming dropout rate of 17.3 percent a year compared to the national average of 1.7 percent for Jews and 2.8 percent for Arabs – and the municipality was doing little to counter it. The municipality replied that it was doing its best and had spent more than $160 million to close the gaps created in the past forty years.

Adding another twist to an already-fraught situation, in 2011 the Jerusalem municipality told private schools receiving subsidies that they had to buy and use only Israeli textbooks, thus paralleling the (unsuccessful) efforts to get Jewish ultra-Orthodox schools to follow the official curriculum. The angry response from Palestinian activists was summed up by the head of the Parents' Committee Union, Abdel Karin Lafi, who said that the Israeli occupation authorities were completing 'the project of achieving total domination over both the Palestinian land and the Palestinian human while depriving him from his culture and his history, thus tampering with the collective identity of Palestinians'.[88]

The municipality stepped into a murky situation: after the 1967 conquest of East Jerusalem, Arab schools had continued to follow the Jordanian educational system; later, after the signing of the Oslo Accords, they began to use the curriculum of the Palestinian Authority. Today, the East Jerusalem education system is governed by four different authorities: Israel; the Islamic Waqf; the private sector; and UNRWA, the UN agency for Palestinian refugees. The Israeli and private schools get varying amounts of state funding; the other two do not. It's all complicated, and a lack of understanding leads to ill-informed criticism.

There is also continuing dispute about the exact situation. As the school year began in September 2013, the Association for Civil Rights in Israel and Ir Amin issued a damning report that the municipality and the Ministry of Education were doing little to meet the 2011 High Court ruling that ordered completion of 2,300 classrooms in East Jerusalem by 2016.[89] Since 2009, only 150 classrooms had been built, they said, and wide disparities existed, such as only 29 counsellors in East Jerusalem compared with 250 in the West. The mayor's office hit back, accusing Acri and Ir Amin of 'recycling the same distorted annual report'. Instead, it said, more than NIS400 million had been spent to build four hundred classrooms, and the municipality was also promoting a 'technology revolution' in East Jerusalem schools.

\* \* \*

Illiteracy in Israel stands at 4.6 percent. That ranks as twenty-seventh among 177 countries. In terms of groups and sexes:

| | |
|---|---|
| Arab women | 13.4 percent |
| Jewish women | 3.4 percent |
| Arab men | 5.5 percent |
| Jewish men | 1.99 percent |

The differences are unacceptable, even allowing for factors such as the conservative nature of parts of Arab society in which women are kept at home instead of going out to work, and the economic pressures of poverty which push Arab youth to drop out of school to seek work. Again, however, a closer look reveals considerable progress.

For example, in 1948 there were 12,000 Arab children in school; by 1990 there were 220,000 – a rate of increase of eighteen – whereas their population had grown only fivefold.[90]

Among Arab Bedouin women aged over sixty, illiteracy is 92.3 percent. That reflects the past. For women aged thirty-five to thirty-nine, reflecting recent years, it is 13.2 percent – not good, but showing how much has been done.[91]

Arabs, once a small minority of school-going children, have become a significant component of the educational system: from 10 percent in 1960 to 25 percent in 2009. They share the rapid increase with ultra-Orthodox Jews, who went from 4 percent of school-going children in 1980 to 15 percent in 2009. The same reasons apply to both: high rates of birth and school attendance.[92]

These are remarkable achievements for a new state, particularly during the decades when it was absorbing many hundreds of thousands of Jewish immigrants from North Africa, Asia and the Middle East: many arrived penniless and illiterate and were taught in Hebrew as the unifying language.

Action to tackle the persistent disadvantages of minorities was begun late in 2012 with the Council for Higher Education putting in US$81 million to enable institutions to offer counselling and personal support to Arab students; websites must be translated into Arabic and workshops must be organised to help Arab students improve their Hebrew and study skills; long-term plans must be prepared with clear goals for accepting minorities and encouraging them to pursue advanced degrees.[93] The council acted after a survey showed that Arabs were disadvantaged from the start: while 44 percent of Jewish students met the minimum requirements for university admission, only 22 percent of Arabs did. Only 57 percent of Arab teens took the school matriculation (*bagrut*) examinations, compared to 73 percent of Jewish teens. The dropout rate was 15.4 percent among Arab students compared to 10.6 percent among Jews. Arabs were 11.3 percent of undergraduates but only 3 percent of doctoral students.

## BEDOUIN

Modernity moves on remorselessly, and the Bedouin people in the Negev are hard hit by it; the problem is exacerbated because it pits the Bedouin against Jews in a contest for land, and Jews command the power of the state. Once again, it's not a uniquely Israeli situation. In 2007 Egyptian police clashed with three thousand Bedouin who were protesting against a government order to demolish their houses along the Gaza Strip's porous border; it was an Egyptian attempt to prevent the smuggling of weapons and people into Gaza.[94]

The same problem arises in other parts of the world, as, for example, in dealing with ancient people in Southern Africa. In Botswana, the indigenous Bushmen – the San – protested bitterly at the government's refusal to provide them with a polling station in their living area in the Kalahari game reserve during a general election. In 2002 the government had evicted San from their ancestral lands in the park and closed a borehole that was their only source of water. The government argument was that it could only provide services to people living in formal settlements and not in the park.[95] In neighbouring South Africa, the post-apartheid African National Congress government has been accused of persisting with 'cultural genocide' against descendants of the Khoisan people, failing to redress the injustices of the apartheid regime's oppressive laws but instead marginalising them even further. The Khoisan demand recognition as a nation and want 'first-nation status' under a UN protocol.[96]

In the Negev, half of the two hundred thousand Bedouin live in limbo; many of the other half live wretchedly. Yet they are all citizens, paying taxes and entitled to health care and services. They also volunteer for army service. The problem begins with land ownership, and that sparks arguments over how long the Bedouin have been there: some academics say they have not been in the area for more than about two hundred years, and others say they have been there much longer. The Bedouin claim private ownership of land and the state refutes this, saying that in Ottoman and British mandate law it was always public land.

In the 1970s the government embarked on urbanisation: it created eight towns with houses and schools and electricity and water on the condition that the Bedouin abandoned their claim to land. Today, those towns suffer from poor infrastructure, high unemployment and poverty, high crime and drug smuggling. Bigamy and intermarriage leading to congenital malformations at birth add to health problems. The Bedouin outside the towns are semi-nomads in clusters of rundown black goat-hair tents with herds of camels, sheep and goats. Others have set up about fifty villages with makeshift houses whose existence is not officially recognised; therefore, they do not have running water, electricity, sewage or garbage collection, and most do not have schools or clinics. (These 'unrecognised' villages are a disgraceful phenomenon in Israel, both in the Negev and in the Galilee in the north, with tens of thousands of Arabs there who have lived in substandard conditions for many decades, some going as far back as the 1948 war when they left or were driven from their villages and settled wherever they could in the neighbourhood.)

The struggle between government and people has continued for more than six decades. Whereas the Bedouin are denied permission to build and what they erect is destroyed, the government aims to create a set of ten new towns to draw Jews to the Negev. A government investigation led to legislation in 2013, heatedly debated in the Knesset, which would accept only 63 percent of Bedouin claims to ownership of land while paying compensation for some claims. The government plans to destroy the homes of thirty thousand to forty thousand people and transfer them to undeveloped plots in 'authorised' locations. Right-wingers oppose it: they object to giving any land rights at all to Bedouin and want to confine them into a smaller space. On the Left, the Association of Civil Liberties in Israel and Planners for Building Rights, Bimkom, say the law is 'dispossessing them [Bedouin] of their property and historical rights to their lands, destroying the social fabric of their communities, and sealing the fate of thousands of families into poverty and unemployment'.

A year before the legislation, a Bedouin expert, Dr Clinton Bailey, gave a clear and sober warning: 'Although the state dealt harshly with Bedouin in the past by moving them from place to place, confiscating their flocks, destroying their homes and even spraying their crops with poison, its actions never resulted in an uprising, perhaps because these violations were small-scale: a family here, a clan there'.[97]

Watch for conflict.

*Chapter Four*

# The Occupation

*To the east of Israel proper is the West Bank. Israeli settlement there began out of idealistic belief. It became zealotry, which has gained its ends through mass deceit, land theft, corruption and abuse of law. The result, in Israel's military occupation, is the oppression of Palestinians.*

\* \* \*

The Israelis who settled the West Bank after the 1967 war did so out of their idealistic belief that they were serving the cause of the Jewish people: they were entrenching the unexpected military victory and fulfilling the Divine purpose. National-religious belief increasingly came to the fore: to the settlers, the West Bank, officially returned to its biblical names as Judea and Samaria, had been given by God to the Jews, was the ancient heartland of the Jewish faith and had to be kept Jewish forever. Later, the economic advantages of settlement – from tax breaks to cheap housing and transport – took on weight, but always on the bedrock of the God-given right to be there. [1]

Unfortunately, countless eras in human history show that religious belief and nationalist passion do not always go with justice, wisdom and truth; zealous adherence to a cause does not necessarily justify the cause. So it has been with the West Bank's settlers: they have pursued their beliefs through deceit, lies, theft, corruption, illegality, cynicism and brute force, and with no regard for the rights and humanity of Palestinian inhabitants. [2]

The settlers have transformed Israel: they have influence in the inner core of government, and they shape profound policy decisions for the future. Many, many millions of shekels are devoted to them in budgets, both openly and secretly. Their existence has been made possible by military occupation, which in its nature is cruel and capricious towards the subjugated Palestinian people. And they have succeeded only because of the connivance and/or political cowardice of successive Israeli governments of all political hues. Even noted peace figures have collaborated: Shimon Peres, seeking reelection as prime minister after the assassination of Yitzhak Rabin in 1995, and Yossi Beilin, his housing minister, promised to build thousands of houses on the West Bank, and their Labour Party entered into deals with settlers.[3] The settlers have created deep divisions among Israelis and between Israel and the world. The ruinous moral, military and economic consequences for Israel are beyond measure.

The settlers have also contributed to and been part of far-reaching religious change among Jews. The Zionism which brought Israel into existence was mainly secular; in contrast, the messianic outlook in West Bank settlement has spurred a national-religious movement which has deeply affected Israeli society, from emboldening rabbis into challenging the authority of the state, to changing the character of the army's officer corps. National-religious Jews project themselves as the carriers of the Zionist torch; adherents of the original Zionism vehemently disagree.

The depth of belief is explained by a well-known rabbi, Shlomo Aviner: responding to the US-initiated Roadmap of 2003, which envisaged a Palestinian state on the West Bank within two years, he noted that it was the government's job to decide on urban planning; however, the 'ideological question' of whether a particular location belonged to the Jewish people or anyone else transcended governments, and the answer instead was provided by 'the Master-of-the-Universe, by the Torah, by Jewish tradition, by history'. (Clearly, as interpreted by the rabbis.) His emphatic declaration was: 'Uprooting a Jewish community is a terrible crime with no parallel throughout Jewish or world history. All the more so that establishing a foreign state in the very midst of our own country is a national crime which surpasses all the bounds of reason and ethics'.[4]

From 1948 to June 1967 no Jews lived on the West Bank and in East Jerusalem; Jews in these areas prior to 1948 were killed or expelled during the War of Independence. But by 2013, an estimated 400,000 were on the West Bank and 250,000 in East Jerusalem.[5]

The Oslo Accords of 1993 split the West Bank into three. Area C has 61 percent of the land with 5.8 percent of the Palestinian population and is fully under Israeli control pending final Palestinian-Israeli agreement – with the proviso that the land would come under Palestinian control six years later, by 1999 (which did not happen). Area B is under shared Israeli and Palestinian control; it has 21 percent of the land and 41 percent of Palestinians. Area A is under Palestinian control. If the Israeli army wants to enter Area A, say, to detain a man in Nablus, it needs to obtain the permission of the Palestinian security authorities.

There are different types of settlements, and they can be roughly defined. 'Settlements', 120 of them, are Jewish civilian communities on land seized in the 1967 war. They are all illegal in international law. 'Outposts' are a second type of settlement. In 1996 the government decided not to build new settlements but went on creating settlements; in order to skirt political and international obligations, it has established – or allowed – more than one hundred unofficial settlements, known as 'outposts' or 'unauthorized outposts'. Some have been the focus of court applications to have them destroyed. The court cases can run for years and sometimes do lead to removal of an outpost. In a third category are outposts which do not have government approval. The government can and does order the police and army to remove settlers and demolish their trailers or buildings. Settlers often resist strongly. Not all the 'illegal outposts' are dismantled; some eventually gain official recognition.

To Israel, the West Bank is 'disputed territory': its lawyers say it was part of the British mandate, and Jordan seized it in 1948, annexed it in 1950 and held it – recognised only by Britain and Pakistan – until evicted by Israel in 1967; its legal status is thus uncertain and Israel can settle it. However, virtually the entire world disagrees and says that the West Bank is 'occupied territory' and Israel has no right to settlements and must get out.

Two points can be made to cut through the thicket of legal claims and counterclaims: first, the West Bank was meant to have been part of the Palestinian state proposed in the UN partition plan in 1947, and had Arabs at that time accepted it instead of going to war, today's problem would not exist; second, the Oslo Accords reached between Israelis and Palestinians were posited on the creation of an independent Palestinian state. And if not on the West Bank and Gaza, then where?

A hunt to justify the settlements legally was mounted by Prime Minister Binyamin Netanyahu in 2012: he appointed a committee of three headed by retired High Court judge Edmund Levy to advise on 'steps to be taken to regularize construction'. The committee obliged four months later by pursuing the 'disputed territory' line and declaring that Israel is not an 'occupying power' in the West Bank, it can really do what it likes, Israelis have the legal right to settle in Judea and Samaria, and establishing settlements cannot be considered illegal. The findings not only flew in the face of world legal opinion but also of Israel's own official attitude and the way its courts have dealt with the territories over the years. Uncomfortably for the right wing, they also contradict the view of Ariel Sharon when he was prime minister: after a life dedicated to pushing for settlement, in 2003, in what CNN described as 'stunning words from the longtime hawk', he said:

> You cannot like the word, but what is happening is an occupation – to hold 3.5 million Palestinians [in the West Bank and Gaza] under occupation. I believe

that is a terrible thing for Israel and for the Palestinians. . . . It can't continue endlessly. Do you want to stay forever in Jenin, in Nablus, in Ramallah, in Bethlehem? I don't think that's right.[6]

* * *

A variety of methods is used to seize land. Land history and laws are often uncertain, so there is scope for ingenuity. First are 'state lands', which means using public lands previously in the control of the Ottoman Empire/British mandate/Jordanian governments. The land is handed to settlers who hire private contractors to build houses and apartment blocks; the Israeli government, through its various departments, provides electricity, water, sewage, roads, *mikvehs* (ritual baths), schools and security through the army and private guards.

Over time, that approach became more refined, with 'state lands' meaning any land that was not being cultivated. To this end, Israeli officials flew over the West Bank in helicopters in search of uncultivated land; once identified, land registries dating back to Ottoman times were checked for private ownership. The inherent flaw in this process is that Israel has no right to 'state lands': it has never annexed the West Bank and remains only the occupying power with rights that do not extend to doing whatever it pleases.

The second method is to decree that land is needed for 'military purposes' or 'military needs'. An army base might or might not then be built on it. The intent is to allow settlers onto the land, perhaps as crypto-soldiers, and in due course, the land becomes a settlement. Another way has been to secretly establish a 'work camp' – that's how Ofra began and in time grew to be a major settlement. Palestinian owners of seized land are supposed to get some payment and even an annual leasing fee – but even this shabby set-up has been poorly administered with years-long delays.[7]

Third, another trick is to claim that the pressure of satisfying 'natural growth' requires creating 'new neighbourhoods' in existing settlements – which, in fact, are new settlements. The 'natural growth' line is in any event dubious: the population of Israel increased at a rate of 1.9 percent in 2012. In the same year, the settlements increased by 5 percent, and 31.5 percent was directly attributable to immigration from Israel and abroad.[8]

The fourth method is the outright grabbing of land which belongs to Palestinians. Prime Minister Menachem Begin ordered a stop to this in the late 1970s and said only 'state lands' must be used. But it continued. Private builders erect buildings, and thus a settlement comes into being. The Peace Now movement revealed the staggering scale of it in a report in November 2006, which drew on official data of the Israeli Civil Administration, the government agency in charge of the settlements. It said that nearly 32 percent of the total land area of the settlements was privately owned by Palestinians: 'The settlement enterprise has undermined not only the collective property rights of the Palestinians as a people, but also the private property rights of individual Palestinian landowners'.[9]

Sometimes the theft is exposed and is so blatant and outrageous that the government is forced, eventually and reluctantly, to enforce the law. This was the case with the Migron outpost built on private Palestinian land in 2001 with government money.[10] It took six years of repeated applications to court – and court eviction judgments repeatedly ignored amid government and settler ducking and diving – before the government finally ordered police to evacuate fifty settler families. Incentives were provided at taxpayer expense to buy off settler anger, including removal costs, temporary housing and $180,000 grants to each family. Even that was not the end: ten structures were left standing because settlers claimed they had bought the land. The attorney-general finally ordered their destruction. The disputing continued.

Fifth, young religious zealots move trailers (it's only possible with the army's knowledge) onto a hilltop and create an outpost. Some become permanent settlements, and others are destroyed by the police and army with the youth furiously resisting evacuation.

Finally, the government simply does what it likes – which is what happened in November 2011 when the Netanyahu government was looking for ways to punish the Palestinian Authority for being accepted as a member of UNESCO. One of the sanctions was to announce a new wave of settlement construction on the West Bank: to build two thousand housing units in East Jerusalem and expedite two settlement areas.[11]

The national-religious are the battering ram in securing and maintaining settlement. But while no exact information is available, it seems that they are a minority among settlers and their power is magnified through their zealotry and commitment. Most other settlers on the West Bank and in East Jerusalem range from secular through religious to ultra-Orthodox and are there for economic and practical reasons: cheap housing, good schooling, subsidised services and clean air. As Gideon Levy reported,

> Whoever imagines the outposts in the West Bank as a handful of trailers perched atop a bald mountain, or a group of settlers with long sidelocks and piercing gazes, is invited to tour Outpost Country, version 2012. Out of a total of about 100 such outposts, there are a few that look like the height of bourgeois life.

One of the outposts he wrote about was built on privately owned Palestinian land (the government promised to legalise it); another was on 'state land' but without any building permits. Soldiers guard the entrances; each settlement has a long list of officials from secretaries and security coordinators to rabbis and ritual bath attendants with most salaries paid by the state. 'The plots are large, the gardens are expansive, and the landscape is breathtaking', Levy wrote about one outpost.[12]

The government spent from $250 million to $400 million on West Bank settlements in 2011.[13] That covered costs such as subsidised housing, school buses, protective fences, security provided by the army and private guards, reinforcing buses that serve settlements and paying for bulletproof windshields for settlers' vehicles, subsidised bus travel, special roads, subsidies for factories to compensate for problems in selling in Europe and elsewhere, ritual baths and the separation barrier. An earlier 2007 estimate put the cost much higher, at about $1.4 billion a year, half paying for military expenses in keeping control and half for civilian costs; $50 billion was estimated to have been spent during the first forty years of occupation – obviously a heavy drain on the ability to provide schools, hospitals, clinics and welfare inside Israel proper.[14]

The extent to which ideology trumps all else was seen in mid-2012 in regard to Ariel College. Its occupation identity is clear by its former name, the College of Judea and Samaria. Ariel is a settlement town of twenty thousand people and growing, a dagger pointing into the heart of the West Bank, twenty kilometres from the Green Line. Of its thirteen thousand students, about five hundred are Arabs. For years, Israel's seven universities through the official Council for Higher Education fought against attempts to upgrade the college, arguing that there was no need for another university and, even more, fearing that their budgets, already reduced, would be further cut.

A contrary view came from the Judea and Samaria Council for Higher Education – which is appointed by Israel's army commander on the West Bank. To no one's surprise, the council voted to upgrade Ariel College, to create the first new university after forty years and the first outside the country's borders. As for the money worry, then finance minister Yuval Steinitz waved that aside by announcing that he would allocate a special amount of $12.5 million over two years which would not come from the universities' budget, with extra funding after that. Others estimated that Ariel would need at least $50 million a year. Right-wing members of Knesset understandably hailed it as a 'historic' victory.

A week later, the government announced rises in taxes and VAT to counter a growing economic crisis. And in due course, the cabinet approved the new university with Prime Minister Netanyahu announcing, 'I love to break monopolies and cartels', and giving Palestinians a poke in the eye with the reminder that Ariel will 'remain an inseparable part of the State of Israel just like the other settlement blocs'.[15] The heads of Israel's universities came under heavy pressure to give way and endorse Ariel, but only Bar-Ilan University buckled. Finally, in an unprecedented move, the Council for Higher

Education was brushed aside and then minister of defence and Labour leader Ehud Barak approved the new university. It is doomed to be shunned by world academia. Still to come could be international fallout for Israeli scholars.

* * *

The first settlement on the West Bank was in September 1967, less than five months after the war. Jews were euphoric, borne aloft by the swift transition from the fear of Arab attack and mass deaths on 5 June to the victory on an unbelievable scale within six days. Motivated by nationalist emotion and historical pain, and messianic belief for some, Jews returned to a site that was a symbol for Zionist heroism and martyrdom: Kfar Etzion, between Jerusalem and Hebron, a farming community destroyed during Arab riots in 1929 and again in 1936. In 1948 it was destroyed for the third time with a large-scale massacre of Jewish civilians and soldiers. The fall of Kfar Etzion was also linked with the February 1948 death of thirty-five young soldiers on their way to relieve the region. It was 'an open wound that needed healing', said Zertal and Eldar.[16] After Israel regained the site, the settlers' descendants – who included children sent to safety in 1948 – told Prime Minister Levi Eshkol that they wanted to return. He gave his approval – despite legal advice that settlement on occupied land would be a contravention of the Fourth Geneva Convention. The Kfar Etzion kibbutz was thus reborn, and in due time the area was populated by twenty-two settlements with seventy thousand people.

The next intrusion was for a different reason: religious zealotry. Rabbi Moshe Levinger asked the IDF for permission to celebrate the Passover seder in 1968 in Hebron, the city revered by Jews and Muslims for the tombs of the patriarchs. He rented rooms in the Palestinian-owned Park Hotel on the main street.[17] After the seder, he refused to leave. Instead of immediately expelling him, the army and government backed away from confrontation and struck a deal that allowed him and his family and supporters to move into a former army base on a hill nearby; with the state's cooperation, this became the settlement of Kiryat Arba.

It did not stop there. In April 1979 Levinger's wife, Miriam, led a march to the centre of al-Shuada Street in Hebron and occupied a building which had been a police station in the Ottoman era. And it went on. Kiryat Arba grew and grew and religious Jews took over al-Shuada Street. Palestinians fought back. Both sides killed; dozens died. The Palestinians were the ones whom the army locked up. Eventually, the street was effectively only Jewish; the IDF welded shut the metal doors of the Palestinian homes and residents had to climb across the roofs to get out. The flourishing marketplace closed down. Jews harassed Palestinians who had to put up wire netting over their windows to guard against stones and garbage; however, this, of course, did not guard against verbal abuse. An army barrier at the end of the street barred access to and from the city of Hebron. A Kiryat Arba resident, Baruch Goldstein, a medical doctor, entered the tomb and shot and killed twenty-nine Muslim worshippers. A mob killed him. Palestinian access to the tomb was restricted even more.

By 2005, a 'routine of violence and harassment' was reported against Palestinians in Hebron by Israeli security forces.[18] In areas close to the settlers, Palestinians by then had abandoned at least 1,014 residences (41.9 percent of the total number of houses in the area) and at least 1,829 businesses (76.6 percent of the total) – 440 closed by order of the army. The centre of Hebron remains a ghost town.

Levinger has been a turbulent player. Most of his eleven children and fifty grandchildren are said to live on the West Bank. He has been arrested at least ten times, according to *Wikipedia*. Things got notably worse after 30 September 1988, when Khayed Salah, a Palestinian store owner in Hebron, was shot dead and a customer was wounded. Levinger claimed to have only shot into the air to defend himself against stone-throwers. He conveyed the flavour of his outlook in telling a press conference that 'the State Attorney's Office knows that I am innocent and that I did not have the privilege of killing that Arab. Not that I may not have wanted to kill him or that he did not deserve to die, but I did not have the privilege of killing that Arab'. He was charged with manslaughter, causing bodily harm in aggravated circumstances and intentionally damaging property. His trial began in August 1989 despite protests by thirteen right-wing Knesset members and hundreds of supporters. Levinger accepted a plea bargain to the lesser charge of negligent homicide. He was sentenced to five months' imprisonment and seven months suspended; he served ninety-two days. On his release he told Israel Radio, 'If I'm in a situation of danger again, I'll again open fire. I hope that next time, I will be more careful and I won't miss the target'.

This is a man who has single-mindedly pursued his religious beliefs with violent and racist views towards Arabs and a scorn for legal process. He has had many admirers and has greatly influenced right-wing and settler activity as a leader of *Gush Emunim* (Bloc of the Faithful), a messianic and political movement to establish Jewish settlements on the West Bank (and the Gaza Strip and Golan Heights) set up in 1974. Members were found guilty and jailed for terror attacks on Palestinians.

The movement faded away, but its attitude of extremism and defiance of law lived on and grew into the 'Hilltop Youth' – gangs of religious teenagers dedicated to exclusive Jewish control. They have become notorious for vicious attacks on West Bank Palestinians, setting fire to mosques and burning olive trees; they also operate inside Israel to intimidate Jews who support peace movements. They stone soldiers and damage army and police vehicles.

Their specialty is the 'price tag' – wreaking retribution on Palestinian people and property in response to any move by government, army or courts which they view as backtracking. The army and police seldom bring any to book.

When Yuval Diskin retired as head of the Shin Bet in mid-2011, he used a press conference to warn that the Arab Spring then shaking the Middle East required the Shin Bet to take a closer look at Jews, not Arabs, on the West Bank. 'We are constantly keeping an eye to see if there is change that will take us somewhere else', he said. He also saw a rising threat by Jewish 'radical right-wing groups', both to the state and to Arabs – particularly the Hilltop Youth, who form communities on isolated hilltops to be closer to nature, as well as being admirers of Rabbi Meir Kahane whose racist party is banned from Israeli elections. 'I detect anti-government, anti-establishment and even delusional messianic processes within these groups', Diskin said. [19]

Settlers kept silent about the violence of the Hilltop Youth. Until, inevitably, the youth began attacking leaders of the settler council, Yesha. Puncturing the car tires of a Yesha leader finally led the council head, Danny Dayan, to call for an end to the silence: 'I shamefully admit that even when a Molotov cocktail was hurled at a children's room in [Arab] Hawara and I presented a condemnation resolution at the Yesha Council, I was told "We do not condemn the harming of Arabs"'. [20] A West Bank national-religious rabbi also condemned the silence and lamented: 'Unfortunately we have woken up too late'. In mid-2013 government alarm about increasing attacks led to action including the promise of stiffer sentencing and longer prison terms. [21]

Settler violence has grown so extreme that it now is featured in the US State Department's annual report on terrorism around the world. Details appeared for the first time in the 2011 report. [22] However, the thuggery is not confined to youth. The official lack of respect for the rule of law has spawned an environment of settler violence; in July 2012 more than fifty reports of assaults on Palestinians were recorded, such as:

July 2, Susya: Hate graffiti in Hebrew: 'Price tag, Revenge, Death to the Arabs'.

July 7, Akraba: Israelis attack Palestinians who were grazing their sheep. Soldiers who came beat up Palestinians.

July 9, al-Tawani: Four masked men attack shepherds and international activists with an iron pipe and stones.

July 11, Burka: A farmer attacked by Israelis, eighteen olive trees damaged and cut down.

July 19, Khan al-Ahmar: An Israeli beats a boy of thirteen grazing sheep.

July 20, Imatin: Twenty saplings cut down and a water cistern filled with sand and stones.

In most cases, if there is an investigation, there is no indictment.

* * *

The hidden truth about settlement on the West Bank was dramatically revealed in March 2005 by none other than the Prime Minister's Office. It was
in a report by Talia Sasson, a former government lawyer.[23] She was an expert
on the West Bank and was chosen by the attorney-general in response to a
request from Prime Minister Sharon for an investigation of settlements.

In her report, she described how, year after year, government departments
had, without authorisation, allocated funding and resources to expanding the
Jewish presence in the West Bank, notably at dozens of 'outposts' that the
government knew were illegal under Israeli law; the 'outposts' were simply
settlements by another name. 'State and public authorities took part in breaking the law', Sasson reported.

> They are the ones who financed construction without a resolution by the politi-
> cal echelon, contrary to government resolutions, with no legal planning status,
> sometimes not on state-owned land, sometimes on private Palestinian property
> or on survey land. . . . State authorities and public authorities broke the laws,
> regulations and rules made by the State.

Officials in the Ministry of Defense and Ministry of Housing and Construction and the settlement division of the World Zionist Organization spent
millions of shekels from state budgets to support the unauthorised outposts: it
was a 'blatant violation of the law'. She laid bare secret cooperation between
various ministries and official institutions to consolidate 'wildcat outposts',
which settlers had begun to erect more than a decade earlier. She spoke of
150 communities in the West Bank with incomplete or nonexistent permits –
and noted that this list was not exhaustive because of the lack of cooperation
of some ministries and government offices which had failed to hand over
important documents. Her report said:

- The Ministry of Housing supplied four hundred mobile homes for outposts
  on private Palestinian land.
- The Ministry of Defense approved placing trailers to begin new outposts.
- The Ministry of Education paid for nursery schools and their teachers.
- The Ministry of Energy connected outposts to the electricity grid.
- Roads to outposts were paid with taxpayers' money.

It was astonishing that Sharon commissioned an investigation into so
sensitive an issue as the settlements. It was astonishing that he made public
so devastating an exposé. It was astonishing that he went on to endorse it.
After all, Sharon was known as the 'father of the settlements'. He was famed
for an earlier statement: when minister of housing in 1998, he urged settlers

to seize hilltops in order to break up the contiguity of Palestinian areas and prevent the establishment of a Palestinian state: 'Let everyone get a move on and take some hilltops! Whatever we take, will be ours, and whatever we don't take, will not be ours!'

Sasson was later asked why Sharon had let her investigate the settlements.[24] 'I never asked him this question', she said.

> There are some questions that you don't ask. But I can assume why. One reason was that he had to explain to the Americans why he didn't fulfill the Israeli commitments to evacuate the outposts. I remember that Mr Dan Kurtzer, who was the American ambassador to Israel at the time, asked me why it was that when every Palestinian goes from his house to his sister's to visit for two hours, the security authorities know immediately, but when a caravan of trailers goes into the territories, nobody's heard of it? Can you please explain that?
>
> The other reason was entirely different. I think Mr Sharon thought the settlers and all the governmental organizations that helped them caused a lot of damage to Israel and, therefore, he thought that it must be stopped. But when he wanted to stop it, he found out that he couldn't. He wanted to show the settlers that he meant business by appointing somebody who will write a report revealing the real truth about what's going on.

Within a week of the release of the Sasson report, the cabinet met to consider it. Sharon backed it. The cabinet approved it by 18–1 and appointed a nine-member committee to decide on action against 'illegal' settlements. The one dissenting voice said there was no need for a committee, and the job of dealing with settlements must be tackled without delay.

The ministerial committee stalled. Settler supporters attacked the report. A leader, Shaul Goldstein, said Sharon should be the one to face questioning over the findings: 'It's obvious that the one who sent us in order to protect the roads and land is the prime minister so he should look in the mirror. Mr Sharon has to be questioned — not us'. The report was swept under the carpet. Whatever hope there might have been of giving it effect ended in the general election campaign of 2009: Talia Sasson stood as a candidate for the left-wing Meretz Party; she had no chance of being elected, and wasn't, but it gave the right wing the final excuse to write off her report as a biased left-wing document. The wrongs and the deceit she revealed to the public gaze not only went unpunished but continued unabated.

Mitzpeh Cramim was one of the illegal outposts named by Sasson and needing urgent action. Yet the opposite happened: a full seven years later, in 2012, the main report on *Haaretz*'s front page was: 'Outpost expanded onto private Palestinian land'. It referred to some twenty prefabricated and permanent houses built in the outpost, seven hundred meters from the Kochav Hashahar settlement, during the past year on land that the state officially recognised as privately owned by Palestinians. Building had continued despite the Civil Administration's orders in 2011 to stop the work.

Dror Etkes, who monitors settlements, said that the new construction 'is one of hundreds of examples that collaboration with the settlers has become part of the Israel Defense Forces and Civil Administration's DNA. . . . [T]hese bodies don't learn any lessons from their past failures, and continue to neglect their duty to protect Palestinians' private property'.[25]

\* \* \*

An equally rotten situation received much publicity during 2012: the Ulpana 'neighbourhood' or 'outpost' whose existence was even more flagrant than its Beit El settlement parent. Beit El itself was established in 1977 near Ramallah. In biblical times, Beit El was the site where Jacob dreamed of the angels coming up and down a ladder. In recent times, it grew to be home to more than five thousand settlers, chiefly national-religious; it acquired a reputation as a right-wing citadel. Detailed information about it came to light through a secret database on settlements prepared by the Defense establishment; this went beyond the Sasson investigation of outposts and covered all settlements. *Haaretz* reported that the database disclosed that about 75 percent of construction in settlements had been carried out without appropriate permits or contrary to issued permits. Additionally, in more than thirty settlements, extensive construction of buildings – including schools, synagogues, homes, roads and police stations – had been carried out on private lands belonging to Palestinians. This ranged from Nokdim, a small settlement where Foreign Minister Avigdor Lieberman lives, to the town of Modi'in Illit, with more than thirty-two thousand residents.[26]

Astonishingly, the *Haaretz* report noted that

> in many of the settlements, it was the government itself, primarily through the Ministry of Construction and Housing, that was responsible for construction, and since many of the building violations involve infrastructure, roads, public buildings and so on, the official data also demonstrate government responsibility for the unrestrained planning and lack of enforcement of regulations in the territories. The extent of building violations also attests to the poor functioning of the Civil Administration, the body in charge of permits and supervision of construction in the territories.

In the case of Beit El, it was established on Palestinian private land seized for military purposes and on state lands that had been seized under Jordan's administration. Construction without approved plans included council offices, about 140 houses and trailers, and an industrial zone of ten buildings.

Out of this came the Ulpana outpost in 1999 with construction by a private contractor of substantial buildings – five apartment blocks with thirty-three families. Later, murky details emerged that the land had been bought, from a dead man, by two prominent local women. In due course, Palestinians said the land was theirs. Their claim was supported by the state prosecutor and upheld after lengthy Supreme Court hearings. It was acknowledged that fraudulent documents had been used to steal the land. The state was ordered to raze the buildings.

Then the game really began. With settlers yelling in outrage and the cabinet in crisis, the government did its utmost to avoid demolition, and failing that, to find an alternative acceptable to the Ulpana residents as well as all other settlers. It led to the surreal sight of Prime Minister Netanyahu assailing those who had gone to court to have the law upheld! 'Those who think they are using the legal system to weaken the settlements are mistaken, since the opposite is actually taking place', he told a press conference.[27] Vice Prime Minister Moshe Ya'alon chimed in that the rule of law would be a casualty of evacuation, as settlers would feel betrayed by the government. Dozens of residents staged a hunger strike, and hundreds, mostly teenage girls, marched towards Jerusalem.[28] A mosque near Ramallah was torched, apparently in a 'price tag' operation. 'The war has started' and 'You will pay the price' was painted on walls. Hundreds of police were trained to remove the settlers in time for the 31 July deadline set by the court.

Netanyahu's escape route was to pile illegality on illegality: Beit El would be expanded by 300 new homes, with another 531 elsewhere on the West Bank. Still further, the Ulpana apartments would not be demolished but would be moved intact to a nearby tract of land confiscated by the army in the 1970s; this was soon revealed to be impractical, so 90 new apartments were promised. Costs involved were said to run at about $12.5 million. Settlers accepted the deal and agreed to move nonviolently.[29] Late in November, acting on the Supreme Court's orders, bulldozers moved in to demolish the buildings.[30] The following February, the Ministry of Defense formally approved the building of 90 housing units in Beit El.[31]

Akiva Eldar made a disturbing point about the state's abuse of its own law: hundreds of houses had been built on land obtained fraudulently. In some rare cases, the High Court had ordered that the plundered assets be returned to their owners: 'But so far, not a single person has been penalised by the courts for fraud, forgery or illegal construction in such cases'.[32]

\* \* \*

Ulpana and Mitzpeh Cramim are not unique. The occupation throws up many equally bad, and worse, events: this is a small but revealing extract from a US State Department annual report on human rights for 2010:[33]

Principal human rights problems related to Israeli authorities in the West Bank
were reports of excessive use of force against civilians, including killings,
torture of Palestinian detainees, improper use of security detention procedures,
austere and overcrowded detention facilities, demolition and confiscation of
Palestinian properties, limits on freedom of expression and assembly, and
severe restrictions on Palestinians' internal and external freedom of movement. Additionally the IDF, in some cases, failed to pursue investigations and
disciplinary actions related to violations. Violence by Israeli settlers was also
reported . . .

Israeli civilians committed violent acts against Palestinian civilians and
their property with reportedly little or no intervention and no subsequent investigation by Israeli officials. Some settlers reportedly used violence against
Palestinians to keep them away from settlements and land that settlers sought
to expropriate. The Palestine Center estimated that between 2009 and mid-
year, settlers committed approximately 1,000 acts of violence against Palestinians and their property. . . .

On November 11, settlers targeted a Palestinian woman and her two children, ages 10 and 11 years old, with rocks as they went to school in Tuqu
village, near Bethlehem in the West Bank, according to media reports. A
Palestinian group later protested the incident by burning tires and throwing
rocks at Israeli vehicles, and a clash with Israeli forces ensued. . . . Settler
violence against Palestinians in the Old City of Hebron continued to decline,
according to local NGOs, attributed primarily to Palestinian video documentation of settler harassment. Nevertheless, residents and several former IDF
soldiers reported that Israeli authorities in the Old City consistently refrained
from protecting Palestinians against settler violence and failed to enforce law
and order on assailants.

Day after day, newspapers, television and radio in Israel and abroad carry
details that give flesh to this summary of the results of occupation. These are
further details:

## LAW

Officially, Israel's occupation is 'temporary', so in line with international
law the former legal system remains in place; military cases are determined
by Jordanian law – except where changed or supplemented by the 1,700 or so
military orders issued by Israel's army since 1967. In general, the penal code
on the West Bank is harsher than in Israel, due largely to the combating of
terrorism. Thus murder on the West Bank carries the death penalty (although
it has never been carried out) while in Israel the maximum sentence is life
imprisonment. Attempted murder in Israel can draw twenty years' imprisonment but life on the West Bank. On the West Bank, Palestinians can be
detained before seeing a judge for longer than in Israel, and there are fewer
restrictions on detaining minors. The Jordanian penal code also differs from

Israel: for example, rape within marriage is a crime in Israel but not in Jordanian law and hence not on the West Bank.[34]

Israeli law does not apply to the West Bank, so settlers in the area are, in theory, also subject to military law; in practice, settlers are usually judged in courts inside Israel. Settlers pay Israeli taxes and are governed by Israeli institutions for education, religion, health, social welfare and so forth. Land law is a confused mix of Ottoman, British, Jordanian, military and Israeli law.

Thus two systems of justice, and administration, run parallel. The UN Committee on the Elimination of Racial Discrimination terms this 'de facto segregation'. While that is correct, it's oversimple: Israel doesn't apply its law to Palestinians, not because it wants to discriminate against them, but because it cannot and dare not do so: it could only do so if it annexes the West Bank, and it has not done so. Palestinians who work legally in Israel, inside the Green Line, and there were fifty-two thousand late in 2013, enjoy the same labour laws as Israelis (another thirty-three thousand are estimated to be working illegally).

An exception arose in mid-2013: a Jerusalem court ruled that Palestinians who worked in industrial zones in West Bank Jewish settlements were entitled to the salaries and benefits provided in Israeli law. 'Public interest', said the judge, meant that ten Palestinians in a stone plant were entitled to the tens of thousands of shekels' difference between the salary they were paid and the minimum wage in Israel and fringe benefits such as holiday pay and pensions paid to workers in Israel.[35]

This was taken further with a government decision to provide full protection to Palestinian workers by 1 January 2014 – and with outrage in the Knesset Public Petitions Committee when members learned that as Israeli law does not generally apply in the West Bank, each law must be individually applied by an order from the army, and this could not be done by the set deadline. 'It cannot be that Palestinian labourers work under slave-like conditions just because ministries can't handle the schedule they gave themselves', protested MP Adi Kol of the Yesh Atid Party.[36]

But the laudable aim of ensuring equality in benefits for Palestinians who work for Jews in the West Bank is a double-edged sword, because it means an extension of Israeli law into the territory and hence it advances a creeping annexation.

Israel also has to be careful about the extent of applying its law to Jewish settlers. That was evident in May 2012 when a Likud member of Knesset proposed a bill to extend Israeli law to settlements as a means of protecting several settlements against Supreme Court orders for the demolition of houses illegally built on private Palestinian-owned land. Cabinet ministers who supported the bill rapidly reversed their votes after intervention by the prime minister when it was realised that extending Israeli law to the settlements would mean a de facto annexation of them.[37] The consequences of that could have been so serious internationally that everyone backed off, including the right wing.

The military courts have a remarkable rate of convictions: 99.74 percent of cases.[38] That would have been a proud record in the political trials of the former Soviet Union. The courts deal with all criminal and security cases involving Palestinians. The military appeals court also favours the prosecution, accepting 67 percent of appeals filed by prosecutors as against 33 percent by the defence. The courts heard 9,542 cases in 2010, of which 2,016 involved terrorism, 763 disorderly conduct and the rest Palestinians staying illegally in Israel, traffic offences and criminal activity.

## ECONOMY

The occupation of the West Bank, and including the Gaza Strip, is an open sesame for Israel to profit from the Palestinian people and their natural resources, apart from the fact that it's a captive market of 3.9 million people. The importance of that market was spelled out by Israel's then agriculture minister Shalom Simhon, saying that Israel produced one and a half times its agricultural needs; half the surplus was exported to the United States and Europe; the rest, half and half, to the value of $1 billion a year, to the West Bank and Gaza.[39] Apart from that, Israel's total sales to the territories were more than $2 billion – more than 6 percent of all exports excluding diamonds – and this maintained 76,000 jobs. In light of these figures, the continuing blockade of Gaza with severe restrictions on the flow of food and goods is extracting a heavy price from Israeli farmers and manufacturers. It makes as little economic sense as the political decision behind it.

The results of Israel's blockade are contradictory. That it imposes hardship is certain. But how much of what is claimed is propaganda? Reuters circulated a photograph from Gaza on 22 January 2008 with the caption: 'The Palestinian parliament was forced to meet by candlelight on Tuesday night'. The effect was spoiled, however, because the curtains were closed but thin, and it was clearly daytime outside. The Hamas cabinet staged a similar stunt, meeting by candlelight, but a chink in the curtains showed daylight.

Gaza farmers suffer savage financial penalties because their exports of strawberries and flowers to lucrative foreign markets are at the whim of the Israeli government; sometimes, however, Hamas leaders inflict punishment on their own because for reasons which are not clear they close the border crossing with Israel and the products of their farmers are left to rot.

Yet while abuse is heaped on Israel for its siege, it is not the sole cause of Gaza's woes. Egypt, and especially in the post–Muslim Brotherhood era, is an even tougher blockader.[40] It has destroyed most of the one thousand tunnels which Gazans used to bring in every conceivable item, from guns to cows, causing shortages of fuel and basic goods. It strictly controls the Rafah crossing in the south, keeping hundreds of Gazans waiting for days at the border to return home. It is as rough as Israel in ordering Gazan fishermen to stay within specified areas. Egypt holds Hamas responsible for attacks on its security forces in Sinai and cooperates with the Israeli army in countermeasures.

## OCCUPATION COSTS

A Palestinian study in September 2011 cited damage caused since 1967 by restrictions on the movement of goods and labour inside the West Bank because of road blocks, checkpoints and extended road trips as a result of diversions; blocked access to the Dead Sea for tourism and minerals; water directed to Israeli settlements, industry and agriculture; and the uprooting of about 2.5 million trees, including olive trees, for settlements, infrastructure and the separation.[41]

The World Bank reported in 2011 that Palestinian economic growth 'has been unsustainable, driven primarily by donor aid rather than a rebounding private sector, which remains stifled by Israeli restrictions on access to natural resources and markets'. In 2012 the budget deficit was $1.25 billion, and the Palestinian Authority was hoping for – and relying for payment of salaries and survival – on donations of $1 billion.

The Oslo Accords gave hope of going forward, and business consultant Sam Bahour says he relocated from the United States to his father's birthplace in al-Bireh, adjoining Ramallah, to help build an economy to serve the new and emerging state of Palestine. But in 2012 he said: 'My dream has become a nightmare'. Any investment is threatened as the Israeli military, directed by the Israeli government, micromanages every aspect of the Palestinian economy. 'Israel will not let us build a real economy', he said.[42]

On the other hand, it's a myth to believe that there was a golden age from 1994 until the start of the second intifada in September 2000: GDP increased only from $3.65 billion to $5.3 billion, per capita income on the West Bank rose from $1,739 to $1,900 a year. Poverty rates fell from 24 percent only to 21 percent.[43] Certainly, Israel's closures during 1995 and 1996 in response to Palestinian suicide attacks caused huge losses to Palestinians. But other factors which prevented Palestinian growth included lack of private investment, reliance on international donor aid, and internally, massive corruption, inefficiency and despotic leadership. Not all of it could be blamed on Israel.

The West Bank is locked in and does not even have its own airport. Israel collects customs levies on behalf of the Palestinian Authority; it is Palestinian money, but every now and again Israel, illegally and immorally, withholds millions of dollars to pressure the Palestinian Authority to do its bidding. The economic exploitation, including theft of resources as in stone quarrying (which Israel's Supreme Court has bafflingly endorsed as valid), is comparable with classical colonialism: a mother country which conquers and exploits another people and their territory, to the extent that its own people move in and usurp land. However, the dominant point is that this stems from the occupation and is not the reason why the occupation was pursued in the first place – even though economic exploitation is now maintained for its own sake because of the profit it generates for Israel.

Separate roads have been built on the West Bank to enable settlers to avoid driving on public roads. The restriction applies to cars: Israeli yellow and black number plates are allowed, whether driven by Jews or Arabs; Palestinian green and white are barred. Additionally, roads in the Palestinian Area A are barred to Israelis.

These are not 'apartheid roads' described by critics but are an expensive, heavy-handed way of dealing with the very real security problem caused by drive-by shootings, roadside bombs and rock-throwing, which have caused many deaths and injuries. Of course the settlers should not be there in the first place but given that they exist in the many thousands, the Israeli government protects them.

B'Tselem reports that Palestinian cars are 'completely prohibited' on fourteen sections of West Bank roads, a total of 46.92 kilometres, and are 'restricted' on five sections, 20.7 kilometres. In Hebron, they are 'prohibited' on eighteen sections, ranging from 0.05 kilometres to 2 kilometres, a total of 6.72 kilometres. On the two-kilometre stretch, the only cars allowed are those whose owners hold special permits. [44]

Water is life and it's an emotive issue. Israel controls the main supplies and allocation is unequal: the daily per capita usage in Israeli towns is 242 litres; the West Bank has about 73 litres per capita for domestic, urban and industrial use; 100 litres a day is the international recommended minimum. [45] While the disparity reflects Israel's far higher industrial and agricultural activity, the contrast between the green lawns of settlements and Palestinian villages short of water, and rationed to only a few days a week, is wrong and offensive. It draws the apartheid accusation – but is, instead, yet another instance of the all-powerful conquerors grabbing as much as they can. The Gaza Strip, under siege, suffers more: it relies on underground water, and 90 to 95 percent is considered unfit for human consumption due to high levels of salts and nitrates. [46]

Water is so crucial to existence that it's no surprise that countries apply their muscle in dealing with weaker neighbours – as in Southern Africa, where landlocked Lesotho wants to scrap 'prejudicial' sections in its agreement with South Africa in building a gigantic dam; South Africa will gain water from the dam. [47] The agreement was signed in 1999 when the Lesotho government was nearly paralysed because of internal discord, and South African troops were stationed in the country.

Misuse of Israeli power is seen in the disposal of West Bank sewage: both Palestinian villages and Jewish settlements need treatment plants, and the Civil Administration has tried to withhold building permission from Palestinian villages and towns unless they agree to link up with nearby settlements; Palestinians refuse to sanctify the stealers of their land, so raw sewage pollutes the land and underground water. It's a grave health hazard for both Palestinians and Israelis: nearly 90 percent of sewage from Palestinian towns and 13 percent from Jewish settlements flow into the environment untreated, contaminating the groundwater and 162 kilometres of streams – which flow into Israel.[48] The Ofra settlement arrogantly built an installation on Palestinian private land; the Supreme Court ordered a halt.

Yet the water issue is not straightforward: Israel is accused of stealing water from Palestinians in drawing so much from the mountain aquifer, which is largely under Palestinian territory; but the western and northeastern parts of the aquifer flow naturally towards Israel, and the water is most easily accessible from within Israel's borders. Further, Israel was using 60 to 70 percent of the aquifer's potential before its 1967 victory – and its usage has continued at much the same rate.[49] Additionally, the allocation of water was agreed between Israelis and Palestinians in the Oslo Accords in 1993. Palestinian needs have since grown because of a rise in population and standard of living, and Israel notes that it is supplying a greater amount than specified.

But when all is said and done, the simple fact is that Palestinians go short and hence B'Tselem argues that Israel 'flagrantly breaches international law which requires Israel to ensure proper living conditions for the local population and to respect the Palestinians' human rights, including the right to receive a sufficient quantity of water to meet their basic needs'.[50]

The rights and wrongs of the water situation are not always easy to understand: a World Bank report in 2009 castigating Israel drew a frosty response from the Ministry of Foreign Affairs on 28 April 2009, saying that, according to interim agreement, 23.6 million cubic meters of water was allocated to Palestinians annually but that they actually had access to twice as much. The authors of the bank's report had met with ministry officials 'and were briefed on all the factual details. They were also presented with the Israeli position paper on the subject, which contained verifiable facts that contradict all the objections presented in the bank's report. Significantly, the authors chose to ignore the ministry's position and declined to take the facts presented to them into consideration in the published report. They rely totally on unsubstantiated information supplied by the Palestinian Authority, which raises a serious question mark over the credibility of the report and the intentions of the authors'.

Revision of the agreement is due in final status negotiations between Israelis and Palestinians, whenever that might happen. But this is one critical issue that lends itself to resolution: a conference in Jerusalem reporting on a joint Israeli-Palestinian water study was told that 'an equitable solution which will involve Israel, Palestine, Jordan, Lebanon and Syria is possible. Agreement on the significant reallocation of water can be a motivation for peace'. It was possible because of Israel's development of seawater desalination plants to provide water at a cost comparable with water from natural sources. A mere $20 to $40 million a year would ensure enough for Israelis and Palestinians.[51]

Israel has built giant desalination plants drawing from the Mediterranean Sea with the aim of providing 85 percent of its drinking water; however, it's not a free lunch because the salt residue presents pollution problems and the treated water needs to be supplemented by expensive chemicals to make it fit for people. Israel is also a world leader in efficient water management and wastewater treatment: it reuses 75 percent of its wastewater, mainly for agriculture. The Palestinian shortages should thus end. The water surplus will also enable Israel to revive the southern Jordan River: the Bible says that the people of Israel crossed there into the Promised Land; it's also central to Christians because Jesus Christ was baptised in its water. But after years of overuse by Syria, Israel and Jordan, the river is almost a trickle – 5 percent of what once flowed along the Jordan Valley from Lake Kinneret to the Dead Sea. Returning water to the Jordan began in 2013 and within ten years 'we will erase our debt (to nature)', says an Israeli leader.[52] As a grim reminder of past wars, the banks of the Jordan River have to be cleared of mines.

In rare and historic action, and hopefully a harbinger of more to come, Israel, Jordan and the Palestinian Authority are cooperating in building a desalination plant in Aqaba, in Jordan, to provide water for that country and for southern Israel. The resulting brine will be piped 160 kilometres to replenish the shrinking Dead Sea, which is of interest to Israel and Palestine.[53]

The security barrier – partly an eight-metre-high wall (about 5 percent) but mainly fences and ditches – runs between Israel and the West Bank. When completed it will be about seven hundred kilometres long. Originally planned for security to block suicide bombers from getting into Israel, that vital purpose became distorted by greed and ultranationalism to enable land grabs from Palestinians. Hence the barrier does not follow the Green Line, the 1967 ceasefire line, but twists and turns according to Israeli arbitrary decisions limited in places by court order. About 8 percent of the West Bank is on the Israeli side.

One of the merciless effects of the security barrier is the double punishment it imposes: Palestinians whose West Bank land and homes have been swallowed inside the barrier are thus 'annexed' to Jerusalem but are denied either permanent or temporary Israeli residency. The military authorities give them residency permits with no right to work in Israel, or to access Israeli health insurance or other benefits of normal residency. About fifteen hundred Palestinians with West Bank IDs are victims. [54]

\* \* \*

Improved conditions of life do not validate occupation. But some good did come out of the early years (and also make nonsense of anti-Israel accusations of 'genocide') as basic health indicators show that the infant mortality rate on the West Bank dropped from 95 per 1,000 live births to 42 – and under the Palestinian Authority has since come down to 13.98.

The Gaza Strip is even more noteworthy. Under siege, with shortages of food reported and alarming claims of severe malnutrition, the estimated infant mortality rate in 2013 was 16.55 per 1,000 live births. This selection shows world standings: [55]

Infant mortality rate: Deaths per 1,000 live births

| | |
|---|---|
| 1. Afghanistan | 119.43 |
| 25. Pakistan | 59.35 |
| 52. South Africa | 42.15 |
| 84. Turkey | 22.23 |
| **105. Gaza Strip** | **16.00** |
| 108. Jordan | 15.26 |
| **120. West Bank** | **13.98** |
| 174. United States | 5.90 |
| 189. United Kingdom | 4.50 |
| **199. Israel** | **4.03** |
| 210. Germany | 3.48 |
| 224. Monaco | 1.81 |

Life expectancy at birth on the West Bank rose from 56 years to 66 years and in 2013 was estimated at 75.46 years. Gaza was close behind with 74.40. This is a selection of world standings:

Life expectancy at birth

| | |
|---|---|
| 1. Monaco | 89.63 |
| **18. Israel** | **81.17** |
| 30. United Kingdom | 80.29 |
| 51. United States | 78.62 |

| | |
|---|---|
| **91. West Bank** | **75.46** |
| **111. Gaza Strip** | **74.40** |
| 124. Egypt | 73.19 |
| 126. Turkey | 73.03 |
| 149. Iran | 70.62 |
| 222. South Africa | 49.48 |
| 223. Chad | 49.07 |

The two indicators reveal that both the West Bank and the Gaza Strip are about halfway between the best and worst in the world. That is not ideal, but it reflects a different story, especially for Gaza, than the catastrophic health conditions claimed by anti-Israel propagandists.

\* \* \*

Very occasionally, truth about government deceit accidentally slips into the open – as with the work of Ramit Zvi, deputy director of the Civil Administration's unit that deals with enforcement of planning and construction regulations. Zvi is a West Banker and lives in the Peduel settlement. In a High Court case, he submitted an affidavit showing that the number of structures demolished in Jewish areas of the West Bank exceeded the number in Palestinian areas, although the incidence of building violations was higher among the Palestinians.

Zvi was already a target for attack by settlers who condemn government officials involved in demolitions, and demonstrations were held at his synagogue in Peduel. Settler outrage now rose further and flyers were distributed against Zvi. He defended himself in his settlement's newsletter, protesting that the Jewish structures being destroyed were not significant: 'The vast majority are not permanent houses, but tents, sheds, tin shacks, temporary structures, light structures that in many cases are not occupied and are in one stage or another of construction'. He added, 'I see myself as loyal to the Torah of Israel, the Jewish people and the Land of Israel, and act according to the principles required by such loyalty'.

Reporting this, *Haaretz*'s headline was: 'Senior Civil Administration official reassures settlers: "We are demolishing tents, not homes"'.[56] So the game was exposed: demolition statistics are designed to fool the world about government action against settlers. The truth is different, and an official describing his loyalties does not mention adherence to the law.

\* \* \*

Stealing land from Palestinians is done crookedly and callously, and with the weight of help from officials. An astonishing illustration came to light in a Jerusalem court case in 2012, reported by Nir Hasson as 'The Palestinian taxi driver crucial to Jewish settlement in E. Jerusalem'.[57] Starting in the 1970s, Mohammed Nabulsi, an East Jerusalem taxi driver, provided settler organisations with affidavits claiming that Palestinian owners of East Jerusalem homes were 'absentees' living in enemy countries, which the state used over and over to expropriate the properties and turn them over to settler organisations.

It appears that Nabulsi provided at least ten to fifteen affidavits. Most homeowners did not know they had been declared absentee. Some found out only when the new, Jewish, residents came to the house in the dead of night to evict them. Because of earlier criticisms, no more affidavits have been taken from Nabulsi since the early 1990s, but the declarations he had already made continued to be used.

According to the law, it is enough to prove that a property owner was residing in an enemy country – including any Arab country or the West Bank – at the time East Jerusalem was annexed to Israel in 1967 for them to lose their rights to the property. The decision is made by the Custodian of Absentee Property, whose department is now part of the Ministry of Finance.

This, said the report, is the way most of the real estate in Jerusalem's Silwan and the Old City was transferred to settlers' associations – via various bodies including the Development Authority (a government agency that manages absentee property), the Jewish National Fund, the public housing agency Amidar and others. Nabulsi provided the custodian with the pretext to declare the landowner absent: a short affidavit that the owner lived in Jordan or the territories. There was no supporting evidence and nothing was checked. An attorney represented settlers' associations and the Jewish National Fund. He obtained Nabulsi's signature on affidavits and defended the procedure in endless court appearances.

\* \* \*

Road 443 is the alternative route between Tel Aviv and Jerusalem, from the coastal plain up to the Judean hills. It's a beautiful drive along mountain ridges. But the route is scarred for considerable sections near Jerusalem by brick and cement walls that shut out the view and by stretches of metal fences and barbed wire. Israel began building Road 443 during the 1980s; about fourteen kilometres runs through the West Bank, and Palestinian properties were unilaterally expropriated for the road. Villagers who lived along the route were promised access – to their advantage because it would cut their driving time to Ramallah in half. Then came the second intifada; six

Jews died in fire-bomb and shooting attacks on cars. In 2002 Israel closed the villages' access roads – illegally. The promised access was ditched.

The Association for Civil Rights in Israel (ACRI), went to court. The court agreed that this was collective punishment and at the end of 2009 ordered the IDF to open the road. Months passed, and finally it was done – but only partly: some villages were given access but restrictions applied to the times when Palestinians could drive. ACRI noted that while the court's decision was seen as a victory for the rule of law and human rights, the IDF's implementation amounted to 'a blatant mockery of these values'.[58]

Meanwhile, two checkpoints were set up, at the western entry to Israel and at the eastern entry to the Jerusalem area. The rudimentary structures grew and grew, and by 2012 they were akin to international border points with armed soldiers on twenty-four-hour duty as cars drove through – that is, vehicles with Israeli yellow and black number plates with either Jewish or Arab drivers.

Checking Palestinian vehicles coming onto Road 443 from the villages can take about twenty minutes, so people sometimes prefer using the side roads.[59] The central problem is that Road 443 leads nowhere if you are a Palestinian: the way to Ramallah is still closed off and Palestinians are not allowed to enter Jerusalem, so the only reason to use the road is for visiting one of the neighbouring villages along the route – and people prefer to do so by using side roads, thus avoiding being checked by the military and having to wait. Additionally, access road checkpoints are open only at certain times; arriving after 10 p.m. means calling soldiers to do the job. These are the reasons why virtually no Palestinian number plates are seen on the forty-thousand-plus vehicles which drive on Route 443 each day.

*  *  *

Lest any doubt remains about government duplicity, there is the boasting by then finance minister Yuval Steinitz who told a West Bank radio station late in 2012 that Prime Minister Netanyahu's government had quietly doubled the portion of the national budget allocated to Jewish settlements on the West Bank. Steinitz had received an award from the settlement movement, honouring him for his contributions, and, perhaps filled with emotion, he spilled the beans: 'During the current government's terms, we doubled the budgets [allocated] to Judea and Samaria. We did it with a low profile, in agreement with the mayors'. The government had done it quietly so that 'elements in Israel and abroad' would not attempt to stymie them.[60]

That nothing has changed in settlement criminality was revealed in mid-2013 in a report by State Comptroller Joseph Shapira: he attacked the absence of criminal investigations into illegal settler building and the loss of millions of shekels in uncollected property fees on the West Bank. The comptroller, who is independent and reports directly to the Knesset, checks on the legality, efficiency, economy and ethical conduct of public institutions. Shapira fired a broadside against the IDF, the Border Police, the Custodian of Abandoned Property and other state bodies, including the health and agriculture ministries, for failing to enforce regulations regarding property, agriculture, water, illegal Palestinian workers, the environment and traffic violations. 'It's a free for all on the West Bank'. He also noted that half a billion shekels a year were being lost because lease fees were not collected. Leases had not been signed and fees had not been collected in eighty-seven settlements created by the World Zionist Organization. [61]

It's to Israel's credit that so senior an official publicly exposed such a wide range of sins of omission and commission to do with settlers; conversely, his report caused barely a ripple – a bit of public outrage but no government alarm or clean-up pledges.

\* \* \*

Heartlessness and bureaucratic inflexibility inevitably go hand in hand with military occupation. Like all misdeeds of occupation, they have become mundane in their frequency and are too many to enumerate. To take but one example: In the Bedouin village of Um al-Kheir on the West Bank, a resident set up a toilet for his brother who had suffered head trauma and was urinating and defecating in a nearby stream bed. He dug a cesspit and placed a tin structure, donated by an aid organisation, on top of it. Civil Administration officials, backed by armed soldiers, arrived and said it violated an order forbidding the movement of mobile structures without a permit. They removed it. [62]

*Chapter Five*

# What Was Apartheid?

*Whites in South Africa believed that they were racially superior to blacks,
mixed-race coloureds and Asians. They imposed 'apartheid', seizing the best
of the country for themselves and driving racial discrimination into every
detail of life. They enacted draconian laws to suppress opposition.*

\* \* \*

Apartheid, Afrikaans for 'apartness', became known to the world after 26
May 1948 when white Afrikaners won the general election in South Africa.[1]
It was, coincidentally but without meaning, less than two weeks after the
State of Israel had been born. Apartheid expressed the political intention to
ensure supremacy for the white minority, and power for Afrikaners, in a
country where blacks, mixed-race coloureds and Asians outnumbered whites
by four to one.

The word was first used in 1929 in missionary work among blacks by the
main Afrikaner church, the Dutch Reformed Church. It was benevolent and
paternalistic. Blacks had to be uplifted 'on their own terrain, separate and
apart'; their 'character, nature and nationality' had to be built up. During the
1940s the word developed as a political concept and grew into a potent
slogan to express *baasskap*, white boss-ship. The fears and emotions it
played to won victory for the Afrikaner Nationalists in the 1948 election
from the overwhelmingly white electorate. The significance of such naked
racism only three years after the end of the World War II triumph against
Nazi racism was not immediately apparent to the world. The word that later
aroused so much emotion wasn't even mentioned in initial reports abroad.
Instead, the shock in the Nationalists' victory was the defeat of the renowned
international elder statesman Field Marshal Jan Christiaan Smuts. He was an

Afrikaner who had fought against Britain fifty years earlier and then became an honoured friend; he had led South Africa into and through World War II. He had the remarkable record of having sat in Britain's war cabinets in both world wars.

'Smuts loses seat in Parliament; Foes, some Pro-Nazi, are swept in', the *New York Times* reported on 28 May. It quoted a Nationalist leader, Ben Schoeman, as having said during the war that 'the whole future of Afrikanderdom [*sic*] is dependent upon German victory'. On 4 June it reported that another leader, Hans Strydom, 'has agitated for many years for white's [*sic*] domination over Negroes'. By 6 June the newspaper was beginning to understand the depth of what had happened: the Nationalist leader Dr D. F. Malan and his party 'are exponents of the Fascist wing of totalitarianism. They believe in racism; they consider the Bantu and Indian to be inferior'.

South Africa and the world were soon to see that put into practice. The Nats, as they were called, had a foundation on which to build: segregation and discrimination were already well established, stretching back to the start of European settlement in 1652. At that time, the Netherlands was a major trading power, and its Dutch East India Company opened a base in what is now Cape Town, at the foot of the African continent, to supply fresh water and food to ships sailing the arduous, months-long passage between Europe and the East. Settler numbers gradually increased, and they went deeper into the country. Contacts with the indigenous hunter-gatherer peoples were violent as they resisted the settlers taking land. The brown-skinned Hottentots, called Khoikhoi today, were driven away, and hunting parties went out to kill the Bushmen, the San. Cape society depended from the start on control of the indigenous people and on slaves brought from Africa, India and the East Indies.

Early in the nineteenth century, Britain, by then the dominant maritime power, seized the Cape Colony to protect the vital South Atlantic sea passage (the Suez Canal did not yet exist). The settlers, who became known as Boers (farmers), and later as Afrikaners, had all the hardy independence of frontier people. They had disliked the authority of the Dutch East India Company when it controlled the Cape and were even unhappier with the British, whose outlook and culture were foreign to them and whose actions increasingly affected their lives. As the Boers went further inland, they were aggrieved because the British reformed the land laws, creating problems and delays in issuing title deeds.

In 1828 they were further enraged by a law issued in London ending all legal restrictions on the movement of the Khoikhoi, who were little more than serfs working on white-owned farms. With freedom, the Khoikhoi, usually badly paid and often badly treated, left the farms en masse, creating a severe shortage of cattle-herders. To the disgust of the Boers, Khoikhoi could now take their masters and mistresses to court for mistreatment. The British also objected to any racial discrimination inside the Dutch Reformed Church, and the Khoikhoi could now marry in the church and receive the sacraments.

Six years later, Britain abolished slavery. It was the last straw, especially as little compensation was paid to slave-owners. A Boer woman, Anna Steenkamp, complained that black slaves had been 'placed on an equal footing with Christians, contrary to the laws of God, and the natural distinction of race and religion – wherefore we rather withdraw in order to preserve our doctrines in purity'.

Mass exodus followed: the Great Trek began in 1835 with parties of Trekkers taking off from their homes in cumbersome wagons drawn by oxen. Within ten years, fifteen thousand Boers and their families had left (25 percent of the whites), along with five thousand servants. The further they travelled, the more they ran into the dark-skinned Bantu tribes; they suffered many losses, from disease and in wars with the Zulu, Xhosa, Ndebele, Basotho and other tribes whose land they usurped. The Boers fervently believed that they were fulfilling God's purpose in overcoming the heathen black masses. Though little educated, they had the Bible: it was at the heart of their existence, with every word accepted as sacred. They went forth with Bible in one hand and gun in the other – muzzleloaders, but deadly. The tribespeople they encountered had spears and shields and were no match for them. By the middle of the nineteenth century, the Boers had seized much land and created their own republics.

Mythologies were created that were to loom large and sustain Afrikaners for many years to come. The most notable followed the February 1838 massacre of a Trek leader, Piet Retief, and one hundred of his followers by the Zulu king Dingane. For Afrikaners it was proof of the perfidy and untrustworthiness of blacks. Ten months later, a Boer force of 470 men, women and children used the *laager* – a defensive circle of wagons – to beat off an attacking force of 10,000 to 15,000 Zulu warriors. About three thousand Zulus died; four Trekkers were lightly wounded. It was called the Battle of Blood River because of the blood that flowed into a nearby river. From then on, it was celebrated as a national holiday. The victory was seen as God-given because the Boers had promised to build a church on the site if they won. Later it was called the Day of the Covenant. It is commemorated in the Voortrekker Monument in Pretoria – once a statement of Afrikaner power, now a tourist site.

The Boers insisted on segregated churches. The Dutch Reformed Church wanted only whites to pray in its churches, so it set up three segregated 'daughter' churches – for black people, for mixed-race coloureds and for Asians (descendants of workers and immigrants from what is now India and Pakistan) – but often with white ministers in charge. Even this was too liberal for some Trekkers, who formed two new whites-only and even sterner Calvinist churches.

The discovery of diamonds on a stupendous scale at the end of the 1860s brought far-reaching changes which determined South African basics for more than one hundred years: British imperialist and commercial interests secured the area and enacted laws for a hut tax on blacks, compelling them to earn cash by becoming migrant workers on white-owned mines and farms; the rural 'reserves' designated for blacks became more fixed; on the mines blacks were housed in closed compounds so that they could be controlled. Everything accelerated after 1886 with the discovery of gold in the Transvaal Boer republic and the need for huge numbers of black workers for pick and shovel work. Gold also drew the covetous British: war between Britain and the Boers from 1899 to 1902 ended Boer rule.

During the war, British soldiers rapidly overran the Boer republics. But the Boers stubbornly refused to recognise their defeat and twenty-five thousand of them, citizen-soldiers, went on fighting a guerrilla war. Britain brought in 250,000 soldiers from its worldwide empire to crush them. It also created the first 'concentration camps': that's what they were called, but they were nothing like the later Nazi death camps. They were meant to give refuge to the old, women and children displaced after the British destroyed their farmhouses and fields to deny aid to guerrillas; but poor hygiene and farm people unaccustomed to being cooped up led to disease and many deaths – and to lasting hatred for Britain.

Out of the conflict grew Afrikaner contempt for *hensoppers* – from the English words, 'hands-uppers' – those who surrendered to the British and made peace with them. Instead, the *bittereinders* – bitter-enders, those who fought to the bitter end, whatever the consequences – were to be admired and honoured.

The Afrikaner national psyche was shaped: suspicion of the world and of outsiders. Their racial ideology was fixed. Their religious ministers preached that the Bible justified separation of races and apartheid. The ox wagon was used as a symbol of the people's struggle to survive and so was the powder horn, a reminder of the Trekkers' muzzleloading guns.

* * *

In 1948, with the Nationalist election victory, blacks had no illusions about what lay ahead. There was 'great sadness mixed with anger and apprehension and we believed blacks were in for a real hard time', according to Nthato Motlana, then a student at the elite Fort Hare University College for blacks. He went on to qualify as a medical doctor and played a leadership role in later freedom struggles. He described life in parts of the country through the eyes of a young black man:

In the 1940s, the attitude of white South Africans was monstrous, appalling. They were boors, animals. We lived a life of subservience, obsequiousness, fear, of obeisance to the white man in a way that nobody can really understand. When you saw a white man you saw God Almighty and you had to get out of his way. He could kick you, he could kill you and get away with it.

Black apprehension was justified. Within a year of the election the Nats put their racism into effect with the Prohibition of Mixed Marriages Act – the 'mixed' referring to whites and people of colour. While marriages across colour lines were not common, they had been happening since the early days of white settlers. Now they were totally barred. The next year, 1950, the Nats really got going and parliament enacted three laws as the foundation stones of apartheid rule:

- Population Registration Act: Every white, coloured and Asian person was to be put into a racial pigeonhole. Blacks had their own gradings into different tribes.
- The Group Areas Act: Divided the entire country into different areas for residence and business by different colour groups.
- The Suppression of Communism Act: Not only did it ban the Communist Party of South Africa, which had been formed in 1922, but it gave the government sweeping power to restrict personal liberties.

\* \* \*

Now followed an avalanche of laws and regulations which reached into every nook and cranny of South Africa, institutionalising racism, entrenching white privilege and wealth, debasing people of colour and blasting their lives. An early action was to get rid of the vestigial voting rights of coloureds so that only whites voted and parliament consisted only of whites. Nat racism enjoyed increasing white support in election after election; most whites enjoyed the privileged and exalted status which apartheid gave them.

Apartheid determined where you were born, where you would live, which kindergarten, school or university you attended – and the quality of your education; if you had access to a library; which entrance to public buildings you could use, which elevators, and which toilets; which jobs you could have and hence what you would earn; with whom you could have sex and whom you could marry; which taxi, bus and train you used; which movie house or theatre, if any, you could attend; which restaurant or hotel you could use; which cell, clothing and food you got if you were jailed; which police and army rank you could attain; the amount of old-age pension or disability grant; which hospital you could use – and the quality of treatment; and ultimately where you were buried. The denial of respect and liberty for black people, the humiliations, the lack of regard for them as human beings, led to the word 'nonpersons'.

There was little room for compassion. The stock answer from government officials when approached to help a victim of apartheid rules was: 'It's the law. There is nothing I can do.' Apartheid was at its height during the next twenty-five years. Then, beginning in the late 1970s, there was a gradual easing until it was all scrapped with the coming of democracy in 1994. But at the height, the scale and depth of the racism and discrimination were over-whelming, and the extent of enforcement was staggering. The minutiae of racism and oppression were written meticulously into law.

* * *

To put the Population Registration Act into effect, an identity number was assigned to every person and two numbers in it recorded racial classification: 00 was a white born in South Africa, and 10 was a white born abroad, 01 was coloured, 02 Malay, 04 Chinese, 05 Indian (also known as Asian), down to 09 for a Nama of South West Africa. Because human beings do not lend themselves to being placed in watertight compartments, the list included what amounted to miscellaneous: 06 Other Asian and 07 Other Coloured.

'Race Classification Boards' were set up to decide 'borderline' cases: the tests used varied over time, with different weight attached to physical appear-ance, family background and social acceptance. At one stage, board mem-bers – all whites – pushed a comb through people's hair on the theory that the crinklier it was, the more coloured the person; in another test, also later discarded, the moons of finger nails were examined in the belief that this revealed the degree of whiteness. By September 1958 the boards had clas-sified 45,024 'borderline' cases.

After centuries of interracial sex, in and out of marriage, many families had different hues of skin colour, from darker to lighter. 'Trying for white' was the goal to gain the highest privileges. Families were split as the lighter-skinned got across the barrier and shunned their parents, brothers and sisters. Malicious neighbours reported those passing themselves off as white, leading to visits by race inspectors. It was ugly and demeaning and led to suicides.

Population classification made the Group Areas Act possible. It took years to implement, and the law was repeatedly amended. Many thousands of people were ordered to leave their homes. Few whites were ordered to move; the burden fell on coloureds and Asians. Government inspectors decided on property valuations and kept them low. City centres were all declared for exclusive white occupation and use. But people of other colours could work there for white employers and, of course, they bought from the white-owned stores. An amendment to the law said that 'disqualified persons' – the officialese in this case for coloureds, Asians and blacks – could buy food and drink in restaurants or cafés as long as they did not sit down to eat.

District Six was a notorious apartheid case, a suburb in walking distance from Cape Town's city centre and home to coloureds for centuries: thirty-eight thousand were evicted for resettlement twenty kilometres away. People feared the zooming sound of the 'GGs', the Government Garage Volkswagen Beetles which officials used to serve eviction notices, driving up and down steep mountainside roads. The entire area was bulldozed, with only a few churches and mosques left standing in the emptiness. The government planned new housing and business blocks for white use – but in one of the few anti-apartheid successes, local public opinion, led by whites, opposed commercial building, and District Six remained largely bare except for police barracks and an office block. The apartheid scar remained even after freedom in 1994: How to return the land? Some residents had been owners, but many were tenants. How to fix property values fifty or more years later? How to recompense those who had lost their homes? Should new houses be built for the children of the original victims? What to charge them?

Blacks underwent their own forced removals under separate laws. Townships – or 'locations', the demeaning word for black residential areas – were established outside cities and villages and filled with tiny, poor-quality houses for the blacks who each day went to work in white-owned factories, offices and homes. Transport was inadequate. Several million people who were deemed 'surplus' to the white need for labour were compelled to move, often at gunpoint, to 'dumping grounds' – open spaces in remote areas, short of basic amenities and with few jobs available. People starved. Death rates among children were high. The same fate befell those expelled from 'black spots' – patches of land in white-owned rural areas.

Asians suffered a specific cruelty: many, especially in the Transvaal province, were shopkeepers inside cities and villages. In the rural areas, they had for many years sustained white farmers, extending credit for buying goods in the hard drought years and getting paid when the rains came. This was brushed aside, and they were ordered to go and trade on the outskirts. With courage and resilience, many survived and over time built up new businesses. At the same time, hundreds were given exemptions and allowed to retain city premises. Opportunities for bribery were many.

Ismail Mohamed, a distinguished barrister who was Asian, was debarred from renting an office in Innes Chambers in Johannesburg, which housed barristers and was located across the street from the Supreme Court. However, he worked there for years, in defiance of the law and aided by his legal colleagues, using the room of a barrister who was often away and moving temporarily to another room when necessary. In due time, when apartheid ended, Mohamed was appointed the first chief justice.

Buildings had to provide toilets for males and females and for each separate race group; in practice, this meant for white men and women and 'non-white' men and women. It led to crazy prohibitions as in the capital, Pretoria, where building laws decreed that sewage pipes in high-rises had to remain separate and could only join up at basement level.

The forty thousand Chinese in the cities were the only group to escape removal. Most were small shopkeepers spread throughout four cities, and the intention was to cluster them together in their own group area. But even official ideologists realised the impracticality of creating an area populated only by shopkeepers trading with each other, so they were left where they were. But in daily life the Chinese were in a twilight zone within wider society, their status uncertain. They did not have the right to vote but could live in white areas. They could get on a white bus but were uncertain whether the conductor would allow them to sit downstairs or order them upstairs. At movie houses they never knew whether they would be allowed in or turned away. They could travel in coaches reserved for whites on suburban trains, but on long journeys special coaches might be reserved for them at the end of the white coach that adjoined those reserved for blacks. They were not admitted to the dining car, but meals were served to them in their compartments.

Japan became an important trading partner, and in the early 1960s about one hundred Japanese diplomats and businessmen were in South Africa. They were given the status of 'honorary white' and were treated as whites. But to the uninitiated, how to know the difference between Japanese, to be treated respectfully, and Chinese, who could be rudely dealt with? A Japanese diplomat said he believed that shopkeepers picked up the difference immediately: Japanese would walk in confidently whereas Chinese hesitated momentarily at the door.

The Nats used the enactment of the Suppression of Communism Act for scaremongering. The Communist Party of South Africa never had a mass membership but had some influence among black workers. However, the Nationalists were obsessed with it: to them, the party wanted to *opstook* (incite) blacks; it was God-less; many of its white members were Jews. Communists were the *Rooi Gevaar*, the Red Danger. This went together with two other great fears: the *Swart Gevaar*, the Black Danger, and the *Roomse Gevaar*, the Roman Catholic Danger. All were handy for emotional and highly effective appeals to white blood by Afrikaner politicians on public platforms.

The Communist Party was always a creature of Moscow. Its political zigzags included following orders in the early 1930s to work for a Black Republic – which was bizarre because the party was a unique pacesetter in having members and leaders of all colours. Later during that period, several of its leaders were summoned to Moscow and were never seen again, victims of Stalin's purges. The party faithfully followed the ordained line and lined up with the Soviet Union in 1939 when it signed a pact with Nazi Germany; hence it condemned Britain – and South Africa – for declaring war on Germany. Then it leaped the other way and enthusiastically supported the war when Germany attacked the Soviet Union in 1941.

Parliament enacted a law to proscribe the Communist Party. The party did not wait: it disbanded itself a few days before, thus achieving the distinction of being the world's only communist party to vote itself out of existence and to actually mean it, rather than being a subterfuge. It was reborn in 1953, underground and illegal, as the South African Communist Party.

The law's definition of communism was so wide that it could be applied to virtually any liberal opposition to the government, and that's exactly how it was used. 'Banning' was the basic tool: the minister of justice, acting on undisclosed Security Police advice, simply issued a notice restricting a person's civil liberties. He or she could not attend meetings, including social gatherings – that is, could not be with more than one other person at a time; he or she could not prepare anything for publication; nothing he or she said could be published; entering schools, universities or factories was barred without permission; membership in named organisations was barred; he or she could be ordered to remain inside a suburb or a town, or be confined to home at night and over weekends, or totally, that is, house-arrested. Loopholes opened by court appeals were closed by amendments rushed through parliament; habeas corpus was one of the early safeguards of liberty to be done away with.

While communists were the first target, non-communists and even known anti-communists, such as leaders of the Liberal Party, were also silenced through banning.[2] Fear of banning became a mighty weapon in dampening opposition to apartheid.

\* \* \*

In everyday life, 'Whites only' and 'non-Whites only' noticeboards proliferated on benches in parks and railway stations. Post offices had separate entrances, queues and phone booths. Magistrate's courts had separate entrances and public seating. Beaches were segregated, with the best of the seaside reserved for whites. Separate buses ran for whites and blacks; in Johannesburg, separate bus stops were a few metres away from each other. Long-distance trains had segregated coaches, and dining cars were for whites only. In Cape Town, unusually, buses and trains had not previously been segregated but were now forced into it; buses were allowed to carry everyone, but separated inside by signs. Segregated seating was ordered in the city hall, with people of colour in the back. Libraries were for whites only.

Prohibition of sex between whites and blacks, in effect since 1927, was widened to forbid all interracial sex. Policemen climbed up trees to peer into bedrooms for evidence of illegal sex. They felt the sheets of beds to check if they were warm and hence evidence of recent sex. A white man and a woman of different colour driving in a car risked being stopped and questioned by police. Yet the sex continued, on a grand scale. In the thirty-five years leading up to 1985, when the Immorality Act was scrapped, there were about 110,000 criminal prosecutions; those were the people who were caught. They included a former private secretary of a prime minister. Whites also went to neighbouring black-run countries for sex. In Swaziland, a Nationalist cabinet minister was found with a black woman and was politely escorted to the border and told not to return; the story was hushed up. Existing segregation in movie houses was strengthened. The same happened in theatres, except for a handful in Cape Town. Taxis were licensed for either whites or blacks. Municipal halls and libraries in cities were for whites only. Hotels and restaurants were for whites only, with a few of low quality catering for people of colour. Whites and blacks could not sit down for coffee together in cafés. Liquor sales to blacks were restricted (leading to large-scale smuggling). Blacks and whites had to use separate elevators in high-rises.

Prisoners were segregated between whites and people of colour. They wore different uniforms, and blacks had less warm clothing, did not always have jerseys and either went barefoot or had rubber sandals. Food was different: blacks had less meat than whites. Black prisoners were usually housed in large dormitories and were victims of assaults by warders as a matter of course.

Control of blacks was vastly extended. Laws ordering black adults to carry a 'pass' had been initiated by the British during the late nineteenth century and were a feature of existence. Now the Nats enacted the Natives (Abolition of Passes and Coordination of Documents) Act. The wording could not have been more cynical because far from 'abolition', the pass laws were made into a heavier burden than ever: every black adult male, and later women, too, carried a document book which had to be produced on demand. Failure to do so, or not having the official stamps showing the permitted place of residence, work and tax payments, meant immediate arrest. People were arrested outside their homes: it did no good to explain that the pass was in a jacket pocket inside the house a few feet away. Arrests and prosecutions ran to 1,000 a day, 365 days a year. Those charged went through special courts which worked like sausage machines, with perhaps three minutes per case. The pass system led to another abuse: sentenced offenders could be hired out to white farmers. Details emerged every now and then of ill-treatment, of prisoners dressed in potato sacks and of beatings and deaths. Bribery was rampant but was seldom reported because publicity would have exposed the victim to official retribution.

Blacks hated the pass above all else. It was the means and the symbol of control over them.

The pass system was integral to the Nationalist ideological drive to keep down the numbers of blacks in cities; they even believed they could reverse the flow so there would be fewer blacks. During the 1960s, this evolved into the policy of 'separate development' which at its heart was an attempt to prettify raw apartheid. The concept was a politicised and distorted version of the Dutch Reformed Church's 'separate and apart' missionary activity in 1929. Separate development led to the creation of 'Bantustans', tribal mini-states. Blacks were stripped of South African citizenship and instead given citizenship in their own tribal 'homelands'. Thus 'separate freedoms in separate areas'. To bring it about, tribal structures and allegiances, on the wane under the impact of modernisation, were forcibly resuscitated with ruthless suppression of opposition. The aim was that 'white' South Africa would no longer have any black citizens and therefore could no longer be accused of oppressing blacks; the world would no longer have a reason to condemn apartheid because it no longer existed. That was the theory, but the world never believed or accepted it. Coloureds and Asians remained in white South Africa, in their own segregated group areas.

It was a gigantic confidence trick. First, it began with the fact that whites, forming at that stage 15 to 20 percent of the population, were holding on to about 84 percent of the land. Second, at least one-third of the black population was by then firmly established in urban areas, and many had lost all connection with their original rural tribal roots and had nowhere to return to. Third, the purpose of the Bantustans was to provide reservoirs of cheap black labour to be drawn into white South Africa as needed and expelled when not wanted (or when causing trouble through protests). Ten tribal Bantustans were created and three were given 'independence'; no one in the world recognised these vassal states except South Africa.

The system of migrant labour, used since the mid-nineteenth century, was strengthened even more, with men allowed to work in the cities but their wives and children left behind in the rural 'reserves'. The pass was the means of enforcement. Family life was devastated. Children grew up fatherless and in poverty. In the cities, malnutrition and crime spread. Prostitution flourished – and helped in the spread of AIDS in the early twenty-first century, whereby some 20 percent of South Africans were HIV positive, as men took the disease home to their wives.

Only blacks whose labour was needed were allowed to remain in the cities. Those who were 'surplus', including the aged, were ordered to go and live in the rural areas, in one of the tribal 'homelands', as they were ideologically called. Poverty there was overwhelming, with widespread malnutrition. Kwashiorkor, a disease caused by protein deficiency, killed countless babies: the exact toll is unknown because for many years there was no proper registration of births and deaths. The few homes for the aged in city townships were closed down, and people were sent to die in the rural areas.

To be 'endorsed out' was a frightening prospect. Any person who was not wanted – or who resisted the government – could be summarily ordered out of the city, and his pass endorsed to show it. That could mean being sent into rural poverty, lonely, amidst strangers and without work. The threat of being endorsed out was used as a quick and cheap way to force people to become informers for the Security Police.

\* \* \*

Hospitals were segregated: those for blacks were often overcrowded and had inferior facilities. Hospitals for blacks had white nurses, usually seniors; hospitals for whites did not have black nurses. Black doctors were debarred from treating their own patients in hospitals if this involved them being in a position of authority over white nurses. Black specialists in large hospitals could not be in a position of authority over white doctors, interns or medical students. Doctors below senior grades were paid according to colour, with whites getting the most, followed by Asians and coloureds, and blacks at the bottom. Nurses were represented by a statutory national association: by law it had separate colour branches, but the controlling board was composed of only whites. Separate ambulances served different colours. If the 'wrong' ambulance arrived at the scene of an accident, which happened sometimes, it could not carry the victims. Black medical students at the two universities which accepted them, Cape Town and Witwatersrand in Johannesburg, had to leave examination rooms when a white corpse was brought in; white students dissected whites as well as blacks. Later, separate medical schools were opened for blacks; students treated only patients who were not white, and that also applied to corpses.

Cape Town and Witwatersrand universities were English-speaking and applied academic freedom so that students of all colours were admitted (but social segregation excluded non-whites from sports and dances). The government insisted on imposing apartheid, and a prolonged battle ensued which the universities eventually lost: they were allowed to admit students who were not white but had to apply for permission for each one. Meanwhile, the government opened universities in rural towns meant to serve specific tribes and also coloureds in Cape Town, although it proved impossible to adhere strictly to the tribal divisions. These universities were derisively known as 'bush colleges', and for years they provided jobs for poor-quality Afrikaner academics. Dissent by students was punished by expulsion.

Among the most long-lasting damage the Nats did to South Africa was in black education. It began by forcing the closing of most of the schools run by 'English' churches, often missionary, which for one hundred years had produced an elite whom the Nats mocked as 'black Englishmen'. Leaders such as Nelson Mandela and Robert Sobukwe came out of these schools. On the one hand, the government ensured that vast numbers of children went to school, albeit totally segregated; on the other hand, it starved black education of funding, insisting that money had to come from black taxation, which was limited because of poverty. It perverted education through the ideological insistence that blacks could not aspire to anything but low-level work in 'white' South Africa. Inadequate facilities were the norm, differing only in their grossness: in Johannesburg townships, black primary schools had pupils sitting on rocks and using benches as desks; textbooks were scarce to the extent that pupils about to sit their final matriculation examination did not have a single textbook. Libraries and laboratories were rare in black high schools.

Statistics reveal the extent of inequality: in 1969–1970, white pupils had 16.6 times more money spent on them than did blacks; Asians and coloureds fell between these poles. By 1978–1979, the gap had narrowed to 10.15. The pupil-teacher ratio for whites was 19.6, for Asians 26.2, for coloureds 29.6, and for blacks 47.6. The standard of black teachers was low: in 1978, only 2.32 percent had university degrees and 15.48 percent had matriculation. Control was strict: any teacher who criticised the government, let alone who took part in a protest, faced being found guilty of misconduct and fired.

The consequences still run deep. Allied with the effects of later political upheaval, the education of blacks remains a fraught area, gravely retarding South Africa's ability to progress.

Under 'Job Reservation', regulations aimed to protect jobs for whites by specifying which colour group could do which job in which area of the country. In Cape Town, for example, jobs which only whites were allowed to do included ambulance drivers and attendants, firemen and traffic policemen above the rank of constable. Even that wasn't enough: Nationalist MPs objected to having coloured constables directing traffic outside parliament, so the municipality removed them. In building, blacks could do skilled work only in black townships and black rural areas – at lower rates of pay than whites. Discrimination was already built into gold mining, in its time the mainstay of the economy. By long usage it was applied by allowing only whites to hold a 'blasting certificate', the right to set off explosives underground. In practice it was usual for the high-paid white miner to sit back while the black workers – who earned perhaps one-tenth of his income – did the forbidden skilled work. The exclusion remained under apartheid, especially because the white mineworkers' union was Afrikaner-run. Only whites could do all the skilled work in mining. That also applied to work throughout the country. In cities, blacks were actually debarred from learning skills.

In social welfare, only whites and coloureds could get family allowances. However, everyone qualified for old age, blind, disability payments, war veteran pensions and maintenance grants for children. But not everyone was equal: in 1972, whites got 6.3 times more than blacks; in 1979, 3.5 times.

Under apartheid, black workers were debarred from going on strike. It was a criminal offence to do so. Trade unions could be formed for blacks – but were not recognised by law and could not take part in official wage talks and conciliation procedures. Employers could recognise an unregistered union and agree to negotiate with it. Few did so and instead, when employers faced protesting workers, the usual style was to call in the police, who would hit a few heads and arrest the ringleaders, charging them with 'incitement'. End of problem. The government set up 'works committees' to represent workers, with white officials handling industrial disputes. Understandably, many black workers mistrusted the system. In Johannesburg, when several hundred municipal workers went on strike, they were summarily fired and shipped to the 'homelands'. They would have been listed as troublemakers, and hence made unemployable forever.

Sports facilities in cities were reserved for whites. Coloureds and Asians had their own, lesser and poorer grounds in their areas. Attendance at sporting events was controlled: anyone who wanted to watch a public sports event by players of a colour group other than his own had to apply for a permit either from the Department of Community Development (which handled Group Areas) or the Department of Planning, or the Department of Bantu Administration and Development in the case of blacks. Permits were usually granted for coloureds and Asians to attend white sporting matches provided they were at a provincial or international level and provided that special entrances, seating and toilets were arranged; blacks were often refused permission. National teams had only whites. That was the reason for international boycotts: South Africa was booted out of the Olympics in 1964, and later excluded from rugby, football, cricket and other world sports.

Blacks who did not live in cities were allowed to enter for only seventy-two hours; after that, if caught, they were prosecuted. It was normal in Johannesburg to see a long line of handcuffed black pass offenders being led by policemen. In turn, whites were not allowed to enter black townships and had to obtain a permit if they wanted to go there. They were also not allowed in the rural 'reserves' without permission, but this was applied selectively to some areas and to only some whites.[3] It was a criminal offence for blacks to stay overnight in a house in a white suburb, but domestic servants could stay – although, for some years, this was not allowed for Asian and coloured employers. In practice, women domestic servants frequently had husbands or boyfriends, or their children, stay illegally with them in backyard quarters – and were subject to raids and arrest by police. Employers who hired illegal blacks faced prosecution. Domestic servants, as well as illegal workers in any area, were victims of exploitation in pay and conditions.

Black professionals – the small number of doctors and lawyers, plus hawkers and pedlars – were ordered to leave the city centre and go to townships. But severe restrictions applied there: notably, no freehold right to land.

Blacks could not own more than one business. They could not erect their own building but had to rent from the municipality. Children could not inherit from parents. Shopkeepers could sell only essential domestic goods – no clothing, no furniture, nothing. No black-owned companies, partnerships, financial institutions or wholesalers were allowed.

\* \* \*

Apartheid in action brought black resistance to life. The African National Congress (ANC) was formed in 1912 by black professionals and tribal chiefs. Over the decades it was eclipsed by new movements but each time rose again as the premier organisation. In its first forty years, it meekly asked and begged whites to give blacks a share in the country but was always rebuffed. The heady ideas about freedom generated by World War II began its transformation: at Fort Hare University College young men – many who would become famous, such as Nelson Mandela, Oliver Tambo and Robert Sobukwe – set up a Youth League inside the ANC to push for militant action. The Nationalist victory in 1948 spurred this. A wave of protests and struggles against white domination were successively put down. In a process of 'action, reaction and counter-action' the government initiated new apartheid action, blacks resisted and the government took ever-harsher suppressive measures. Each conflict left South Africa more authoritarian than before.

Detention without trial began in 1960, starting at twelve days. That was extended to three months. Then six months. By 1967 it was indefinite detention without trial. Under the Terrorism Act almost any opposition to the government could be a crime; the onus of proving innocence was placed heavily on the accused. Torture was routine. By the time detainees were brought to court their wounds had healed.

The media were choked. Radio was controlled by the government and was his master's voice. Television, which began with one channel, was the same. Afrikaans-language newspapers were for years faithful servants of the National Party. English-language newspapers opposed apartheid to varying degrees but faced mounting restrictions. Mind control was pursued through the banning of books in the thousands and censorship of movies. One of the many restricting laws, dating back to 1927 legislation, made it an offence to 'incite hostility' between different population groups. It was a reasonable weapon to have against hate speech. But its application had far-reaching, inhibiting effects on criticism of the government because its threat hung over the opposition; it was never applied to any of the Nationalist leaders who day after day poured out racist views. Yet despite the strangling of dissent, more than enough was published so that no South African could ever say he did not know about the merciless application of laws in subjugating blacks.

The Defiance Campaign Against Unjust Laws in 1952 was the first of the major onslaughts on Nationalist rule: ten thousand people of all colours deliberately broke apartheid laws, sitting on park benches and going into railway stations; the offences were minor, so sentences were light. The government acted swiftly with a new law which elevated a minor offence into a major one if it was committed as a protest: leaders backed off when faced by imprisonment for up to five years plus whipping for repeat offences. The ANC totally failed to halt the government as it surged ahead to put its apartheid stamp on the country.

An ANC breakaway group, the Pan-Africanist Congress, derided ANC leaders for lack of action and called on blacks to leave their passes at home and to offer themselves for arrest at the nearest police station. On Monday, 21 March 1960, thousands responded in Cape Town and, fatefully, the township of Sharpeville, less than an hour's drive from Johannesburg: police there opened fire on unarmed demonstrators and killed sixty-nine; many were shot in the back as they tried to flee. Sharpeville catapulted South Africa onto the world stage in a way that had not happened before; it brought loathing for apartheid to a new pitch and accelerated boycott calls. At home, the ANC called for a strike. Amidst widespread unrest and riots, the government declared a state of emergency, giving it the power to do what it pleased; it rushed through laws to ban the PAC and the ANC and detained some twenty thousand people without trial. The PAC leader, Robert Sobukwe, was jailed for three years for incitement. As his imprisonment was ending, the government, fearing his opposition and his charisma, passed a special act of parliament which kept him in prison on Robben Island, in virtual solitary confinement for six years; he was then banished to the town of Kimberley and died of cancer nine years later.

A year after Sharpeville, the government beat down a national strike call by Nelson Mandela. He then announced that nonviolent resistance was pointless. The underground ANC and Communist Party switched to armed resistance. Mandela left the country, but he was captured – apparently betrayed by an informer – when he returned and was jailed. Later charged with seeking to overthrow the government by violence, he was given life imprisonment, narrowly escaping the death penalty.

The next turning point came in 1976: the underlying rejection of apartheid was triggered by government insistence on greater use of Afrikaans – hated as the language of the oppressor – for teaching subjects such as mathematics. School pupils went into the streets to protest and were shot down. The official death toll was about five hundred; journalists spoke about reports of truckloads of bodies being moved at night and estimated perhaps as many as one thousand died; with unknown numbers escaping the country for military training, no exact count was ever possible. Children boycotted schools under the slogan of 'No education without liberation'. They could not have been braver and more committed to gain freedom – and it proved a disastrous legacy for the future, with much of a generation depriving itself of education and skills. Eight years later, black anger again burst out and, despite heavy suppression, it went on boiling until the Nationalists recognised that they could not continue as the masters. Mandela was released from prison in 1990, the underground organisations were unbanned, negotiations got underway, and in April 1994 South Africa held its first democratic elections. White rule and apartheid ended. The ANC won overwhelmingly.

No single factor can be said to have ended apartheid. The refusal by US banks to roll over loans in August 1984 was a giant blow which exposed the inner weakness of the economy, caused by apartheid. There weren't enough skilled whites to keep the country going. The end of the Cold War was crucial: the United States no longer felt the need to support the status quo of white rule while the ANC lost support from the Soviet Union, so everyone was driven to seek a deal. The black townships were ungovernable, and police could enter them only in force. A war in South West Africa against blacks demanding freedom from South African rule was straining the army and bleeding the economy. The ANC's guerrilla warfare did not pose a great threat, but it put more strain on the army and finances. Disinvestment was hurting, although import substitution was filling gaps. International sports boycotts had deep psychological effects on white morale. Cultural boycotts also had their impact. So did the widespread world distaste for South Africa: whites who went abroad were made to feel like pariahs.

Afrikaner Nationalists wanted division and partition; some black tribal leaders went along with them and benefited. But fundamental to the struggle against apartheid was the goal of a single, nonracial and democratic South Africa. Blacks wanted it, as did the vast bulk of coloureds and Asians and the minority of whites who opposed apartheid. There was unity of belief and purpose. And that is what was achieved in 1994.

Some Afrikaner bittereinders have retreated to their own all-white enclave. They bought land in an arid part of the country and named it Orania. About 1,500 people live there and do all the jobs, from management to physical labour. The neighbourhood for more affluent residents is called *Grootdorp* (Big Town); the lower-income section is called *Kleingeluk* (Little Luck). The government leaves them alone. They are a curious hangover from the vanished terrible past.

\* \* \*

Shuffling people from one racial pigeonhole to another went on into the dying years of apartheid. 'Race Classification Boards' made the decisions, with far-reaching effects on lives. The *Star* (Johannesburg) reported on 21 March 1986:

More than 1,000 people officially changed colour last year.

They were reclassified from one race group to another by the stroke of a government pen.

Details of what is dubbed 'the chameleon dance' were given in reply to Opposition questions in Parliament.

The Minister of Home Affairs, Mr Stoffel Botha, disclosed that during 1985:

- 702 coloured people turned white.
- 19 whites became coloured.
- One Indian became white.
- Three Chinese became white.
- 50 Indians became coloured.
- 43 coloureds became Indian.
- 21 Indians became Malay.
- 30 Malays went Indian.
- 249 blacks became coloured.
- 20 coloureds became blacks.
- Two blacks became 'Other Asians'.
- One black was classified Griqua.
- 11 coloureds became Chinese.
- Three coloureds went Malay.
- One Chinese became coloured.
- Eight Malays became coloured.
- Three blacks were classed as Malay.
- No blacks became white and no whites became black.

## Chapter Six

# Are They the Same?

*A point-by-point comparison of Israel inside the Green Line with apartheid South Africa.*

\* \* \*

## VOTING

*South Africa*: Blacks, coloureds and Asians – most people – did not have the right to vote.
*Israel*: All citizens have the right to vote – Jews and Arabs, men and women.


*South Africa*: Only whites could be elected to parliament.
*Israel*: The Knesset (parliament) has Arab members, representing both Jewish and Arab parties.

## DEMOCRACY

*South Africa*: Whites oppressed the majority of people – blacks, coloureds and Asians. A vast range of laws curtailed civil liberties of everyone, including whites.
*Israel*: Jews and Arabs have democratic rights.

## FREEDOM OF MOVEMENT

*South Africa*: Blacks were severely restricted in where they could live or work. They needed permission to enter cities specified for whites. Whites were not allowed to enter areas for blacks without permission.

*Israel*: Everyone has freedom of movement throughout the country – Jews and Arabs alike.

## FREEDOM OF SPEECH

*South Africa*: Freedom of speech was restricted. The press was muzzled. State radio and television were government mouthpieces.

*Israel*: No restrictions except in security issues. Newspapers, radio and television are free, vocal and critical.

## FREEDOM OF ASSOCIATION

*South Africa*: Severe restrictions on people of different skin colours being able to meet.

*Israel*: Jews and Arabs can meet where and when they please.

## FREEDOM FROM WANT

*South Africa*: Hunger and malnutrition were rife among blacks. Vast numbers of blacks lived in dire poverty, with little government help for them.

*Israel*: Large numbers of Jews and Arabs live below the official poverty level. There is no starvation. Government social welfare helps all.

## SEX

*South Africa*: Sex between people of different skin colours was a criminal offence.

*Israel*: No restrictions.

## MARRIAGE

*South Africa*: Marriage between people of different skin colours was prohibited by law.

*Israel*: Marriage and divorce are controlled by religious communities – Jewish, Muslim and Christian. Each imposes its own restrictions. But anyone can go abroad and have a civil marriage that is recognised in Israel.

## HEALTH

*South Africa*: Hospitals were segregated, with the best reserved for whites. Black hospitals were invariably overcrowded with lesser facilities. Some major city hospitals admitted patients of all colours but in segregated wards. Doctors treated everyone but nursing was segregated. Clinics throughout the country were segregated. Ambulances were segregated: ambulances for whites were not allowed to carry people of other colours.

*Israel*: Jews and Arabs are treated alike in hospitals and clinics. Same wards, same facilities, same doctors, same nurses. Doctors and nurses are Jews and Arabs.

## HEALTH INSURANCE

*South Africa*: Most whites had medical insurance coverage through employers. Most blacks did not and were treated in public hospitals and clinics.

*Israel*: Jews and Arabs have the same rights to National Insurance coverage, pay the same rates and enjoy the same benefits.

## SOCIAL WELFARE

*South Africa*: Whites received higher old-age pensions, and blacks received far less. It was the same for other social benefits including disability grants and unemployment pay.

*Israel*: Jews and Arabs get the same benefits. There is preferential payment of allowances to *yeshiva* (Jewish religious seminary) students.

## PRISONS

*South Africa*: Prisons were segregated, with different sections for whites and blacks and a descending order in the type of food, starting with whites, then coloureds and Asians and then blacks. For many years, blacks were denied warm clothes for winter such as long trousers, jerseys and shoes.

*Israel*: Jewish and Arab criminal prisoners have equal facilities. Security prisoners are kept separate in their own prisons and/or sections.

## THE RIGHT TO WORK

*South Africa*: Laws barred blacks from doing many skilled jobs.
*Israel*: No restrictions.

## TRADE UNIONS

*South Africa*: Trade unions for blacks were not recognised by law. It was a crime for blacks to strike. Trade unions were not allowed to hold joint meetings of white, coloured and Asian members.
*Israel*: No restrictions.

## FREEDOM OF RELIGION

*South Africa*: The main Afrikaans church was segregated between whites and 'daughter' churches for coloureds, Asians and blacks. The two other Afrikaans churches barred anyone who wasn't white. Blacks played a subservient role in many other churches. Blacks were often discouraged from attending 'white' churches in cities; whites were not allowed to attend church services in 'black' areas.
*Israel*: The practice of religion is open. But Orthodox Judaism is recognised by the state, which finances its rabbis and courts. So, too, are Muslim religious courts, but judges earn lower pay than Jews. Muslim access to the Dome of the Rock in Jerusalem for Friday prayers is restricted to married men above a specified age.

## SCHOOLS

*South Africa*: Schools were totally segregated. Only whites were allowed to teach in schools for whites.
*Israel*: No legal restrictions for admission, but each religious community has its own schools. Free compulsory education for all.

## HIGHER EDUCATION

*South Africa*: Universities were segregated. A limited number of blacks were allowed to study at 'white' universities. At 'white' medical schools, black students had to leave when white corpses were brought into anatomy classes.
*Israel*: Open to all.

## ARMY

*South Africa*: Whites only. People of other colours were used for support services.
*Israel*: Conscription applies only to Jews, Druze Arabs and Circassians. Bedouin Arabs volunteer. National service open to all.

## POLICE

*South Africa*: Whites and blacks were members, but blacks were in subordinate ranks. White policemen did not salute blacks who held any senior position above them.
*Israel*: Open to everyone.

## LAND

*South Africa*: About 84 percent of land was reserved for ownership and occupation only by whites.
*Israel*: About 13 percent of the land reserved for ownership and occupation only by Jews. Social pressures discriminate against Arab ownership in some parts of the country.

## CITIZENSHIP

*South Africa*: Blacks were deprived of South African citizenship and were forced into tribal Bantustans.
*Israel*: All have citizenship, except East Jerusalem Arabs who rejected it. The Right of Return (to immigrate) is reserved only for Jews.

## PUBLIC FACILITIES

*South Africa*: Libraries, beaches, park benches, municipal theatres, toilets and so forth were segregated, with facilities in cities for whites only.
*Israel*: Everything open to everyone.

## PRIVATE FACILITIES

*South Africa*: Hotels, restaurants, night clubs, coffee bars, theatres, cinemas and toilets were segregated by law. In cities, this meant for whites only.
*Israel*: Everything is open to everyone.

## TRANSPORT

*South Africa*: Trains, national and suburban, were segregated with different carriages for whites and blacks. Buses were segregated with separate buses or sometimes with internal segregation. Taxis were segregated.

*Israel*: Open to everyone. On some bus routes serving Jewish ultra-Orthodox neighbourhoods, women sit at the back and men at the front. It is supposed to be voluntary.

## LANGUAGE

*South Africa*: Afrikaans and English were the official languages; no tribal languages.

*Israel*: Hebrew and Arabic are official languages, although Arabic has a lesser status.

## IDENTITY DOCUMENT

*South Africa*: Everyone had an ID card, but only blacks were required to carry their special 'pass' at all times, showing where they were allowed to live and work. Instant arrest and prosecution followed failure to produce the pass to a policeman.

*Israel*: Everyone has ID. It doesn't have to be produced on demand.

## SPORT

*South Africa*: Total segregation at all levels. Blacks were excluded from national sports teams.

*Israel*: Open to all.

## CURFEW

*South Africa*: In cities and villages, blacks were not allowed on the streets of 'white' suburbs after a specified time, often 9 p.m.

*Israel*: Doesn't exist.

## LEGAL SYSTEM

*South Africa*: Judges, magistrates, prosecutors: whites only.

*Israel*: Everyone can hold any post, including on the Supreme Court.

REPUBLIC OF SOUTH AFRICA

28/03/1973

Sy Ed., Prof., Dr., Ds., Mnr., Mev., Mej.
The Hon., Prof., Dr., Rev., Mr., Mrs., Miss.

B POGRUND,
P O BOX 1138,
JOHANNESBURG.

Neem asseblief kennis dat —
Please note that —

VAN
SURNAME        POGRUND

VOORNAME
FIRST NAMES

IDENTITEITSNOMMER
IDENTITY NUMBER    730106 5123 00 7

geklassifiseer is
has been classified

AS A WHITE PERSON

vir die doeleindes van die Bevolkingsregistrasiewet, 1950.
for the purposes of the Population Registration Act, 1950.

OP LAS VAN DIE SEKRETARIS VAN BINNELANDSE SAKE
BY ORDER OF THE SECRETARY FOR THE INTERIOR

**A South African identity card issued at birth. The racial coding determined everyone's life, from where you were born to where you were buried. The majority of black people had a different coding based on tribal divisions.**

| Population group | S.A. Citizen | Non-S.A. Citizen |
|---|---|---|
| (i) White | 00 | 10 |
| (ii) Cape Coloured | 01 | 11 |
| (iii) Coloured person of South-West Africa | 20 | 21 |
| (iv) Malay | 02 | 12 |
| (v) Griqua | 03 | 13 |
| (vi) Chinese | 04 | 14 |
| (vii) Indian | 05 | 15 |
| (viii) Other Asian | 06 | 16 |
| (ix) Other Coloured | 07 | 17 |
| (x) Baster of Rehoboth | 08 | 18 |
| (xi) Nama of South-West Africa | 09 | 19 |

**Racial categories and official codings.**

A beach notice in Afrikaans and English. Apartheid notices were placed on park benches, court entrances and seats, post office and railway station entrances, libraries, buses and trains, taxis, public toilets, sports stadiums, and for a time also on elevators. (*Courtesy Times Media Library*)

Ms Debora Manana with her class of 110 black pupils in a makeshift classroom in a garage, circa the 1970s. School education was segregated, with far less money allocated for blacks. (*Mike Mzileni; courtesy Times Media Library*)

Police with protestors during a demonstration, circa the 1980s. This was mild compared with the usual mass shooting and killing. (*Courtesy Times Media Library*)

Shacks in Crossroads, a squatter settlement outside Cape Town, circa the 1980s. These were the homes of black people who defied apartheid laws by leaving their impoverished rural homes to seek work in cities. Today, blacks can move freely around South Africa, but many hundreds of thousands still live miserably in shacks. (*Courtesy Times Media Library*)

Erecting a shelter after spending the winter night cold and wet in the KTC squatter camp near Cape Town, circa 1984. Black people were there illegally, defying apartheid orders to stay in poverty-stricken rural areas. They put plastic sheeting over sticks pushed into the soggy ground. Each day the police raided the camp and seized the sheeting and each day Christian priests replaced it. (*Riaan de Villiers; courtesy Times Media Library*)

Russian savagery against its Jewish people pushed US president Theodore Roosevelt in 1904 to protest to Tsar Nicholas II: 'Stop your cruel oppression of the Jews'. (*Library of Congress*)

'With one hand he does his work, in the other he holds his weapon'. The Hebrew text from Nehemiah 4:11 features at the head of this World Zionist Organization poster to typify the early Zionist ethos. Below it says: 'Creativity = Struggle'.
(*Central Zionist Archives, Jerusalem*)

1945: Jewish children who survived the Holocaust and arrived in Palestine illegally were taken to the Atlit detention camp, near Haifa. They were guarded by armed British police. (*Wikimedia Commons*)

Below a photograph of Theodor Herzl, Zionism's founding father, David Ben-Gurion announces Israel's independence in a hall in Tel Aviv on 14 May 1948. (*Israel Ministry of Foreign Affairs; Wikimedia Commons*)

Brooms to sweep away tacks thrown on roads by strikers during Arab riots, 14 May 1936. (*John D. Whiting; Library of Congress*)

A Palestine refugee family waits to receive a tent at an UNRWA emergency distribution centre after a severe winter storm damaged their makeshift shelter. Tyre camp, Lebanon, early 1950s. (*UNRWA photo by Myrtle Winter-Chaumeny*)

# NO TO KANGAROO COURTS

# YES TO CONSTRUCTIVE DIALOGUE

The South African Jewish Board of Deputies dismissed the Russell Tribunal's 'hearings' in 2011 accusing Israel of apartheid practices as a 'kangaroo court'. The tribunal made little impact on media or public.

What If I had Won?

| the good things | the bad things |
| --- | --- |
| THERE WOULD BE NO ISRAEL AND NO PALESTINIAN'S BLOOD SHED | I WOULD'NT HAVE ALLOWED THE MAKING OF THE NEW BEETLE |
| THE REST IS YOUR GUESS | THE REST IS YOUR GUESS |

A flyer distributed in the streets of Durban, South Africa, during the UN anti-racism conference in 2001. The conference of NGOs which preceded the meeting of governments produced vitriolic anti-Semitism and attacks on Israel.

Israel's Qalandia checkpoint, the main crossing to the West Bank. Palestinians must have permission to enter Israel. (*Raphaela Meli*)

Propaganda for boycotting Israel: it's dishonest 'Israeli apartheid' message is followed by misuse of Nelson Mandela's image and name through partial use of a quote about Palestinian freedom.

*Chapter Seven*

# Comparing Israel and Apartheid South Africa

*Do apartheid accusations against Israel bear up against reality?*

\* \* \*

Israel proper and Israel's occupation of the West Bank are separate but closely linked. Some issues are relevant to only one of them; some are common to both. How do they compare with apartheid South Africa? Studying the details in six spheres shows more differences than similarities. [1]

### RELIGION

*In South Africa*, Christianity was dominant. The white Afrikaner rulers proclaimed their belief in God and in South Africa as a Christian country, and most people of all colours went along with that. The disagreement was over how honestly and correctly Christianity was being applied. Most whites were adherents of one or other of the churches which had originated in Europe, ranging from Roman Catholic and Anglican (Episcopal) to Methodist, Lutheran and Dutch Reformed. The largest number of blacks belonged to the multiplicity of what were called 'independent' churches and which practised Christianity with an African and evangelical flair.

While Christianity was in theory a giant unifying force, in practice apartheid distorted its message. For many years, the Afrikaner creed was that the Bible supported apartheid. In response, an essential part of the anti-apartheid struggle stemmed from private and public agonising and argument over the moral meaning of Christianity and its challenge to white rule. Christian morality won and was a powerful factor in giving strength to the anti-apartheid opposition and also in persuading Afrikaners that they were wrong in relying on biblical support. Jews and Muslims (who were among apartheid victims) had limited impact on the national scene, but individuals in both groups played influential roles out of proportion to the sizes of their communities.

*In Israel*, Judaism versus Islam is fundamental and divisive in the Jewish-Arab struggle. Christianity is on the sidelines and barely features. The conflict is grounded in the fact that Jews and Muslims claim title to land and sites which they say are holy to them in terms of their history and religious faith; each disputes and is quick to disparage the other's claim to the same land and sites. Religion thus works as a highly divisive force: it not only keeps people apart, but it arouses fierce and angry passions which can and do rapidly spill over into violence.

Jerusalem is at the heart of the conflict. Hebron also features largely and so do holy sites such as Rachel's Tomb on the edge of Bethlehem. In Jerusalem, the Noble Sanctuary/Temple Mount is a dominating physical presence, which more than anything else is the focus of desire, sensitivity and rage for Muslims and Jews throughout the world. Its significance is conveyed by Moshe Amirav in writing about the Camp David II summit in July 2000 where the United States brought together Jews and Palestinians for peace negotiations: 'The more it went on, the more it became the "Jerusalem summit". Towards the end it could even have been called the "Temple Mount summit" for this was perhaps the sole substantial issue that remained in dispute'.[2] It wasn't resolved and the summit failed. Six weeks later, Ariel Sharon, then the opposition leader, demonstratively visited the Temple Mount. It led to violent clashes with Arabs and set off the second intifada.

The Wailing/Western Wall – the remnant of the Second Temple – and the Temple Mount complex are explosive-filled, always waiting for a fuse to be lit by one or the other side, in either actions or words. One episode was an official paper published by the Palestinian Authority Ministry of Information in Ramallah late in 2010 saying that the Western Wall belonged to Muslims and was an integral part of al-Aksa Mosque and the Temple Mount complex. The paper was prepared by al-Mutawakel Taha, a ministry senior official, to 'refute' Jewish claims to the Western Wall. 'The Zionist occupation falsely and unjustly claims that it owns this wall, which it calls the Western Wall or Kotel', it said. It also stated that 'Muslim tolerance allowed the Jews to stand in front of it and weep'.[3]

This wasn't a new theme for Palestinians: leaders have repeatedly denied Jewish rights to the wall, insisting that the Temple of biblical times never stood in the area. But it set off new Jewish alarm and fury. Hence the Jewish Council for Public Affairs, the national umbrella for US Jewish policy groups, in one of the milder comments, said: 'We intend to share with Palestinian leaders our worry that this study could resurrect a false narrative that

Jews have no connection to the land and could reignite ugly religious battles over free worship and access'. The particular offence of the Palestinian Authority paper at this time was that it came in the midst of one of the US attempts to restart peace negotiations between Israelis and Palestinians and Washington quickly stepped in to reject the paper as 'factually incorrect, insensitive and highly provocative'.

The pressures led to an unusual Palestinian backing away: two days later, the Palestinian Authority removed the report from its official website. But author Taha said that he stood by his work.[4]

Mahmoud Abbas's Presidential Guards also lay claim to the Western Wall: a picture on its Facebook pages in August 2013 showed the Wall with the Palestinian red, green and black colours imprinted on it; plus an ultra-Orthodox Jewish man praying and next to him a youth wearing a keffiya and giving a victory sign, and the inscription, 'Palestinian youth know their rights'.

Jewish zealotry matches the other side with sundry groups demanding free access to the Mount. They reject rabbinical decrees that Jews must not set foot on the Mount because of its holiness. However, only limited access is allowed to both Jews and other non-Muslims, and Israeli police ensure that they cannot pray on the Mount; visitors must be careful about moving their lips. Jewish extremists fuel Muslim anxieties by talking about destroying the mosques on the Mount and rebuilding the biblical Temple on the site of the Noble Sanctuary.

Of course, religion is supposed to be about peace and harmony between people, and dialogue groups constantly work to bring together Jews and Muslims for joint study of each other's religious beliefs so as to engender acceptance and respect. Valuable as this is, it is repeatedly offset by the religious and political leaders on both sides who, whether out of zealous belief or for political manipulation, use religion to fan the flames of rejection and hatred.

It is not a simple divide between Jews and Muslims. Among Jews there is acute division between different streams of Judaism, and also within the Orthodox section. Among Muslims, Israel and Palestine are spared the murderous fight between Sunnis and Shi'as in Islamic countries. However, Palestinians have Hamas with its fundamentalist Islamist and anti-secular beliefs on the bedrock of denial of Israel's existence and its chilling commitment to murder Jews wholesale.[5] Christians, too, are divided: Roman Catholics, Greek Orthodox, Armenians and Copts have fragile relations in sharing control of the Church of the Holy Sepulchre in Jerusalem, Christianity's holiest church, and every now and then their priests come to blows over, literally, which inch of space belongs to whom.

## ECONOMIC

*In South Africa*, blacks and whites were intertwined in a single economy. Factories, mines, offices and farms were almost exclusively owned by whites but would have collapsed without black workers – who were generally poorly paid and treated. Whites also relied on having and exploiting black servants in their homes to clean, cook and look after the children. The Afrikaner Nationalist government did its utmost to reduce dependency on blacks, introducing laws which reserved jobs for whites only, and debarring blacks from doing them. The government efforts failed. In the process, severe damage was inflicted on the economy, creating shortages of skilled labour, inflating the wages of protected white workers, and stunting growth. These eventually proved to be factors in the ending of apartheid.

Strikes by black workers were illegal, but workers did go on strike for better pay and conditions and then for political rights. They defied tough police action, firing by employers, arbitrary restrictions on personal liberty and eviction from cities into rural poverty. Eventually, the government was forced to allow unionisation to blacks. Because of their numbers, black workers had the power to endanger the economy. By withholding their labour, or threatening to do so, they forced whites to negotiate and finally to capitulate. After years of oppression and paying heavy personal penalties for daring to strike, black workers organised themselves and defied the white rulers and thus helped to bring down apartheid.

Blacks, although most were poor, were the consumers who provided the mass market for the overwhelmingly white-owned factories and stores. For example, more than 90 percent of toothpastes and bicycles were bought by blacks. In reverse, blacks were dependent on whites for jobs and money, and they needed to buy food, clothing and furniture from white-owned stores.

The government tried to foster factories in rural areas, on the edges – the borders – of the tribal mini-states it created, the Bantustans. The scheme flopped because employers and skilled white workers refused to move away from the cities and the facilities and standard of living they had there.

Bantustans were used as reservoirs of labour, with blacks penned in them so that they could be hauled into 'white' South Africa when needed and sent back in due course, after months or years of work. An octopus-like network of labour bureaus in cities and rural areas directed supplies of black workers to white-owned factories, offices, homes in cities and towns and to farms.

*In Israel*, there is no dependency on Arab workers and no threat from them. Israeli Arabs are in no way a commanding proportion of the workforce and have no influence except in localised disputes. Until 2000, tens of thousands of Palestinians worked in Israeli construction and in agriculture, in hotels and restaurants, and as cleaners in Jewish homes; they went back and forth freely from the West Bank into Israel. Workers from Gaza faced regulation and control with long queues every day; most returned home at night, which saved Israel the cost of ensuring housing and social support. Exploitation of workers was rife.

The violence of the intifada caused dramatic change, totally the opposite of the South African Bantustans: Israel did not want Palestinian workers. It set up border checkpoints to keep them out. The numbers were reduced to a trickle. Loss of income seriously degraded Palestinian lives and reduced their economy. Israel made it a criminal offence to employ a Palestinian without permission.

Foreign workers replaced Palestinians, such as Chinese for the construction industry; Thais and Africans to harvest fruit and vegetables and for restaurants; Filipinos for fields, restaurants and hotels and as caregivers and cleaners; and Romanians as cleaners and caregivers. They, too, are often exploited with underpayment and poor conditions. Importing foreign workers has introduced its own social problems: temporary workers whose numbers can only be estimated remain in the country, working illegally; they have relationships with other foreigners or with Israelis, forming families with children. The government has toughened up on enforcement and arrests and deports as many illegal workers as it can find.

The strict exclusion of Palestinians was later eased, but far smaller numbers are allowed in. By mid-2013, about thirty-five thousand had permits to work in Israel, many in construction. The cabinet increased this by 15 percent 'despite anger at the Palestinian Authority's economic warfare against Israel'.[6] A report by the Palestinian Bureau of Statistics estimated that thirty-four thousand Palestinians were working in Israel without permits, and about twenty thousand were working in Israeli settlements.[7] Workers are at the mercy of officials, whether of the civil administration or contracted private security companies, who wield rubber stamps in deciding their fate. In this sense, Israel and apartheid South Africa are alike – as are all the countries in the world where people without power are helpless victims of bureaucratic cruelty.

Palestinians with work permits can enter Israel through eleven checkpoints. B'Tselem reports that, especially at the start of the week,

> lengthy lines that build up outside the checkpoints force laborers to arrive in the middle of the night in order to ensure their place in line, and then wait until dawn to cross into Israel and travel to their workplaces. When their turn to enter the checkpoint itself finally arrives, the laborers and their belongings are scanned with a metal detector. Then, they move on to staffed stations where security guards check their fingerprints and their papers, including their entry permits.[8]

The essential point is that there is no total dependency on Israeli Arabs or Palestinian workers, and there is no political threat from them. Israel consumes some fruit and vegetables from the West Bank but loss of this would be no more than an irritant. Conversely, Palestinians rely in great measure on buying food and goods, such as cars and gas, from Israel. The West Bank is surrounded by Israel and permission is needed for everything that goes in and out. That applies partially to the Gaza Strip, where Israel's blockade has been in place since 2005.

The Israeli and Palestinian economies are separate but linked. Israel is in no way dependent on the other, and the connection is in its favour. However, there is close cooperation at top levels between Israeli and Palestinian businessmen in monopolistic areas, such as gas and cement, which have to come from Israel.

## INTERNATIONAL

*South Africa* was the polecat of the world. Its membership of the UN General Assembly was suspended, and it was evicted from many international bodies, political, cultural and sports. No country was willing to speak up for it in international forums.

Yet the country had considerable power: first, it was a treasure chest of minerals which the world, and especially the industrialised West, had to have, and second, during the era of the Cold War the West was determined to ensure that it did not land up under Soviet control or influence. So, although publicly treated as a pariah and the target of UN and individual country sanctions, South Africa, in fact, was sustained and protected.

However, this changed as soon as the Soviet Union and its communist bloc collapsed: the worldwide abhorrence of apartheid came to the fore. Combined with domestic pressures and grave economic difficulties, the white rulers were pushed into yielding to majority rule. Whites were left to hang out to dry in a lonely and friendless world. In contrast, the African National Congress was able to occupy the moral high ground, overcoming the 'terrorist' tag affixed to it by Britain's prime minister Margaret Thatcher. It achieved recognition as a legitimate contender for power.

*Israel* has very different standing and support. It is a member of the United Nations and takes full part in debates – although, through Arab pressure, it is denied its rightful place in the Asian regional group and is barred from involvement in many UN bodies. In sports, it is also excluded from the Asian region and participates in the European zone. It even participates in the annual Eurovision song contest – and has won one of them.

The United States has been its powerful protector since the beginning. Over the years, other countries, such as Germany, France and Canada, have shielded it from attack in international forums. This is out in the open for all to see. When Israel has come under military attack, its friends – mainly the

United States but at one time, France and, earlier, Czechoslovakia – have rushed in arms to enable it to defend itself. These friends do not always like Israel's behaviour regarding the Palestinians, but they respect and support the country as a democracy and as the home of Jews after centuries of persecution and rootlessness. Christian evangelicals are uncritical supporters, especially when Israel is at its most hawkish. And the Jewish Diaspora is ever-present, sending money to help good causes and acting as potent lobbying groups to influence governments in Israel's favour.

Palestinians lack Israel's wide international acceptance. The Arab bloc is behind them, but its members are frequently at odds with each other and the help they promise does not always come through. Palestinians draw only fractional support from their Diaspora, even though it is considerable and spread around the world and certainly includes many who are wealthy: apart from organisations which operate politically to foster action against Israel, little, it seems, is given to help Palestinians at home or in exile. Palestinians also suffer from their own actions: they have undermined their international moral status by setting the fashion for hijacking passenger aircraft, leading to incalculable problems, inconvenience and cost for the entire world; they have resorted to suicide bombings and attacks on schools and buses in indiscriminate murder of civilians; they have used extremist hate-filled language in threatening to get rid of Israel's Jews.

## THIRD-PARTY INTERVENTION

*South Africa* personified the twentieth century's worldwide struggle against racism. The world was outraged to find apartheid installed as official government policy a mere three years after the defeat of Nazism with its poisonous racist ideology and the Holocaust it perpetrated. In addition, countries with their own racial discrimination – notably the United States and to lesser extents, Canada and Australia – played out their domestic consciences through condemnation of South Africa. The African National Congress, the Pan-Africanist Congress and other liberation movements turned to the world for support in international bodies to apply pressure for change, whether the United Nations or the Olympic movement, and for financial help and military training. The white government in turn worked to counter their influence and to make friends abroad.

But with all this, it was always a one-country problem: South Africans did not want outside forces stomping in. The African National Congress and the government were willing to accept help from countries such as Britain to facilitate their early face-to-face encounters; once past this stage, blacks and whites wanted to negotiate their own solutions between themselves, and this they did.

*Israel* is at the centre of unceasing international peace efforts. It cannot avoid being so: its conflict with Palestinians has far-reaching implications for the region and the wider world and is a worry for the West and Muslim states. Middle East oil is a crucial element; Israel's geographical position at the crossroads between Europe and Asia is a factor; so, too, is the potential for unrest among Palestinian refugees in Arab lands; there is also the effect of the conflict on the West's relations with the Muslim world.

Israel relies on friendly nations to help it in time of need. It sometimes speaks defiantly but is anxious lest its friends, and the United States more than anyone else, try to apply pressure to make it do something that it doesn't want to do, or make it stop doing something. It takes part in conferences, sometimes unwillingly, with Palestinians hosted by the United States. A special grouping, the Quartet – the United States, the United Nations, the European Union and Russia – has tried to mediate in the conflict. United Nations forces are stationed in the south and in the north to keep the peace. How effective they are is a good question. However, bringing in other peace-keeping forces as part of possible solutions to the conflict is regularly discussed.

## VIOLENCE

*South Africa*'s whites maintained their control over the black majority through violence. Wide-ranging laws, enacted to keep white rule in place, were mercilessly applied and gave the police and army all the power they needed. Blacks in opposition did not respond in kind. Until the second half of the twentieth century, black political movements asked, pleaded and begged the white rulers to share power and privileges with them. They were repeatedly spurned, their peaceful protests were violently put down and their oppression grew worse.

Finally, in 1961 the premier black movement, the African National Congress, which was by then proscribed by the government, turned to armed resistance. But it was guided by belief in Mahatma Gandhi's creed of nonviolence and by the strategic principle of embracing whites. So the switch to violence went with the caveat that the African National Congress would attack property, not people: it would not launch random attacks on white civilians; farmers on the borders were possible exceptions because they were viewed as being part of the military framework. The policy was adhered to for the next thirty years or more, until apartheid ended – except on only a few occasions when civilians were killed in bomb attacks.

There were no suicide bombings, no assassinations, no drive-by shootings, no roadside firing at cars and no knifings. Domestic servants did not try to poison their employers, and there was no random violence by blacks against whites for political reasons. No rockets or mortars were fired at residential areas. Only a small number of whites died. Whites did not have to fear for their lives. They were also assured that they did not have to be afraid of being swept into the sea when majority rule triumphed. Thus, when circumstances changed, notably the end of the Cold War, most white people were relatively at ease about negotiating with blacks to end white rule and apartheid. They were given further assurance during negotiations because of 'sunset' clauses which guaranteed continuation of pension rights for white government officials who were running the country. And when the new majority government led by the African National Congress took over, the idea of staging Nuremberg-type trials was rejected; instead of calling the perpetrators of apartheid-era human rights abuses to account, a Truth and Reconciliation Commission was set up with the intention of exposing abuses but also to effect conciliation between whites and blacks.

*In Israel*, Jews maintain control through violence. It has been reactive to the violence by Arabs through the twentieth century and up to the present, first against the growth of Jewish immigration to Palestine and then to the existence of the Jewish state. The Arab violence has gone together with threats to wipe out Jews and Israel. The Israeli counter-violence has built up its own momentum so that it is now not only defensive but aggressive.

Whether Palestinians had any choice but to turn to violence is a moot point. However, having done so it has had catastrophic effects in shaping Jewish outlook. Instead of pushing Jews to agree to Palestinian demands, it has hardened attitudes and strengthened determination not to yield. It has switched off many Israelis from feeling sympathy or compassion for Palestinians. Suicide bombers in indiscriminate murders on buses, in hotels, in coffee bars and on the streets drove most Israeli Jews to the Right, as did roadside killings and rockets coming out of the sky.

Israeli tough responses and retribution – including assassinations, bombings, air attacks and artillery fire, mass detention without trial, prosecution and imprisonment, destruction of houses of families of perpetrators – have, in turn, embittered Palestinians, setting off more violence and hence even tougher Israeli responses including drastically reducing contact with Palestinians. Negotiating a deal to meet the aspirations of both sides and effecting reconciliation has been made infinitely more difficult. The country has had to become an armed camp with gun-carrying guards protecting hotels, post offices, banks, supermarkets, government and office buildings, bus and train terminuses, shopping malls, restaurants and coffee bars. Security for Israeli aircraft in the air and for passengers at airports, at home and abroad, is at levels like nowhere else in the world.

For Israelis, vigilance never ends. Flying out of the country means going through a series of airport security checks; boarding a flight to return home by El Al means going through tight security, with Israeli guards and local armed police or army keeping watch, and usually going to the furthermost gate in terminals for boarding; visitors complain about intrusive security vetting. Aircraft of El Al, the national airline, are equipped with expensive anti-missile devices. While sitting on the beach at Tel Aviv or other resorts in the summer, there is the knowledge that a ceaseless watch is kept on the sea, because terrorists have used that route before to get ashore for murder. Taken together, the impact on the psyche of Israelis is immeasurable.

## PERSONAL

*In South Africa*, whites and blacks rubbed shoulders all the time. Although it was a master and servant relationship, there was contact, whether it was the black nanny caring for white children or the waiter serving tea or the office messenger bringing the mail or the factory worker with the skilled white foreman. The existence of the mixed-race coloured community was testimony to sexual relations and marriage when these had been allowed, and the intercourse continued during apartheid. Whites and blacks of like mind cooperated at the political level – not in great numbers but significant enough for the Afrikaner Nationalists to try to halt it. Despite the barriers to normal contact set up by apartheid, friendships developed among elites. When the basic circumstances changed, there were blacks and whites of stature who had overcome difficulties to sustain friendship and contact over the years; there was trust between them, and they were able to play important roles in the negotiations for change. When it came to sitting down together to talk, whites and blacks of whatever background and political outlook invariably found that they enjoyed an easy familiarity because of love of their country, shared language and, often, religion.

This helped to overcome the apartheid policy, contrived and artificial, to divide South Africa into a large white area and ten or so black tribal ministates. Instead, the sense of South Africanness always existed – it was fundamental to black aspirations – and eventually helped to sweep aside the divisions for most people.

*In Israel*, the 1948 war and its aftermath all but effaced the kinds of personal relations and dialogues that existed in the mandate years. The occupation, the continuing failure to achieve peace and the second intifada in 2000 deepened clefts in relations. The fear factor is significant, brought down to the elementary level where anyone who looks like an Arab entering a bus in Israel during the intifada was watched with suspicion. That continues in many aspects of everyday life today.

In physical terms, Israelis are debarred from entering Palestinian towns and other areas without permission from Israeli authorities, and Palestinians are severely restricted from entering Israel. It is difficult to meet, far more so than under apartheid. Yet links remain and many people work together for peace and human rights and to improve daily existence – even though they must contend with widespread Palestinian opposition to 'normalisation', which means refusal to meet or talk to Israelis, and also to support boycotts at home and abroad of everything Israeli. This parallels but goes way beyond the growth of Black Consciousness in apartheid South Africa with rejection of contact, and especially political cooperation, with whites.

The mass of Jews and Palestinians do not have contact. They are ignorant of each other's living and thinking and that opens the door to prejudice and rejection. Nor is it all that much better between Jews and Israeli Arabs: there is some contact in daily existence, but it is limited and mutual suspicions have grown.

The security barrier/fence/wall and checkpoints created because of the violence exceeds anything under apartheid. The barrier is immoral, exploitative and damaging to the lives of hundreds of thousands of Palestinians, and the wall part of it is an ugly sight, disfiguring the landscape as a statement of oppression. The original purpose of the barrier, which remains relevant, was to protect against would-be suicide bombers (other barriers for the same and other purposes are in the north, east and south of the country).

Critics repeatedly condemn Israel as though it is the only country which has erected barriers. However, it's an international phenomenon. The *Guardian* (London) reports that separation barriers have been going up 'at a rate perhaps unequalled in history' – at least 9,650 kilometres in the last decade alone.[9] A website, 'A world of barriers', lists thirty-one barriers for anti-immigration, anti-terrorist or anti-smuggling purposes. They range from the 20 kilometres around Sharm el-Sheikh in Egypt to the 3,268-kilometre barbed-wire fence which India is building on its border with Bangladesh. According to the *Guardian*, 'Though it is not fully completed, the twists and turns of the metal curtain already separate families and communities, with those who live on the border often finding their homes in one country and their paddy fields in the other. Watch towers, floodlights and armed border guards dot the landscape'.

Botswana and Zimbabwe have a barrier; so do South Africa and Mozambique; also inside Belfast in Northern Ireland between Roman Catholics and Protestants; Saudi Arabia is protected against Yemen; there are barriers between Iran and Pakistan, the United Arab Emirates and Oman, the United States and Mexico, China and North Korea, South Korea and North Korea, Iran and Pakistan, and between Greeks and Turks in Cyprus. There is also the little-mentioned 2,700 kilometres long, 1–3 metre high earthen wall backed by a trench and surrounded by bunkers, fences and landmines to separate the part of Western Sahara controlled by Morocco from the eastern Free Zone controlled by Polasario; all along this barrier are forts, airfields, artillery emplacements and radar stations.[10]

None of this prevents wrong or malicious reporting about Israel's barrier. For example, Asim Rafiqui, described as a US-based photographer and blogger on the Mondoweiss website, goes over the top with 'one of the greatest physical structures of political, cultural, historical and social segregation and negation concocted in modern history'.[11] The *Guardian* perpetrates its own error in describing Israel's barrier as '[m]ade of concrete, steel, razorwire'. Well, yes and no – concrete forms about 5 percent of it.

The claim by critics that Israeli security control is 'even worse' than apartheid is thoroughly misleading. The two are as different as apples and oranges. Resistance to apartheid in South Africa, as noted, never used suicide bombers or drive-by shootings, and there was only a tiny number of wholesale terror attacks against whites. Hence there was never any call for the range of defensive responses that Israel resorts to. The occupation is cruel and despotic, and there is no need for the sake of propaganda to use untrue comparisons to make it seem even worse. Yet why is this done, and on such an immense scale?

## CONCLUSIONS

Looking at Israel inside the Green Line (chapter 3) alongside apartheid South Africa (chapter 5) shows two radically different countries. Yes, Israel's Arab minority does suffer discrimination, but their lot is not remotely comparable with blacks under apartheid. To claim they are the same is to stretch, bend, twist and contort truth. The West Bank (chapter 4) is more complex. Yes, it is a tyranny whose existence casts a pall over the image of the State of Israel. That it is colonialism is obvious and hence an international offence: the settlers come from a mother country and serve its interests; they deny civil rights to the local people and exploit the natural resources. But to claim that this is the same racist rule as apartheid South Africa is without substance or truth.

Intentionality is the key test. In South Africa, the white rulers deliberately set about forcing segregation and discrimination into every aspect of life; that was their intention from the start, with the aim of securing power and privilege for the white minority.

That is not Israel on the West Bank. There is no ideological aim to discriminate against Palestinians. Occupation of as much of the land as possible is the overarching principle and everything flows from it. The checkpoints, detentions, separate roads, security barrier, economic and water exploitation and the rest are not ideological goals; they are the consequences of occupation and resistance to it. End the occupation, and they will end.

The occupation has taken on a life of its own because it has become submerged in the messianic mission to control much of the West Bank.

Perhaps this brings Israelis closer to South Africa's white Afrikaners, with some in each group subscribing to the Chosen People belief, the Jews a people whose history stretches back four thousand years, and Afrikaners who emerged as a people during the nineteenth century. Also common to them is the total commitment to survival (although the long-term future of the Afrikaners under black majority rule is not certain). Both, at least the highly religious among them, believe in the literal interpretation of the Bible. And there are many Israeli Jews who are as racist in their view of Arabs as Afrikaners were (and some still are) of blacks.

That is as far as it goes. With all the oppression and harsh consequences of the occupation, it is nothing like the meticulously organised and institutionalised racism of apartheid South Africa. The unscrupulous liars among the settlers who draw a religious cloak over immoral behaviour are exactly that.

It is also not correct, as critics claim, that Israel's treatment of Palestinians on the West Bank is racism. How can it be? The Palestinians are family of the Palestinians who live in Israel and who are Israeli citizens with the rights of citizens. They are from the same stock.

Gideon Shimoni, South African born and emeritus professor at the Hebrew University, Jerusalem, is an authority on Zionism and on Jews in apartheid South Africa. He dismisses the Israel apartheid analogy as 'malicious slander'. However, he says, comparison with South Africa could be relevant in one respect – the Afrikaner Nationalists' ruthless enforcement of their tribal Bantustan policy to ensure white supremacy. The analogy is with the Jewish national-religious right wing, who want to maintain West Bank occupation as a permanent annexation, whether de facto or de jure, while denying the Israeli vote to its Palestinian residents. The South African experience is a warning to Israel because it 'proved to be not only morally reprehensible but also realistically untenable'.[12]

Apart from this, some try to apply the apartheid label to the theft of West Bank land, because Jews are the perpetrators and Palestinians the victims. Doing that misses the point and confuses the issue. Instead, it's a bunch of Jewish crooks driven by religious zealotry who are abusing the law. They enjoy influence inside government, and the agents of law drag their feet in doing their job. But none of this is the implementation of formal government racism policy. It is renegade behaviour. One sign of this is in the frequent condemnatory views and decisions of the courts in upholding the law. Another is that government officials and agencies feel obliged to behave in surreptitious and underhand ways: they know full well that they are acting illegally and contrary to the rule of law.

The West Bank is not apartheid, and certainly not at this stage when a political process is still underway, however haltingly, and the future remains unresolved. It is not apartheid while a two-state solution with a Palestinian state on the West Bank remains the official stance of Israel, Palestine and much of the international community, and while so many in civil society believe in it and press for it.

*If* settlement expansion continues, *if* no Palestinian state comes into being, *if* Israel annexes the West Bank, *if* Israel denies rights to Palestinians and *if* it enforces rigid separation and discrimination, then it will be time to talk about apartheid. Until then, it is not apartheid and use of the label is inappropriate and wrong. It is misleading and creates confusion because it distracts attention from the occupation.

## A PERSONAL NOTE

I was treated for stomach cancer at one of Israel's leading hospitals, Hadassah Mt Scopus in Jerusalem. The surgeon (he was the head surgeon) was Jewish, the anaesthetist was Arab. The doctors and nurses who cared for me were Jews and Arabs. During four and a half weeks as a patient, I watched Arab and Jewish patients get the same devoted treatment. A year or so later, the head surgeon retired; he was replaced by a doctor who is an Arab.[13] Since then, I've been in hospital clinics and emergency rooms. Everything is the same for everyone.

Israel is like apartheid South Africa? Ridiculous.

## Chapter Eight

# The Critics (1)

*Israel is relentlessly criticised. Even its right to exist is questioned. However, deconstructing the criticisms reveals that, overwhelmingly, they are based on falsehoods, distortions, prejudice or lack of knowledge. They often emanate from people with tendentious motives who hate and reject Israel as the Jewish state.*

\* \* \*

The point must be made and made again: Israel, despite awesome achievements, is not a perfect society. As with any other country, it has problems; like any country, it deals well with some, badly with others. Its record of handling an Arab minority population is both positive and negative. The country's two most acute problems are: first, external – rejection by the Arab world; and second, self-inflicted – its military occupation of the West Bank and maintaining the oppression of Palestinians, plus the siege of the Gaza Strip. Anyone who wants to criticise the country has abundant material available: Israelis, both Jews and Arabs, are open and unstinting in exposing Israeli errors and injustice. Day after day Israeli media are full of detail, as are foreign newspapers, television and radio. But there is a world of difference between condemnation and calumny, between angry, honest protest and malevolent, destructive attack.

For a country so small in size and population, Israel receives exceptional attention. In the media, for example, the BBC's onsite news coverage during 2010 of Egypt, Libya and Tunisia combined and doubled was still less than what was given to Israel; the BBC's Middle East editor devoted 95 percent of his coverage of those four countries to Israel. In Britain's *Guardian* and *Daily Telegraph* newspapers – at different ends of the political spectrum –

the coverage of Egypt, Libya and Tunisia doubled and tripled still amounted to less than what was written about Israel. The *Independent*, the *Times* and the *Financial Times* showed the same interest. The *Guardian* published sixteen editorials about Israel that year and not one on the other three countries. [1] Apart from anything else, the figures show how the media, as much as intelligence agencies and the ruling dictators themselves, were caught unawares by the outbreak early in 2011 of the Arab Spring in Egypt, Libya, Tunisia, Syria and elsewhere.

People who care about their world have their favourite causes, whether protection of cats or human rights abuses in one country or another. But Israel is unique in the passions it arouses and in the venom with which it is assailed by so many different people in so many parts of the world. It's not only a one-issue cause for many, but any sense of proportionality is swept away so that truly horrendous deeds elsewhere are ignored.

Unlike any other country, Israel is not merely criticised for mistakes and wrongdoings, whether real or alleged, but its very existence as a state is questioned. That comes from both the Left and Right in the West and parts of Africa, chiefly from non-Jews but also from Jews apparently embarrassed about being Jews and hence linked with Israel, and from the Arab world. The right wing is driven by hatred of Jews. The left is more complex, with a combination of angry disappointment that Israel has failed to carry through on its founding socialist dreams and those still engrossed with Marxist hostility towards nationalism, plus anti-Semitism, whether open or hidden. The critics, both at home and abroad, can be roughly divided into five groups:

First, those who cannot bear the fact of Israel's existence. They want it dead and gone. Some frankly admit to this. Others do not: it reeks too much of repellent anti-Semitism for them to own up to it. Some Christians carry within them a centuries-old rejection of Jews as alleged Christ-killers.

Criticisms from this group must be treated with great caution. They are highly motivated propagandists with a goal. Their accusations might have a basis of fact, and indeed often do because of Israeli abusive actions. But that is not enough for them, and they inflate and exaggerate, taking the truth and distorting and bending it, all to present Israel in the ugliest possible light. They selectively use quotes which suit their purpose, omitting to mention that other quotes balance out or cancel what they claim to be official policies. Their true beliefs and aims are easily brought to the surface through a simple test: asking them about '1948' and/or the 'Palestinian demand for the return of refugees'. These are code words – disguises – for denying the legitimacy of Israel's founding and existence. They do not want a two-state future with Israel and Palestine living side by side in peace.

Second are those who do not deny Israel's existence but are affronted and angry about aspects of its behaviour, in particular the abuse of human rights in its occupation of the West Bank and siege of the Gaza Strip. Their opinions are rational and intelligent and are formed by newspaper reports and what they see and hear on television and radio.

Third are others – probably the majority of people – who also react to reports of Israel's abuse of human rights but follow their heart; they are well meaning and are prone to being caught up by propaganda. An Arab proverb can apply to some of them: 'Allah protect us from the error of the intelligent'.

Fourth are Jews, from both Israel and the Diaspora. Their criticisms are often well founded, but they seem to be driven by the need to show that they are more condemnatory than any non-Jew. In doing so, some lose their balance: they overstate the ills and problems and end up presenting a monster-like Israel which is not related to reality.

The fifth group comprises South Africans, and especially the black majority, who emerged from apartheid in 1994 and have a high sensitivity to racism and oppression. Their influence stretches far beyond the borders of their country. The few South African journalists and politicians who visit Israel/Palestine – and especially those who came during the height of the violence and harshness of the second intifada at the start of the 2000s – often relate their past experience to what they see, and are told, about the occupation and all that goes with it in regard to armed soldiers and police, checkpoints, mass arrests, detentions without trial and other denial of rights. They contrast the debased lot of Palestinians with the privileges and separate lifestyles of the Jewish settlers.[2]

To them, the settler Lords of the Land look much like the white masters of the apartheid era. Hence the reaction of Gaye Davis, a South African journalist: 'Confining people to their own territory, controlling their access to yours through permits and checkpoints is painfully familiar to a South African and sounds as much of a political dead end as the Bantustans of South Africa'.[3] Never mind that the analogy is false because the aim of an independent state of Palestine is in no way comparable with apartheid's Bantustan tribal mini-states and that Israel and Palestine-to-be are separated by border controls; it's her feeling and emotion which are relevant and telling.

The analogies are correct in that Palestinians are oppressed and blacks were oppressed. But oppression does not automatically or necessarily mean apartheid, and to attempt to make the two the same is invalid. Too many elements are different. But at first sight, and superficially, the comparison can be made – and it is made, and distorted, by people who are malevolent towards Israel and who hate the existence of the Jewish state. They play to the emotional feelings of black South Africans to build political campaigns against Israel.

Other South African media visitors have shown a deeper understanding of the complexities. Such as Sibusiso Ngwala, who returned home from a visit and wrote in human terms in the *Sunday Times*, South Africa's largest-circulation newspaper, about the need for a two-state solution: 'Such an agreement will mean the children of Sderot and Gaza could roam the streets without the fear of a rocket landing on their heads or an air strike robbing them of their future'.[4]

Apart from this, there are obvious reasons for the wider world's intense interest in Israel and the conflict with Palestinians and the Arab region. The monotheistic religions, Judaism, Christianity and Islam, have roots there and especially in Jerusalem. Jewish and Arab lobbies compete for attention and support from governments, peoples and media. Arab states continue to reject Israel's existence as a non-Muslim state in the region – adding to their feelings of humiliation at being bested in a succession of wars by the Jews, over whom they lorded for centuries – and with such command of the world's oil, their resentments can translate into dangerous threats and instability. News is accessible. Reporting out of Israel and the West Bank is easy: Israel's high degree of press freedom and its open society give journalists space and freedom with the bonus of comfortable and safe living conditions.

The additional critical factor at work, anti-Semitism, is defined by historian Milton Shain as 'unprovoked and irrational hostility towards Jews'.[5] Some Jews sometimes exaggerate the extent of it and use it to whip up popular support by playing to Jewish fears; at the same time, the continuing existence of this age-old plague is worrying. In the United States, a 2013 poll showed that 12 percent of people harboured deeply anti-Semitic attitudes, according to the Anti-Defamation League.[6] That was better than the 15 percent in 2011 and 17 percent in 2002. In world terms the 686 incidents of anti-Semitic violence and vandalism recorded in 2012 (obviously, many instances are doubtless not recorded) might not seem so serious. But, in fact, it reversed two years of decline with an increase of 30 percent over the previous year. There were worrying signs in the rate in France jumping by 60 percent and in opinion polls showing that 63 percent of Hungarians held anti-Semitic views (up from 47 percent in 2009) and that an average of 30 percent of people held anti-Semitic views in ten European countries.[7] A study by the EU Fundamental Rights Agency covering 2012–2013 reported that 20 percent of Jewish respondents in nine European Union states said they had experienced an anti-Semitic incident during the past twelve months; 4 percent spoke of physical attack or threats of violence and 64 percent of these respondents said they had not told the authorities because they considered doing so ineffective. Asked to define an anti-Semite, 34 percent of all respondents indicated that it referred to a 'non-Jewish person if he or she criticizes Israel'.[8]

Shain puts it well, noting that while enmity towards Zionism and the Jewish state is rooted in the Israeli-Arab conflict,

It would be simplistic to equate hostility towards Israel with anti-Semitism. The Arab-Israeli struggle is a political conflict over real issues and such clashes are invariably characterised by negative stereotyping of, and bitterness towards, the 'enemy'. However, a careful analysis of anti-Zionist rhetoric (including that in the West) reveals that much although not all of the propaganda against Israel has employed classic anti-Jewish motifs. A special hatred seems to go beyond the bounds of normal political conflict. Jews or Zionists have become, at least for some critics, diabolically evil. The Muslim/Arab world in particular has employed motifs and language long associated with modern antisemitism. This is especially the case among Islamists (Muslim fundamentalists).[9]

\* \* \*

The first use of the 'apartheid' tag appears to have been in the United Nations General Assembly on 9 December 1971, four years after Israel's victory in the Six-Day War. A debate telling Israel to withdraw from all occupied Arab territory (Israel insisted there must first be agreement on 'secure and recognised borders'), according to the *New York Times*, 'took on a vitriolic tone when the Soviet Union accused Israel of pursuing "a racist policy of apartheid against the Palestinian people"'.[10] Apartheid in South Africa was then in full flow and the country was abjured by the world. So the accusation by the Soviet's Yarov A. Malik was a calculated insult. Since then, of course, the Soviet Union has fallen and so has apartheid South Africa, but the accusation has become standard fare for Israel's enemies.

The 'Zionism is racism' charge was the mainstay of attack during the next few years, culminating in the notorious UN General Assembly resolution in November 1975 pushed by the Soviet Union and Cuba. Although the General Assembly rescinded it sixteen years later, it was given new life in the run-up to the UN World Conference Against Racism, Racial Discrimination, Xenophobia and Related Intolerance scheduled for Durban, South Africa, in 2001. At the time, the violence and counter-violence of the second intifada was roiling emotions in the Middle East and the wider world. The United Nations had held two earlier conferences against racism, in 1978 and 1983, aimed at getting rid of South Africa's apartheid. Durban was to be a celebration of the coming of democracy in South Africa seven years earlier and was intended to develop the worldwide struggle against racism.

The conference was preceded by regional meetings, with each continent drawing up recommendations. Tehran was the meeting place for Asia. The Iranian government did not bother with the nicety that this was a United Nations event: it did not recognise Israel and refused to allow the Jewish state to send a delegation. Nor did it allow the Kurds or anyone from the Baha'i faith. Under pressure, it gave visas to Jewish NGOs, but issued them so late that no one could get there. The world kept silent. The conference adopted a Declaration and Plan of Action, much of it written in advance, which condemned Israel for 'its ethnic cleansing of the Arab population of historic Palestine', described Israel as 'a new kind of apartheid, a crime against humanity' and said that Zionism was 'based on racial superiority'.

The regional recommendations went for coordination to a conference in Geneva. The UN's High Commissioner for Human Rights, Mary Robinson, a former president of Ireland, promised that the outrageous Tehran words would be weeded out. They weren't. Arab and Muslim states insisted they remain and added still more: that Holocaust be in the plural to include what Israel was, allegedly, doing to Palestinians. All the offending words were included in the draft for Durban – set between brackets to signify 'tentative, proposed but not agreed'. At the same time, African states targeted slavery – condemning the trans-Atlantic trade in people but not the Arab role – and demanding an apology, which meant reparations, from the West and the United States in particular. To which the (black) US secretary of state Colin Powell said words to the effect, 'Will I pay or be paid?' Powell objected to the fact that Israel was the only country singled out by name, noting that the Israel-Arab conflict was political, not racial, so why was this on the agenda? Alarmed that the conference was going to run out of control, Powell stayed away and sent a low-level delegation; Israel's delegation was led by a Foreign Ministry senior official instead of the deputy foreign minister.

The Durban Forum opened with a massive gathering of seven thousand people from three thousand NGOs from around the world. It rapidly became a wild assault on Israel, taking in, too, the United States, the West, colonialism and globalisation. The driving force was an unlikely alliance of Palestinian NGOs, Arab and Muslim activists, Leftists and Cubans. Some Jewish anti-Israel groups, from the Left and from the Right (in the form of Neturei Karta), aided and abetted them. The tone at the opening ceremony was set by large banners: 'Stop the massacre of the Palestinians' and 'Racism = Israeli rule'. Street marchers chanting anti-US and anti-Israel slogans carried posters: 'Israel is an apartheid state'.

Dissenters were shouted down, abused and pushed out. Jewish participants felt fear for their physical safety. The Arab Lawyers' Union distributed pamphlets depicting hook-nosed Jews, blood dripping from their fangs, shown as Nazis spearing Arab children. A Durban Muslim, Yousef Deedat, printed and distributed Hitler flyers. Copies of the nineteenth-century tsarist police forgery Protocols of Zion were on sale. The Jewish Caucus of NGOs proposed a change in a section on anti-Semitism to denounce attacks on synagogues and Jews anywhere in the world motivated by anti-Zionism spilling over into anti-Semitic acts and violence. No less than the World Council of Churches, speaking for the Ecumenical Caucus and acting at the request of Palestinian NGOs, opposed it – seemingly a resurfacing of ancient Christian rejection and hostility towards Jews.

The concluding Declaration and Plan of Action contained all the original vitriolic language against Israel. It also accused Israel of 'genocide' against Palestinians. It called for the dismantling of all Israeli settlements and bringing Israelis before an international war crimes tribunal. The Plan of Action sought to revive the worldwide coalition that had worked against South African apartheid through the launch of 'an international anti-Israeli Apartheid movement' that would 'impose a policy of complete and total isolation of Israel'.[11]

The NGO resolutions were handed to the conference of world's governments which began immediately afterwards.[12] Robinson could not live with the extremism and the hatred directed at Israel. She refused to let the resolutions and Israel attacks go to the conference – the only time in UN history that NGO recommendations have been so fully rejected. But Arab and Muslim states and the countries of the Non-Aligned Movement pressed for the inclusion of the same sort of condemnations singling out only Israel. The United States walked out, followed by Israel. The European Union and other countries were on the verge of going. South Africa, panicked as its celebratory conference went sliding down the drain, worked with Belgium for a solution. The final texts contained no attacks on Israel or Zionism. The only references were to 'the plight of Palestinian people under foreign occupation' and the recognition of the Palestinian right to an independent state. With the NGO and government conferences concentrating on Israel/Palestine, the cries for help by many groups which suffer discrimination were ignored or had little attention: Dalits in India, Kurds, slaves, Roma in Europe, and indigenous groups around the world.

The Durban NGO Forum was so much a hatefest against Israel and Jews that it proved counterproductive. The forum discredited itself. Its actions and resolutions were so unbalanced and filled with venom that they could not be put before the conference of governments. Despite this, the people behind the forum might have been fuelled by their own excesses and could perhaps have launched punitive action against Israel. But it did not happen. Three days after the end of Durban, Muslim terrorists flew aircraft into the Twin Towers in New York and the Pentagon in Washington, DC, killing three thousand Americans. September 11 overtook everything. Only four years later did Palestinian NGOs pick up again on the Israel equals apartheid theme.

Meanwhile, the South African government realised how much damage the NGO Forum had done to the country and to the cause of fighting racism. Aziz Pahad, then deputy minister of foreign affairs, asked the Zionist Federation to invite him to its annual conference in Johannesburg. In a remarkably frank speech, he condemned the 'disgraceful events' at the Durban NGO meeting, 'on the fringes' of the UN meeting, as he put it.

I wish to make it unequivocally clear that the South African Government recognises that part of that component was hijacked and used by some with an anti-Israeli agenda to turn it into an anti-Semitic event. Recognition of this, however, was precisely the reason for the refusal of the world's governments . . . to accept the final statement of NGO proceedings into the final document of the Conference. Additionally, the South African Government as Chair, worked hard to ensure an acceptable and honourable outcome of the final document which avoided singling out Israel for exclusive criticism in regard to the current crisis in the Middle East. [13]

For good measure, Pahad affirmed South Africa's longstanding policy of support for a Palestinian state and support for Israel's right to exist within defined borders and in peace and security with its neighbours. He decried Israel's use of 'military might' against a people struggling for freedom and said, too, that Palestinians would not achieve liberation through 'brutal and horrendous acts of terrorism committed against the citizens of Israel in their streets, suburbs and cities'.

With those views and such openness, South Africa could and should have been a powerful bridge-builder between Israel and Palestinians. It tried but unfortunately was unintelligent and insensitive and was dismissed by Israel as not being serious. Outside the government, in civil society, South Africa went on to become a critical player in mounting the apartheid accusation against Israel: it has been the fount from which Arabs, Muslims and Leftists in the world draw their inspiration and strategy. Also, many of the key writers and speakers against Israel are South Africans, who claim moral strength and special understanding. That claim, however, is not always justified by their knowledge. Whether because of mental laziness or inbuilt prejudices they do not explore and try to understand. The government formally supports both Israel and Palestine but in practice has become increasingly hostile towards Israel. Of course, none of this has happened in a vacuum: since the 2001 Durban conference Israel has stoked up opposition to itself in South Africa and in the world through its vast expansion of settlements on the West Bank, its continued occupation of the West Bank and its responses to violence from Lebanon and the Gaza Strip.

\* \* \*

*Criticisms pour out against Israel. This is a selection, and an examination of their validity . . .*

Jimmy Carter was a liberal and well-intentioned US president but failed to secure reelection. One singular success was in fathering a peace accord between Israel and Egypt which effectively ended the threat of another concerted Arab attack. Carter went on to work determinedly to make the world a better place, achieving a Nobel Peace Prize. Building on his Christian beliefs, he pursued Middle East peace and gave expression to it in his 2006 book, *Palestine: Peace Not Apartheid.*

Using the word 'apartheid' in the title linked Israel's behaviour towards Palestinians with the racism of apartheid South Africa. Yet it is not a major theme in the book, and the word occurs only twice in the index and three times in the text – when Carter uses it to explain that he doesn't mean to equate Israel with South Africa's racism but means the acquisition of land.

So if he didn't mean 'apartheid', why did he use that emotive word? It was certainly an advertising winner and, together with the power of his name, drove the book into the best-seller lists. Carter explained that he chose the title to be 'provocative' because he wanted to publicise the 'horrible treatment' of Palestinians which was not known in the United States.[14] He insisted that using 'apartheid' to describe Israel's West Bank policies 'should give no aid or comfort to any of those who have attempted to equate racism with Zionism'. Which drew the comment from *New York Times* writer Roger Cohen: 'Nice try, Jimmy. Trying to take race out of the word "apartheid" is as far-fetched as trying to take Jew out of the word "Zionism". It doesn't work'. But Carter succeeded in provoking: while many applauded him, an angry backlash saw rejection by former supporters and the resignation of board members from his Carter Center in Atlanta, Georgia.

The thrust of the book is its repeated attack on Israel, and particularly its occupation of the West Bank. Nothing wrong with that, except Carter simplistically presents sixty years of conflict as though one event has not led to another, with many culprits. Carter nags away, page after page, that Israel is to blame for everything wrong in the Middle East and for the lack of progress towards peace. In addition, the book contains factual errors, some as elementary as saying that Israel launched a pre-emptive strike against Jordan in 1967 (it was the other way round). Its chronology of crucial historical events, astonishingly, does not list Zionism or Theodor Herzl.

Perhaps the most dubious material (the accuracy of which was additionally disputed by former aides) concerns Carter's conversations with Arab leaders. He reports them with little challenge or comment: the sweet words of Syria's late president Hafez al-Assad about his desire for peace are wildly at variance with the way he actually behaved. Carter quotes the late Yasser Arafat as telling him: 'The PLO has never advocated the annihilation of Israel'. That was in 1990. He does not say whether he asked Arafat to justify that statement in light of the Palestinian National Covenant of 1964 enshrining annihilation as the goal.

Although apartheid does not feature largely in the book, Carter addressed it strongly when he went on a publicity tour, saying that on the West Bank, 'apartheid exists in its more despicable forms, that Palestinians are deprived of basic human rights'.[15]

Yet, amidst the controversy, Carter preaches peace in the book and presents basic principles to do with a two-state solution. His message was powerful, and he could have played a mediating role in the cause of peace. For the sake of a huckstering and misleading title, and because of sloppy research and confused thinking and writing, he lost all chance of making an input. Not only was it a lost opportunity, but his name linked with the word 'apartheid' is a primary weapon used in attacks on Israel.

Carter stepped in again to criticise Israel after the parents of Rachel Corrie lost the civil action they brought against Israel for the 2003 death of their daughter in Gaza. Rachel Corrie, an American pro-Palestinian activist, was killed while trying to halt a bulldozer. Judge Oded Gershon ruled that the State of Israel was not responsible for her death. To which Carter said, 'The killing of an American peace activist is unacceptable'. He hoped that 'justice is done for the Corrie family'.[16]

The bulldozer driver testified that he had not seen Rachel Corrie in front of the machine. He was either telling the truth or lying. The judge accepted that he was telling the truth and dismissed the case. For Carter to attack the ruling meant that he believed the driver was lying and/or that the judge was crooked. He produced no evidence. That's questionable behaviour by a former president of a great democracy grounded on law.

\* \* \*

The United Nations Human Rights Council is a prime example of perverted attacks on Israel. It's the UN body with the job of promoting and protecting international human rights, but, as Irwin Cotler, Canada's former minister of justice and attorney general, has said, 'it has become a human rights violator'.[17] The council was created in 2006 to take over from its discredited predecessor, the UN Human Rights Commission, but has maintained the same biases – which means it latches onto Israel above all others as a human rights abuser. From 2006 to 2010 it adopted forty condemnations of countries, of which thirty-three focused on Israel, more than 80 percent of the total. Cotler comments that 'while the council has selectively singled out one member state, it continues to grant the major violators [in the world] exculpatory immunity'. Israel is also the only country with its own permanent agenda item: number 7 speaks of 'Israeli human rights violations in the occupied Palestinian territories'; every other country is lumped into agenda item number 8, which speaks about 'human rights violations in the rest of the world'.

The *Mavi Marmara* deaths in the 31 May 2010 Turkish-led flotilla attempt to breach Israel's blockade of the Gaza Strip drew the council's condemnation, and it called for an international commission of inquiry. 'Surely the order should have been the reverse', commented Asher Susser, a noted Israeli academic, 'an inquiry first and condemnation later, if and when justified by the investigation'. He noted there was much international outrage about the *Mavi Marmara*: Ban Ki-moon, the UN secretary-general, condemned the violence and called on Israel to give a full explanation.

> Oddly enough no similar international outrage and demand for explanations was recently evident in reference to other even more tragic events: not when Iran again hanged political dissidents, bringing the total to nearly 300 since early 2009; nor when the North Koreans sunk a South Korean ship killing 36 seamen; nor when attacks on two Ahmadi mosques in Lahore killed at least 93 worshipers. International outrage is awfully selective. [18]

The United States long refused to take part in the forty-seven-nation council; it finally joined in 2009 but is drowned by the majority votes of member countries notorious for human rights abuses such as Bangladesh, Qatar, China, Saudi Arabia, Senegal, Uganda and Cuba. The Asians and Africans who dominate the council block criticisms of countries like Zimbabwe and Sudan or support, as they have done, a proposal by Muslim countries to protect religion from criticism. Even Libya has been a member – elected late in 2010 despite Muammar Gaddafi's known record as an international killer, until his murderous excesses at home finally brought suspension by the UN General Assembly in March 2011.

The Human Rights Council's obsession with Israel led to the debacle involving Judge Richard Goldstone and his investigation into Israel's onslaught on the Gaza Strip in 2008–2009. The attack, from 27 December to 18 January, caused international outrage. The deaths and maimings seen on television and in newspapers of more than 1,200, of whom Hamas later acknowledged 600 to 800 were its own fighters, drove innumerable people in many parts of the world into the streets to protest. But there was a background: the ruling Hamas rejected Israel's existence and refused to forswear violence. Rockets and mortars from Gaza had first struck Israel on 16 April 2001 followed by more than 6,300; the count that year was more than 3,000. A million people lived under threat of a terror attack, rushing to air raid shelters when sirens gave them less than a minute's warning of a missile. No help or protests came from abroad, but the Israeli public demanded government action.

Israel was the target of extreme condemnation with accusations of 'genocide', 'Holocaust' and 'Warsaw Ghetto'. An official of UNRWA, the UN's relief agency for Palestinians, went on television with a passionate call to end the Israeli attack. But he did not say a word about what had led to it and spoke as though the Israeli onslaught came out of nowhere, without reason or cause. Nor did he refer to Hamas's firing of missiles from the heart of civilian areas.

None of these troubling questions seem to have bothered the Organisation of the Islamic Conference (OIC) or the UN Human Rights Council. On 3

January, OIC asked the council to send a fact-finding mission to Gaza, and on 12 January the council resolved to do that, 'to investigate all violations of international human rights' by Israel. The wording made it an open and shut case against Israel, finding it guilty without any investigation. Mary Robinson, former UN high commissioner for human rights, was asked to head an inquiry; she refused, saying that the resolution was 'one-sided' and 'guided not by human rights but by politics'.

Goldstone was approached: South African born, he had a distinguished record in human rights during and after the apartheid era and then worked internationally; he was also active in Zionist bodies. At first he, too, said the resolution was 'biased'. The council's chairman agreed to broaden the terms of reference to allow for investigation of 'all violations of international human rights law and international humanitarian law that might have been committed at any time'. The change was never formally adopted by the council, so, whatever the chairman said, the mandate remained one-sided against Israel. But it was enough for Goldstone to agree to lead the inquiry – even though the Human Rights Council had such a dreadful, unbalanced record against Israel that its motives and actions had to be suspect. Because of these factors, and despite Goldstone's pleas, Israel refused to have anything to do with the inquiry.

Goldstone bought himself even more trouble by retaining Christine Chinkin as one of the three other commissioners: a professor of international law at the London School of Economics, she had already made her views known in January by co-signing a letter published in the *Sunday Times* (London) describing Israel's attack as 'an act of aggression'. Not only was her status as an unbiased investigator put into question but so, too, was Goldstone's judgment in leaving her in place.

Goldstone could not but know that he was accepting a poisoned chalice. Yet he went ahead. On 15 September his commission issued a 574-page report: it damned Israel for war crimes, for deliberately killing civilians, and criticised Hamas in more general terms. Israel was the target and Goldstone served it up.[19] Everyone who hated Israel now loved Goldstone. Everyone who wanted an excuse to condemn Israel for its occupation of the West Bank, or for its right-wing government, or for its discrimination against its Arab minority, or for simply existing, suddenly had a big stick ready to hand – and, wonderfully, provided by a Jew who put all his Jewish and Zionist and judicial and South African credentials behind the report. His name gave it infinitely more power than any of the usual international reports assailing Israel. His accusations became imprinted on the world's consciousness. The findings left many Israelis and friends of Israel who admired and trusted Goldstone shaken and ashamed. The damage inflicted on the country's image and standing was beyond calculation, and this remained so even though the report's defects and poor quality loomed larger the more the details were examined.[20]

Israel and vast numbers of Jews and others throughout the world condemned Goldstone – some hysterically and abusively, with phrases like 'this Jewish self-hater' and 'traitor'. The United States rejected the report, its ambassador at the United Nations speaking of 'very serious concerns about many of the recommendations'. However, Goldstone stood by the report amid widespread admiration and television and media interviews. Meanwhile, the Israeli government rejected calls to set up its own judicial inquiry to investigate why the Israel Defense Forces had killed so many Gazans and had inflicted so much damage for so long, as well as such worrying questions as allegations about the killing of fleeing civilians carrying white flags and the use of white phosphorus.[21] The government mulishly refused to heed arguments that Israelis needed an independent investigation for their own moral peace of mind, or if wrong had been done, to recognise and address it. Instead the government ordered the army to investigate its own actions – which it did, over many months, concluding that, apart from a few episodes, its soldiers had behaved properly and not disproportionately.

Out of the blue, Richard Goldstone recanted his main accusation against Israel. It was 1 April 2011. It looked at first like an April Fool's Day joke. But it was true: the *Washington Post* published an article by Goldstone in which he withdrew his claim that Israel had deliberately targeted civilians in Gaza as a matter of policy. 'If I had known then what I know now, the Goldstone Report would have been a different document', he wrote. Immediately the enemies he had made through his condemnation of Israel were triumphant and gloating; those who had backed him were dumbfounded and angry, or scrabbled around to justify their one-time support. Clearly the pressures on him had exerted their toll. One erstwhile supporter wrote of a 'shameful u-turn' and 'it is his wish to return to the Zionist comfort zone that propelled this bizarre and faulty article'. The *Guardian*, unwilling to let Israel off the hook, tried to switch tracks, arguing that 'indiscriminate warfare, as opposed to deliberate killing, was undoubtedly state policy'. Jews were split about his coming clean: 'Some consider him a hero, some congratulate him, some will never forgive him'.[22]

The previously adoring Arab camp turned with a vengeance: Goldstone was no longer a good Jew, and newspapers depicted him unpleasantly, as in a cartoon in Saudi Arabia's *al-Watan*: Goldstone shovelling earth to cover a grave filled with corpses; the headstone said 'Stone' and sitting on it was an Israeli soldier – hook-nosed – holding a bar of 'Gold'.[23]

\* \* \*

Created through a vote of the United Nations and admitted as a member in May 1949, Israel has an uneasy and often adversarial relationship with the world body. That has been so from the start: Arab states opposed partition, and lost, and went to war to destroy the fledgling Jewish state, and lost. Frustrated, they have ever since waged unceasing battle against Israel. In the Security Council, the United States has applied its veto power to block attempts at punitive international action. But in the General Assembly, Israel has faced a host of resolutions each year on a wide range of issues, including its handling of Palestinians, the Golan Heights, its nuclear programme and the Gaza Strip, and specifics such as its attack on Iraq's nuclear installation and its attacks on Lebanon. Israel has rejected or ignored them. None have carried sanctions, but they have served cumulatively to help shape a view of Israel as a rogue state which does not respect international norms.

Israel is certainly open to criticism: the ferocity of its 2008–2009 onslaught on Gaza is but one example. However, it has ample reason to resent and mistrust the United Nations. The UN did not try to prevent the invasion by Arab states immediately after the new state had proclaimed itself in 1948; while the UN did later mediate and ratify the General Armistice Agreements between Israel and four neighbouring Arab countries, thereafter it regularly condemned Israel's retaliatory attacks in response to terrorist incursions across its borders, instilling in Israelis the belief that it favoured the Arabs. The UN found it hard going: Secretary-General Dag Hammarskjold in 1955 likened Middle East diplomacy to 'being in a madhouse'.[24] Israel's dismissive attitude, attributed to Prime Minister David Ben-Gurion, came the same year: he said *Oom Shmoom*, meaning 'United Worthless', a play on *Oom*, the Hebrew abbreviation for UN. Forty-three years later, in 1998, Kofi Annan, then the UN secretary-general, threw the phrase back while on a visit to Israel: using Hebrew, he made the point that without the *Oom* there would be *Kloom*, nothing.

These days the Israeli government speaks of the General Assembly's 'numerous and one-sided narrow resolutions that single out Israel. These resolutions not only fail to recognise Israel's desire and work towards peace, but they categorically reject Israel's right to live in security and defend its citizens. Furthermore, these resolutions are adopted year after year in an automatic manner – often recycling the identical language time and again. Such work reflects a desire to condemn and isolate Israel while ignoring the changing facts on the ground'. Even more, it says, no other countries – even those which systematically deny basic freedoms to their citizens – face such a barrage.[25] Kofi Annan added his voice: in his farewell speech in 2006, he asked whether any of the resolutions 'had an effect on Israel's policies, other than to strengthen the belief in Israel, and among many of its supporters, that this great Organisation [the UN] is too one-sided to be allowed a significant role in the Middle East peace process'.

Over a period of more than sixty years, such UN resolutions have run to nearly three hundred. That's a deceptive figure as it includes the ritual annual repeat of previous resolutions, such as 181 of 1948 about refugees. But the total figure is used to feed on itself and becomes a weapon for the country's enemies: look how Israel repeatedly ignores the UN, they cry, it does not deserve to sit among the civilised nations of the world.

Arab states have used their growing numbers and influence in the General Assembly to keep up unremitting hostility towards Israel. The assembly has blocs of countries with overlapping members: the Arab group has 22 countries, the Organisation of Islamic Cooperation (formerly the Organisation of the Islamic Conference) has 57 countries and the Non-Aligned Movement has 118 countries. The Soviet Union and its satellites joined in. The USSR supported the creation of Israel but changed sides because of Cold War politics and cooperated with Arab states. Its turning was given substance in 1955 by a massive arms deal between Czechoslovakia, then its pawn, and Egypt, opening the Middle East to communist penetration.

Right up to May 2000, Israel was the only country excluded from the UN's formal regional groupings. The country's natural geographic place was, and is, in the Asian Group, but Arab states have never allowed it to take part. As a result Israel was debarred from sitting on the Security Council or the important Economic and Social Council. Israel was finally admitted to the Western European and Others Group but is confined to taking part only in meetings held in New York. There are also UN bodies, with costs running into many millions of dollars a year, specifically tasked with dealing with Palestinian refugees and which are platforms for keeping up attacks on Israel: UNRWA, the UN Relief and Works Agency for Palestinian Refugees in the Near East, which uniquely cares for only one group of people and whose definition of a refugee is unlike anything else within the UN or the world; the UN Committee on the Exercise of the Inalienable Rights of the Palestinian People; the Division on Palestinian Rights; the Special Committee to Investigate Israeli Practices affecting the Human Rights of the Palestinian People and Other Arabs of the Occupied Territories; the UN Office for the Coordination of Humanitarian Affairs, which in 2013 had five offices and sixty-eight staff; and the UN Human Rights Council, with its focus on Palestinians. In 2005 at the United Nations Annual Day of Solidarity with the Palestinian People, the main ceremony featured a map of the region with Israel labelled 'Palestine'!

There is still much more reason not to trust the United Nations. Israel has bitter memories of 1967 when the UN meekly accepted an order from Egypt to withdraw its peacekeeping force from Sinai so that the Egyptian army could take its place – confirmation to Israel that it was about to be attacked, and hence its pre-emptive strike which dramatically changed the region.

A cruel blow was inflicted on Israel and Jews in November 1975 with the passage of General Assembly Resolution 3379, by seventy-two votes to thirty-five with thirty-two abstentions: this was the resolution which declared that the country's founding belief, Zionism, was 'a form of racism and racial discrimination . . . [and] is a threat to world peace and security'. Israel's ambassador, Chaim Hertzog, responded: 'For us, the Jewish people, this resolution based on hatred, falsehood and arrogance, is devoid of any moral or legal value. For us, the Jewish people, this is no more than a piece of paper and we shall treat it as such'. He tore up a copy of the resolution.

Hertzog's view came to be widely recognised, at least outside the Arab camp. The resolution was rescinded in December 1991 by 111 votes to 25 (mainly Islamic states) with 13 abstentions. It is the only General Assembly resolution ever rescinded. Gone but not forgotten. As described earlier, it was dragged out again for the Durban anti-racism conference in 2001. It apparently went on lurking inside Turkey's prime minister Recep Tayyip Erdogan and burst into the open when he spoke at a meeting of the United Nations Alliance of Civilisations in Vienna, a framework for West-Islam dialogue. He grouped Zionism with anti-Semitism, fascism and Islamophobia as a 'crime against humanity'.[26] No one at the meeting rebuked him, but the White House attacked his view as 'offensive and wrong' and the UN said it was 'wrong' and 'hurtful'.

After fifty-nine years of membership, Israel finally scored a victory in the General Assembly: a resolution it proposed was accepted. The usual automatic anti-Israel majority of Muslim and non-aligned countries was not activated, and the resolution was passed by 118 votes with 29 abstentions. It encouraged states to improve agricultural technology and plant species for the good of humanity, especially in developing countries. Israel's ambassador Dan Gillerman hailed it as 'this first historic resolution'.[27]

* * *

John Dugard did sterling and clever work in applying the law to undermining apartheid while professor of law at the University of the Witwatersrand in Johannesburg. He later moved to the University of Leiden in the Netherlands. He led a commission of inquiry to Palestine/Israel for the UN Human Rights Commission in 2001 and was appointed special rapporteur to investigate and report on Israeli violations of human rights in the Occupied Palestinian Territories. For eight years he presented annual reports condemning Israel's occupation. Much of his findings drew on investigations by Israeli human rights groups and Israeli media and accurately described mass arrests, assassinations and detention without trial; restrictions on freedom of movement and the humiliation of checkpoints; the effects on health and schooling; and the traumatising of children.

Yet there was an inherent flaw. His master, the Human Rights Commission, had already entrenched itself not only as a highly questionable defender of human rights but as targeting Israel above all others. Dugard knowingly became part of the apparatus and went on to serve it well and achieved repeated reappointment.

In his first report, Dugard explained that he focused on the military occupation 'as the root cause of the present conflict in the OPT and Israel; as the cause of the violation of human rights and humanitarian law in the region'.[28] That was a narrow and limited view: it was as though the world had begun on 6 June 1967 when Israel counterattacked into the West Bank; it ignored the fact of Jewish-Arab violence since the early twentieth century or the creation of the state of Israel and continuing Arab attempts to destroy it. Nor did he mention the UN's nineteen-year silence during the previous military occupations, from 1948 to 1967, of the West Bank by Jordan and the Gaza Strip by Egypt. For someone of Dugard's calibre the lack of any context was inexplicable.

Dugard also said he was only investigating Israeli violations of human rights in the military occupation because that was the mandate given to him by the Human Rights Commission. This, again, was peculiar: if his mandate was deficient, did he ask for it to be altered? That he had misgivings seemed evident because the next year he castigated *both* sides for the violence of the second intifada which was then raging, and his recommendations included that 'both Israel and Palestine should make every endeavour to respect the rule of law, human rights and humanitarian law'.[29]

But he shifted his position. In 2006 Dugard referred to Israeli air attacks in Gaza 'in response to Qassam rockets fired by militants'. This was the only context he offered, otherwise damning Israel wholesale as though it was not in any way responding to murderous attacks. He also offered this bit of haughtiness about the Palestinian execution of five Palestinians: 'The Special Rapporteur's mandate does not extend to human rights violations committed by the Palestinian Authority. It would, however, be irresponsible for a human rights special rapporteur to allow the execution of Palestinian prisoners to go unnoticed'.[30]

Dugard continued his job when the Human Rights Commission was reconstituted as the Human Rights Council. But the United States, the European Union and others, not to mention Israel, continued to dismiss his reports as one-sided. He was criticised for repetitiveness, failure to address terrorism and failure to consider human rights violations by Palestinians. Dugard's response was a defence of Palestinian suicide bombs and rockets as 'acts committed in the course of a war of national liberation against colonialism, apartheid or military occupation'.[31] This superficial entry into a complex issue which engages the world in an era of terrorism does not reflect well on him as a professor of law and champion of human rights. In addition, dragging in a link with apartheid was inaccurate, as he must have known, because the African National Congress had waged its liberation struggle in South Africa with a principled decision not to use terror against civilians.

Dugard seemed to feel the need to explain to the Human Rights Council why it was devoting such a disproportionate amount of attention to the Israel-Palestine conflict – together with other international forums and the media – so he argued that the 'Occupied Palestinian Territory' was of special importance to the future of human rights in the world. After the end of apartheid in 1994, he said,

> Palestine became the only developing country in the world under the subjugation of a Western-affiliated regime. . . . There are other regimes, particularly in the developing world, that suppress human rights, but there is no other case of a Western-affiliated regime that denies self-determination and human rights to a developing people and that has done so for so long. This explains why the OPT has become a test for the West, a test by which its commitment to human rights is to be judged. If the West fails this test, it can hardly expect the developing world to address human rights violations seriously in its own countries, and the West appears to be failing this test. [32]

Never mind what China does in Tibet, what Turkey does to its Kurds, what happens in Sudan or Rwanda or Nigeria or what Russia does in Chechnya. Nor the three million Burmese who escaped their country and the eight hundred thousand Muslim refugees in western Burma, the Rohingya. They are not 'Western-affiliated' so do not have to be held accountable to the same standards of behaviour. That is called paternalism, a carryover from colonial times, and is a weak attempt at an excuse for focusing on Israel/Palestine above all else. And speaking only of the 'developing world' evades Europe's problems – for example, Spain's Catalan and Basque heavily suppressed independence struggles.

In dealing with anything Israeli, Dugard seems to have lost the sense of decency and rightness he had in fighting apartheid. How else can we understand these statements:

Referring to the start of Israel's onslaught on Gaza in December 2008, he said: 'And one must remember that the opening salvo, which was very much like an attack on Pearl Harbor, was an attack directed at a police parade in which fifteen new recruits were killed'. [33] The killing of the police recruits can be, and has been, criticised. But like Pearl Harbor? What sort of outlook is able to relate that act of international infamy against an unsuspecting United States with Israel's widely predicted Gaza attack after months of enduring a rain of missiles from Hamas?

Even more was Dugard's use on the same occasion of the plight of the captured Israeli soldier Gilad Shalit to score a point about the occupation. He began his statement:

At the outset I wish to make it clear that I have every sympathy for Corporal Gilad Shalit; and indeed for all Israel's young soldiers compelled to serve in the army of an occupying power. I hope that he is well treated as a prisoner-of-war and released in good health. I hope, too, that the Palestinian prisoners in Israeli gaols will also be well treated and released in good health.[34]

This was cynical and lacking any factual basis because (a) Shalit was not part of an occupying force but was seized on Israeli soil while defending his country's border; (b) Hamas treated him with utmost callousness, denying communication with his family or the world and even refusing access by the International Red Cross; and (c) as Dugard must know from public reports, there is no comparison with conditions of Palestinian prisoners in Israeli prisons, and to suggest otherwise is a lie. And again illustrating his prejudices, the best condemnatory, inadequate words he could muster about the firing of literally thousands of missiles on Israel from Gaza were: 'Deplorable as such Palestinian actions may be'.[35]

Late in 2011 Dugard even took part in the 'Russell Tribunal' in South Africa, lending his prestige as a lawyer to that tawdry propaganda exercise against Israel with its self-called 'jury' and 'court' and 'findings'. He made himself into a feature on the international circuit for attacks on Israel.

\* \* \*

In John Dugard's 2007 report to the UN Human Rights Council condemning the occupation, he did not claim that Israel had inflicted apartheid or colonialism; rather, he hinted and suggested it, using oblique language: '*elements* of the occupation constitute *forms* of colonialism and of apartheid' (my emphasis). But that was enough of a start for some South Africans with an established record of hostility towards Israel. The Human Sciences Research Council of South Africa (HSRC) was the vehicle they used. After fifteen months, a report appeared which elevated Dugard's tentative words into an emphatic statement: the occupation 'has become a colonial enterprise which implements a system of apartheid'.[36]

The report tries to convey the impression that it is a weighty document. The language tries to be serious and academic. It says it is 'based on fundamental concepts and principles of international law and draws on diverse branches of substantive international law'. But it is a hatchet job whose outcome was certain. Given those involved it would have been astonishing if this wasn't so: Virginia Tilley, American-born, who ran the project for the HSRC, writes incessantly to damn Israel; so does Ronnie Kasrils, former cabinet minister and a communist from the Soviet era who gave the keynote speech at the report's launch in Cape Town. Among the fifteen or so 'international experts' recruited for the project were five Israelis – all activists from the Left and beyond of the political spectrum. All their views were predictable.

The report falls at the first hurdle: every Israeli action is painted in the most severe terms as though they are the direct results of orchestrated designs by evil and rapacious Jews. There is no hint that Israeli behaviour comes out of the conflict between Israelis and Palestinians. There is no mention that some of the Israeli actions were responses to suicide bombers and drive-by shootings; no mention that border crossings became increasingly fortified with concrete walls and reinforced glass to protect soldiers who were being bombed and knifed. The report refers to Israel's 'regular large-scale military attacks on the Gaza Strip'. True of course – but surely it's worth mentioning they were a response to missiles fired into Israel?

The report is at its most inventive about apartheid. It refers to the UN Apartheid Convention's listing of six categories of 'inhuman acts' as comprising the 'crime of apartheid' (see appendix 3). But, it goes on to say, not all the listed acts need be present; also, other 'similar' policies and acts can be included. In other words, the definition of apartheid can be stretched, adapted and manipulated as wanted – in this case, to be fixed to Israel in the occupied territories. The report's same lack of sense is found in saying that practices in South Africa 'are not the test or benchmark for a finding of apartheid elsewhere' and then proceeding to attempt (unsuccessfully) to draw exact parallels between South Africa and Israel. That even includes sly analogies to the 'reserves' in South Africa within which the black majority were penned from the late nineteenth century and which, to anyone with even minimum knowledge, haven't the slightest relevance to the Israeli-Palestinian conflict.

Lewis Carroll described it in his classic book *Through the Looking Glass*, first published in 1871:

> 'When I use a word', Humpty Dumpty said, in rather a scornful tone, 'it means just what I choose it to mean – neither more nor less.'
>      'The question is', said Alice, 'whether you can make words mean so many different things.'
>      'The question is', said Humpty Dumpty, 'which is to be master – that's all.'

Sooner or later, the report had to get to the nub of its attack on Israel, and two-thirds of the way through, there it is, the usual code words for questioning Israel's existence as a Jewish state: 'Palestinians are denied their right to leave and return to their country. Palestinian refugees displaced in 1948 . . . are not allowed to return to their former places of residences'.

Nor is the report always accurate, even in describing well-known details. It merely takes a quick reading to come across errors so serious that one has to ask how much those who wrote the report actually know about Israel.

Take, for example, the statement that 'about 93 percent of land inside Israel . . . cannot be leased by non-Jewish citizens of Israel'. *(Untrue: In fact, about 13 percent of 93 percent of the land cannot be leased or sold to non-Jews – and the situation has been under challenge and before the courts for some years.)* Also, on the West Bank, 'Palestinian trade unions exist but are not recognised by the Israeli government or by the Histadrut, the main Israeli trade union, and cannot effectively represent Palestinians working for Israeli employers and businesses'. *(Untrue: In fact, until 2011 there hadn't been any Palestinian trade unions for workers in Israeli firms on the West Bank, so there weren't any not to be recognised, partly because Jordanian labour law applied and made strikes difficult. The first Palestinian trade union was formed in mid-2011 and launched a strike against the Jewish owner of quarries on the West Bank. The workers won an Israeli-court sanctioned payout.)*[37]

The Human Sciences Research Council is a government research body to ensure that democratic governance empowers South Africans to deal with issues such as poverty, inequality and national identity; it is also concerned with crime and corruption, AIDS, local government delivery of services and African integration. The Middle East Project was commissioned by the Foreign Affairs Ministry, now International Relations and Cooperation, because of South Africa's 'bitter history of apartheid' and wanting to ensure that 'other peoples must not suffer in the way the populations of South Africa and Namibia have suffered'.[38] In which case, presumably, the same interest will be shown in a host of other relevant areas of the world, such as Tibet, which the People's Republic of China seized as far back as 1951 and which it has colonised, including, according to exiles, sending in Chinese to swamp the Tibetan population; also Turkey, where oppressed Kurds fight for freedom; Kashmir, split between India and Pakistan; and the Alawite murderous oppression in Syria. But thus far, only Israel.

The project must have been expensive with all the international experts flying around for more than a year, a launch in London in May 2009 and another launch and conference in Cape Town the next month. The ministry funded the project – in a country struggling for resources to overcome abject poverty and deprivation. As a trade union leader has said: 'The 2010 United Nations Development Programme report shows that 44 percent of workers in South Africa live on R10 a day . . . this amount can barely pay for a dry loaf of brown bread'.[39] Other statistics show that most of the country's schools do not have a library, laboratory or computer, 14 percent have no electricity, 10 percent have no water and nearly 4 percent do not have toilets.[40] Yet money was splurged on this project. How were South African taxpayers suckered into it? And in any case, whatever hopes the ministry might have had, the report is so one-sided and inadequate that it is no source for authoritative reference. All the report can do is confirm the prejudices of anyone who already believes that Israel is really wicked.

The HSRC report has had a spin-off in a summary which it says 'draws partly' on it. It uses Virginia Tilley's name, but whether she was actually involved in writing it is not said. Dated 8 March 2010 it appears on a grotesquely named website, Shoah: The Palestinian Holocaust, and makes its outlook plain with the headline: 'Is Israhell really an apartheid state?' and phrases like 'Zio-Nazi Knesset'.

\* \* \*

Talk late in 2009 that the Palestinian Authority was considering a unilateral declaration of independence drove Virginia Tilley to oppose it vehemently as an Israeli plot, with the United States involved too, to emulate the Bantustan 'Homelands' of apartheid South Africa.[41] Undermining her view, however, was poor knowledge about the Bantustans, causing her to perpetrate at least two basic errors: first, by saying that 'The only state to recognise the Homelands was fellow-traveller Israel' (*it didn't; the only recognition came from South Africa and fellow Bantustans*); and second, that 'Well-meaning white liberals in apartheid South Africa – yes, there were some of those, too – held the same earnest candle burning for the black Homelands' (*apart from her distasteful sneer about white liberals – some very brave people who stood up to apartheid rule and suffered for it – she was plain wrong: no liberals of consequence supported the Bantustans*).

\* \* \*

Even by the standards of the UN's special rapporteur on Palestinian rights, Richard Falk was a way-out choice to succeed John Dugard. While his academic title seems impeccable – emeritus professor of international relations at Princeton University – he has been given to outlandish statements, such as claims that the George W. Bush administration was complicit in the 9/11 attacks on New York's Twin Towers and supporting a denial that an aircraft hit the Pentagon that day. UN secretary-general Ban Ki-moon has said Falk's comments were 'preposterous'.

In July 2011 Falk's blog carried an Arab-drawn cartoon to illustrate his claim about the supposed anti-Arab and pro-Israel hypocrisy of the United States and the International Criminal Court. It showed Lady Liberty taking her dog for a walk; the dog wore a shirt labelled 'USA', had a Jewish *kippah* (skullcap) on its head and was gobbling a pile of bloody human bones while wetting Lady Liberty's foot. As protests came, Falk responded: 'It is a complete lie. I know nothing about such a cartoon, and would never publish such a thing, ever'. However, later the same day he admitted to the cartoon, saying: 'Maybe I do not understand the cartoon, and if it offends in this way I have removed it from the blog. It may be in bad taste to an extent I had not earlier appreciated, but I certainly didn't realize that it could be viewed as anti-Semitic, and still do not realize'. He blamed his imperfect eyesight, at age eighty, for causing him to think that the dog's Star of David–adorned kippah was a helmet. The head of the Human Rights Council, Navanethem Pillay, eventually rebuked Falk. But, despite his deformed outlook, Falk remained in place to pass judgment on Israel, which is yet another commentary on the council.

In 2013 the European Union again denounced his latest report to the UN Human Rights Council as inaccurate and biased. Yet Falk remained in his job.[42] He retired in 2014.

\* \* \*

The marvel of the Internet in making information available has its downside in opening the gates to anyone anywhere who wants an outlet for hate or madness. There's a super-abundance of such sites dealing with Israel, both for and against. One among the many sites is soundofegypt.com, which under the headline 'Fact' says: 'Back when the UN created Israel, the very same resolution also created a Palestinian state. Israel immediately refused to recognize Palestine since it sat on land Israel coveted, namely Jerusalem. Arab nations (and the Palestinians) responded by refusing to recognize Israel'.

These facts are so wrong that they can be laughed off. Other material is so bizarre that it is also beyond any response, such as 'Radio Islam' in Sweden, which says it appears in twenty-two languages and presents itself as wanting to improve relations between the West and the Arab and Muslim world. It declares: 'Israel constitutes by its mere existence a complete defiance to [*sic*] all international laws, rules and principles' and 'Israel is the last outpost of apartheid'. Radio Islam runs the Protocols of Zion, denying that it is the nineteenth-century tsarist police forgery which it is. Radio Islam vents the basest, and maddest, views, with headlines such as: 'Jewish manipulation of world leaders'; 'The Jewish hand behind Internet'; 'Jews who want to be human beings have to renounce being Jewish'; 'Britain under Jewish occupation!'

\* \* \*

A group of eleven 'Women of Color Feminists' visited the West Bank in June 2011.[43] Among them were Angela Davis, well known for her militancy, and Rabab Abdulhadi, born in Nablus and at one time the director for Arab-American studies at the University of Michigan, Dearborn. They issued a strong statement to condemn Israel, but for such a high-powered group, it was a disappointing mix of fact and misinformation. On the one hand, for example, they were justifiably angry, among much else in the occupation, at seeing 'vast numbers of Israeli settlements ominously perched in the hills, bearing witness to the systematic confiscation of Palestinian land in flagrant violation of international law and United Nations resolutions'. On the other hand, they were shallow about the complex events of the 1948 war in speaking of refugees 'whose families had been evicted from their homes by Zionist forces, their land confiscated, their villages and olive groves razed'. That's the standard anti-Israel propaganda line which avoids the facts of what actually happened.

Thus too: 'In defiance of United Nations Resolution 194, Israel has an active policy of opposing the right of Palestinian refugees to return to their ancestral homes and lands on the grounds that they are not entitled to exercise the Israeli Law of Return, which is reserved for Jews'. The reference to the Law of Return is correct; the reference to the UN resolution is inaccurate because the wording is not as emphatic as they claim. It's an offhand, unthinking reference to the core of the conflict – the existence of Israel as a Jewish state.

Nowhere does the statement reveal knowledge, let alone any attempt to understand the ramifications of the decades-long conflict. The women leap on 'the Israeli project of apartheid and ethnic cleansing'. Did they come to the West Bank with predetermined views, already certain about Israeli guilt and Palestinian innocence? If they did, then this was simply a propaganda exercise; if not, then this was, like Jimmy Carter, a chance thrown away for an honest examination and search for ways to help.

\* \* \*

Also in June 2011, Alice Walker, Pulitzer Prize–winning author, wanted to sail to Gaza. The trip was aborted, but she gave her views in advance: she wrote about Israel 'murdering' activists on the Turkish ship *Mavi Marmara*, which had tried and failed to get to Gaza the previous year.[44] As plentiful reports show, Israeli soldiers mishandled that situation, seriously underestimating the violence they would encounter in boarding the ship; but you have to twist yourself into knots and have some warped emotions to accuse them of 'murdering' in defending themselves.

Ms Walker later again confirmed the strength of her imagination in speaking of the occupied territories: 'It's so much like the [American] South of 50 years ago, really, and actually more brutal, because in Palestine so many more people are wounded, shot, shot, killed, imprisoned. You know, there are thousands of Palestinians in prison virtually for no reason'.[45] There are more than enough reasons to condemn the occupation without such spurious claims, where nearly every word is nonsense. Yet it is on such basis that Walker uses her name and her skin colour to issue moral edicts for singers and others to boycott Israel.

\* \* \*

'Ronnie Kasrils likened restrictions on passengers flying on international airlines to Israel to the meticulous lists and photographs compiled by the Gestapo'. That's how the *Cape Times* began its report about a media briefing in Cape Town, South Africa, on 19 July 2011. Kasrils presented his Gestapo analogy in relation to Israel's action earlier that month in blocking hundreds of Palestinian supporters from flying in from European airports; it did so by ordering airlines not to carry them to Ben-Gurion airport. Kasrils called for an end to the 'crime of silence' by the international community – although about what or by whom wasn't clear.[46]

The analogy was so far removed from reality and was really so obscene that it would not merit publication in a newspaper except perhaps to illustrate a bizarre outlook. Yet not only was it said by a former South African cabinet minister, but it was the main report on page six of Cape Town's morning newspaper, with headlines across six columns: 'Kasrils raises his voice: Call for an end to "crime of silence"'.

Could it be that both Kasrils and the *Cape Times* did not know that the United States compels every international airline to submit lists of passengers before take-off to the United States? And didn't they know about worldwide screening and profiling practices to keep out terrorist and political suspects and to trace drug-runners? If Kasrils is concerned about freedom of movement, why is he silent about the wholesale discrimination against Israelis by Arab countries, from Saudi Arabia to Syria: no one with an Israeli passport can board an aircraft to these countries, with discrimination also against US passport holders born in Israel. Some Arab countries do not admit anyone whose passport bears an Israeli entry visa, so travellers such as journalists and business people carry several passports and zigzag their way around, flying into and out of Israel via nearby countries which do not discriminate, like Jordan and Cyprus.

Yet here was Kasrils in a prominent report accusing Israel of Nazi Gestapo lists – used to identify Jews meant for extermination – to keep out critics. It was revealing in once more confirming his extreme, but poorly informed, attitudes towards Israel, as well as the *Cape Times*' level of journalism.[47]

The Kasrils report appeared in the context of a media briefing about the intention of the 'Russell Tribunal' – described as an 'international peoples' tribunal' – to meet in Cape Town later in 2011 'to determine if the treatment of Palestinians in Israel and the occupied territories' met the criteria of the UN convention against apartheid. What was called a 'jury' was to hear testimony and give its 'findings' on Israel.[48] The members were to include Kasrils. During an interview, the tribunal's secretary, Terry Crawford-Browne, said the tribunal had a long history: the philosopher Bertrand Russell had established the first one on war crimes in Vietnam in the 1960s. Crawford-Browne claimed successes that will surprise anyone with a cursory knowledge of history: 'That led to a change of attitudes and eventually the American withdrawal', he said. There was a tribunal on war crimes in South America and 'Obviously, there's been a major change in South America'. The Russell Tribunal achieved all that!

After the boasts the interviewer asked him if the tribunal had focused on other countries in the Middle East where human rights 'are at least equally abused'. He replied: 'We don't dispute that at all. What happens in Syria and Saudi Arabia is a nightmare. But Israel does claim to be a democracy'.

This is the same line peddled by John Dugard: Israel must be singled out and punished because it is a democracy. No need to do anything about abuses in Syria and Saudi Arabia and other tyrannies because they are not democracies!

In due course, in November 2011, the Russell Tribunal met and behaved as expected. The Jewish community rightly derided it as a 'kangaroo court'. It received little attention. What was the cost of carting a few dozen people around the world, to sessions already held in Barcelona and London with New York and Brussels still to come? The players did not stay in youth hostels or live on hamburgers. According to the organisers, the Cape Town event alone was budgeted at $250,000 of which $150,000 had been donated. Who was behind it? Who paid the huge costs? And why?

In any event, the tribunal people are confused in using their founding father's name. While their existence is devoted to getting rid of Israel, they are, in fact, acting contrary to the views of Bertrand Russell who wrote in 1943:

> For a long time I was doubtful as to the importance of a Jewish national home in Palestine as an element in such reparation [the creation of a state], but I have gradually come to see that, in a dangerous and largely hostile world, it is essential to Jews to have some country which is theirs, some region where they are not suspected aliens, some state which embodies what is distinctive in their culture.[49]

* * *

'Who said nearly 50 years ago that Israel was an Apartheid State?' is a favourite start to speeches and articles by Kasrils.[50] He triumphantly answers his question: Dr Hendrik Verwoerd, the South African prime minister who was a notorious apartheid apostle. He says that Verwoerd 'emphatically stated as far back as 1963 that "Israel is an apartheid state"'. Of course it is strange to have Kasrils speak approvingly of anything that Verwoerd said, and it is not known to what extent he looks for inspiration in Verwoerd's violent, racist views. But in this case Kasrils's choice of a quote is misleading because he uses it out of context. He even got the source wrong by claiming it appeared in the *Rand Daily Mail* of 23 November 1961; it didn't. The background to the Verwoerd statement was that Israel had voted at the United Nations to criticise South African apartheid; Israel had also just issued a joint statement in the same terms with the African state of Upper Volta, whose president had been visiting Israel. Verwoerd was not referring admiringly to Israel but spoke out of anger and pique, trying to score points – and to give warning to the Jewish community in South Africa that they had to put pressure on Israel to back off.

Kasrils goes on to tie Israel to Verwoerd in every possible way. The more detail he gives, the greater truth suffers. As with: 'To be sure Verwoerd was correct. Both states preached and implemented a policy based on racial ethnicity; the sole claim of Jews in Israel and whites in South Africa to exclusive citizenship' (*untrue: Arabs share full citizenship with Jews*); 'monopolised rights in law regarding the ownership of land, property, business' (*apart from a part-restriction on land, all entirely untrue*); 'superior access to education, health, social, sporting and cultural amenities, pensions and municipal services at the expense of the original indigenous population' (*untrue comparisons, including the reference to the indigenous population*); 'the virtual monopoly membership of military and security forces' (*a simplistic and untrue description*); 'and privileged development along their own racial supremacist lines – even both countries [*sic*] marriage laws designed to safeguard racial "purity"' (*straight-out lies*).[51]

Then follows this claim, also wholly removed from the reality of life in Israel:

> The so-called 'non-whites' in apartheid South Africa, indigenous Africans, others of mixed race or of Indian origin – like second- or third-class non-Jews in Israel – were consigned to a non-citizenship status of Kafkaesque existence, subject to bureaucratic whims and the laws prohibiting their free movement, access to work and trade, dictating where they could reside and so forth.[52]

Kasrils has also said: 'The occupation reminds me of the darkest days of apartheid, but we never saw tanks and planes firing at a civilian population. It's a monstrousness I'd never seen before. The wall you built, the checkpoints and the roads for Jews only – it turns the stomach, even for someone who grew up under apartheid. It's a hundred times worse'.[53] And in another version: Any South African who goes to Palestine today and visits the West Bank and Gaza, or Palestinians living in the State of Israel, 'come away shocked and, shaking their heads saying, "This is far worse than the apartheid we knew." South Africans in great numbers are saying, "What we went through is like a picnic compared to what Palestinians are going through"'. [54]

He is correct about the occupation. The checkpoints, plus the tanks and planes during periods of violent conflict. But the comparison with apartheid South Africa? How can there be? Blacks did not use a single suicide bombing in their struggle. They did not drive past cars and open fire, killing men, women and children, etc. Palestinian violence against Israel has been of an entirely different nature and Israel has used different countermeasures. Whether always rightly or not is another issue. His claim that apartheid was a 'picnic' compared with the lot of Palestinians is so economical with the truth that the only charitable explanation for it is that Kasrils was in exile abroad for so many years, fighting in the freedom struggle, that he does not know the full horrors of apartheid.

Kasrils's disparagement of the security barrier – the wall – would ring truer if, in an earlier time, he had also condemned the Berlin Wall erected by East Germany's communist rulers. That structure, and the many killings that went with it, was a genuine reason for stomach-turning, but he was silent.

Kasrils is of Jewish descent and seems to have rediscovered his roots late in life. While minister of intelligence in the South African cabinet, he had the practice of assailing Israel during parliamentary debates, using hostile language that went far beyond the government's official policy. He explained that he was speaking in his 'personal capacity' – an unusual departure from the principle of cabinet responsibility. It might be that Kasrils was a willing tool as a 'tame Jew' for anti-Israel attacks which the government wanted expressed but did not wish to say officially because of its formal policy of friendship and trade with Israel. That could explain why even his most strident attacks were never repudiated by then president Thabo Mbeki.

Kasrils was mocked by a genuine authority, Israeli historian Bennie Morris, who said in response to one of Kasrils's articles that he 'uses history to advance a political agenda. The problem is that his history is skewed; factual errors piled on top of ideologically-motivated distortions. The outcome is lamentable'. [55]

There is, unfortunately, no shortage of examples of Kasrils's lamentable combination of ignorance and distortion. For instance, his version of the Deir Yassin massacre: 'On 9 April 1948, 254 men, women and children were butchered there by Zionist forces to secure the road', he wrote.

> Because this was one of the few such episodes that received media attention in the West, the Zionist leadership did not deny it, but sought to label it an aberration by extremists. In fact, however, the atrocity was part of a broader plan designed by the Zionist High Command, led by Ben-Gurion himself, which was aimed at the ethnic cleansing of Palestinians from the British mandate territory and the seizure of as much land as possible for the intended Jewish state. [56]

Not only is he inaccurate about the death toll but his so-called explanation for what happened is fantasy: the Irgun and the Stern Gang were responsible for the massacre, and there was no 'broader plan' behind it.

This is a man who can fairly be described as an unreconstructed Stalinist: he applies all the baleful techniques that he learnt and admired in Soviet propaganda to vilify Israel. He is on the international circuit to attack Israel and question its existence.

\* \* \*

Palestinians who tried to breach Israel's borders with Syria and Lebanon in May 2011 might have been driven by idealism – although there was speculation that they were put up to it by the Syrian government wanting to divert attention from its growing domestic opposition. However, anyone who climbs over a border fence, and also cuts it, is likely to get into trouble, and especially so when the fences are between Israel and countries with which it is in a state of war and when the soldiers on guard are on alert because one of their number was a kidnap victim for more than five years. Twenty Palestinians were shot and killed when they did just this in May 2011. Lamis Andoni, a commentator on the Middle East, sought to make capital out of the tragic episode by perpetuating historical myth: 'Most non-Arab Israelis are afraid to face their original sin of deliberately expelling the native Palestinian population'.[57] This bit of dream fiction was the lead-in to saying: 'New generations of Palestinians . . . understand that the Palestinian right of return is the crux of the struggle for their independence'. Which, as always, is the honeyed disguise for aiming to destroy Israel.

The Palestinian Authority's official newspaper, *al-Hayat al-Jadida*, uses crossword puzzles to deny that Israel exists. Thus the clue, 'A port in occupied Palestine', and the solution, 'Haifa', an Israeli city.[58] The offence is all the greater because this was published in February 2014 when US secretary of state John Kerry's peace initiative was at a critical point and the basis of it was a secure Israel alongside an independent Palestine. It doesn't help to reassure Israelis about Palestinian intentions.

Palestine Media Watch reports that it has documented 'numerous examples' of the same crossword denial: Israeli cities such as Acre, Safed, Lod and even Tel Aviv have been presented as 'Palestine' or 'Occupied'.[59]

\* \* \*

In an astonishing lapse from the usual propaganda line that Israel is the unique inheritor of the apartheid label, Electronic Intifada in February 2014 noted that other countries also merit it. Reporting that Harvard University's Palestine Solidarity Committee, in preparing for Israel Apartheid Week, was collecting testimonies about apartheid from students, it said: 'A simple Google search confirms that situations as diverse as the US to Rhodesia, the north of Ireland to Brazil, Latin America to Saudi Arabia all have the word apartheid attached to them in ways old and new.'[60]

Correct. But any hope that this acknowledgement signaled a new era of truth-telling was dashed a mere two days later with a comment about the Kerry peace initiative and Palestinian claims to a right of return: 'The US political establishment is about to embark on a gamble that it can sell the idea of a colonial-settler, exclusivist state in Israel and a bantustan state in the West Bank and Gaza while denying human rights to Palestinian refugees and Palestinians with Israeli citizenship.'[61]

That's five distortions in one sentence: Israel is not a colonial-settler state; it can choose to be as exclusivist as it pleases (like Saudi Arabia or Pakistan or any Muslim state); the West Bank and Gaza are nothing like South Africa's bantustans; whether it is Israel or the host Arab states like Lebanon which deny rights to Palestinian refugees is debatable; and Israel does not deny human rights to its Arab citizens.

*Chapter Nine*

# The Critics (2)

*The attacks on Israel and questioning its existence come from many sources and take many forms . . .*

\* \* \*

For some critics, any stick will do. Hence, the *Independent* in London used its Christmas edition on 23 December 2006 for a large front-page report by Johann Hari: 'In two days, a third of humanity will gather to celebrate the birth pains of a Palestinian refugee in Bethlehem'. The purpose of Hari's rewriting of history, conferring (a nonexistent) Palestinian identity on the Jewish Jesus Christ, was to tell a story about a Palestinian mother in the town who said she had lost a baby because Israeli soldiers had refused – while allegedly laughing at the sight of her bleeding – to let her through a road-block at night to get to a hospital. According to Hari, the twenty-seven-year-old 'gap-toothed' woman speaking 'in broken, jagged sentences' gave him the well-crafted quote which enabled him to ram home his political point: 'What would happen if the Virgin Mary came to Bethlehem today? She would endure what I have endured'.

It was a muddled report because Hari, a well-known left-wing writer, wasn't really sure whom to accuse for what. While Israel was the target, he also said that the world had choked off funds for the Palestinian Authority after Hamas's electoral victory; the Palestinian Authority had been unable to pay its doctors and nurses, so they went on strike and for three months the maternity wards 'were empty and echoing'.

Another Hari special was headlined: 'Israel is suppressing a secret it must face'.[1] What secret? According to Hari, it was 'Plan Dalit' [*sic*], which had been used to evict Palestinians in 1948. That's actually Plan Dalet (Operation

D), the early 1948 military plan devised by the Haganah to end the Arab insurgency and to break the Arab control of roads between cities. The plan has been written about extensively in hundreds of books and countless articles. It needs a great ignorance to claim, sixty years later, that Israel was concealing it.

Hari's reporting sins went beyond Israel/Palestine, and he came unstuck in 2011 when angry revelations on the Internet led him to admit his habit of recycling quotes in writing interviews. He was also accused of inventing quotations.[2] The *Independent* sacked him, and the Orwell Prize for journalism, awarded to him in 2008, was revoked. What was never explained was why and how he had gotten away with his lying for so long. The *Independent* had promoted him as a star columnist.

\* \* \*

Even medieval-era blood libels are used – as in a report by Donald Bostrom in *Aftonbladet*, Sweden's biggest circulation daily, accusing Israel Defense Forces soldiers of abducting Palestinians to steal their organs.[3] It followed on the unrelated arrests in New Jersey of several Jews, including rabbis, on accusations of brokering the sale of human organs for transplant. Bostrom and *Aftonbladet* quoted Palestinians as saying: 'Our sons are used as involuntary organ donors'.

A columnist in another Swedish newspaper, *Sydsvenskan*, rightly noted: 'Whispers in the dark. Anonymous sources. Rumors. That is all it takes'. For, once started, the 'grotesque throwback to the blood libels of the Middle Ages', as the Israeli Foreign Ministry put it, rolled on. Within weeks, the *Jerusalem Post* reported: 'The anti-Semitic blogosphere and many Arab and Muslim media outlets are aflutter in recent days over accusations of an international Jewish conspiracy to kidnap Algerian children and harvest their organs'. It referred to a sensational report in an Algerian newspaper that bands of Moroccans and Algerians were roaming the streets of Algeria's cities kidnapping young children for sale to Israelis and American Jews for their organs. A Dr Mustafa Khayatti was apparently the source of the allegations; he was described as head of the 'Algerian National Committee for the Development of Health Research'.[4] Closing the circle, the Iranian news agency PressTV linked the accusations with the New Jersey arrests.

The *Guardian* (London) allowed itself to be caught up in the libel, reporting:

> Israel has admitted that pathologists harvested organs from dead Palestinians, and others without the consent of their families – a practice that ended in the 1990s, it emerged at the weekend. The admission, by the former head of the country's forensic institute, followed a furious row prompted by a Swedish

newspaper reporting that Israel was killing Palestinians in order to use their organs.[5]

So the prestigious *Guardian* confirmed the harvesting of Palestinian organs, and its report rapidly circulated through the Internet. But note the two words, '*and others*', in the first sentence, which the reader's eye would tend to skim over but which, in fact, gave the lie to the sentence and to the headline above the report: 'Israel admits harvesting Palestinian organs'.

The truth appeared halfway into the report:

> Channel 2 reported that in the 1990s, specialists at Abu Kabir (forensic institute) harvested skin, corneas, heart valves and bones from the bodies of *Israeli soldiers, Israeli citizens, Palestinians and foreign workers*, often without permission from relatives. The Israeli military confirmed to the programme that the practice took place, but added: 'This activity ended a decade ago and does not happen any longer' (emphasis added).

Thus *everyone* was the victim of the forensic institute's aberrant behaviour. Not only did the *Guardian* distort the truth and propagate a group libel that could stoke up dangerous prejudices against Jews, but the report was written by none other than its Middle East editor, Ian Black.

Organ-harvesting claims were again in the news within two months. The scene changed to Haiti, but Israelis were again the alleged offenders. Britain's Liberal Democrats dropped Baroness Jenny Tonge as health spokesperson in the House of Lords after she gave credence to ugly, baseless rumours that the Israeli army's team working to aid Haitians in an earthquake crisis had stolen human organs. She said, 'To prevent allegations like these . . . going any further, the IDF and the Israeli Medical Association should establish an independent inquiry immediately to clear the names of the team in Haiti'.[6] Whether Tonge was concerned about the good name of the IDF or had other motives cannot be said. But two years later, at an Israel Apartheid Week event at Middlesex University, London, she said Israel would 'not last forever' and would 'lose support and then they will reap what they have sown'. She lost her party link in the House of Lords.[7]

Gaddafi's Libya also got in on the act. It's sobering now to recall that its international Organisation for the Elimination of all Forms of Racial Discrimination (EAFORD) was accredited as an NGO by the United Nations Human Rights Council in Geneva. EAFORD picked up the *Aftonbladet* article and submitted a document calling for investigation of allegations that 'Israeli physicians, medical centres, rabbis and the Israeli army' may be stealing the organs of 'dead, kidnapped and killed' Palestinians for sale on the black market.[8] Shamefully, and no doubt something everyone would like to pretend never happened, the Libyan document was screened by the UN's

Office of the High Commissioner for Human Rights, Navanethem Pillay, and was circulated as an agenda item for the council.[9]

Also in a vicious, but barmy, mould is a report by the Palestinian Authority's official news agency, Wafa, that Israel was using rats to drive Arab families out of their homes in Jerusalem's Old City. Dozens of Jewish settlers had been coming with iron cages full of rats, it said; they released the rats to find shelter in open sewage systems.[10] Sam Bahour, a Palestinian businessman, spread the story further through his online network, with the heading: 'Israel using rats to drive away Arabs?' He did not seem to take on board the inherent absurdity of the report: Arabs, Jews and Christians live in adjoining areas in the Old City's one square kilometre, and it is unlikely that rats would respect any boundaries.

A newspaper, *al-Hayat al-Jadida*, with a tiny circulation but supposedly a voice of the Palestinian Authority, also stands accused of repeatedly publishing blood libels: that Israel conducts 'horrific Nazi-like medical experiments on Palestinian prisoners'.[11]

Going further into lunacy was an article in the Saudi Arabian government daily, *al-Riyadh*, by Dr Umayma Ahmad al-Jalahma of King Faysal University about the Jewish festival of Purim, which features Queen Esther saving the Jews from a tyrant, Hamman. He was correct in saying that Jews celebrate Purim by eating 'very special pastries'. But whereas the pastries – triangular-shaped and called *Hammantashen* (Hamman's ears) are filled with crushed poppy seeds, or cheese or chocolate or whatever – he repeated the age-old libel that human blood is used: '[T]he victim must be a mature adolescent who is, of course, a non-Jew – that is, a Christian or a Muslim'. He went on with lurid fictional details about a needle-studded barrel the size of a human body: 'These needles do the job, and the victim's blood drips from him very slowly. Thus the victim suffers dreadful torment – torment that affords the Jewish vampires great delight as they carefully monitor every detail of the blood-shedding with pleasure and love that are difficult to comprehend'.[12]

The hatred and prejudice behind these reports are so intense that they defy rational discussion. That also applies to Iran's Mahmoud Ahmadinejad, who, while president, regularly dismissed the Holocaust as a 'myth'. While speaking at a pro-Palestinian rally in Tehran, he said that the Western powers 'launched the myth of the Holocaust. They lied, they put on a show and then they support the Jews'.[13] This was not the first time that Ahmadinejad spoke in these terms, and he went on saying much the same, and worse.

But a full three years earlier, Virginia Tilley in South Africa was denying that he said anything of the sort. A lengthy and tortuously argued article in 2006 asked the question in the headline: 'Is Iran's President a Jew-hating, Holocaust-denying Islamo-fascist who has threatened to "wipe Israel off the map"'? Her answer was to repudiate a report by the US Congress Subcommittee on Intelligence Policy that he had said: 'They have invented a myth that Jews were massacred and place this above God, religions and the prophets'. No, said Tilley, 'he actually said, "In the name of the Holocaust they have created a myth and regard it to be worthier than God, religion and the prophets." This language targets the myth of the Holocaust, not the Holocaust itself – i.e. "myth" as "mystique", or what has been done with the Holocaust'.

She equally defended him in regard to reports that he called for Israel to be 'wiped off the map'. He was being 'prophetic, not threatening', she said, and what he actually said was 'this regime that is occupying Jerusalem must vanish from the page of time'. The accuracy of the 'wipe off the map' translation from Farsi has been argued over, but Tilley's authority as a commentator has not been helped because Ahmadinejad, seemingly unaware that she denied that he made extremist and hate-filled statements, went on saying them. This is a tiny selection from a host of his statements readily found via Google:

- On Israel's sixtieth birthday, Ahmadinejad said: 'Those who think they can revive the stinking corpse of the usurping and fake Israeli regime by throwing a birthday party are seriously mistaken. Today the reason for the Zionist regime's existence is questioned, and this regime is on its way to annihilation'.[14]
- 'The Zionist regime is dying', and '[t]he criminals imagine that by holding celebrations . . . they can save the Zionist regime from death'. And, 'They should know that regional nations hate this fake and criminal regime and if the smallest and briefest chance is given to regional nations they will destroy [it]'.[15]
- At a gathering of foreign guests marking the nineteenth anniversary of the death of Ayatollah Ruhollah Khomeini, Ahmadinejad said: 'You should know that the criminal and terrorist Zionist regime which has 60 years of plundering, aggression and crimes in its file has reached the end of its work and will soon disappear off the geographical scene'.[16]

To cap it, Iran's presidential website said that 'the Zionist Regime of Israel faces a dead end and will under God's grace be wiped off the map', and 'the Zionist Regime that is a usurper and illegitimate regime and a cancerous tumor should be wiped off the map'.[17]

The words could not be found after Ahmadinejad ceased to be president in August 2013. But the country's supreme leader, Ayatollah Ali Khameini, kept up the refrain, telling a crowd of militiamen in November 2013 that Israel was doomed to collapse and describing the 'Zionist regime' as the 'sinister, unclean rabid dog of the region'. 'Death to America' and 'Death to Israel', shouted the crowd.[18] Khameini spoke his frank, brutal words as his negotiators were at work in Geneva on reaching agreement on easing sanctions, so no wonder that Israel's belief in Iran's murderous intentions towards it were confirmed, again.

Hezbollah, based in Lebanon, has the same evil aim. According to its leader, Hassan Nasrallah, Israel is a 'cancerous gland' that needs to be 'excised'. The Jewish state's demise was in the interest of Lebanon and the region, he told a crowd of cheering supporters in Beirut in August 2013, saying, too, that 'all of Palestine, from the sea to the river, must return to its people'.[19] Thus the open declaration, beyond the usual disguised words, to get rid of Israel – and carrying the threatening weight of the sixty thousand or more missiles which Hezbollah is said to have aimed at Israel.

* * *

Leaders in Egypt after the Arab Spring are also culpable. Fathi Shihab-Eddam, holding the job of appointing editors of all state-run newspapers, called the Holocaust a hoax cooked up by US intelligence agencies to justify war and destruction of Axis military and civilian facilities. Six million Jews had not been murdered, he said, but had moved to the United States.[20]

He made these statements shortly after revelations of earlier statements, in 2010, by Mohammed Morsi, that Jews were 'bloodsuckers' and 'the descendants of apes and pigs'. Morsi was president when the information surfaced, and his office said he had been reported out of context.[21] But his political opponent, Mohammed el-Baradei, former head of the International Atomic Energy Agency, said: 'We are all aware that those statements were not taken out of context and that this discourse is very common among a large number of clerics and members of Islamist groups'.[22]

* * *

Virginia Tilley, again: 'Is Israel really an apartheid state? YES' was the headline.[23] Someone who is so emphatic surely knows the facts. But she provides wide-ranging statements that are either factually incorrect or so one-dimensional that they are also incorrect, such as her comparison of South Africa's 'Grand Apartheid' with Zionism, 'which holds that Jews and Palestinian Arabs who live in the same land cannot live together as one nation'. She overlooked the fact that not only Zionism, but also the United Nations voted for partition in 1947 to separate Jews and Arabs; that the Palestine Liberation Organization and Yasser Arafat later accepted partition; that it's been the policy of the United States and Russia and the European Union and many other countries including South Africa, and also the Palestinian Authority.

She writes that the 'Israeli-delineated cantons in the West Bank are often called Bantustans'. What cantons? They don't exist, except in the minds of some Jewish right-wingers. She says Arabs are banned from leasing 93 percent of Israel – which is wrong. So it goes on. Yet she presents herself as an expert on the Middle East, writes and talks about it a lot and, sitting thousands of kilometres away, promotes policies intended to harm Israel and which, if anyone were ever to listen to her, would have devastating effects on people's lives there.

\* \* \*

As the world worried about what to do about Iran's apparent pursuit of nuclear weapons, Günter Grass, the German Nobel Prize writer, created uproar when he attacked Israel as a threat to world peace and said it must not be allowed to launch military strikes against Iran.[24] *Die Welt* newspaper in Germany called him 'the prototype of the educated anti-Semite',[25] and Israel's Prime Minister Netanyahu railed: 'It's Iran, not Israel, that threatens to destroy other countries. It's Iran, not Israel, that supports terror organizations that fire rockets at innocent civilians. It's Iran, not Israel, that endorses the Syrian massacre. It's Iran, not Israel, that pelts women with stones, hangs homosexuals and brutally suppresses tens of millions of its citizens'. He added the stinging reminder of the notorious fact that it had taken Grass sixty years to own up to having been a member of the Waffen SS – 'and it therefore comes as no surprise that he regards the only Jewish state in the world as a threat to world peace and opposes its procurement of means of self-defense'.[26]

\* \* \*

Uri Geller, the man with reputedly spoon-bending power, was said to have made possible Israel's famed Entebbe hostage rescue in 1976, according to the *Independent*.[27] Absurd as the story was, it drew readers' comments. Among them, from 'halfbeing': 'The Nazis believed in all kinds of mystical b—— s—— so it would be no surprise that their Zionist successors would believe the same sort of crap'. A copyeditor let that through on a mediated site. That's not freedom of speech but reflects worryingly on the *Independent*'s readiness to give validity to a nonexistent Zionism-equals-Nazism claim by someone who has crawled out from under a rock.

\* \* \*

Recent years have seen the rise of the phenomenon of Jews issuing public statements to distance themselves from Israel. The names of those known to want Israel's destruction usually appear. But the lists include Jews sincerely upset by Israeli actions. It doesn't matter whether they have always been connected to Judaism or have more recently rediscovered their roots. What, time and again, makes them remarkable is how little they know about what they are condemning. Take, for example, a collection of British Jews who signed an article, 'We're not celebrating Israel's anniversary', which appeared in the *Guardian* on 30 April 2008, ahead of the celebration of Israel's sixtieth birthday. Their statement included: 'In April 1948, the same month as the infamous massacre at Deir Yassin . . . Plan Dalet was put into operation. This authorised the destruction of Palestinian villages and the expulsion of the indigenous population outside the borders of the state'.

These are slipshod views of documented historical events. First, as anyone interested in Israel should know, Deir Yassin was a maverick killing by Jewish extremists, the Irgun and Stern Gang, and it was immediately denounced by the Zionist leadership. So why tar today's Israel with it? Second, they were equally wrong about Plan Dalet. It was not, as they say, a plan for expulsion but (as outlined in chapter 2) its purpose was to counter Arab attacks on roads and the shelter given to them by neighbouring villages.

The statement ends: 'We cannot celebrate the birthday of a state founded on terrorism, massacres and the dispossession of another people from their land'. With that insulting pomposity, these British Jews threw aside, as if none of it had ever happened, the United Nations decision for partition, Jewish acceptance, Arab rejection, Arab invasion and the terrible consequences of war.

Who wrote this? Did all the signatories understand to what they were giving their names? Or were they simply following the politically motivated who were intent on scoring propaganda against Israel?

Jews in South Africa have been led several times into the same trap, as with a statement in April 2007 dealing with John Dugard's latest UN report about the West Bank and Gaza.[28] It reasonably referred to Israeli destructive actions, condemned the building of the security barrier and the growth of settlements. But all of it was stated in a vacuum as though a conflict hadn't been ongoing for nearly sixty years, with Israel under ceaseless threat of annihilation. It also said: 'In a particular six-day attack by Israel on Beit Hanoun, Gaza, 82 Palestinians were killed and 260 were injured'. That looks really bad and would merit strong condemnation of Israel. But a closer look tells a very different story.

After Israel withdrew its army from the Gaza Strip in August–September 2005, its civilians were the target for indiscriminate attacks by Hamas, Islamic Jihad and others; they fired hundreds of Qassem rockets, Grad missiles and mortars – many of them primitive but still able to damage and kill: 757 from the withdrawal until the end of June 2006. Israel used artillery to try to stop the barrage, going for the missile-firers. The missiles kept coming. On 25

June Hamas militants crossed into Israel through an underground tunnel they had dug. They attacked an army post, killing two soldiers, wounding four and kidnapping Corporal Gilad Shalit. The Israeli bombardment increased, and on 1 November the army crossed into Gaza and occupied the town of Beit Hanoun and its thirty-two thousand people. During the next six days, Israel sought to seize militants in the town and to trace Shalit. In fierce fighting, fifty-three Palestinians died – sixteen were civilians – and one Israeli soldier.[29]

The army withdrew on 7 November. The missiles kept coming: more than twenty of them, wounding three Israelis. Less than twenty-four hours after withdrawing, Israeli tanks responded by shooting at militants firing missiles in an open field one kilometre from the town. But the shells hit a row of houses in the town, killing eighteen or nineteen people and wounding more than forty.

Had that been a deliberate aiming of the guns to kill civilians, it would have been horrific and laid Israel wide open to the gravest possible charges. But Israel immediately said it was due to a technical malfunction of the guidance system. Prime Minister Ehud Olmert issued statements and went on television to apologise and to offer humanitarian assistance. At the United Nations, the country's representative expressed 'deep sorrow and regret' over the killing of innocent civilians; he blamed Hamas terrorism for creating the situation.

Much of the world rejected Israel's explanation and apology. Why this was so strange: it's a fact of war that shells go off target with terrible results; in recent years alone, the United States, Britain, France and Germany have shown that in Iraq, Afghanistan and Libya, and earlier, Iran and Iraq showed it during their years-long conflict. Yet Beit Hanoun opened floodgates of condemnation starting with Hamas's Ismail Haniya, calling it an 'awful massacre'. The UN Security Council met, the Islamic Conference had an emergency session and a BBC television presenter said Israel's explanation was suspicious. Bloggers had a field day. One said it had been a deliberate, premeditated killing and spoke of Israel as a 'criminal nation' and that 'US officers planned the massacre'.[30]

Were the Jews in South Africa – and elsewhere in the world – who expressed their moral outrage aware of the background? Or did they simply sign a statement because it seemed to give them a reason to distance themselves from Israel? Did they go on to read and, even more, to understand, the conclusion in the statement they had signed, which was, clearly, its chief purpose? To hang around Israel's neck the charge that its actions contained 'elements' of 'colonialism, apartheid and foreign occupation'. Whether they realised it not, the Jewish signatories played the game devised by Israel's most fervent enemies whose aim was, and still is, the destruction of the country.

* * *

More naked in intention was a large advertisement in South African news-papers to condemn Israel's sixtieth birthday.[31] The several dozen signatories ranged from the Palestine Solidarity Committee and the Muslim Youth Movement through the Congress of South African Trade Unions, Jewish Voices, the South African Communist Party, Council of Churches and the End Occupation Campaign. The advertisement aimed to equate South African apartheid with Israel and to try to make something out of what did not exist. It was, line by line, dishonest propaganda. Examples include:

- '60 years ago, 750,000 Palestinians were brutally expelled from their homes and suffered persecution, massacres and torture'. *That's a misstatement of what happened in the 1948 war: many thousands of Palestinians were indeed forcibly expelled; and many thousands of Palestinians fled out of fear before and during the war.*
- 'When we think of the Sharpeville massacre of 1960, we also remember the Deir Yassin massacre of 1948'. *Sharpeville was perpetrated by the police, the agents of the state, and was to do with the suppression of black protest. Deir Yassin was a maverick killing by extremist groups and in any event was connected to breaking the Arab siege of Jerusalem.*
- 'When we think of South Africa's Bantustan policy, we remember the bantustanisation of Palestine by the Israelis'. *The Bantustans were so totally different in purpose and practice from Israel's actions on the West Bank that trying to compare them is irrelevant.*
- 'When we think of the Group Areas Act and other such apartheid legislation, we remember that 93 [percent] of the land in Israel is reserved for Jewish use only'. *First, it's 13 percent of 93 percent of Israeli land that is confined to Jews – and not only is it due to historical factors going back more than one hundred years, it's being challenged. There is no comparison with the giant social engineering and forced removal of millions of South Africans under the Group Areas Act and related laws.*
- 'We . . . demand that millions of Palestinian refugees must be accorded the right to return to the homes from which they were expelled'. *There, near the end, was the coded message, wrapped up nicely, for the destruction of Israel. Anyway, it's false: there were about 750,000 refugees in 1948 and the numbers have grown into millions only because of the definition of refugees applied only to Palestinians.*

* * *

Stock phrases are repeatedly used with the aim of making bad situations look even worse than they are, to Israel's discredit, of course. Hence the repeated refrain that the Gaza Strip is the world's most densely populated place. But it isn't. With 3,090.71 people per square kilometre, it ranks number 6, a long way behind Macau with its 20,824.4 per square kilometre. Between Macau and Gaza are Monaco, Hong Kong, Singapore and Gibraltar. Out of 232 listed countries and areas, the West Bank ranks number 37 with 285.66 people per square kilometre. Israel is number 39 with 282.82.[32]

It is also often said that Israel 'maintains the longest occupation in modern history'.[33] This is also deceitful propaganda. First, Kashmir has been occupied by military forces since the break-up of India in 1947, the year before Israel's creation; India, Pakistan and China each control a part of it, and the local people have no say. Second, Tibet has been under Chinese occupation since 1951, which is sixteen years before Israel occupied the West Bank in 1967. Tibetan resistance has never stopped, and the world is regularly reminded of it by the self-immolation of protesters.

\* \* \*

The US Campaign to End the Israeli Occupation should be reported for breaching advertising standards' rules: its name is deceptive. The detail goes much further than the name, notably the 'right of return', the usual code phrase for destroying the Jewish state. Wrapping it up inside a listing of international covenants – the Universal Declaration of Human Rights, the Fourth Geneva Convention, and so forth – does not make it any less misleading. It wants the United States to end aid to Israel (but says nary a word about Israel's right, or ability, to defend itself against countries that have attacked it or want to attack). And it carries the dishonest slogan, illustrated by barbed wire, 'Wrong for South Africans, APARTHEID, Wrong for Palestinians'.

\* \* \*

Al-Aqsa Mosque on the Noble Sanctuary/Temple Mount is the third holiest mosque in Islam. It's a cause of simmering tension between Israel and Arabs, which erupts from time to time. During Binyamin Netanyahu's first term as prime minister, his opening in 1996 of a nearby new entrance to a tunnel set off Muslim protests and gun battles in which sixty Palestinians and fifteen Israelis were killed. In 2011 deep Muslim suspicions about Jewish intentions halted construction of an access bridge to replace a temporary structure which was deemed unsafe. Threats by Jewish zealots of their intention to ascend the Mount and even to take it over understandably fuel Muslim anxieties; but they are no reason for telling so many lies and for inciting religious hostilities.

On 21 August 1969, an Australian, Dennis Michael Rohan, started a fire in the al-Aqsa Mosque. It was put out but caused considerable damage. The *New York Times* reported: 'Old-City Mosque badly damaged – Arson is charged by Arabs in Jerusalem – Israel denies responsibility'. The report said that Israeli firemen 'were beaten and stoned as they sought to enter the mosque' and crowds of Arabs shouted 'Death to Jews'. Later in the day, Prime Minister Golda Meir arrived, and 'pale and visibly shocked, expressed her sorrow in the mosque to a Muslim leader'. Even before the identity of the arsonist was known, young Arabs took to the streets with calls for a strike 'in protest against the mosque fire and amid implications, rejected by the Israeli government, that the arson had been committed by an Israeli'.[34]

The Israeli police tracked down Rohan; he was tried, judged insane and sent to a psychiatric hospital. When asked why he had started the fire, he said: 'To prove to the world that God wants me to build his temple and that he will set me up as king over Jerusalem and Judea'. In 1974 he was returned to Australia and died in psychiatric care there in 1995.[35]

Rohan was not Jewish, but a Christian. He was obviously deranged. There is not the slightest evidence that Israel had anything to do with the arson. Yet, in line with the initial Arab protest, Israel was blamed – and this is regularly repeated as the anniversary of the event comes round. The accusations were quickly taken up in the world: twenty-four Muslim nations demanded UN Security Council action. Jordan's representative, Mohammed El Farrar, spoke darkly of the 'criminal' and the 'accomplice' and said: 'According to news that originated from Israeli sources, the Australian subject is a friend of Israel who was brought by the Jewish Agency to work for Israel'. The Muslim nations finally settled for a Security Council resolution, passed by eleven votes to none with four abstentions, which '[r]ecognises that any act of destruction or profanation of the Holy Places, religious buildings and sites in Jerusalem or any encouragement or connivance at any such act may seriously endanger international peace and security'.[36] The import in the veiled language was clear, and Israel's Ministry of Foreign Affairs understandably accused the Security Council of a 'new level of irresponsibility and irrelevance' in a resolution that was 'a concoction of ambiguous phrasing, intended to deceive and cast aspersions'. It accused Arab governments of fabricating a libellous charge of arson against Israel and of trying to further their political and war-like designs under cover of a holy war.[37]

The libel has never stopped and has become part of the never-ending attacks on Israel. It doesn't matter what Israel says or whatever evidence does not exist. Thus, according to the website Palestine Facts, 'Even while Israel has repeatedly denied that Rohan was a Jew, facts have proved him to be a Zionist, recruited by the violating parties to commit this sinful task'. Among the never-ending unjustified statements, Arab News, based in Saudi Arabia, reported thirty-three years later: 'On that day in 1969 Zionist aggressors set fire to al-Aqsa . . . in an attempt to destroy all Islamic landmarks in occupied Palestine. . . . The crime of setting fire to the al-Aqsa Mosque was part of the ongoing Israeli aggressions against the mosque. . . . Since the Zionist, Dennis Rohan, committed the crime . . . Zionist Jewish spite against al-Aqsa Mosque has been growing'.[38]

The fortieth anniversary was marked by the *Jordan Times*, which wrote about the arson attack by 'a Jewish extremist'.[39] In Dakar, Senegal, a news agency wrote, amidst heavy hints of Israeli complicity, about 'this Christian (some say he is a Jew) of Australian nationality'.[40]

The lies have grown with the years: another 2008 version peddled by al-Jazeera claimed Rohan was 'an Australian Jew' and went on: 'Eyewitnesses said that the Israeli police cut the water supply immediately after the mosque was set on fire, and barred hundreds of Arabs, and the firefighters from reaching the area'.[41] Palestinian Authority TV perpetuated that fiction with a slide broadcast on 5 March 2010 with text at the top: 'Israeli aggression against the holy places' followed by: '[T]he Jew Dennis Michael [*sic*] set fire to the al-Aqsa Mosque, with the support of the Jewish government, which cut off the water supply from the neighbourhoods close to the al-Aqsa Mosque with a view to delaying the operations to extinguish the fire'.[42]

What invented story will come next? Golda Meir, box of matches in hand, walking into al-Aqsa Mosque? Nothing is too far-fetched for propagandists in the guise of journalists who want to stir up religious rages.

One outcome of the fire was the creation the same year of an organisation intended to do harm to Israel: 57 Muslim states formed the Organisation of the Islamic Conference (OIC). Their 650 million people make up 21 percent of the world's population; they possess 70 percent of the world's crude oil reserves and 50 percent of the natural gas reserves. In 1981 the OIC decided to redouble efforts 'for the liberation of Jerusalem and the occupied territories' and to institute an economic boycott of Israel. But the Muslim world is not monolithic and the OIC's members span a wide range of religious views, and some do have economic ties with Israel. So in regard to Israel, the OIC does little but issue statements. (It has been rebranded as the Organisation of Islamic Cooperation.)

* * *

Jacqueline Rose is a British academic who happens to be Jewish and doesn't want Israel to exist. So much so that she has written that 'we believe Zionism to be a form of collective insanity'.[43] She goes even further, raising the possibility that Adolf Hitler and Theodor Herzl both attended the same performance of Wagner in Paris and this inspired the separate writing of Hitler's *Mein Kampf* and Herzl's *Der Judenstat*. There is no evidence for this improbable linkage.

She and other Jewish intellectuals don't merely reject Zionism but use violent and extremist language. Such as the late American poet, Adrienne Rich, who wrote that Zionism was 'so incendiary, so drenched in . . . ideas of blood and soil, in memories of victimisation and pursuant claims of the right to victimise' that it 'needs to dissolve before 21st century realities'.[44] Joel Kovel, an American academic, has written a book, *Overcoming Zionism*, and argues that 'to be a true Jew', Jews must 'annihilate or transcend Zionism' and 'annihilate the Jewish state'.[45]

Jonathan Pollak is among the Israeli Jews who travel abroad and slang off the country. He was in South Africa twice within a year. In a discussion at the University of Cape Town, he commented on Hamas's attitude: 'I also say that Israel shouldn't exist'.[46] It's his right to say what he likes, and he is able to return home knowing he faces no retribution. However, there's a twist: Pollak is a founder of an Anarchist group (he has been in jail for protests and was deported from the Netherlands) and represents only a tiny slice, probably infinitesimal, of Israeli public opinion. So who elevates him to the role of an international speaker about Israel? He was in South Africa again in September 2012, and his sponsor was the Boycott, Disinvestment and Sanctions movement. They like what he says and he says what they like. For good measure, Pollak threw in a special whopper: he said Palestinians on the West Bank and Gaza 'are subjects living under military law without the right to vote'.[47] That, of course, is untrue: Palestinians have the right to vote and the Palestinian Authority on the West Bank and Hamas in Gaza can hold elections; whether they do or don't has nothing to do with military law.

Professor Nurit Peled-Elhanan of the Hebrew University's School of Education vehemently criticises what she says is the negative depiction of Arabs in Israeli school textbooks. She speaks about mourning on Nakba Day and damns 'the mendacious Zionist myth'. Her anger takes her into incomprehensibility: 'I will mourn for the democracy in this country, half of whose subjects live in conditions that are forbidden even for beasts in other democratic countries'.[48]

She exhibits the syndrome common among Jewish critics in Israel and abroad: they are so angry about real or perceived misdeeds by the state that they go over rational boundaries, they lose sight of the trees for the forest and lose all sense of proportion; they are so anxious to press their case and to put space between themselves and what they reject in Israel that they exaggerate and misstate; they land up seeing nothing that is good in Israel, only bad, bad, bad. Anything which might be accurate in their criticisms is submerged and lost in their emotional exaggerations.

\* \* \*

Among the more abrasive Israel attackers is the British writer John Pilger. He started an article about the 2008–2009 Gaza war with a quote from the Soviet dissident Yevgeny Yevtushenko: 'When the truth is replaced by silence, the silence is a lie'. To describe the worldwide clamour set off by Gaza as 'silence' makes one wonder where Pilger was at the time. He then gave his version of the truth. Thus his statement that every Israeli war since 1948 'has had the same objective: the expulsion of the native people and the theft of more and more land'. Yes, like Israel handing back Sinai to Egypt as part of a peace treaty; its offer to return the Gaza Strip, which Egypt declined; its offer of 'land for peace' after the Six-Day War, which the Arab League rejected in Khartoum in September that year; plus negotiations with Syria for the return of the Golan Heights, which foundered not because of principle but through failure to agree on details.

Pilger also writes in sinister terms about a 'holocaust-in-the-making' – picking up from the Nazi-made ghettoes for Jews in Poland – which he claims began with Plan Dalet in 1948 and is ongoing. He seems unaware of the growth in the numbers of Palestinians in Israel and the occupied territories, which makes his talk of 'genocide' a joke. According to his version of history, Israeli propaganda says that the Arab states 'struck first' in 1967. That's untrue: Israel openly acknowledges it struck first – because it had every belief that Egypt was about to invade; however, on the eastern border, Jordan did attack first, despite being warned not to get involved.[49]

Among other comments was the response by a reader in the *Independent* to news that the financier Nathaniel Rothschild, a scion of the famed dynasty, had lost a libel action against the *Daily Mail* newspaper, which had described seedy behaviour by him and Lord Mandelson, the former Labour cabinet minister, in a giant business deal in Russia. The comments were standard anti-Semitism at its lowest level; what was worrying was that a British national newspaper – and once more it's the *Independent* – decided to give them space: 'Rothschild's Zionism is far worse than Nazism. The Zionists even used to bomb Jewish refugee boats if they weren't going to occupy Palestine. . . . We know who the real terrorists are. . . . They hide behind a religion to commit a genocide. The Palestinian Holocaust proves that their corruption and greed rule the world'.[50]

\* \* \*

Apartheid in South Africa was at its height when, on 30 November 1973, the UN General Assembly approved the International Convention on the Suppression and Punishment of the Crime of Apartheid. It expressed the outrage which many in the world felt about the racism of the country's white rulers. With the name of the United Nations behind it, the convention became the basis for campaigners to attack South Africa.

As can be seen in the full text – in appendix 3 – the Apartheid Convention was worded so broadly as a crime against humanity that it could be applied to many situations anywhere. The danger of misusing it was recognised at the time, and it did not draw total support. The United States was among those countries which voted against the Convention. Its ambassador, Clarence Clyde Ferguson Jr, explained: '[W]e cannot . . . accept that apartheid can in this manner be made a crime against humanity. Crimes against humanity are so grave in nature that they must be meticulously elaborated and strictly construed under existing international law'.[51]

In 1998 the Rome Statute established the International Criminal Court. Apartheid was included in its list of crimes and was again defined broadly, albeit more restrictively than in the UN Convention. In brief: inhumane acts of a character similar to other crimes against humanity 'committed in the context of an institutionalized regime of systematic oppression and domination by one racial group over any other racial group or groups and committed with the intention of maintaining that regime'.

Over time, the anxieties of 1973 have proved to be fully justified because there is indeed an ongoing attempt to cast the apartheid net wide – with Israel as the specific target. Of some two hundred countries, only Israel. In a world replete with countries that practise savage discrimination and oppression, you don't have to be paranoiac to smell a rat in the singling out of Israel.

In addition, however worthy the Apartheid Convention might be, and though approved by a vote in the UN General Assembly, it has not gained universal acceptance. Presenting it as though it has is questionable. To this day, many countries share the reservations expressed by the United States and, like it, have not signed up to the convention. They include the world's outstanding democracies: Canada, France, Germany, Italy, the Netherlands, the United Kingdom, Australia and New Zealand. The same applies to the International Criminal Court. By May 2013, while 122 states had ratified the Rome Statute which created it, nonsignatories included a hefty part of the world: China, India, Israel, the United States, Indonesia and Pakistan.

In the *European Journal of International Law*, the lawyer John Dugard and an Irish academic, John Reynolds, write about 'Apartheid, International Law, and the Occupied Palestinian Territory'.[52] The Apartheid Convention is the foundation in their argument for applying 'International Law'. But as the convention is anything but international in practice, they can be said to be using a sky hook. They also refer approvingly to condemnation of Israel by South Africa's Human Sciences Research Council, the Russell Tribunal, UN Special Rapporteur Richard Falk and Dugard's own reports as special rapporteur. But the view of each of these, as earlier discussed, is in its own way a substandard mix of prejudice and error. To base a legal case on these sources is to forego credibility. Dugard and Reynolds end up doing what they say they do not want to do: they provide 'fuel for the deligitimisation of Israel'.

* * *

Much effort goes into trying to justify calling Israel an apartheid state. Lots of articles appear. Reading them is like hacking through a thick jungle because what they share in common is that they are not only confused and confusing but are often based on inaccurate information. For example, Hazem Jamjoun, editor of al-Majdal, Badil Resource Center for Palestinian Residency and Refugee Rights, said that whether to apply the apartheid label could not be determined by comparison with South Africa, although a comparative study could be useful; hence he rejected tags like 'apartheid-like' and 'apartheid analogy'. Instead, it had to be done by 'legal analysis', which, of course, meant the all-things-to-all-people United Nations definition.[53]

But how much credibility should be given to someone like him, who is so ideologically driven? He irrationally equates the 'settler-colonialism' which created white-ruled South Africa with the Zionist process which brought about Israel. He speaks of the 'unabashed alliance between Israel and the South African apartheid regime', and thus ignores the fact that there was probably not a single country which did not treat with apartheid South Africa and many far, far more so than Israel, and especially the Arab oil states. He speaks of the aim of the Bantustans to create a South Africa of '100 percent white minority', and thus shows himself ignorant of the existence, inside white South Africa, of millions of black workers, plus mixed-race coloureds and Asians. He speaks of the Bophuthatswana Bantustan having had an 'embassy' in Tel Aviv, whereas there was no such thing but merely a private business office not recognised by Israel's Ministry of Foreign Affairs.

The purpose of all this stuff finally comes to light in the last paragraph: what Jamjoun was opposing was not only Israel but the goal of a two-state solution. To him, this was Israel's version of a Bantustan, and the leaders of the Palestinian Authority who were working for it were collaborators and puppets. This was political nonsense when he wrote in 2009, and events since then, with Israel undermining, rather than supporting, the possibility of a Palestinian state, have made it more so.

Also from Badil, by Coordinator for Legal Advocacy Karine Mac Allister, is another Israel-apartheid article. To her, the 'crime of apartheid' applies to all of Israel and the occupied territories; she damns the whole lot.[54] But in reading her work, one might wonder what contact writers like this have with real life. For in writing the following, Allister is like Hazem Jamjoun in seeming to be unaware that the original 176,000 Arabs who remained inside Israel after 1948 had by 2013 grown into an alive and vigorous 1,670,000 people, who, although suffering discrimination, are full citizens of the state of Israel. If she is to be believed then none of this has actually happened (and incidentally, the quote she describes as the Zionist movement's slogan has never been that but has been used by some and is often misquoted):

> At the heart of Zionism is thus an exclusivist project: the creation of a Jewish state for the Jewish people. Such a project involves or necessitates the denial of the other; of their presence, rights and existence on the land and reconstruction of the past, namely that the land was empty before the advent of Zionist settlement, hence the movement's slogan describing 'a land without people for a people without land'.[55]

Allister also says, 'In order to acquire land, a number of laws and measures were enacted. These include, for instance, the 1943 Land (Acquisition for Public Purposes) Ordinance'. Nineteen forty-three? Does she know that Israel did not exist then and the law was enacted by the British mandate government? And in her presentation about land, she seems to convey the elementary mistake repeatedly made by critics that 92 percent (93 percent is the figure usually used) is for Jews only. While she correctly reports many undesirable aspects of Israeli society and behaviour, she again reveals ignorance in saying, for example, that in the Jewish Agency's promotion of agriculture, 'it shall be deemed to be a matter of principle that Jewish labour shall be employed'. The statement is correct, but she doesn't seem to know that 'self-labour' was the creed in the early formation of kibbutzim and was integral to getting out of the ghettoes of Europe and creating the new Jew; it meant that kibbutz members themselves did all the work, however menial. In practice, the creed was weakened many years ago because of the need for workers, which led to the hiring of non-kibbutz labour, both Jews and non-Jews, including Arabs.

\* \* \*

Amneh Badran has written a book entitled *Zionist Israel and Apartheid South Africa*. In setting out her views, she seeks to link Israel with apartheid South Africa.[56] This leads her on to strange paths: there is the claim that both were founded on 'colonialism', which is certainly true about white settlement in South Africa but does not apply to the Zionist movement in then Palestine for the simple reason that there was no exploitation of the local land or people for the benefit of a mother country, which is the essential first ingredient of the colonialist concept. Predictably, she uses the 'Zionism is racism' slur.

She goes on to even stranger terrain in trying to spin a web linking Britain, Zionism and white Afrikaners. Hence she says,

It is important to note that the British didn't support the Whites and the Zionists each separately from the other. A tri-partite alliance brought the three together at least until 1950 when the close connection began to fade away after the establishment of Israel and the Afrikaners seized political power in South Africa in 1948 (an interdependent relationship has developed from that time). Different leaders at different periods came together in planning and implementing their colonial schemes e.g. Theodor Herzel [*sic*], Cecil Rhodes and Joseph Chamberlain (British Colonial Secretary) were the partners in the first phase which began in the late 1890s. The second phase (1917–1950) was dominated by figures including Chaim Weizmann, General Ian [*sic*] Christian Smuts, Lord Balfour and Lloyd George. The third phase witnessed a close association of interests between the two colonial outposts. [57]

With this curious recital of history, which bears no relation to any reality, Amneh Badren graduated with a PhD degree at Exeter University in Britain (the book was her thesis); she was then appointed to head the Department of Political Science at al-Quds University on the West Bank.

\* \* \*

If not ridiculous, use of the 'apartheid' word can also be mindless, as seen in an article by a noted American commentator, Robert D. Novak, who wrote reasonably and critically about the plight of Palestinians under occupation. [58] But he included, almost as a throwaway line, that Palestinians alleged that it was 'worse' than South African racial separation. There was nothing to back this up or to show that he or whoever he was quoting had the slightest idea what they were saying. It was enough, however, for a copyeditor to write the headline, 'Worse than Apartheid?'

The same unthinkingness is displayed by people who should know better, such as Uri Avnery, father of Israel's peace movement and a skilled political commentator. Yet in his anger against Israeli oppression, he takes the easy way out by going for apartheid analogies. Thus, for example, in drawing a comparison between the West Bank and Bantustans, he shows that he does not know what the Bantustans were. He ends up with the ludicrous noncomparison: 'And, most importantly, the Wall, which is officially called the "separation obstacle". In Afrikaans, "apartheid" means separation'.

Yet Avnery knows enough to go on to totally reject any notion of real similarities between Israel/Palestine and South Africa. He speaks of the 'fundamental differences' between the two conflicts and scoffs at those who say that methods of attacking apartheid South Africa can be applied to Israel/Palestine: 'That is reminiscent of a classical fallacy, which used to be taught in logic classes: an Eskimo knows ice. Ice is transparent. Ice can be chewed. When given a glass of water, which is also transparent, he thinks he can chew it'. [59]

Avnery's (mis)statements about apartheid draw approving noises from the South African anti-Israel brigade. But his talking of the differences drives them to denouncing him, at length, in Soviet-era speak, for 'glaring logical and factual errors', 'profound misconception', 'flawed analysis', an 'even deeper mistake' and so forth. They are really upset with him for having said the obvious – that South African racial separation was a white agenda universally rejected whereas in Israel/Palestine, opinion polls repeatedly show that the majority of both peoples want separate states.[60]

\* \* \*

Other Israelis also speak loosely and incorrectly about apartheid. *Haaretz*, the liberal newspaper, does so from time to time as in an editorial in 2008 condemning Israel's occupation of the West Bank, saying that the 'interim political situation in the territories has crystallised into a kind of apartheid'.[61] Ten days later, Yossi Sarid, former left-wing Meretz leader and usually an incisive and urbane commentator, seemed to be overcome by his emotions in damning the occupation and wrote that 'what acts like apartheid, is run like apartheid and harasses like apartheid is not a duck – it is apartheid'.[62] *Haaretz* and Sarid need to do some homework about apartheid before offering these slick judgments.

In the same way, *Haaretz* needs to watch advertisements it carries on its website: Fred Schlomka of Green Olive Tours offers 'alternative tours' to Jerusalem, the West Bank, the Dead Sea and Tel Aviv. The advertisement includes the line, 'settlements, Apartheid wall'. By publishing that, *Haaretz* unthinkingly allows itself to be used to normalise the incorrect use of 'apartheid'.

The media often censors hate speech, whether to accord with the law or out of a perceived public good. Can false statements be checked and withheld in the same way? Magazines, with time to spare, can employ fact-checkers, but that is impossible in the rush of everyday news, unless an editor happens to spot mistakes dealing with a topic which he/she knows about or is glad to let through because it fits his/her beliefs. One example was a feature in the *Guardian*'s Comment Is Free by Joseph Massad, headlined: 'The UN vote to recognize Palestine legitimizes a racist status quo'.[63] Perhaps the harshness of the viewpoint, with its damning of the Palestinian leadership, should have sounded an alarm to editors that this was an article needing special scrutiny. Instead, Massad was allowed to get away with falsely labelling the Palestinian Jews of 1947–1948 as 'colonists', going on to turn history upside down by saying that on 30 November 1947 'colonists embarked on the military conquest of Palestine' (is he referring to the United Nations' two-thirds vote for partition?) and that Arab armies 'intervened' (is he talking about the invasion by Arab armies?). He also misquoted the United Nations, saying that it 'has affirmed the right of the refugees to return to their homes and be compensated for their losses (the UN resolution is more shaded than that).

* * *

Electronic Intifada purports to provide news and views about the conflict from a Palestinian viewpoint.[64] But it remorselessly carries anything – anything – that might, in its view, cast Israel in a poor light. That naturally means some of its material is justified and correct, but invariably it cannot contain itself and its inbuilt animus is evident. Such was the case in reporting Hana al-Shabati, a West Bank Palestinian woman whom Israel seized on 7 February 2012 and detained without trial. She had previously been detained for two years. She went on a hunger strike. After forty-three days, Israel capitulated, and she entered into a deal whereby she ended her hunger strike and agreed to be banished to the Gaza Strip for three years.

Not content with reporting al-Shabati's courage and strength of character, Electronic Intifada's knee-jerk response was to drag in apartheid South Africa: 'When the news of the deal broke, the name of another woman immediately came to mind: Winnie Madikizela Mandela' who 'once shared Hanabi's fate under the South African apartheid regime – banishment to a different region'.[65]

Winnie Mandela was a victim of repression more than thirty years ago. Why not use a more recent victim of banishment like Myanmar's famed Aung San Suu Kyi? Or the host of dissident women in China, such as Ding Zilin, Duan Chunfang and Fan Yanqiong, in prison on trumped-up charges or held without due process, or the women undergoing forced 're-education' through labour in Shinali River Women's Labour Camp in Hunan Province? Or among Iran's many persecuted women like Nazanin Khosravani or Roya Tolouee? At least one Electronic Intifada reader was unimpressed by the contrived South African link and wrote: 'To compare Winnie Mandela to Hana is an insult to Hana! Winnie Mandela: kidnapper, torturer, child killer, liar'.

* * *

Israel uses detention without trial. Apartheid South Africa used detention without trial. Therefore Israel is apartheid. That's the loopy logic applied by Electronic Intifada and Eron Davidson in an article about his film *Roadmap to Apartheid*.[66]

They were so intent on smearing Israel – the title of the film is a giveaway in itself – that they did not get round to mentioning Sri Lanka's abysmal use of detention without trial as described by Amnesty International less than four weeks earlier: 'Sri Lanka's shameful record on detention without trial'.[67] Nor did they mention detention without trial in Saudi Arabia, Syria, Russia, Indonesia, Eritrea, Cuba, Moldova, Haiti and the United States. Nor did they mention Gaza, Serbia, Tajikistan, Iran, Egypt, Sudan, Bahrain, Turkmenistan, Ethiopia, Equatorial Guinea, Libya, Yemen, Zimbabwe, Jordan, Myanmar, China, Somalia, Colombia, Ukraine, Belarus, Cambodia, Burundi, and so on.

\* \* \*

Children who hurl stones at passing cars or soldiers are dangerous; they can hurt or kill.[68] How to deal with them is a problem and a UN committee lambasted Israel for its 'harsh treatment of Palestinian children held in custody'. It said that the continued denial of fundamental human rights was totally unacceptable. This serious charge came from the UN Special Committee to Investigate Israeli Practices in the Occupied Territories, which was set up in December 1968.[69]

But what moral force does the condemnation carry in light of the three members who constituted the committee? The chairman was Palitha Kohona, Sri Lanka's ambassador to the United Nations. His country, unhappily, is not a shining example of human rights. The US State Department Report on Human Rights for 2011 refers to abuse of children and child labour in a long litany of what's not good in Sri Lanka. That includes unlawful killings by security forces, torture, disappearances and lack of accountability for thousands who disappeared in previous years, arbitrary arrest and detention, harassment of journalists, violence and discrimination against women. The second member was a Senegalese diplomat, Fod Seck, who represents a country characterised by discrimination against women, child abuse, child marriage, infanticide, child labour and female mutilation – plus torture; limits on freedom of speech, press and assembly; and corruption, rape, domestic violence and impunity for security forces.

The third member was Dato Hussein Haniff, Malaysia's ambassador to the United Nations. His country's abuses include restrictions on freedom of speech, assembly and association; on rights of migrants and refugees; violence against women; and vulnerabilities to child labour, especially for migrants. In addition, his country stands accused of apartheid, of '[d]iscrimination from womb to tomb'. Hindraf Makkal Sakthi, an NGO, has been lobbying Washington, DC, to classify Malaysia as an apartheid state no different from South Africa and based on 'a subtle, pervasive and increasingly aggressive form of racism'.[70]

Each one of the diplomats must surely know what is happening at home. So perhaps some *mea culpa* breastbeating, a bit of humility, even embarrassment, would have been appropriate in pointing an accusing finger at Israel about anything? Instead, Ambassador Kohona also attacked Israel's blockade of Gaza as having 'a devastating impact on the lives of people'. That is true, but perhaps he could have added that he has special understanding because of the devastation inflicted by his government on its Tamil people who sought their own state. And he could have mentioned that Egypt also blockades Gaza.

Less than a year later, another UN body, the Committee on the Rights of the Child, condemned Israel for torture of children, arbitrary arrest and their use as human shields.[71] Israel responded that it wasn't a report 'that aims to promote any real improvement, but only to grab headlines'. Be that as it may, the report contains serious charges. Once again, however, the message is obscured by the messenger because the eighteen-member committee includes notorious human-rights abusers like Saudi Arabia, Sri Lanka, Tunisia, Egypt, Ghana and Bahrain.

That is a great pity because dealing with child misbehaviour in a political context is a fraught issue which needs advice and scrutiny. A boy of five who throws a stone cannot be ignored – he could hit someone in the eye or cause a driver to lose control of a car – but the way Israeli soldiers reacted in Hebron to Wadi Maswadeh raised worrying questions. A video released by the human rights organisation B'Tselem showed him surrounded by six armed soldiers; he cried and struggled as they put him in a military jeep with a Palestinian adult. They took him home, picked up his father, bound and blindfolded him in front of his son, and after half an hour handed them to Palestinian police who questioned and released them. B'Tselem noted the soldiers acted illegally as the age of criminal responsibility in Israel and the West Bank is twelve.[72]

A balance is needed between the malevolence of critics and the validity of some or all of their accusations. The United Nations and its spin-off organisations are the best the current world can offer, and, imperfect as they may be and are, they reflect the state of the world; they cannot be totally rejected.

Israel has shown itself to be willing to change; hence two reports in October 2013. First, UNICEF announced that the IDF was cooperating with it and would test a new approach in arresting children wanted for questioning by going to their homes during the day and not at night. (The IDF said it was still working on the policy.)[73] Second, the government told the High Court of Justice that it had further shortened periods of detention for Palestinians on the West Bank, and particularly regarding minors. The shortened periods refer to the amount of time that suspects can be held without charge.[74]

* * *

Wrong history: 'In 1947, the US-dominated United Nations called for the splitting of Palestine'. That's in an 'educational booklet' produced by the Canadian trade union CUPE British Columbia.[75]

The swipe at the United States in the founding of Israel is inaccurate: it omits that the Soviet Union belonged to the United Nations and joined the United States and a two-thirds majority of General Assembly members to vote for splitting Palestine. It also ignores that the United States was not wholly supportive of a Jewish state: President Harry Truman overrode his State Department to back it.

The same falsification of history is on the website of the Institute for Palestine Studies, Photograph Collection. The caption of a picture of a crowd in Cairo in December 1947 claims that the partition resolution was 'virtually forced through the UN General Assembly by the United States'.

* * *

There is no way to deal rationally with the depth of prejudice against Israel reflected in those who say that PEPSI (as in Pepsi-Cola) is actually an acronym for 'Pay Every Penny to Save Israel'. As reportedly said on TV by Hazem Abu Ismail, a Muslim cleric in Egypt: 'They say: Donate the small change you don't need, but give it to the right cause. If you collect small change you can buy this drink'.[76] He is not a lone nutter. The same statement is attributed to a Hamas member of Parliament, Salem Salamah.

Equally, a newspaper report about Britain's chancellor George Osborne giving evidence to the Leveson inquiry into phone-hacking somehow triggered a primitive hatred from a reader. Among the scores of comments which dealt with the inquiry he or she wrote: 'Friends of Israel huh? Zionist control of western media presently stands at 96%. They want it to be 100% so they can take complete control of all institutions without anyone realizing. Meanwhile they're doing a fantastic job of supporting terrorists in Syria who are slaughtering the locals'.[77]

In the same nutty spirit, As'ad Ramlawi, director of Primary Health Care in the Palestine Authority, blamed Israel for the increase in the number of AIDS patients (there were seventy-seven) in the Palestinian territories. Previously, Egypt had accused Israel of spreading AIDS in the Arab world by dispatching prostitutes to these countries.[78] In Lebanon, the Ministry of Agriculture found it necessary to deny media reports that imported Israeli tomatoes were injected with cancerous cells. In Egypt, the government investigated Israeli tomatoes to check if they contained solanine, a chemical harmful to the liver, after a report in the *al-Ahram* newspaper.[79]

* * *

Also beyond understanding or debate is Professor Arnd Kruger, a sports historian at the University of Gottingen in Germany. According to him, the murder of eleven Israeli athletes during the Munich Olympic Games on 5

September 1972 was not the work of Black September, the Palestinian terrorist group with ties to Fatah; nor could any blame be placed on incompetence on the part of German authorities. Instead, he has claimed that the murdered Israeli athletes had prior knowledge of the planned massacre and consciously decided to stay at the Olympic village to sacrifice themselves for the Jewish state.

Kruger supported what a journalist described as 'nothing but anti-Semitic conspiracy theories' by saying that there was 'a different perception of the human body' in Israel compared to other industrialised nations, and that Israel was 'trying to prevent at all costs living with disabilities' and had a higher abortion rate than other Western countries.[80]

\* \* \*

The photograph on the al-Jazeera television website showed three grim-looking policemen in riot gear holding strengthened shields.[81] Distributed by the international Gallo/Getty agency, it could have come from anywhere in the world, whether New York or Paris, Cairo or Johannesburg. That's what police who deal with civil unrest look like these days. But the accompanying report by Cairo-based Ahmed Moor, 'The front line of ethnic cleansing', gave it a vicious twist, saying: 'A brutish black-clad Israeli police hoard [*sic*] marched up and down a narrow, dusty Silwan street'.

\* \* \*

The BBC's Radio 4 reported that an Israeli hospital in the north was treating scores of Syrians suffering from wounds or illness. The Israeli army allowed them across the border and brought them to the hospital. It's a fractional number of people in terms of the destruction in Syria, with 126,000 deaths and two million refugees reported at the end of 2013. But Syria and Israel are in a state of war, have been so for more than six decades and the border is closed. That made the care given to Syrians an unusual and strong news story about human goodness at work.

But Electronic Intifada did not see it in that happy way. It could not bear to have anything nice said about Israel. In its bile-filled view, 'Israel's PR machine staged a masterclass in how to manipulate a willing media into whitewashing its stained reputation'. The 'easy puppets' were BBC reporters, editors and producers. It was enraged that Radio 4 gave the story five minutes of airtime and, even more, that a TV version was put on the BBC website, to stay there forever.[82]

It was also choleric that Israel had recently sent humanitarian aid to the storm-devastated Philippines. No matter that many countries sent aid and that their media reported it. But to Electronic Intifada, Israel was 'playing up' its aid 'to burnish its image'.

Electronic Intifada propaganda depicting Israel as all bad and to be blamed for just about anything nasty in the region went all the way in the same report: Gaza was at a point of near catastrophe, it said, because a shortage of industrial fuel had stopped waste pumps from working and raw sewage was flooding the streets. And whose fault was it? 'Israel's occupation and seven-year siege has reached a point where it is causing unprecedented suffering'.

That was an enormous untruth. Gaza was indeed in agony, and Israel's siege was continuing as before, but, as widely reported, the November 2013 crisis was caused because Egypt destroyed hundreds of tunnels that had carried fuel and just about everything else into the territory from the south and also closed the border. It did so because it accused Gaza's ruling Hamas of interfering in its internal affairs and specifically of involvement in deadly attacks on Egyptian soldiers in the Sinai.

* * *

Muslims in South Africa went down to the depths in their anti-Israel activities by importing Dr Abdul Aziz Umar to speak at mosques. Released in the 2011 swap of Palestinian prisoners for Gilad Shalit, he was exiled to Gaza. He was the guest of the al-Quds Foundation of South Africa and the Muslim Judicial Council to promote a forthcoming 'March on Jerusalem' and to raise awareness about Palestinian political prisoners in Israel. He told the media that Israel had sentenced him to four life sentences and another thirty years: 'the charge was that I was spreading "new and strange ideas" in my intellectual and academic works'.[83]

The truth rapidly emerged: he was a liar and a murderer. He was a Hamas leader jailed for seven life sentences for dispatching the suicide bomber who blew up the Café Hillel in Jerusalem on 9 September 2003: seven people died and forty were wounded; among the dead was Nava, whose wedding was scheduled for the next day, and her father, Dr David Applebaum, much-admired for his work in extending emergency medical services to everyone, Jews and Arabs.

* * *

Dark beliefs about Israel's power to direct the United States government are not far below the surface, even in high circles; hence Charles Freeman Jr, former ambassador to Saudi Arabia and China, was nominated to chair the Obama administration's National Intelligence Council. This immediately drew questions from Congress members about his suitability in view of his having chided Beijing for not crushing the Tiananmen Square democracy protests sooner and offering sycophantic paeans to Saudi king Abdullah.

Freeman withdrew from consideration for the job and issued a two-page statement describing himself as the victim of a shadowy and sinister 'Lobby' which was 'intent on enforcing adherence to the policies of a foreign government'. An editorial in the *Washington Post* noted: 'Yes, Mr Freeman was referring to Americans who support Israel – and his statement was a grotesque libel. . . . Crackpot tirades such as his have always had an eager audience here and around the world'.[84]

\* \* \*

A lawyer, Marwan Dalal of Adalah, the Legal Center for Arab Minority Rights in Israel, has spoken about the 1948–1966 period: 'Curfews were imposed on non-Jews. There was restriction of movement, banning of political parties, and enactment of laws aimed at the dispossession of the native community of historic Palestine'.[85]

All, of course, correct, and all obviously about the martial law during that time, which stemmed from the internal war in 1948 in which many in the Arab community had taken part and were thus viewed and treated as hostile by Israel's government – a straightforward, and not unique, situation of civil war, conquest and control.

Yet to Dalal, none of this was relevant. To him, 'the reality on the ground was that Israel was a classical apartheid state'! To make that claim, he must be wholly ignorant about what apartheid in South Africa was.

\* \* \*

Complaints are regularly heard that Palestinian television and books use maps which omit Israel. One of many instances was a children's show, *Chicks*, on Palestinian Authority TV, which included all of Israel yet was labelled 'Palestine'.[86] Also the privately published English brochure, 'This Week in Palestine', aimed at tourists. It has an advisory board of distinguished Palestinians. Its July 2012 issue had a full-page 'Palestine Road Map' – stretching from the Mediterranean to the Jordan. No mention of Israel.

Such denial of Israel's existence is both false and stirs Jewish fears about Palestinian intentions. On the other hand, Israel perpetrates the same in reverse: less than a year earlier, the Israel Government Tourist Office had to remove posters on London Underground stations which had maps showing the occupied territories as part of Israel.[87] Two years earlier, the tourist office was accused of using a map of Israel showing Qumram, which is on the West Bank.

* * *

Words are often misused and quotations are invented to besmirch Israel and its leaders. They spread like wildfire through the Internet and are accepted as gospel. To check them can be a considerable exercise in hunting through newspapers and books and is not always successful. One distorted quote repeatedly used in propaganda material is Nelson Mandela's words in support of Palestinian freedom. Pro-Palestinian organisations quote him as saying: 'But we know too well that our freedom is incomplete without the freedom of the Palestinians'. President Mandela did indeed say that, on 4 December 1997, on the UN International Day of Solidarity with the Palestinian People. But it's actually half of what he said, according to the African National Congress website.

Mandela's other, omitted, words explain the context – and the invalidity in singling out Israel – because, in fact, he related the Palestinian struggle to the worldwide struggle for freedom for everyone. 'But we know too well that our freedom is incomplete without the freedom of the Palestinians; *without the resolution of conflicts in East Timor, the Sudan and other parts of the world*' (emphasis added).

The Palestinian Authority's President Mahmoud Abbas played the same selective game in commenting on Mandela's death in December 2013: 'The Palestinian people will never forget his historic statement that the South African revolution will not have achieved its goals as long as the Palestinians are not free', he said.[88] So did others writing in *Haaretz* – Khalid Diab and Gideon Levy. The latter is given to making the Israel-equals-apartheid comparison. His eagerness led to him seriously misreporting an opinion survey: his claim that it found that most Israelis wanted an apartheid regime was wrong; he wrote an apology which wasn't an apology.[89] Hanoch Marmari, a former editor of *Haaretz*, castigated Levy in the *Seventh Eye*, an Israeli media journal, concluding: 'Levy has relinquished his journalist credentials'.[90]

Allister Sparks, a South African journalist, does the opposite, inserting words, presumably with the aim of denigrating Israel.[91] He says he is quoting from the diary of the Zionist founder Theodor Herzl for 12 June 1895: 'We shall try to spirit the penniless (Palestinian) populations across the border . . . while denying it in Palestine'. However, the words 'Palestinian' and 'Palestine' are not in that diary entry![92] Inserting them falsifies Herzl's views. Instead, historians note that in 1895 Herzl was still developing his Zionist ideas, and he was thinking of colonial settlement of Jews in Latin America; Argentina was uppermost in his mind. It is described as his period of 'manic ruminations'.

Sparks is a well-known political commentator but compounds his sin of commission with the sin of omission: he says Hamas 'contains a clause in its charter declining to recognize Israel's right to exist'. He puts it so politely. However, he omits the words of the charter's Article 7: 'the Hamas has been looking forward to implement[ing] Allah's promise whatever time it might take. The prophet, prayer and peace be upon him, said: The time will not come until Muslims will fight the Jews (and kill them); until the Jews hide behind rocks and trees, which will cry: O Muslim! there is a Jew hiding behind me, come on and kill him!'[93] No polite 'declining' there and nothing to persuade Jews that they should entrust their life and liberty to Hamas.

Sparks is among those Westerners who seek to sanitise Hamas. Do they really approve of a terrorist movement which has kept itself in office by throwing people off high buildings and enforcing oppressive sharia laws? Would they be willing to live under such a regime? How do they end up supporting such an anti-freedom stance? Is it simply a response to loathing Israel and/or Jews?

* * *

Israeli leaders who have to confront war and terror make tough statements. But invention and distortion add a spin that is intended to present the leaders as inhumane.

The abusive statement that Palestinians 'are beasts walking on two legs' is attributed to Menachem Begin when he was prime minister. It's in an article, 'Begin and the Beasts', by Amnon Kapeliouk in the *New Statesman* of 25 June 1982 (and spread further in anti-Israel propaganda such as Professor Mona Baker's website). But Begin didn't say it. His original very different and emotional words are recorded in the Knesset on 8 June 1982:

> I want to declare to all nations: The children of Israel will happily go to school and joyfully return home, just like the children in Washington, in Moscow and in Peking; in Paris and in Rome; in Oslo, in Stockholm and in Copenhagen. The fate of . . . Jewish children has been different from all the children of the world throughout the generations. No more. We will defend our children. If the hand of any two-footed animal is raised against them, that hand will be cut off, and our children will grow up in joy in the homes of their parents.

Yitzhak Shamir, another right-wing prime minister, is widely reported to have said: 'The Palestinians would be crushed like grasshoppers . . . heads smashed against boulders and walls'. Rough words, indeed. However, Shamir did not speak about Palestinians but about 'rioters'.[94]

Mazim Qumsiyeh, on 6 January 2008, and many others quote Prime Minister Ariel Sharon as telling Shimon Peres on 3 October 2001, as reported on Radio Kol Israel: 'Every time we do something you tell me America will do this or that . . . I want to tell you something very clear: Don't worry about American pressure on Israel. We, the Jewish people, control America, and the Americans know it'.

It's an invention, as the late Ami Isseroff checked and discovered. Sharon never said it and the radio never reported it.[95]

There was also: 'We have to kill all the Palestinians unless they are resigned to live here as slaves', attributed to 'Chairman Heilbrun of the Committee for the Re-election of General Shlomo Lahat, the mayor of Tel Aviv, October 1983'.

Isseroff noted this, too, was an invention. There was never anybody named Heilbrun on any committee to reelect Lahat. And anyway, Lahat was a moderate who supported the peace process.

\* \* \*

Farid Esack, described as a writer, scholar and human rights activist, has written feelingly: 'As South Africans speaking up about the life or death for the Palestinian people is also about salvaging our own dream of a moral society that will not be complicit in the suffering of other people. There are, of course, other instances of oppression, dispossession and marginalisation in the world. Yet, none of these are as immediately recognizable to us who lived under South African apartheid and fought for liberation from it. . . . Palestine reflects in many ways the unfinished business of our own struggle'.[96]

These words from the heart deserve respect. But they do also lead to questions: Why is the Palestinian struggle uniquely relevant in a world beset by human misbehaviour and so many victims? Why not, as noted earlier, the heroic struggle of the Tibetan people against Chinese oppression for more than sixty years? Why not the Kurdish unremitting struggle against Turkey for independence? What did Farid Esack have to say while the (Christian) South Sudanese were fighting for freedom, and suffering so intensely, against the (Muslim) North Sudanese? And the Copt victims of persecution in Egypt? Why are they not 'immediately recognizable' as worthy of support?

His attempt elsewhere to explain this is derisory: the West backs Israel and that makes the situation unique, he says. Like so many others, he lists horrors of the Israeli occupation – 'barbaric and diverse forms of collective punishment', the 'macabre' wall, and so forth – as though all of it is due to the evil Jews acting cruelly and wilfully. He shows no awareness of the history of conflict in the region, what each people has done to the other over the years and how the past has determined the present.

Esack is a Muslim scholar who studied in Pakistan and has been visiting professor in Islamic studies at Harvard University's Divinity School. Yet where does he stand in the horrifically violent struggles between Shias and Sunnis in Pakistan, Iraq and Iran? Does he condemn and urge international action against the Islamist al-Shabaab, which has been terrorising Somalia since 2007 and threatening Kenya? Does he support the United Nations and the African Union in opposing this movement whose terrorism has led to mass starvation and which has prevented Western aid groups from helping victims? Did he show his anger at the leaders of Libya and Syria who, starting in early 2011, started killing their own protesting people en masse? It might be that Esack is as active in these spheres as he is, with far less reason, in condemning Israel; but if so, the information is not readily available in the public domain.

Whatever Esack's academic quality might be, it deserts him when he deals with Israel. He wrote to Salif Keita, Mali's 'Golden Voice of Africa', urging him not to perform at Jerusalem's sacred music festival in August 2013. He signed the letter as 'Head of Religion Studies at the University of Johannesburg and Chair of BDS South Africa's Management Board' – an unusual linkage of university teaching with an extremist political stance, which must raise academic eyebrows and give pause to potential students. Nor is there evidence of academic standards in his array of distorted and wrong claims, such as the apartheid canard, repeating Ronnie Kasrils's mis-use of the words of apartheid architect Hendrik Verwoerd, an overblown reference to so-called full-fledged race riots in Israel, and the same crude misquoting of Nelson Mandela described earlier. Anyway, it failed: Salif Keita ignored him and sang to a capacity audience in Jerusalem.

\* \* \*

Among critics are doctors who are experts in their field and thus dedicated to checking facts; but they lose it when it comes to Israel and are open to believing the worst. This was the case with Dr Derek Pounder, a British forensic expert from Dundee University who went with Amnesty International to the West Bank city of Jenin after Israel's Operation Defensive Shield in April 2002. Apparently carried along on the tide of Palestinian claims of five hundred dead, he told the BBC that he had seen bodies lying in the streets and received eyewitness accounts of civilian deaths; the Amnesty investigation had only just begun, but Palestinian claims of a massacre were gaining foundation as the team continued its analysis:

> The truth will come out, as it has come out in Bosnia and Kosovo, as it has in other places where we've had these kinds of allegations. I must say that the evidence before us at the moment doesn't lead us to believe that the allegations are anything other than truthful and that therefore there are large numbers of civilian dead underneath these bulldozed and bombed ruins that we see.[97]

In fact, the death toll proved to be about fifty-five Palestinians and twenty-three Israeli soldiers. Terrible, but nothing remotely like what had been alleged. There is no record available on Google that Pounder ever explained himself.

\* \* \*

Sabeel, the Ecumenical Theological Liberation Center in Jerusalem, explains that it emerged in 1990 out of the need for Palestinian Christian clergy to respond to the cries of their people about their physical suffering and their question, 'Where is God in all of this oppression and injustice?'[98] While rabbis have in the past had to face the same fraught question, and so do imams today, Sabeel says it speaks for Christians of different denominations who occupy their own niche: Jerusalem has been the focus of their faith for two thousand years, yet their numbers are declining. Sabeel adds that another reason for coming into existence is that many Palestinian Christians wanted to abandon the Bible, particularly the Old Testament, because of its use to justify their suffering: 'As Christians, however, the Bible is essential to our faith, so it was necessary to find in the Bible the God of justice, the God who is concerned with the oppressed'.

This is a dimension little heard among Jews. It's a striking turning point in history because for many centuries Christians used the Bible to motivate and justify the terrible prejudices and cruelties they heaped on Jews. And Jews survived because of their faith in the God of the Bible.

Sabeel has grown into an influential voice in the Christian world and beyond. Its Kairos Palestinian declaration on 15 December 2009 – the Christian Palestinians' 'word to the world' – is heard at church assemblies, especially in the United States and Europe, with its passionate support for the rights of Palestinians and condemnation of the occupation. Sabeel says that nonviolent resistance is 'a right and a duty' for all Palestinians. It urges economic sanctions and boycotts – to treat Israel 'exactly as most of the world treated apartheid South Africa . . . as a pariah state'.[99]

The 'apartheid' accusation is a regular theme and is as incorrect as it always was. It could be that Sabeel derives its view from what it is told by other Christians, especially in South Africa. If so, it needs to be more careful, as with the interview reported in Kairos Palestine with Dr Alan Boesak, who was once a charismatic and brave leader in the anti-apartheid struggle.[100] Boesak was also a leader in the apartheid-era section for mixed-race coloureds in the Dutch Reformed Church and went on to become president of the World Alliance of Reformed Churches.[101]

According to Boesak, '[W]hat's happening in Israel today is a system of apartheid that in its perpetuation of that system is more terrifying in many ways than apartheid in South Africa ever was'. This is a serious charge, all the more coming from Boesak's eminence in fighting apartheid. But even in his own words, there is no basis to the charge. Either he has lost his memory of what apartheid was like or he is inventing. He says, 'We carried passes as the Palestinians have their ID documents but that did not mean that we could not go from one place in the city to another place in the city'. (*As a coloured, he did not carry a 'pass'; only the majority black people did and they were subject to instant arrest if they could not produce the document when demanded by a policeman; there is not the slightest similarity to the ID carried by Palestinians, whether in the West Bank, or Israeli Arabs in Israel; in South Africa, despite what he says, blacks did indeed have problems going 'from one place in the city to another place in the city'; the relevance to Palestinians is obscure.*)

Boesak also claimed that the apartheid system was skewed but did not 'openly, blatantly have two separate judicial systems as they do for Palestinians'. (*There was indeed a separate system of laws and courts for blacks: these were the Bantu Commissioners' Courts which applied the laws specific to black people and dealt with pass offenders en masse.*)

Other claims in the interview are equally startling: the Arab Spring of 2011 would not have happened, he says, 'if it had not been for the perennial struggle of the Palestinian people'; he also blames Israel for the exodus of Christians from the Holy Land – with not a word about any Muslim responsibility. Yet it seems that it is on the basis of such jaundiced and inaccurate information that Kairos formulates policy.

Kairos Palestine describes itself as 'a moment of truth' and carries scores of articles about Israel. Virtually each one is unremittingly hostile, selected to show the country in the worst possible light. That includes an article from the website 'Shoah: The Palestine Holocaust', whose title is obscene and which talks of 'Zio-Nazi racism' by Israel. In this case, the website's article was a criticism of Rowan Williams, then Anglican archbishop of Canterbury, for having dared to mention Muslim pressures in the exodus of Christians from Bethlehem.

Further light on Sabeel is cast by the Rev Dr Naim Ateek, an Anglican priest who is its founder, president and director. In an Easter 2001 message, he resurrected the worst, and now formally abandoned, Christian calumnies against Jews; he used imagery linking the modern Jewish state with the deicide accusation that for centuries led to the murder of so many Jews. His words were:

> In this season of Lent, it seems to many of us that Jesus is on the cross again with thousands of crucified Palestinians around him. It only takes people of insight to see the hundreds of thousands of crosses throughout the land, Palestinian men, women, and children being crucified. Palestine has become one

huge golgotha. The Israeli government crucifixion system is operating daily. Palestine has become the place of the skull. [102]

Given the prejudices and violent antipathy of Ateek and Sabeel, it is no surprise that to many Israelis they are an enemy whose views are of no account. That is a pity because well-founded Christian criticisms should be part of the debate inside Israel. It's also a pity because Ateek and Sabeel are a long, long way from their declared commitment to Jesus Christ's message of 'justice, peace and reconciliation', at least as far as their relations with Jews are concerned. And it is surprising and disturbing that their views draw support from other Christians.

* * *

Desmond Tutu, Anglican archbishop emeritus of Cape Town and Nobel Peace laureate, is famed for his moral stand against apartheid, for his courage in opposing the Afrikaner government as well as vigilante murders by anti-apartheid protestors. [103] Even after the end of apartheid, he continued to speak in moral terms against the ruling African National Congress. He enjoys immense international credibility. He has increasingly applied his moral strictures to Israel, condemning the occupation and supporting boycotts as a means to put pressure on Israel. That has drawn angry, really vicious, attacks on him from some Jews. Anyone who knows Tutu is aware that many of the criticisms of what he has said, or is alleged to have said, are either misunderstood or are taken out of the context of the time in which they were expressed. [104]

As Tutu would himself readily admit – no doubt with a laugh – he is not God and he is not infallible. He insists that he believes in Israel's existence and that he says so repeatedly. [105] As against that, he seems to have become so imbued with a sense of mission that, in person or by video, he has become a standard fixture at conferences around the world, organised by people who are intent on destroying Israel. He is probably the world's leading voice in castigating Israel, hence the view of him among many Jews as someone who, whether consciously or naively, lines up with Israel's implacable enemies.

There is reason for uneasiness about some of the premises on which Tutu bases his criticisms. One of them is his oft-said statement (which others also make) that Israel is 'worse than apartheid'. This apparently comes out of short visits he has made to the West Bank and the Gaza Strip during times of unrest and refers to what he has seen or been told about Israeli checkpoints, controls on movement, mass arrests and jailings, assassinations, separate roads for Palestinian and Israeli cars, and using overwhelming firepower on the ground and from the air, especially during periods of open conflict.

The 'worse than apartheid' label makes a comparison which is entirely invalid. During the anti-apartheid struggle inside South Africa, as earlier noted, blacks did not resort to suicide bombings and roadside shootings as Palestinians have done. Blacks, with only a handful of exceptions, did not attack hotels, restaurants, buses or private homes and kill indiscriminately, including babies. Unlike Israel, South Africa was never subject to rocket attacks, in the thousands, from neighbouring areas. The anti-apartheid resistance never made it necessary to have armed guards outside hotels, bus and train stations, restaurants, supermarkets, banks and office blocks. Unlike Israel, it was never necessary to guard the coastline night and day against terrorists trying to infiltrate to kidnap and murder. It was never necessary to apply stringent controls at airports, both at home and abroad, to protect against terrorist attacks, nor was it necessary to fit the national airline's aircraft with expensive and weight-consuming protection against ground-fired missiles.

These are the differences between the freedom struggles in South Africa and in Palestine. The levels of violence against civilians have driven Israel to adopt anti-terrorist measures and to apply controls that were never remotely thought of in South Africa. And in any event, the comparison is meaningless because Israel's behaviour has nothing to do with apartheid but stems from its occupation. Using the apartheid label confuses and detracts from the fact of the occupation.

Not only does Tutu seem unaware of the fundamental differences between Israel and South Africa, but he also does not seem to understand the difference between Palestinians in Israel and Palestinians on the West Bank and Gaza. In supporting the boycott by the University of Johannesburg of Ben-Gurion University in September 2010, he said: 'Israeli universities are an intimate part of the Israeli regime, by active choice. While Palestinians are not able to access universities and schools, Israeli universities produce the research, technology, arguments, and leaders for maintaining the occupation.[106] Leaving aside his inexplicable use of 'regime', a word usually reserved for a government not considered entirely legitimate and thus contradicting his assurance that he supports Israel's existence, he doesn't make sense: doesn't he know that Israeli Arabs/Palestinians have full access to Israeli schools and universities, whereas Palestinians on the West Bank and Gaza are not Israeli citizens, have no automatic right of entry to Israel or its universities and have their own eleven universities (all, incidentally, opened during the occupation)?

A month later, Tutu backed another boycott, calling on Cape Town Opera to call off its coming tour of Israel with 'Porgy and Bess' 'until both Israeli and Palestinian opera lovers have equal opportunity and unfettered access to performances'.[107] He thus perpetrated the same mistake because all Israeli opera lovers, whatever their group or religion, can attend the Tel Aviv Opera

House; however, Palestinians from the West Bank need permission to enter Israel, whether to go to the opera or for anything else. Tutu gratuitously added an insulting comment, accusing the state-sponsored Tel Aviv Opera of furthering Israel's 'fallacious claim to being a civilised democracy'. He was also confused about 'Porgy and Bess', speaking of 'its universal message of non-discrimination'. Of course it's nothing of the sort but is about a disabled black beggar in fictitious Catfish Row, in Charleston, South Carolina, in the early 1920s. Its music is by George Gershwin, a Jew. The opera is criticised by some as a racist portrayal of African Americans.

Cape Town Opera rejected Tutu's call and went on to give eighteen successful performances in Tel Aviv. Yet, clearly, vast numbers of people throughout the world heed the archbishop's moral advice and follow his lead. He lends his name to students, activists and churches who want to boycott Israel. But isn't it alarming that a person of his high status, who repeatedly urges others to harm Israel, is so mistaken in his facts?

* * *

There is more to question. 'Mine is a *cri de coeur*', Tutu told a Sabeel conference in Boston in the United States on 27 October 2007, 'a cry of anguish from the heart, an impassioned appeal to my spiritual relatives, the offspring of Abraham like me – please hear the call of your noble scriptures, of our scriptures'. He urged Jews to

> deal with the oppressed, the weak, the despised compassionately, caringly, remembering what happened to you in Egypt and much more recently in Germany. Remember and act appropriately. If you reject your calling, you may survive for a long time, but you will find that it is all corrosive inside and one day you will implode. [108]

It's a theme to which he returns, and he puts it so eloquently. Many Jews agree with Tutu and argue that their Judaic belief and historical anti-Semitic experiences impose a natural obligation to be acutely aware of the suffering of others, to help them and not hurt them. Ervin Staub, professor emeritus in psychology at the University of Massachusetts–Amherst, agrees with that view but also puts another side. His expertise is the study of why people do terrible things to each other and, conversely, why people do good things for each other without hope of reward and even imperil their lives. [109]

Staub argues that any people who have been traumatised by suffering, or who carry knowledge of the suffering of their group, could well be more sympathetic to the plight of the other. However, in sharp contradiction, people who have survived attempts to injure or kill them, or whose people have so suffered, could be resolutely determined not to allow it to happen again.

They will stop at nothing to survive. The more they are cornered and threatened, the greater their resistance.

Hence the behaviour of Israeli Jews. Many of them – plus Jews elsewhere in the world – are angry, ashamed and embarrassed about any discrimination against Israeli Arabs and vehemently oppose the injustice in the occupation. Others, however, view it all as vital for their own survival and that of the Jewish people; they do not acknowledge any moral failings on their part but believe instead that they are engaged in a just and holy struggle against a hostile world to ensure the future of the Jewish people.

In Staub's words,[110] he believes, 'on the basis of research and observations of individuals and groups of people who have been victimized, and have been the objects of violence, that they feel vulnerable and see the world as dangerous. In the face of new threat, danger or attack, they have a strong need to defend themselves. This is natural and even right. But because of their vulnerability and sense of danger, they tend to react more forcefully than necessary for self-protection.

'Identity, a sense of community, can be built around past trauma and woundedness. The culture can maintain and transmit it. It is therefore not only members of the group who have suffered, but also their descendants, who often feel vulnerable and may react to threat with an unnecessary level of force'.

Staub also points to what is possible:

> But this is far from inevitable. Individuals and groups can heal from psychological wounds. Because the group suffered as a whole, because the focus of the suffering is maintained by the group, healing ideally will be group healing. Commemorations that focus not only on the wounds of the past but also on the possibilities of a better future are useful. Acknowledgement by perpetrators, and/or the rest of the world, of the harm done to the group, is helpful. Exploring how the past shapes the perception of and reactions to current events, creating awareness, can limit overreaction to threat.
>
> People can move beyond healing, in what I call 'altruism born of suffering'. This makes possible the kind of empathy for the other that Tutu hoped for. Caring and support for each other within the group, and by outsiders, can help, as it makes people feel that the world does not have to be as they once experienced it. A central thesis is that both violence and caring and helping evolve, as individuals and groups change as a result of their own actions. Beginning to help others can further altruism born of suffering. Leaders, the media and opinion-makers can lead a group to be sympathetic to, altruistic in relation to, the suffering of another group.
>
> It is tragic that Jews and Palestinians are both wounded people, facing each other. Overreactions can therefore come from either group, leading to strong reciprocal violence. Someone has to begin to act in ways that can generate positive reciprocity.

Amid such human complexities, Desmond Tutu's emotional and worthy *cri de coeur* looks oversimple. It is flattering for Jews to be told to act as super-humans. But Jews – and Palestinians – would benefit from better-informed criticisms, greater understanding and compassion, and help, from him.

# Chapter Ten

# Boycotts

*The extent to which boycotts of Israel can effect change is debatable. In any event, boycott calls can be misleading: they are not always intended to push Israel into changing but are a cover for seeking to destroy the country.*

\* \* \*

Boycott, as a means of nonviolent protest and action, is meant to persuade the targeted group that it is better to change their ways than suffer damaging sanctions. It's a tactic, not a principle: boycott cannot be applied always, to every situation. It's to be used when appropriate, intelligently, with clear goals; otherwise not only will it fail to achieve its aims, but it can be counter-productive by stiffening resistance to change.

Calls for boycotting Israel cite apartheid South Africa. Yet the South African experience is not as certain as some believe or claim. In discussing possible pressures on Iran because of its nuclear activities, Natasha Bahrami and Trita Parsi cited studies showing low success rates for sanctions.[1] They said:

> While broad economic sanctions rarely achieve their goals, especially with respect to regime change, the question remains whether they aid in democrat-ization. Unquestionably, they aren't necessary: of 35 authoritarian states that successfully transitioned to democracy since 1955, only one – South Africa – did so under broad economic sanctions. Even in the South African case, it is not clear whether sanctions helped the transition to democracy or if they actu-ally prolonged apartheid. Economist Mats Lundahl suggests that sanctions against the industrial sector contributed to the longevity of the agrarian-based apartheid regime. The trade, investment, and oil boycotts were harsher on industry, thus inadvertently advancing the agricultural sector by strengthening its grasp on the unskilled labor market.[2]

Lundahl argues that if industrial capitalism had been allowed to flourish, a labour market shift to the industrial sector would have organically accelerated the end of apartheid, a system that relied on the availability of large masses of cheap unskilled labor and suppressed the emergence of a numerically strong skilled labor force. Thus, even the most widely cited case of sanctions' success is, at best, debatable.

To which can be added that the United Nations oil boycott which began in 1979 could and should have been crucial in forcing the apartheid regime to its knees. The boycott did not succeed because, as far as is known, except for one period of about three weeks, South Africa was never short of oil.[3] It was able to buy oil direct or on the spot market on the high seas from Saudi Arabia, the Gulf states, Iran and Iraq, and any other country willing to sell. Foreign correspondent Robin Knight, who later worked for the BP oil company, describes its 'prolonged involvement in circumventing' the UN oil embargo and 'its 20-year denial that it had broken UN sanctions'.[4] During the Iran-Iraq war (1980–1988), both countries sold oil to South Africa in return for arms. South Africa paid perhaps up to 20 to 30 percent above market prices for oil, but it got what it needed. Middlemen became multibillionaires.

Just how ineffective boycotts can be was also illustrated by South Africa's northern neighbour Rhodesia, also white-ruled, which declared independence (UDI) in November 1965 and immediately became the target for extensive international sanctions, notably oil. But it never ran short. At first, gas poured over the border from South Africa on such a vast scale that Rhodesians had a storage problem. Later, oil was supplied by BP – then partly owned by the British government – through the Mozambique port of Beira. This was done even while British warships spent years sailing up and down the Mozambiquan coast to stop sanctions-busting! Marxist Mozambique, the enemy of Rhodesia, connived and an overland pipeline carried oil from Beira to Rhodesia. Another instance of an ineffective boycott is Cuba: fifty years of a US trade embargo might have weakened the government there, but it has not fallen.

Iran and Syria also have been subject to international boycotts as the means of forcing their respective governments to change their policies. The boycotts certainly had results. The significant factor is that the breadth and strength of the boycotts far outstripped what was done to apartheid South Africa. UN resolutions did not only receive lip-service but were actually implemented, in particular by the United States and other powerful nations. The most effective actions were the blocking of international financial transactions and the threat of military attack.

Again in regard to South Africa: it is doubtful that a single country in the world didn't trade with it, and that includes Africa. Israel's total trade with apartheid South Africa in 1986 was about $214 million with an estimated additional $272 million to $544 million in arms, that is, a total of $480 million to $788 million.[5] That was little compared with others: boycotts and disinvestment were spreading rapidly at that time, and South Africa concealed trade details. But the available statistics showed that in 1986 two-way trade with the United States was about $3.32 billion; with Japan, $3.27 billion; and with Britain, $2.52 billion. Exports totalled about $19.14 billion and imports $12.2 billion. Israel was thus a small player. Yet critics persistently single it out for having traded with apartheid as though it was the world's only sinner.

South Africa is said to have bought arms from the United Kingdom, France, Italy, West Germany, the United States, Israel and Spain. Nuclear cooperation up to 1975 was provided by France, the United States and West Germany; Israel became a major partner with South Africa.

Trade with everyone continued apace even though foreign corporations were leaving in droves. The country suffered some deprivation, especially in technological know-how, but trade gaps were rapidly filled by others. When the US Kodak left, Japan's Fuji did well; the US Ford and General Motors left to the benefit of Japan's Toyota and Nissan and Germany's Volkswagen and Mercedes.

Cultural and academic boycotts did have an effect. They did not directly bring down apartheid but were a contributory factor; over an extended period of years they helped to undermine the morale and self-confidence of whites, who were made to feel like pariahs. However, whether these boycotts were appropriate or wise is open to argument. That is because their chief victims were the liberal intelligentsia, the people who did so much to expose and to oppose apartheid. The academic boycott in particular kept liberal academics abroad from taking up posts at South Africa's English-language universities; the lack of them, and narrowing access to world writing and thinking, were among the factors which contributed over time to a lessening of anti-apartheid activity inside some universities. Sports boycotts, however, definitely helped to undermine white morale: the sports-loving white community was deeply hurt by being expelled from the Olympics, rugby, cricket and football.

\* \* \*

Israel has lived under boycotts since even before its birth: on 2 December 1945, three years before the state was created, the Arab League declared all Jewish and Zionist products 'to be undesirable to the Arab countries'. The Organisation of the Islamic Conference (now the Organisation of Islamic Cooperation) did the same in 1969. Sundry Arab states announce boycotts from time to time: thus in April 2004 the Central Boycott Office drew nineteen Arab countries to meet in Damascus.

The everyday effect has been seen in difficulties for the national El Al airline in not being allowed to overfly Arab countries, causing operational and cost problems; but El Al has survived and has flourished. Israeli passports are not accepted in many Arab states; all travellers, no matter their country of origin, are barred if their passports have Israeli visas. The boycotts have limited Israeli trade and people contact with neighbours and the wider Arab world; the Arab states lose in being deprived of ready access to Israeli goods and inventiveness and having to pay for what they want through under-the-counter dealings. It's an open secret that trade continues: Israeli tomato seeds are sold to Arab countries and Iranian dates can be bought in Jerusalem shops; joint financial deals between Jews and Arabs flourish in New York.

Trade is so extensive that in 2008 an Arab commentator complained about 'a growing culture of numbness and complicity towards Israel and its financial backers which is being cultivated at the highest levels of Arab governments. . . . Arab governments can no longer be, if ever they were, considered reliable champions of the boycott'. He was worried about undermining divestment attempts in the West.[6] In late 2012, even after changes brought by the Arab Spring, Tunisia was writing a boycott of Israel into a new constitution.

With all this, the bottom line is that boycotts have thus far failed to impede, let alone strangle, Israel.

* * *

This has not deterred opponents. Calls for boycott and divestment have rumbled on. The Palestine Solidarity Campaign was launched on 4 July 2001, urging 'boycott Israeli goods and leisure tourism'. Boycott was intended to be pushed wider into the world four months later, at the 2001 UN Anti-Racism Conference in Durban; it didn't happen because the anti-Israel schemers overreached themselves with their anti-Semitism and grotesque rhetoric, and in any event, within a week they were sidelined by 9/11 in New York.

The first concerted boycott attempt came in Britain in 2002 with a letter in the *Guardian* by British academics led by Professors Steven and Hilary Rose, both Jews.[7] In a statement economical with the facts – indeed it turned out to be hysterical and utterly wrong – they claimed that Israel had carried out a massacre in the Jenin refugee camp. A few weeks later there was similar action in Australia. By October 2002 petitions for divestment had been circulated on more than fifty US campuses. A small boycott call in France dwindled.

This was the prelude. Boycott got going in earnest on 5 July 2005: the Palestinian Campaign for the Academic and Cultural Boycott of Israel (PAC-

BI), meeting in Ramallah, backed the Boycott, Divestment and Sanctions campaign (BDS). The timing was understandable: Palestinians had failed to dislodge the occupation of the West Bank through the violence of the second intifada. Suicide bombers not only failed to force Jews to change but actually entrenched Jewish obduracy by confirming their fear that their very existence was threatened. The bombings also lost the Palestinians whatever moral standing they might have had in the world. The alternative strategy of nonviolent passive resistance requires high levels of discipline and organisation; it has been applied in protests against the seizing of Palestinian land but has been localised and without mass participation; heavy-handed Israeli army responses often ensure that it ends in violence.

BDS has been the obvious road to follow. It does not need any popular mobilisation in the occupied territories as it can be driven by a small number of the elite. It does not need any dangerous direct confrontation with Israeli rule and instead recruits external forces in the big wide world in the cause of Palestinian freedom. It can be publicised by playing to emotions, without bothering too much about facts or accuracy.

Omar Barghouti, born in Qatar but said to be a resident of Ramallah, is a founding member of the BDS movement and plays a prominent role in promoting it at meetings around the world and in media interviews and articles. He seeks to put campaigning against Israel on a lofty moral level, saying that BDS should be 'endorsed by any self-respecting (morally-consistent) liberal, not just by progressives'. It sounds good, but he does not practise the same morality himself. He graduated in electrical engineering from Columbia University and went on to a postgraduate degree in philosophy from Tel Aviv University. This does not chime with urging boycott. Some Tel Aviv students petitioned the university to expel him; the university refused, citing academic freedom.

Asked about his contradictory behaviour, Barghouti responded, 'My studies at Tel Aviv University are a personal matter and I have no interest in commenting'.[8] Barghouti's supporters defend him, saying that Nelson Mandela studied at the University of the Witwatersrand in Johannesburg which was subject to apartheid. But this is yet another instance of ignorance and mendacity because no academic boycott was in place when Mandela was a student in the 1940s; in addition, if Barghouti is not an Israeli citizen, he has studied at Tel Aviv University out of choice and not through necessity.

Barghouti at least showed some embarrassment in responding to a Tel Aviv University statement: they '"cannot and will not" expel me based on my political views and activism', he said in a 'Dear all' e-mail on 9 May 2009. How can he berate a university for denial of academic freedom when it has upheld his academic freedom? His gaggle of words dealing with that problem spoke about the 'well-documented complicity of Israel's academic institutions in the state's colonial and racist policies' and that expelling him 'would have added a bit more fuel to an already blazing fire!'

Not very convincing.

Barghouti's questionable morality is not unique. A number of Israeli Jewish academics also urge the world to boycott but choose to remain in their university jobs, such as Professor Neve Gordon at Ben-Gurion University. Gordon's strong support for boycott has angered donors to the university, leading to calls to fire him. The university has refused to do so. Gordon continues to receive his salary. He tells others to boycott but does not do so himself.

* * *

Israel provides would-be boycotters with all the propaganda ammunition they need. It does so through its occupation of the West Bank with all the consequent injustice, harshness and cruelty together with the creeping settlement of Jews in the territory and East Jerusalem, plus its siege of the Gaza Strip. And if anyone wants more material, it can be found in discrimination suffered by Israel's Arab minority. There are grounds aplenty for justifiable criticism, and the information is readily available. Enemies can make a damaging case against Israel simply by telling the truth. But that is not enough for them. Instead they habitually exaggerate, twist and pervert, and time and again the result is a caricature of Israel, at home and in the occupied territories. It is astonishing to read them. Such attitudes are so far beyond what actually exists that they can only come out of a deep, deep hatred for Israel and/or Jews and a huge, overwhelming, even uncontrollable urge to destroy the Jewish state.

BDS's three demands for Israel, repeatedly presented with slight variations in words by Barghouti and others, are: 'withdrawing from all Arab lands it occupied in 1967, including East Jerusalem; implementing full equal rights for the Arab-Palestinian citizens of Israel; and respecting the right of Palestinian refugees to return to their homes as stipulated in UN Resolution 194'.[9]

The 'right of return' is the demand that reveals the real intention: as always, it's the code phrase for getting rid of Israel. For not only is it a misreading and an enlargement of the wording of UN Resolution 194, but the practical effect of anything of up to six or seven million Palestinians returning would end the Jewish majority and the Jewish state. That is the BDS's ultimate aim.

The 'apartheid' label is the weapon. BDS says it draws its inspiration from the South African experience. 'Our South African moment has arrived', is a favourite phrase. The same sources in South Africa and the world are quoted all the time: Desmond Tutu, South Africa's Human Sciences Research Council, John Dugard, Richard Falk, Ronnie Kasrils, Jimmy Carter and the Human Rights Watch.

Their messages are carried around the world by organisations which have signed up to BDS. Such as Britain's War on Want charity, whose declared purpose is to fight poverty in developing countries. It stretches itself to the Israeli-Palestinian conflict and levels justifiable criticisms of Israeli actions in destroying Arab houses in Silwan, Jerusalem. However, it also makes a statement which is way-out even by the standards of the anti-Israel brigade: 'Israel's siege of Gaza has condemned its 1.5 million inhabitants to levels of poverty more commonly associated with sub-Saharan Africa'.

This charge raises questions: has anyone from War on Want ever seen any Palestinian skin-and-bone babies dying from kwashiorkor, the starvation disease of sub-Saharan Africa? Has anyone from War on Want ever seen Palestinians in the rags that pass for clothing in many parts of sub-Saharan Africa? Has anyone ever seen a Palestinian who can be remotely compared with the victims of war in the Central African Republic of Darfur? Palestinians certainly suffer, especially in the Gaza Strip, but has anyone from War on Want ever seen masses of Palestinians reduced to the level of poverty, hunger and disease that is the lot of many millions in sub-Saharan Africa? Of course not, because none of it exists in Gaza (and even less so on the West Bank).

Two statistics further discredit War on Want. Crucial health indicators for Gaza are infant mortality per 1,000 live births is 16.00 (number 105 in the world out of 224 countries, better than Turkey and Brazil) and life expectancy is 74.40 (number 111 out of 223 countries, better than Russia and Iran). [10]

So here is a well-known British organisation, with official status as a charity, sending out false propaganda and soliciting public money for doing it. It receives large amounts from the British government for its work. It also supports the deceptive 'right of return' and mimics the usual inaccurate information about the status of Israeli Arabs.

Britain's workers have been receptive to Palestinian claims. The Trade Union Council (TUC) – which brings together 60 unions with 6.5 million workers – has a tradition of supporting international action in defence of workers' rights. But it has been careful about what it actually does, and hence its Fair Play campaign for decent wages and conditions for workers in the global sports good industry has not called for boycotts because 'these workers need their jobs'. Yet it has moved away from that stance in regard to Palestinians.

The TUC's policy, as with the British government, has been support for two states and 'an agreed, just, fair and realistic solution to the refugee issue'. But some unions have gone further, as at the TUC annual conference in September 2006, with Sully Munir of Amicus giving the standard left-wing rant which brings in traditional dislike and envy of the United States: 'Israel is an apartheid state. . . . During South African apartheid the government of South Africa was armed by Israel. . . . [W]e all know that Israel is acting as an agent of the US in the Middle East . . . the brutal Israeli regime'. The motion adopted by the conference confirmed the TUC's two-states commitment – but, at the instigation of the Fire Brigades Union, included a demand for 'the right of Palestine refugees to return to their homelands'. It cannot be said whether this union, or the mass of delegates, realized that this addition was in direct contradiction of the TUC's two-states policy. Did delegates pass it knowing what they were doing, or were they hoodwinked?

Israel's war against Gaza in December 2008/January 2009 had a profound effect in Britain as elsewhere in the world. However justified Israel's response to thousands of missiles fired at it, the duration and death-filled ferocity of the assault persuaded many people that the country was running amok, and they became more receptive to calls to act against it.

The TUC annual conference in 2009 saw a wave of motions protesting Gaza. The Fire Brigades Union called for a general boycott of Israel. TUC leaders opposed this and tried to hold the line. The conference ended up condemning both Israel's attack and the rocket attacks on it and urged the British government to work for a negotiated settlement based on 'justice for the Palestinians and on security for Israel' – which reflected TUC's existing support for a two-state solution.[11]

But unions demanded more, and the conference voted for a boycott of Israeli goods from illegal settlements so as to step up pressure 'for an end to the occupation of Palestinian territories'. The Palestine Solidarity Campaign (PSC) rightly hailed it as a 'landmark decision' – and even more because the TUC voted to work with the organisation. The TUC not only affirmed previous boycott motions but also called on unions to review their 'bilateral relations with all Israeli organizations, including Histadrut'. It doesn't need a conspiracy theorist to note the links: the motion was proposed by the Public and Commercial Services Union whose deputy secretary-general, Hugh Lanning, was chairman of the Palestine Solidarity Campaign. Six months later the TUC and PSC issued a leaflet, 'Would you buy stolen goods?' with a briefing to unions to urge consumers not to buy goods from illegal Israeli settlements.

Despite all this publicised activity, British-Israel trade rose by 21.9 percent between the first quarter of 2012 and 2013, and Britain's imports from Israel rose by 55.6 percent! Britain is Israel's second biggest export market, second to the United States.[12]

\* \* \*

Dr Derek Summerfield, a South African–born psychiatrist in Britain, has led the charge against Israeli medical doctors, accusing them of complicity in the torture of Palestinian prisoners. A Cairo newspaper reported in 2008 that Summerfield had spent the previous sixteen years 'exposing Israeli war crimes and publishing scathing critiques in Britain's leading medical journals on the complicity of Israeli doctors'.[13]

However, the problem which Summerfield has faced is that few of his peers agree with him. He has been singularly unsuccessful in drawing any mass support, despite writing many letters and articles and giving speeches to try to link Israel with apartheid South Africa, even throwing in the canard that Israel 'has gone further than the excesses of the apartheid era'.[14] One of his attacks on the World Medical Association (WMA) drew the tart reply from secretary-general Delon Human that 'we seriously take issue with even the inference' made by Summerfield that WMA was condoning the involvement of doctors in torture.[15]

Summerfield's particular target has been Dr Yoram Blachar, the long-time president of the Israeli Medical Association (IMA). In 2003, Summerfield, all his anti-Israel efforts in vain, wrote to the *Lancet* to complain that Blachar had been elected chairman of the council of the World Medical Association, the international watchdog on medical ethics. The WMA ignored him.

Not only did the WMA consistently treat Summerfield with disdain, but in 2008 it elected Blachar as its president! That drove Summerfield to get 725 doctors in 43 countries to sign an open letter to the WMA demanding that Blachar step down as 'a matter of priority' because he had (allegedly) turned a blind eye to the involvement of medical staff in torturing Palestinian prisoners.[16] That seems like a lot of protesting doctors. But it was, in fact, a puny number: the WMA's membership was nine million. The WMA ignored the letter. Blachar himself said he had responded many times to the torture accusations: 'We are faced with an obsessional person'.

Worse was to come for Summerfield: when Blachar's one year in office ended in November 2009 he remained as a member of the triumvirate at the top of the WMA. A further Summerfield protest was ignored.

Earlier, in 2007, Blachar and a legal colleague, Malke Borow, wrote on behalf of the IMA about Summerfield's 'never-ending campaign against Israel. . . . Unfortunately it is next to impossible to refute baseless accusations'. On torture: 'unequivocally we state that we completely oppose the involvement of physicians in anything that can be construed as torture'.[17]

\* \* \*

Summerfield has had some kind of a platform because the *British Medical Journal*, the *Lancet* and the *Journal of the Royal College of Medicine* have been launch pads for protracted attacks on Israeli doctors – who have countered by accusing them of 'publishing political rhetoric disguised as medical articles' and 'the articles detailing human rights abuses seem to focus on Israel to an almost distorted fashion'.[18]

Inevitably, a prejudiced political agenda opens the door to sloppiness and distortion, as with a letter in the *Lancet* which said that the 1948 Israeli-Arab war had 'generated the largest refugee population in the world . . . 4.6 million Palestinians with refugee status'. Which, of course, blithely ignored the fact that there were actually some 750,000 refugees – and their numbers have only grown over the decades because of the definition, unique to Palestinians, that refugee status means the original victims *and* their descendants.

The *Lancet*'s editor-in-chief, Richard Horton, has often written and spoken aggressively against Israel. Perhaps it was because of diminished critical faculties that the Lancet Global Health website allowed publication of a bizarre article about the Israeli 2008–2009 assault on Gaza; never mind that there was not a single reference to the missiles fired at Israel which triggered the onslaught, but its factual errors were so gross that it was formally withdrawn three weeks later (but remained available on the Web). The article was presented as: 'Two surgeons from the UK, Dr Ghassan Abu Sittah and Dr Swee Ang, managed to get into Gaza during the Israeli invasion'.[19]

They actually wrote and Lancet Global Health actually published these words:

> Silent Bombs
> People in Gaza described a silent bomb which is extremely destructive. The bomb arrives as a silent projectile at most with a whistling sound and creates a large area where all objects and living things are vaporized with minimal trace. . . .
> Executions
> Survivors describe Israeli tanks arriving in front of homes asking residents to come out. Children, old people and women would come forward and as they were lined up they were just fired on and killed. Families have lost tens of their members through such executions.

It's all fantasy. Clearly Drs Abu Sittah and Swee Ang swallowed whole whatever rubbish they were told in Gaza: hence their other claim that Israel had murdered five thousand people in the town of Khan Younis during the Sinai campaign of 1956. In fact, what actually happened there remains disputed, but a partisan website, soundofegypt.com, whose headline 'Israeli massacres' reflects its mission, reports 275 deaths.

* * *

A leading British cancer surgeon, Professor Michael Baum, challenged the accusation that the Israel Medical Association was complicit in torture – and this set off a campaign to have him struck off as a doctor. 'The views I got were extremely hurtful and extremely abusive, not to mention the hate mail I got both electronically and by post. It was also the first time I had experienced anti-Semitism in my life. . . . Any attempt to defend myself provoked more anti-Israel and anti-Semitic rhetoric'.[20]

Baum's experience is not unusual. Anyone who argues in favour of Israel about anything is sneered at as an 'apologist'. Only full-blooded condemnation of Israel is acceptable. There is much on record to show that at anti-Israel meetings anyone who dares to offer a counterview risks being yelled at and abused and told to get out.

It must be said that it's no better on the other side of the fence: there's an army of Jews who stand with Israel, right or wrong, and are quick to denounce critics as anti-Semites.

\* \* \*

In Norway, some elements display high hostility towards Israel. The 2009 action programme of LO, the country's leading trade union confederation, singled out Israel in a call for 'firm measures'. Its leader, Roar Flathen, focused on one country – Israel – for criticism in his 2009 report.[21] The logo of the Norwegian Association of NGOs for Palestine shows a Palestinian flag flying over what is Israel/Palestine – but there is no sign of Israel. Attitudes like these are perhaps more understandable in light of the strange information peddled in that country, as in a report about a May 2008 visit to Israel by two Socialist Youth League members, Thea Schjedt and Nora Ibrahim, who reported: 'We have heard stories of Palestinians who are at checkpointen [*sic*] and waiting to get through, when two female Israeli checkpoint guards line up in front of them and have sex'. They concluded: 'Boycott apartheid, free Palestine!'[22]

Fortunately, there are enough sensible Norwegians who do not fall for this weird stuff even though, disconcertingly, many have a negative view of Israel, as shown in a survey that 38 percent feel that the treatment of Palestinians is similar to how Nazis treated Jews.[23] In 2011 a new record was achieved for goods imported from Israel, and exports to Israel increased.[24] The organisation With Israel for Peace nearly tripled its membership over five years. And, of course, Norway was the behind-the-scenes player in bringing about the mould-breaking Oslo Accords in the early 1990s.

In France, BDS adheres to the standard distortions of history by declaring that 'Israel was established by the Zionist movement . . . with the intention and effect of achieving the permanent removal en masse of the indigenous, predominantly Arab population of Palestine'. It accuses Israel of 'a system comprising apartheid, occupation and colonialism' and speaks of 'permanent removal en masse'. It does not explain how this squares with the growth in Israel Arab numbers from 156,000 to 1,670,000.

BDS in France has been split between a group which backs boycott, whether of settlements or totally; but at least up to the time of writing, had not gone any further towards the more militant, who frankly proclaim that their aim is to wipe out Israel. Palestinian rights, they say, 'are incompatible with the existence of a Jewish state which practises apartheid'. They want the 'right of return' for Palestinian refugees, which is the same thing in different words.

* * *

COSATU, the Congress of South African Trade Unions, joined with many in Israel and abroad in the justifiable call for an international investigation into the death of Arafat Jaradat while in Israeli detention. But COSATU went even further in making use of the death to promote BDS, and with a depth of abuse that has become its hallmark: 'We must isolate anything to do with the apartheid state of Israel and its murderous security regime'.[25]

Within less than a week COSATU had to deal with a dreadful murder on its home ground – the death of a taxi driver, Mido Macia. In full public view, policemen tied Macia to the back of a van and drove off at speed. Widespread outrage followed, with statements pointing out that this was but the latest 'barbarity' by police who were an 'ill-disciplined and brutal rabble' and 'operated in the same brutal manner as their apartheid-era counterparts'. COSATU issued a statement: there was none of the condemnation it had levelled against Israel; instead, COSATU said it was 'appalled'.

* * *

Desmond Tutu is given pride of place in the Palestine Solidarity Campaign booklet, 'Palestine – the new apartheid', saying:

> I am a black South African, and if I were to change the names, a description of what is happening in the Gaza Strip and the West Bank could describe events in South Africa under Apartheid.[26]

It is difficult to believe that Tutu ever said that. If he did, it must have unthinkingly slipped out of him. The comparison is unfounded and is insulting to the black people of South Africa. Only two decades later, it is impossible to believe that Tutu has forgotten the depth of the oppressed and debased lives of blacks under apartheid. Could he know so little about Palestinian existence, even under occupation, as to make the comparison?

However, the quote is a gift to the Palestine Solidarity Campaign. Its 'apartheid' booklet, as is usual with its propaganda material, is entirely one-dimensional. It is written as though there is no history of conflict between

Arabs and Jews, no wars, no suicide bombers, no anti-Semitism, nothing. It is simply Jews bad, Palestinians good. That is the base from which to present the usual lies, starting with the stock one that the Palestinians who remained in 1948 'do not enjoy the same rights as Jewish Israelis'. There is also the flat-out untruth that Palestinian members of Knesset 'who campaign for a more democratic system have been stripped of their parliamentary immunity and tried for subversion'. The 'apartheid' word is repeated and repeated, as though repetition will make it true. 'Zionism' is a dirty word. 'Racism' is another regular word, and the 'right of return' is the repeated theme, as always concealing the aim of destroying Israel.

\* \* \*

Boycotters have brought out a special book, *The Case for Sanctions against Israel*, to promote their cause.[27] Its worst sin is that it is boring: the usual people combing over the usual material with the usual untruths and twisting. Hence, Israel's establishment 'through a deliberate and systemic process of forcible displacement of a majority of the indigenous Palestinian population' which could hardly be a more inadequate and distorted description of the events of 1948. The same writer says that Israel operates 'a more sophisticated, evolved and brutal form of apartheid than its South African predecessor, according to authoritative statements by anti-apartheid leaders'. And who are the two quoted for this way-out claim? Desmond Tutu and Ronnie Kasrils, both of whom have repeatedly shown only limited knowledge of Israel and the occupation.[28]

\* \* \*

Five Indian artists announced they would not take part in an exhibition at the Tel Aviv Museum of Art in 2012. They were among about twenty artists invited to show at the exhibition 'Deconstructing India'. They said they refused 'to legitimize the illegal racist and apartheid policies of the Israeli government against the people of Palestine'.[29]

So they began with a double error for, as earlier noted, Israel is neither 'racist' nor 'apartheid'. They followed what others abroad, in Palestine and Europe, told them. Hence too the common error of claiming as a reason for boycott that Palestinians would have difficulty getting to the exhibition because they would have to pass through blockades and security checks – which is perfectly true because the West Bank is under occupation and the Gaza Strip is under siege – but they are also not part of Israel, and Palestinians need permission to enter Israel just as Pakistanis need permission to enter India to go to an exhibition.

Indeed it is worse than this. An article in the *Guardian* complained about the Indian embassy in London:

> Explicit discrimination can be found on the website for visas for India: 'Processing time for UK Nationals is a minimum of 2–3 working days. . . . Processing time of applications received from persons of Pakistani origin (including British citizens) will be minimum 7–8 weeks'. . . . Disclosing a link with Pakistan triggers demands for extra information and a long processing period, which in many cases makes travel to India impossible. India is effectively banning more than half a million British citizens of Pakistani origin from travelling to India as tourists, on business, or to participate in academic conferences or student exchange programmes.[30]

A reason given for the visa toughness is the 2008 terrorist attack in Mumbai perpetrated by Pakistanis – which seems like Israel's response to Palestinian suicide bombers.

\* \* \*

There is no doubt that boycotts are spreading; more slowly and restricted than campaigners claim, but the circle has widened in recent years, from Sweden to Canada, South Africa to Britain, with highlights such as the refusal in 2013 of the eminent British scientist Stephen Hawking to attend a conference in Israel. BDS is bound to keep growing, at least for as long as Israeli repressive actions feed the crocodile.

Meanwhile, the same inaccurate theme recurs in campaigns: 'The situation has rightly been compared to apartheid South Africa'. ('218 Signed Call for a Swedish Academic Boycott of Israel', Palestinian Campaign for the Academic and Cultural Boycott of Israel, 2 October 2011.) Several Christian churches have decided to disinvest from commercial companies which operate on the West Bank or even in Israel. Some calls are specific, such as boycotting a regional conference in Tel Aviv of the International Geographical Union. (Electronic Intifada, Palestinian Campaign for the Academic and Cultural Boycott of Israel, 2 July 2012.) Eleven members of the organisation's executive committee signed the statement, including one Israeli, Professor Aharon Kellerman of Haifa University. They objected strongly to Israel's treatment of Palestinians and the occupation of the West Bank. They also spoke of 'the massacre of nine human rights activists' – a reference to the *Mavi Marmara* ship which tried to break Israel's Gaza Strip blockade. That refers to a tragic event, but the word 'massacre' does not even remotely apply, and its inaccurate use is puzzling coming from a group of academics.

BDS scored a significant victory at the end of 2013 when the American Studies Association (ASA) endorsed a boycott of Israeli universities (but not of individual academics), after the Association for Asian American Studies had taken the same step in April.[31] The ASA council gave the lead by voting not to work with Israeli universities 'as an ethical stance, a form of material and symbolic action'.[32] The ASA also condemned the United States in 'aiding and abetting' Israel's violation of human rights in Palestine and its occupation.[33]

The decision is contradictory and full of holes. Why Israel, and only Israel, when so many countries perpetrate dreadful deeds on immense scales? Why condemn your own government but not follow up with rational and courageous action and boycott your own country's universities? It's Ivory Towerism at its woolly headed worst. But it could open the US door to wider boycott.

\* \* \*

Pop singers and bands have been susceptible to pressures not to perform in Israel, but while some have gone along with this, many notable artists, such as Madonna and Leonard Cohen, have visited. South Africa's Nobel Prize writer Nadine Gordimer, well known for opposing apartheid, travelled to Israel despite pressure at home by pro-Palestine groups not to attend the Jerusalem Writer's Festival in 2008. She went and spoke about 'the writer's role in a time of crisis'.

The language can be violent: a 'Dear John Lydon' letter to the British punk legend who was formerly known as Johnny Rotten urging him not to tour said that Israel, like apartheid South Africa, exercised 'racism, land dispossession and murderous atrocities'.[34] Lydon replied robustly in the *Independent*: 'I really resent the presumption that I'm going there to play to rightwing Nazi Jews. If Elvis-f\*\*king-Costello wants to pull out of a gig in Israel because he's suddenly got this compassion for Palestinians, then good on him. But I have absolutely one rule, right? Until I see an Arab country, a Muslim country, with a democracy, I won't understand how anyone can have a problem with how they're treated'.[35]

\* \* \*

Oscar-winning actress Emma Thompson and writer and director Mike Leigh were among thirty-seven leading British arts personalities who urged London's Globe Theatre to withdraw its invitation to Tel Aviv's famed Habimah Theatre to perform there. Habimah was to stage *The Merchant of Venice* as part of Globe to Globe, a six-week festival of thirty-seven Shakespeare plays, each in a different language.

Other British arts luminaries rejected the boycott and asked about the presence of theatre companies from other countries.[36] It was a good question: Habimah was open to attack because it had performed in Israel's Ariel settlement on the West Bank, an action which brought it criticism inside Israel's arts circles; but what about festival troupes from countries with odious human rights records such as China, Zimbabwe, Turkey, Belarus, Afghanistan, Bangladesh and Georgia? The thirty-seven did not explain why they chose only Israel. Time and again this selectivity is worrying and raises questions about motivation.

\* \* \*

Anyone who seeks peace between Israelis and Palestinians will surely welcome contact and cooperation across the lines of division. It could hardly be more basic. How else to break down stereotypes, prejudice and fear of the other? How else can trust between enemies be created?

Yet BDS demands exactly the opposite: 'Over and over again, champions of the boycott movement have condemned cooperation with apartheid Israel in acts of normalization', says the Palestinian Students Campaign for the Academic Boycott of Israel and the University Teachers' Association in Palestine. They were really enraged to discover that the Italian Development Corporation (DGCS), with the support of UNESCO, had arranged a partnership of three Israeli universities with the Palestinian al-Quds University to learn about 'cooperation, humanitarianism, peace and cultural preservation' ('among other things', which they did not specify). [37]

Not only were the would-be boycotters in denial of human interaction as the most elementary factor in achieving progress, but they were ignorant of the South African apartheid about which they always preach. For over the years in South Africa, numbers of blacks and whites had defied government-imposed racism and they maintained contact and friendships; despite qualifications and contradictions, these proved significant in ending apartheid.

\* \* \*

Electronic Intifada, with its addiction to saying anything to make a political point, claimed in an opinion/editorial: 'Apartheid in South Africa was abolished through a successful global BDS campaign, and a successful BDS campaign can put an end to Israeli apartheid. . . . We are borrowing a model that led South Africa to freedom'. [38]

As any South African of that era will know, this greatly overstates the effectiveness of the boycotts. If only the freedom struggle there had been as simple as Electronic Intifada claims!

The same exaggeration and hyping goes into the annual Israel Apartheid Week (IAW) on university campuses. It is very slowly spreading; in 2012, eight years after starting, it made a lot of noise but the gains thus far were limited. The IAW website proclaimed that 'more than 100 universities' were taking part. However, this did not amount to much: about twenty were in the United States – out of some four thousand universities and colleges. South Africa did better with billboard and newspaper advertising for about eleven campuses – but scored little media attention. In Britain, where the week has been gradually spreading, it reached twenty-four campuses; a minor scuffle was reported at one university. In Canada, where IAW is probably at its strongest, about twenty-four campuses took part.

The events provide a platform for peculiar talk, as at Britain's Middlesex University where American Ken O'Keefe, described as a former US Marine, said Israel and its Mossad 'were directly involved' in 9/11 – and stuck to it despite laughter and jeering. In South Africa, Ahmed Kathrada, an African National Congress leader and former political prisoner, spoke in ignorant terms about Israel's 'apartheid' and 'separate roads, de facto Mixed Marriages Act'.[39] Another former prisoner, Dennis Goldberg, reclaiming his Jewish origin, said he was 'ashamed' Israel perpetrated 'the same kind of brutality' on Palestinians as Jews had suffered in the Holocaust; he did not offer any evidence of gas chambers and ovens for killing Palestinians. Goldberg's background is worth noting: he was sentenced to four life imprisonments in the same trial in 1964 as Nelson Mandela; he was released after twenty-two years after Israeli intervention. He went to Israel but attacked the country for cooperating with apartheid South Africa and its treatment of Palestinians; he did not like Israel and Israel did not like him. He moved to Britain, which was then the world's second biggest trader with apartheid South Africa, and lived there for years.

The Apartheid Week 2013 was the platform for trying to exploit Israel's problem with migrants. Scheduled speakers included Dennis Goldberg and Professor Farid Esack, the Muslim scholar mentioned earlier. Their publicised subject:

> Israeli 'racism' toward Palestinians has increasingly been turning toward African refugees. Last year, in June 2012, Israeli anti-African protests turned into full-fledged race riots against Africans. Israeli racism and xenophobia against Africans is shared and even encouraged by leading Israeli politicians.

A recent African National Congress conference decision was quoted, abhorring 'recent Israeli state-sponsored xenophobic attacks and deportation of people of African origin and request that this matter should be escalated [*sic*] to the African Union'.[40]

Yes, Israel indeed has a migrant problem, along with most of Europe and other countries, too. But it is far from the inflated and distorted description above. Even more, it pales into insignificance compared with the situation as described in a Johannesburg newspaper a mere month later under the headline 'Xenophobic demons linger in South Africa'. The report said:

During 2012, at least 140 foreign nationals were killed, many of them grotesquely and intimately, and 250 seriously injured. In 2013, at least three major
incidents are being reported each week, most rooted in business competition;
almost all are shrouded in the language of hatred and discrimination. [41]

With that mess on the doorstep, it needs gross insensitivity and an aver-
sion to truth to upbraid Israel, or any other country.

Kathrada was later at it again at a Palestine Solidarity Campaign meeting,
saying he had recently visited the West Bank and the occupation was 'worse
than apartheid because it reduces human beings to animals'. After that balo-
ney it was probably inevitable that he went on to misuse Nelson Mandela's
name, as others have done and as discussed earlier, by quoting only half his
words about South African freedom and Palestinians and thus inaccurately
conveying his views. [42]

BDS supporters sometimes feel the need to offer an explanation for why
they focus on Israel and not on North Korea, Zimbabwe, Syria, China, Turkey, Myanmar, Sudan, Somalia, Russia, Iraq, Yemen or many of the well-
known, flagrant abusers of human rights. Naomi Klein, a Canadian writer,
had a go at it, saying in regard to Western countries: 'Boycott is not a dogma;
it is a tactic. The reason the BDS strategy should be tried against Israel is
practical: in a country so small and trade-dependent, it could actually
work'. [43]

Klein's argument is spurious and morally bankrupt. Hit Israel because it
is easy pickings? Ignore the mass killings in Syria which began early in 2011
(the later boycotts of it were at government level, led by the West, with no
sign of great popular street protests led by people like Klein)? Look the other
way at China's occupation of Tibet? Were Stalinism and its horrors to be
ignored because the Soviet Union was too big to tackle? Was Gaddafi's
Libya so powerful that its brutalities were beyond attack? And Egypt's dic-
tatorship? And scores of other tyrannical countries?

Even the claim about Israel's vulnerability to boycott is fake. Its international status is nothing like that of apartheid South Africa: instead it enjoys
the goodwill and support of many countries, however critical some are, as
well as several million Jews. Its Jewish citizens believe their survival is at
stake and that invests them with extraordinary stubbornness and strength.

Klein is also quoted as saying in an interview that individuals around the
world are not boycotting but rather they are responding to a call for boycott
coming from Palestinian civil society, which was what happened during the
South African struggle against apartheid. [44]

Does this mean: Don't bother about North Korea because its terrorised
people are too afraid to ask the world to boycott? Ignore Saudi Arabia because the rulers jump on anyone who dares to send a protest into the world?

This is disingenuous and dishonest. It's a cop-out for failing to fulfil principles of human rights.

A third argument is advanced for singling out Israel, to counter the obvious view that boycott is a denial of dialogue. 'Boycott is dialogue . . . BDS enables a discourse that moves beyond "ending the occupation" to place demands for the right of return and equal rights for Palestinians in Israel as top priorities'.

Inside these convoluted words what emerges, finally, hidden in the nice-sounding code phrases 'right of return' and 'equal rights', is the true purpose of BDS: the destruction of the Jewish state.

\* \* \*

The ostensible BDS purpose is to persuade/push/pressure Israel to end the occupation of the West Bank. With that, often, go demands for 'democracy' inside Israel, for rights for the Arab minority. There are also demands for the return of Palestinians who left in 1948 and 1967 – which, as noted, means destroying the Jewish state.

However, none of it takes into account Jewish history and fears: centuries as victims of a baleful world have made Jews ultra-sensitive to criticism. They are quick – too quick, many times – to see anti-Semitism. When critics question the right of the Jewish state to exist, defensive aggression is a natural response. [45]

Jewish history, filled with murders and expulsions over centuries, has traumatised the Jewish people. They are often acutely suspicious of the world, and have reason for it. Their paranoia is justified. The creation of the state in 1948 was supposed to overcome that but has not done so. Israel is a successful and true haven for Jews, but it has been under never-ending violent assault, starting even before its birth date, and when that is not happening, it is the target for denigration and questioning of its existence.

Given this history, a BDS threat does not easily frighten Israelis – Jewish Israelis, at least – and does not cause them or their government to change direction. Might BDS perhaps threaten the economic livelihood of Israelis? Might that make them pause and change? Unlikely. For Israel is strong economically and can also sustain itself relatively well, especially in food. Of course exports are vulnerable, but the countries of the European Union are the chief buyers, and while pressures are likely to build for boycotts and disinvestment, it is also unlikely in the foreseeable future that all of Europe would take part, especially Britain, Germany, France and Italy.

Israel enjoys a high degree of immunity from commercial boycotts because of the quality of its hi-tech and other inventiveness: it is rated as the second Silicon Valley and anyone who wants to seriously boycott would have to worry about the extent of Israeli technology and Israeli-made chips in the modern necessities of life, in computers, cell phones and cameras. Arab states know that it all works because of Israeli technology and could be operating on Israeli-made chips. Israeli inventions, among much else, include instant messaging, the USB memory stick, the firewall and the secure data links that enable most of the world's banking transactions and TV signal decoders, the *Guardian* reports.[46] And the country is a decade ahead of the United States and Europe in consumer apps based on crunching vast amounts of information.

Anyone who wants to save money on life-saving drugs would have to be careful to stay away from Teva, the world's biggest generic drugs-making company. In agriculture, Israel is a world leader, from drip irrigation to varieties of fruit. That's just the start. Oil is vital, but as the South African and Rhodesian examples showed, this can be overcome – and not only does Israel have access to far more oil supplies than did those two countries, but in 2012 it achieved its own bonanza with the finding of vast amounts of liquid gas off its coast in the Mediterranean Sea, enough for its needs and for export for a quarter-century and more.

A peep into the backroom trade emerged in a British government report about Israeli requests to sell its electronic warfare systems which contained British parts. It listed Egypt, Morocco, Pakistan, Algeria and the United Arab Emirates. Pakistan denied it.[47]

Those behind the boycott movement are aware of all this. It does not faze them, at least not in public. They say that agitating for this or that boycott serves a purpose in itself because it is a means of creating activism for political mobilisation against Israel. And as always, that goes far beyond the ending of occupation and is aimed at Israel's existence.

\* \* \*

Not all boycott calls are ill motivated. In the United States, Peter Beinart, a noted political pundit, used his website early in 2012 to convey the essence of his book *The Crisis of Zionism*.[48] Beinart articulated the anger and the ambivalence of those Jews in America and elsewhere who stand solidly with Israel but are deeply pained and anxious about its oppressive actions:

> In Israel, the deepening occupation of the West Bank is putting Israeli democracy at risk. In the United States, the refusal of major Jewish organizations to defend democracy in the Jewish state is alienating many young liberal Jews from Zionism itself. In the next generation, the liberal Zionist dream – the dream of a state that safeguards the Jewish people and cherishes democratic ideals – may die.

Whether this assessment is accurate or an overstatement remains to be seen. And of course Israel might change direction. But for now, many Jews, and non-Jews also, are certainly heartsore about the occupation and face dilemmas in giving unstinting support to Israel. Beinart's response to the situation he sees is to reject BDS and boycott of Israel and instead to urge US Jews to refuse to buy settler-produced goods. Focusing on the settlements for boycott has been around for some time, but Beinart gave it immediacy. Whether it could be restricted to settlements is unlikely: the BDS movement would certainly embrace it – and use it to bolster arguments for total boycott of everything Israel.

That indeed was spelt out by Andrew Kadi of the US Campaign to End the Israeli Occupation. It is 'simply dishonest to perpetuate the myth that the settlements or the occupation are somehow disconnected from the Israeli state', he said. It is the very government that funds, equips and protects settlements – and discriminates against its Palestinian citizens. Therefore, it's full boycott – economic, academic and cultural.[49]

In any event, could a restricted boycott by American Jews – with BDS enthusiastically joining in – persuade or drive Israelis to abandon settlements? It's unlikely. First, because a restricted boycott could not in its nature generate enough power to be effective and second, because most Israelis, it can safely be said, would dismiss it as interference in their affairs and it would only create irritation and resentment among settlers and in the government.

However, Israel is not immune to pressure in regard to settlements. The simple point is that it has not annexed the West Bank and enjoys no international recognition of its occupation of the West Bank, East Jerusalem and the Golan Heights. It has no right to label goods from the West Bank, such as beauty products, wines and fruits and vegetables, as 'Made in Israel'. Opposition to it doing so has been gradually spreading in the European Union and elsewhere and will continue to do so because there is no legal or moral basis on which settlement products can be falsely labelled. Right-wing arguments that thousands of Palestinians work in producing the goods and will suffer from boycotts are amoral; they might as well, equally absurdly, demand that settlement construction be approved because the number of Palestinians working in settlements increased by 25 percent to twenty-four thousand in mid-2013. The anti-Semitism cry is also heard but carries no weight, and nor should it, because the European Union is applying elementary law and common sense in insisting that the West Bank be distinguished from Israeli products for purposes of import rebates.

The possibilities in substantial international pressure were dramatically shown in mid-July 2013 with news that the European Union's bureaucrats in the European Commission had followed up on policy decisions taken the previous December by their political foreign ministers and had prepared directives that agreements the EU signed with Israel would exclude all territories beyond the Green Line – which meant no funding under the EU's prestigious Horizon 2020 programme for scientific research and innovation for any Israeli institutions working there. Israeli left-wingers hailed this, but it caused consternation and panic among right-wingers. The details came into the open just as US secretary of state John Kerry was working to bring Israelis and Palestinians together for peace talks after three years of nothing, and the Israeli government saw this as predetermining borders within the pre-1967 Green Line, and thus boosting Palestinian demands.

Prime Minister Netanyahu declared, 'We will not accept any external dictates regarding our borders'.[50] 'Hypocrisy, Hostility and Blatant Prejudice' was the headline on the response by Alan Baker, former legal adviser to the Foreign Ministry, writing for a right-wing think tank.[51] 'More kids, more trees, more vineyards, more homes – that is the real answer to the EU', said Naftali Bennett, head of the Bayit Yehudi Party, who accepted government talks with Palestinians only because he believed they would not achieve anything.[52]

The practical financial effect of the EU guidelines, if put into effect, would be insignificant – of the E800 million of aid to Israel over seven years, about 0.5 percent went to the territories, according to a German spokesperson.[53] But the possible loss in terms of scientific research and contact was described by an Israeli scientist as an 'irreversible disaster'. Coming so suddenly, the guidelines created shock, and even more because they were such a blunt challenge to the occupation. The government and its supporters had become accustomed to an easy ride, to ignoring the condemnations of the Sasson report, Supreme Court judgments, warnings from the peace movement and the countless books and newspaper reports exposing the unlawfulness of occupation and the evils it spawns. It broke open the delusional world of the settlers and their supporters, who believe they can do whatever they want.

For the challenge to come from the European Union, usually derided as a toothless non-player in the Middle East, was too much to bear. Europe, where Jews suffered such persecution for centuries!

Four months of negotiation at the political level led to Israeli capitulation. The EU guidelines stood. The blustering counted for nothing. National interest won over ideology and the settlers. The best that Israel could achieve was to be allowed a facesaver in appending a letter saying it did not accept the guidelines.

Once started and having breached the wall, the Europeans might push ahead with widening sanctions, if not now then later. Their action carries within it the seed of even greater punishment – entry by the United States. Washington has consistently and repeatedly condemned the spread of settlements. But that is as far as it has gone: mere words of reproach, which Israel ignores. If the European Union cracks down, might the United States be obliged to follow, especially if it has to deal with an insulting, recalcitrant Israel? Current unswerving support for Israel cannot be guaranteed forever.

Targeted action by friends and directed specifically at the occupation could prove deadly. Justice Minister Tzipi Livni said the European Union had given a 'wake-up call'. It soon became an alarm bell with an unnamed 'senior European official' in Brussels telling the *Jerusalem Post* that half the European Union's members – fourteen out of twenty-eight – support labelling West Bank settlement products.[54]

Meanwhile, Israel's trade and contact with the world flourishes. During November 2013 alone, large business delegations came from India and China wanting to access Israeli technology and to increase trade. The same message came from France, Mexico and Paraguay, and an Israel-Russia trade agreement was being sought. During December, China's foreign minister visited and so did Guatemala's president. CERN, the European Organisation for Nuclear Research, admitted Israel as a full member. The presidents of Romania and Sri Lanka visited in January, and economic links were signed with Georgia. Canada's prime minister came with a sterling message of support.

In February 2014, Peru's president was followed by Germany's chancellor Angela Merkel. She came for one day – with sixteen members of her cabinet. Despite, or possibly because of, this unprecedented backing for Israel, she spoke bluntly: 'We do not support the demands for a boycott. This is not an option for Germany'. But she endorsed EU policy on products from West Bank settlements: 'We have certain rules of labeling and we have to adhere to those rules'.[55]

Less than two months earlier Palestinian Authority president Mahmoud Abbas said exactly the same in South Africa while attending Nelson Mandela's funeral: 'We do not support the boycott of Israel, but we ask everyone to boycott the products of the settlements'.[56] Abbas's words caused consternation and rage in BDS circles and he was attacked: his rejection of boycott was 'shocking'; he lacked a democratic mandate; he was 'aloof' from his own people's aspirations. And, saying openly what is often played down, BDS wanted not only to boycott settlements, but its aim was total boycott of Israel.[57]

Within the Israeli government there is dawning realisation of the danger in international boycotts and sanctions – even though it was reported early in 2014 to be 'sharply divided' about what to do. The Strategic and Intelligence Affairs Ministry was said to be urging an aggressive public relations counteroffensive, wanting to spend $28.5 million on public diplomacy and legal measures against groups advocating boycotts. The Foreign Ministry, on the other hand, was said to argue that this would play into the hands of boycott activists. The diplomats believe the threat is overblown and that legitimate criticisms from foreign governments and NGOs of policy in the territories, especially settlement building, are wrongly branded as 'delegitimisation'.[58]

Whatever the response, it's inescapable that mislabelling settlement products as 'Made in Israel' cannot be defended, and that international rejection of settlements and West Bank occupation is growing, with the possibility of punitive action looming somewhere down the road. But Israel behaves on the West Bank as though none of it matters: in 2013 the number of new housing starts in settlements soared by 123.7 percent over the previous year, a ten-year high: 2,534 starts were officially approved. Illegal building in outposts, said to be a significant number, were not in the statistics.[59]

No amount of public relations campaigns can sanitise these facts and the oppression of occupation. With so much to feed on, the boycott movement is bound to spread. The Israeli government has yet to understand this.

## Chapter Eleven

# The Big Issues

*The obstacles to achieving peace are immense and complex. They must be confronted and resolved: two states with agreement on borders, refugees, Jerusalem.*

\* \* \*

The core issues must be resolved for peace between Israelis and Palestinians: creating a Palestinian state, which means deciding borders, the refugees, and Jerusalem. Time and again they have defied agreement and stymied peace possibilities.

### THE PALESTINIAN STATE

The United Nations General Assembly voted in November 1947 for two states, Palestinian and Jewish, to adjoin each other. That remains the aim. The Israeli government endorses it and so does the Palestinian Authority. The United Nations backs it as does the United States, the European Union, Russia and most countries, including many Arab states. At least they all do so formally. In practice, Israeli actions and Palestinian Authority foot-dragging undermine making it happen.

For two states to come into being, Palestinians demand that Israel return to the borders before the 1967 war. However, Israel will not do that, arguing that they are not defensible. It will also not return to the 1967 division of Jerusalem, not only because of ideology but for practical reasons: in one of many instances, Jordan in the 1948 war captured the Hebrew University and the Hadassah hospital on Mount Scopus; while they laid derelict, Israel created a new university campus and a new hospital in West Jerusalem; Mount

Scopus was reclaimed in 1967 and the university and hospital were brought back to life. They will remain Israeli. There is not the slightest chance that Israel would leave the Western Wall and the Old City's Jewish Quarter.

Israel has already made the 1967 borders irrelevant through building the separation wall/fence/barrier which intrudes into the West Bank and seizes 6 to 8 percent of the land. In theory, the barrier can be moved and does not define the future border, but for Israel it effectively supersedes the 1967 Green Line and creates a new reality.

The even bigger reality is the growth of Jewish settlements and settlers on the West Bank and in East Jerusalem. They are facts on the ground to establish Jewish ownership. Each house that is built diminishes the possibility of a viable Palestinian state. The number of settlers on the West Bank – from zero in 1967 to an estimated 400,000 in 2013, plus another 250,000 in East Jerusalem – tells the story.

Inevitably, because Israel is undermining the possibility of a viable Palestinian state, there is support for an alternative – a single Jewish-Palestinian state, either unitary or binational with internal division of power. The one-state road has been around ever since Israel came into existence: it was the goal of Israel's most fervent enemies, the Arab and Muslim states. They did not want a Jewish state to come into being and insisted on a single state: at that early stage, Jews were in the minority in the population and, clearly, Arabs expected that they would occupy the same position as they had for centuries in the region: Jews would be treated well (apart from the possible occasional eruption of violence against them) but would have a lesser, subservient role.

It was an impossible goal, especially after World War II, during which some Arab leaders were pro-Nazi and the Mufti of Jerusalem spent several years as an honoured guest in Berlin, helping with broadcasts to the Arab world and recruiting soldiers for Germany. Jews could not place themselves at the mercy of an elite led by the Mufti.

The ferocious feelings towards Israel turned into a political goal: attaining Palestinian freedom meant the elimination of the Jewish state. It only began to wind down, at least for the mainstream Palestine Liberation Organization, in 1988 with the start of recognition of the reality of Israel's existence; this became formalised with the Oslo Accords in the early 1990s. It is not always a wholehearted acceptance, and Israelis are quick to see aberrations. But it's enough to be friends, and Israel reciprocated in the Oslo Accords by effectively accepting the existence of the Palestine Liberation Organization and the right of the Palestinian people to their state. There is no total unanimity on either side: on the Israeli side, opposition to a Palestinian state is intense among the right wing; among Palestinians, rejectionists like Hamas and others want to destroy Israel, and in recent years they have been joined and strengthened worldwide by a motley spread of left-wingers, Jews who dislike the notion of a Jewish state and/or are angry and embarrassed by Israel's behaviour, and outright anti-Semites.

Denying the promise of a Palestinian state by building settlements is a gift to the rejectionists. It gives them the opening to pump the one-state approach of a single, shared democratic state in which Jews and Palestinians will live happily alongside each other.

It seems so simple, and the creation of the South African post-apartheid unitary state is quoted to support it.[1] Against this is the fact that the whole point in creating Israel was to have a state for Jews; it remains that despite uncertainty about its exact definition and the role of religion. It is a safe guess that at least 98 percent, perhaps more, of Israeli Jews will not yield on this. They will not agree to destroy the Jewish state of Israel in favour of a single Israeli-Palestinian state. It would spell national suicide for them. There is not the slightest prospect, at least in the foreseeable future, that this could happen. The only way Jews could be made to enter into a single state would be at gunpoint and/or by killing most or all of them or by driving them out. Any comparison with post-apartheid South Africa is, as previously discussed, facile and irrelevant.

The truism that history determines the present and the future is totally relevant. Arabs bitterly opposed the creation of Israel and went to war in an attempt to stifle it at birth. Both sides suffered many deaths; both sides committed atrocities. One war followed the other, initiated or provoked by one or the other side. Palestinians resorted to terrorism, attacking Israelis in their homes, in factories, on the roads, on beaches and at the Olympics. They began the modern plague of airplane hijackings. They turned to suicide bombings, trying to murder as many Israeli civilians as possible. From the perspective of Jewish Israelis, Palestinians have spent more than sixty years seeking ever-new ways to kill them. Israeli retribution has been harsh and preventive measures rough and far-reaching.

The result, understandably, is that the gap between Israelis and Palestinians has widened. Mistrust, fear, hatred and rejection dominate the attitudes of many. Additionally, there has not been leadership – on either side – working to calm passions and to persuade their peoples to go along new roads. Indeed, tragically, more often than not the opposite is true. Language also separates these two groups: Jews speak Hebrew and Palestinians speak Arabic. Then there are the deep religious differences between Islam, to which most Palestinians adhere, and Judaism; plus the vast differences in culture in books, music and theatre; plus the entirely opposite experiences and perceptions of society, whether in the rule of law or aggressive exposure and questioning in the media; plus the levels of economic development and technical knowledge, which are massively lopsided in favour of Israelis.

In time, these factors could no doubt be overcome and the gaps bridged; that is the pattern in human history. Meanwhile, Israel is a country with a

Jewish majority, and that is what makes it fundamentally different from any multicultural single state. Jews will not imperil that, certainly not after only some six decades of existence.

All this is disappointing to anyone who believes in the unity of people and sincerely wants to see people coming together and living peacefully. Unfortunately, in recent times alone, Kosovo, East Timor, Chechnya, Sri Lanka, the former Czechoslovakia, Korea, India, Pakistan, Bangladesh, the Sudan, Spain, Belgium, Turkey, the Sahel, Syria, Iraq, Scotland, Tibet, China, the Central African Republic, the Democratic Republic of the Congo and a host of other places are instances, some acutely distressing and violent, of people who want to get away from each other.

For Israel and Palestine, the negative realities are so powerful and inescapable that they make nonsense of calls for a one-state solution. The prospect of one state is so impossible that it is surprising that anyone even goes on talking about it.

## REFUGEES

Palestinians speak about 1948 as the *Nakba* (the catastrophe), and it is recorded in photographs and words of long lines of women, men and children laden with possessions, wretchedly walking away from their homes into exile. It was the start of a refugee problem that instead of diminishing over the years has grown into a critical obstacle to peace. After more than sixty years, many hundreds of thousands of those Palestinians, and their children, grandchildren and great-grandchildren, eke out their lives in poverty and with few rights.

Yet, wherever they might be, belief and hope remain about returning home. Exactly how many cling to that cannot be said, but, clearly, it is widespread: 'I learnt about Palestine through stories', said Samia, a woman born in Lebanon. She captured the feeling of it in saying: 'In the refugee camps we never missed an opportunity – a marriage, a funeral – to tell these stories, often with tears in our eyes. Palestine was a sort of Paradise Lost'.[2] The late Dr Iyad Saraj, a psychiatrist in the Gaza Strip, conveyed the depth of the trauma: 'The identity of the Palestinians, who are mostly peasants, was linked to the land. Thus, to lose your land and house was also to lose your honour and identity'.

Salim, twenty-two, from the Ain al-Hilweh refugee camp in Lebanon, took part in the 2012 'Global March to Jerusalem' to mark Land Day in 1976 when six Palestinians were killed by Israeli soldiers. The Lebanese army stopped the two thousand marchers – far fewer than had been expected – several kilometres north of the border with Israel. Salim spoke poignantly:

I came today to see my land, my country. It's tormenting to be so very close to our land and yet we cannot go. . . . Life as a refugee, as a Palestinian, is really difficult. The humiliation we endure every day from the Lebanese army at the entrance of the camp is itself a reason that makes me want to go back to Palestine regardless of the danger it might bring. I'm 22, jobless and cannot foresee my future or the near future for me and my family.[3]

\* \* \*

More than sixty years after their traumatic parting, when five hundred thousand died in communal conflict, India and Pakistan live side by side. They are not friendly, and suspicions and tensions sometimes break into heated accusations and counter-accusations, and very occasionally they go to war with each other. The return of refugees is not an issue. A Pakistani man cannot return to his birthplace in India's city of Mumbai and claim Indian citizenship and his ancestral home. An Indian man cannot return to Rawalpindi and claim Pakistani citizenship and get back the key to the house that he left behind – nor can the descendants on either side.

So it has been in the world down the ages. From distant eras of existence, one group has supplanted another, driving them away or killing or absorbing them. It has happened throughout every continent and among all peoples, whether the Native Americans in the United States and in Canada; the Aborigines in Australia; the San, Khoi and Basotho in South Africa; the Saxons in Britain and the successive conquests by Romans, Vikings and Normans; the Maya in Latin America; Poles in Russia and Russians in Poland; the Ottomans in the Middle East; or the Mongols in Asia.

Europe during and after World War II went through the biggest migrations in its history, culminating with the mass movement of some 12 million Germans: 7.6 million had left Poland by the end of 1947, through transfer and escape, with 400,000 dying on the way back to Germany; another 2.5 million had left Czechoslovakia and 200,000 were expelled from Hungary. They also left or were evicted from Ukraine, the Baltic states, Romania and Yugoslavia.[4]

It's cruel, pitiless, and total tragedy for the losers. Always, however, healing comes with time and acceptance of changed reality, even though memories of pain and loss might linger. However, knowing the terrible facts of human history does not make it any easier for victims of today; there is no comfort in being aware of the suffering of countless numbers in the past and of vast numbers at present. The Israeli-Palestinian experience has been unusual and remains so because time has not only failed to end trauma but has deepened and intensified it.

Early in the twenty-first century, the world has about 45.2 million people who have been forcibly uprooted from their homes. That was the figure for the end of 2012 given by the UN High Commissioner for Refugees (UNHCR).[5] The refugee agency was created in December 1950 to deal with 2.1 million Europeans displaced by World War II. It was supposed to complete its task and go out of existence within three years, but more than six decades later it is responding to unending and widening need as civilians on every continent suffer the catastrophic effects of conflict: in 2010 they were defined as 15.4 million refugees, 27.5 million internally displaced people and 850,000 asylum seekers.

The tally included 170,000 refugees in Yemen, mainly from Somalia, plus hundreds of thousands of local internally displaced people. More than 1,700,000 Afghans are cared for inside Pakistan. Iraq has 1.7 million, Somalia 770,000 and Democratic Republic of the Congo 477,000. Algeria shelters 165,000 Sahrawu refugees, and some 300,000 Vietnamese are said to be well integrated in China. Many of these numbers are already overtaken by events such as massive outflows of people in Africa. Syrian refugees exceeded 2 million by the end of 2013 and were increasing by 5,000 a day; another 2.25 million were displaced inside the country. Rising tension was reported in neighbouring Lebanon with accusations that refugees were taking jobs for lower pay and food and house prices were rising.[6]

Palestinians feature largely among the uprooted with nearly five million registered refugees, plus perhaps another two million spread around the world. They are unique among the dispossessed in having an agency that serves only them, the United Nations Relief and Work Agency for Palestinian Refugees in the Near East. It was set up a year before UNHCR, in December 1949, to deal with Palestinians who had fled or were chased from their homes. It has grown into the United Nations' biggest agency, operating in the West Bank and Gaza Strip, Lebanon, Syria and Jordan with a budget of about $1 billion a year, nearly half of which is paid by the United States and the European Union (but which doesn't earn them much street cred among Palestinians). It has nearly 39,000 staff members, 99 percent of whom are Palestinians, and provides education through 663 schools, health care through 122 clinics, and also social services, cash, loans and emergency aid.

These many years later, about 1.3 million of the Palestinians live in fifty-nine refugee camps, still called that although the original tent towns have given way to concrete breeze-block apartments. The United Nations Relief and Work Agency for Palestinian Refugees in the Near East (UNRWA) attends to water, refuse and sewerage. It is often a low-quality existence, overcrowded and often with open sewers and unpaved roads.

The second unique fact is the definition of a refugee, which goes beyond anything applied to anyone else in the world: Palestinian refugees are those 'who lost both home and means of livelihood' as a result of war in 1948 and

1967 – and, significantly, 'the descendant of someone who had'. The original 726,000 refugees have mushroomed to about 5 million, and the number increases by the day. No limit is set on how many generations will be classed, and treated, as refugees.[7]

Third, it's also unique to Palestinians that their status remains unresolved even while so many other refugee situations, some involving far more people than did the Palestinians initially, have ended and the victims have made new lives for themselves. And not only is it an active issue, but it is at the core of the Israeli-Palestinian conflict.

Dispute begins with the very origin of the refugees. Among many or most Palestinians, it's a basic truth that they were driven out of their homes in a preconceived and deliberate Zionist plan; they were violently and illegally dispossessed of their homes and property. Yes, they say, many thousands did leave of their own accord, but that was understandable because people were frightened and they had every intention of returning home when the fighting ended. As Khalil Shikaki, a Palestinian political scientist, has put it: 'What do you do when a war is coming to your village? Do you leave your wife and kids there? . . . And if someone promises that if you leave, they'll fight for you, then bring you back, does that mean that you have no right to return there ever again?'[8]

So Palestinians continue to demand the right to return home in accordance with UN General Assembly Resolution 194 of December 1949, article 11, which said:

> The refugees wishing to return to their homes and live at peace with their neighbours should be permitted to do so at the earliest practicable date, and that compensation should be paid for the property of those choosing not to return and for loss of or damage to property which, under principles of international law or in equity, should be made good by the governments or authorities responsible.

The resolution also urged the warring parties to make peace and called for protection for the Holy Places in Jerusalem, UN control over the city and free access to it. Although 194 is now the bedrock of Arab and other demands for the return of refugees, it was at the time actually opposed by Egypt, Iraq, Lebanon, Saudi Arabia, Syria and Yemen. Six months later, in May 1949, Israel was accepted as a UN member after agreeing to implement UN resolutions, including 194. But it has not done so, even though the General Assembly has repeated the resolution scores of times.

To Israel, the use of the word 'should' instead of 'must' in the resolution made it far less imperative; the requirement that refugees had 'to live at peace with their neighbours' was never realistically in prospect because of the rejection and continuing hostility and threats by Arab states and refugees themselves; and, in any event, the refugees were not only Arabs but also the

1,500 Jews who had been expelled from their homes in Jerusalem's Old City by Jordanian soldiers in 1948. Israel can also point to the wording of resolution 194, which does not single it out for blame but speaks of 'the governments or authorities'.

The Palestinians' loss is their own fault, as far as Israel was and is concerned. As Ambassador Abba Eban told the United Nations in 1958, in words which express today's Israeli attitude as much as they did then: 'Let there be no mistake. If there had been no war against Israel, with its consequent harvest of bloodshed, misery, panic and flight, there would be no problem of Arab refugees today'.[9]

Early on, in 1948, David Ben-Gurion placed the refugees within a wider context: 'When the Arab states are ready to conclude a peace treaty with Israel the question of refugees will come up for constructive discussion as part of the general settlement, and with due regard to our counter-claims in respect of the destruction of Jewish life and property'.[10]

By that, Ben-Gurion was referring to the country-wide effects of the Arab attacks plus the eviction of Jews from the Old City. The same counter-claim came into play after some seven hundred thousand Jews fled to Israel from Arab lands during 1949–1951 and were resettled in Israel; many lost all their property. Set off our claims against yours, Israel has said. Palestinians contest this, arguing that it's a matter for Israel to resolve with the Arab states concerned and not with them and that, in any event, many Jews left of their own accord and Israel eagerly wanted them to come on aliyah to swell population numbers.

It's a knotty issue because of allegations of Israeli undercover disruptive actions in some Arab countries to provoke Jewish flight; on the other hand, Jews suffered deadly attacks by Arabs immediately after the UN partition vote on 29 November 1947 and felt mortally threatened when Israel's coming into being inflamed Arab anti-Jewish sentiment.

Sporadic attempts to resolve the refugee problem have been made over the years, starting in 1949 at a conference in Lausanne, Switzerland, when Israel and Arab enemy states were brought together – not face to face but, at Arab insistence, in separate rooms with messages carried back and forth. Israel offered family reunification for one hundred thousand refugees as part of a comprehensive peace. The Arabs rejected the peace offer, so the proposal fell away. Also that year, the United States proposed that Israel allow the return of one-third of the refugees (a figure of about two hundred thousand was assumed) and the United States would pay the costs of resettling the other two-thirds in Arab countries. Ben-Gurion rejected such numbers but offered financial compensation – not to individuals but into an international fund of which Israel would be one of the sponsors and which would carry out collective resettlement projects in the region. This, too, went nowhere. The most that Israel has been willing to do is for humanitarian reasons, in the cause of family reunification, to admit some refugees. Many thousands have been admitted, but it is not an open door – for example, of 70,000 who applied from June 1947 to June 1994, only 22,179 were admitted – and has grown more restrictive in recent years for reasons which include fear of letting in potential suicide bombers.

Rejecting a mass Palestinian return is not only a negotiating stance but 'a national narrative', says Israeli political scientist Dr Mark Heller.[11] What that means was amplified by Shlomo Gazit, a former army general and the first civil administrator of the occupied West Bank: if Israel

> recognizes the "right" of return it would also be admitting responsibility, and perhaps even culpability for creating the problem. But Israel categorically denies any responsibility for the War of 1948. On the contrary, the guilt and responsibility are all Arab-Palestinian, and it is completely irrelevant whether Arab leaders encouraged the local population to leave their homes, or whether they departed to escape the fighting.[12]

Gazit also noted that Israel rejects return for material reasons:

> There is no possibility of allowing the refugees to return to their original homes and lands without completely undermining the fabric of Israel's society and people. Many Israeli towns and villages, both rural and urban, are built on former Arab-Palestinian land. One cannot hand back these lands and proper- ties without uprooting hundreds of thousands of Israelis, if not more, thus opening up a Pandora's box and courting disaster for Israel.[13]

The impracticality was also tellingly noted by a Palestinian – Hazem Jamjoum of Badil – in arguing in favour of reparations:

> A Palestinian village depopulated by Zionist forces in 1948 that had, let's say, one thousand inhabitants would now have tens of thousands of Palestinians who want to return to it as their home. If we think only in terms of restitution, only those who owned property before they were displaced would have a strong claim for restitution; and even that claim would have to be divided up between all the heirs of the refugee landowner who initially had title to the land. So we'd end up with a massive majority of returning refugees who would be completely landless, a minority who would end up with small bits of land divided between their siblings and cousins, and a very tiny minority, the de- scendants of the biggest landlords, who would have land that you could do something with. (Rich refugees would also have an upper hand with things like access to top lawyers and resources to ensure they got the most out of a restitution process.) Also, if the focus was just on land and property, it could end up destroying productive farms, factories etc.[14]

It is also not feasible, as is suggested, to think in terms of a mass return of refugees not necessarily to their original homes but to more sparsely populated parts of the Galilee or the Negev.[15] This gets to the core of the refugee issue: Israel is a state created for Jews and a mass influx of Palestinians would undermine and even destroy a majority Jewish presence. As matters stand at present, it is inconceivable.

While neighbouring Arab countries admitted refugees in 1948 and 1967, the treatment of them has varied greatly. Part of that comes from reluctance to allow permanence to refugees because that would mean accepting Israel's existence – and that view has been shared by many refugees. In 1965 the Arab League decided to preserve Palestinians' refugee status by not granting them citizenship but also said that they be given the same rights as nationals.[16] However, there is also widespread wariness about them as a potential threat to the stability of the host country, and even outright hostility.

In Jordan, perhaps up to 60 percent – the exact figure is unknown – of the people are of Palestinian origin; most have the right to vote and citizenship and have the right to public services; they can work in government but are discriminated against in appointment to high office in the government and military. But the hard memory remains of 'Black September' in 1970, when the Jordanian army, after months of violent conflict, crushed the threat to King Hussein's rule by Palestinian militants. Between three thousand to five thousand people were estimated to have died, although Yasser Arafat, head of the Palestine Liberation Organization, spoke of ten thousand. Palestinian leaders and fighters were expelled to Lebanon the next year. These days, Jordanian intelligence keeps a careful eye on local Palestinians as well as West Bank Palestinians visiting or passing through the country.

Egypt and Saudi Arabia host refugees: they are granted limited rights to residence, education and jobs and are kept under surveillance. Syria does not allow refugees to vote, hold government office or get passports; Kuwait and the Gulf states expelled more than three hundred thousand Palestinians during the 1990–1991 Gulf crisis; those who have been allowed to return are watched. Libya threw out thirty thousand Palestinians in 1995 after the Palestine Liberation Organization entered into the Oslo Accords with Israel.

The worst off are the estimated 416,000 Palestinians in Lebanon (i.e., before the later influx from Syria): they are stateless and endure harsh conditions. They are denied any social rights, such as access to government health services. They are debarred from working for the government and in scores of professions, including medicine, law, engineering and journalism. They need permission to do any building or repairs in the refugee camps, to own property, open a business or invest.

UNRWA is contentious. Its existence, and especially its definition of who it serves, ensures that refugees remain refugees forevermore. It implicitly keeps alive the refugees' belief that they can someday return to their original homes, and it thus exerts a direct influence in relieving pressure which might otherwise apply for Palestinians to compromise on their demands. Whether that is good or bad is another matter. In addition, through its decades-long existence, UNRWA has bred a culture of dependency among the refugees it helps. Its ratio of about one staff member to 164 refugees compares with about one staff member to 2,800 of the UNHRC.

On the other hand, hundreds of thousands of refugees have survived only because of UNRWA's support in providing food and services: in Gaza, for example, unemployment is so high that UNRWA is crucial; in Lebanon, there is not only a lack of jobs but also the harsh restrictions that prevent refugees from earning a living.

Right-wingers in Israel rail against UNRWA. They not only blame it for continuation of the refugee problem but say that its schools are breeding grounds for violent anti-Israel teaching and that it fosters terrorism. They attack it for its definition of refugees and for exaggerating the number of refugees. It is accused of giving jobs to terrorists, of demonising Israel and misusing money. The Israeli government also criticises UNRWA for providing cover for Palestinian terrorists, including hosting meetings of militants in UN buildings. But the government must also be ambivalent because it needs the organisation: without UNRWA, Israel as the occupying power on the West Bank, and previously in the Gaza Strip, would be responsible for ensuring food, shelter and health care for hundreds of thousands of refugees. UNRWA does the job for it.

The most damaging accusations have come from people who know the organisation from the inside. In January 2009 James G. Lindsay, UNWRA's former legal adviser in Gaza, went public with a wholesale attack in a report which said the organisation had taken

> very few steps to detect and eliminate terrorists from the ranks of its staff or its beneficiaries, and no steps at all to prevent members of organizations such as Hamas from joining its staff. UNRWA has no pre-employment security checks and does not monitor off-time behaviour to ensure compliance with the organization's anti-terrorist rules.

He also said: 'No justification exists for millions of dollars in humanitarian aid going to those who can afford to pay for UNRWA services'.[17]

Lindsay said that failure to match the success of UNHCR in resettling refugees 'obviously represents a political decision on the part of the agency' and 'seems to favour the strain of Palestinian political thought espoused by those who are intent on a "return" to the land that is now Israel'. He argued that UNRWA's education system was highly problematic and quoted a number of American research agencies that defined UNRWA's schools' curriculum as 'highly nationalistic' and not a 'peace curriculum', and that textbooks failed to identify Israel on maps and avoided 'discussing Jews or Israelis as individuals (which critics argue would make them more "human" to the reader)'.

UNRWA responded by repeating what it often says: it is merely carrying out the mandate which it has been given, and it is not responsible for the political decisions behind the mandate. On textbooks, it noted that it is obliged to use the textbooks of the host country.

Unsurprisingly, Lindsay came under attack from UNRWA senior officials, including Andrew Whitley, director of the New York office, who shortly after criticised his report as being 'tendentious and partial' and for using a 'narrow range of sources'.[18] But in October the next year, Whitley, then the outgoing director of the New York office, spoke in different terms, raising the taboo subject of return: Palestinians must start acknowledging that the refugees will almost certainly not be returning to Israel.[19]

Palestinians, he said, had long maintained a 'right of return' to Israel and the homes they – or their ancestors – fled during the 1948 war. The issue had been one of the most difficult to resolve in peace negotiations. 'If one doesn't start a discussion soon with the refugees for them to consider what their own future might be – for them to start debating their own role in the societies where they are rather than being left in a state of limbo where they are helpless but preserve rather the cruel illusions that perhaps they will return one day to their homes – then we are storing up trouble for ourselves'. He acknowledged that few Palestinians or even officials in his own organisation had been willing to publicly discuss the issue. 'We recognize, as I think most do, although it's not a position that we publicly articulate, that the right of return is unlikely to be exercised to the territory of Israel to any significant or meaningful extent'.

That drew a strong protest from Saab Erekat, the Palestine Liberation Organization's chief negotiator. 'The Palestinian refugees' right to return to their homes and lands is one of the most important rights. The Palestinians haven't given up this right since the Nakba . . . [a]nd they will never give this right up'.[20] This, of course, confirmed UNWRA's role in perpetuating Palestinian hopes and also validated the deep-felt suspicions of those Israelis who argue that many Palestinians have not yet accepted the reality of the Jewish state's existence but still want to overwhelm it through demographics.

UNRWA has to contend with other critics: Canada expressed its displeasure in January 2010 by withdrawing its annual grant, instead giving the money directly to Palestinians. In September 2011, under pressure from Hamas, the organisation made all its summer camps in the Gaza Strip single sex and also suppressed teaching Holocaust studies in its schools.

A final point: critics attack Israel for failing to carry out General Assembly Resolution 194 in regard to refugees and accuse it of defying the United Nations. But the critics, both Arab states and others, are not equally respectful of General Assembly Resolution 181, which called for partition and the creation of a 'Jewish state' and an Arab state. They have yet to accept that Jewish state.

## JERUSALEM

The Holy City is perhaps even more critical to achieving peace. Jews and Muslims each demand that it is their spiritual capital. Christians play a lesser role but have their own hefty attachment to the city in which fifteen different Christian communities live alongside each other, representing millions of adherents. Known as the City of Peace, Jerusalem's history contradicts that: devotion to it down the ages by hundreds of millions of people, usually driven by religious zealotry, has made it a city of strife. The city has changed hands thirty-six times during its known history, usually in a bloody war. Conquerors from different countries and nations have slaughtered or expelled residents, destroyed structures sacred to other faiths and built their own holy sites. Israel is an honourable exception: it has respected places sacred to Muslims and Christians, albeit with restrictions on access in the name of security.

The UN 1947 partition decision for a Jewish and an Arab state proposed that the city be internationally controlled as a *corpus separatum*. It never happened. Jews and Arabs fought for the city even while British soldiers were still there. On 15 May, minutes after the British left, the Jordanian Legion entered the fray. It seized East Jerusalem and the Old City and expelled 1,500 ultra-Orthodox Jews from the Jewish Quarter, among them families who had lived in the Holy Basin for centuries. Jewish graves were desecrated and headstones used for paving; fifty-eight out of fifty-nine synagogues were destroyed, and no Jew was allowed to pray at the Western (Wailing) Wall.[21]

Colonel Abdullah el-Tal, who led the Jordanian assault, later recorded shelling the Jewish Quarter with mortars, 'creating harassment and destruction'. He reported to his superiors: 'For the first time in 1,000 years not a single Jew remains in the Jewish Quarter. Not a single building remains intact. This makes the Jews' return here impossible'.[22] A concrete wall and barbed wire were erected to separate Jordanian-held land from Jewish-held West Jerusalem, part of it running down what is today's Road No. 1 past the New and Damascus gates of the Old City.

Israel's dazzling and unexpected victory in the June 1967 war got rid of the Jordanians. Since then, Israel has striven hard to entrench its possession of the city and to gain international acceptance and legitimacy for its rule over the whole of a united Jerusalem. It has failed. To the world, Israel is in illegal occupation of East Jerusalem as much as it is of the West Bank.

Jerusalem is immersed in myths and propaganda. A sharp-eyed view is provided by Moshe Amirav, a professor of political science at the Hebrew University, in a book, *Jerusalem Syndrome: The Palestinian-Israeli Battle for the Holy City*.[23] Amirav is uniquely placed: his passionate love for the city goes back to his boyhood days and membership of the right-wing Herut movement. He was a paratrooper in the 1967 Six-Day War and although injured in fighting for Jerusalem, he took himself, bandaged, out of a hospital bed to go to the Western Wall to celebrate its liberation. He went on to work for Mayor Teddy Kollek in charge of the city's planning and development and was adviser on Jerusalem to then prime minister Ehud Barak at Camp David II.

The 'Jerusalem Syndrome' of the book's title is the psychological condition which afflicts scores of visitors to the city: they suffer religious delusions and believe that they are, for example, God or Jesus Christ. They seek the redemption of Jerusalem, but the contradiction between 'heavenly Jerusalem' and 'earthly Jerusalem' appears to disturb their mental balance. About one hundred people a year are admitted for treatment to the mental hospital in the Givat Shaul suburb. Amirav explains,

> Jerusalem's dazzling light blinds all of its heroes and rulers. Memories of past glories and grandiose dreams for the future throw them off-balance. They liken themselves to the city's earlier conquerors and are confident they will succeed where all their predecessors have failed. Captive to the myth of the holy city, they crash against the rocks of Jerusalem's reality and are afflicted with 'Jerusalem Syndrome'.

This delusional illness, he says, seems to have affected mayors, cabinet ministers and prime ministers, hence the muddled, contradictory, unrealistic, counterproductive and harmful policies and actions in dealing with Jerusalem, which he blames on a succession of Israel's leaders. He argues that the 'pervasive euphoria and self-confidence' which followed 1967's military triumph led government ministers to believe that they only need to set goals for the city's unification and it would follow, sooner or later, hence a series of 'utopian, unrealistic goals' which were given the weight of 'national objectives' – and all of which have been marked by 'monumental failure'.

The first goal, he says, has been territorial: the consolidation of Israeli control in East Jerusalem by settling more Jews there. The immediate step after victory was to vastly expand Jerusalem's municipal boundaries. West Jerusalem consisted of about thirty-seven square kilometres and the conquered Old City added one square kilometre. East Jerusalem (i.e., Jordanian Jerusalem) was seven square kilometres – and not only was this annexed, but the area was expanded to encompass seventy square kilometres of the West Bank. Overnight, Jerusalem grew to three times its former size and stretched over an area larger than Tel Aviv.

Jewish settlement has meant investing billions of dollars in building residential neighbourhoods in most of the eastern parts of the city – while also seeking to loosen the hold of Arabs on these areas and cutting off the Arab neighbourhoods from the Arab population centres surrounding the city. But, notes Amirav, 'not only did the construction fail to secure the territorial objective, it also undermined the demographic objective by increasing the proportion of Arabs in the city'.

The Jewish neighbourhoods, he says, occupy only one-third of the area while the Arab neighbourhoods have greatly expanded in the other two-thirds and are home to a majority of more than 240,000 East Jerusalem Arab residents. In addition, the Jewish territorial drive set off an Arab counter-reaction with a wave of illegal construction. People needed houses so they built them. The Israeli authorities lost control: during the 1980s and 1990s, about twenty thousand housing units were built without approval of building plans and without proper attention to infrastructure needs such as water, electricity, sewerage and roads. East Jerusalem was turned into a 'Wild West'.

The second goal has been demographic: to increase the Jewish majority to 80–90 percent. Amirav notes that had Israel been content with annexing Jordanian Jerusalem in 1967, Jews would today be a majority of some 82 percent in a united city. But the annexation of wide areas of the West Bank, including twenty-eight Arab villages, pushed up the number of Arab residents. 'Ironically', he points out, 'it was the government's construction of the "outer ring" neighbourhoods in the 1970s that created employment opportunities for the city's Arabs. Israel's relatively liberal policy granted them more advanced health services and numerous social benefits from the National Insurance Institute. Jerusalem therefore became a magnet for the Arab population from the West Bank'. The ratio of Arabs in the population rose to 34 percent, and the Jewish majority fell to 66 percent.

On top of that, the coming of the right-wing Likud party to power in 1977 led to a clash in national objectives – creating settlements on the West Bank, as opposed to increasing the Jewish majority in Jerusalem. As a result, some 120,000 Jews abandoned Jerusalem during the 1980s and 1990s and moved to the new communities such as Maaleh Adumim, Betar Illit, Givat Ze'ev and Efrat.

The third objective has been political: 'Israelisation' of, equality for, and coexistence with the city's Arabs. The initial policy was clear: the newly acquired Arab residents were to be an inseparable part of the unified city. It was expected that they would integrate into the life of the city as Israeli Arabs had integrated into the state after 1948. Thus the government decided to allocate special resources for this and also enacted liberal legislation regarding Arab status and rights.

But it went sour because the intentions were not implemented, and it wasn't long before the resources that were needed to improve the level of services and infrastructure in East Jerusalem were being directed solely to strengthening and increasing the Jewish majority. The Israelisation policy that touted 'equality' for Jerusalem's Arabs was soon displaced by a new policy that imposed numerous hardships upon them, with the aim of spurring them to leave Jerusalem and thereby reduce their percentage of the city's population.

Housing has been a glaring expression of this: Amirav records that about 30,000 requests for building permits were submitted by Arab residents of East Jerusalem from 1967 to 2001; only about 3,100 (10 percent) were approved – and these few were first subjected to a 'bureaucratic runaround lasting several years on average'. It is also revealing, to the discredit of the city, as councillor Meir Margalit has pointed out, that though Palestinians are 38 percent of Jerusalem's population, their share of the municipal budget is only 11 percent. [24]

The 'Israelisation' policy was supplanted by 'Palestinisation'. Amirav explains that 'the Palestinians in Jerusalem identified with the struggle for national liberation. They no longer sought equal rights or services or benefits. They sought to separate from Israel and to establish their capital in East Jerusalem!' Meanwhile, any hopes for coexistence were undermined by the Palestinian suicide bombings during the second intifada.

In any event, as anthropologist Dr Ali Qleibo notes insightfully:

Jerusalemites are proud of their Arab identity and their historical roots in Palestine. Five decades after the annexation of East Jerusalem to Israel, and despite the Israeli-enforced demographic changes meant to transform the Arab character of al-Quds, Jerusalemites remain staunch Palestinian nationalists. Despite the pragmatic conveniences that would ensue from obtaining full Israeli citizenship, the like of which no Arab state provides for its citizens, most Jerusalemites have chosen to keep the Jordanian passport. Of the estimated 350,000 Jerusalemites, statistics reveal that less than 10 percent of East Jerusalem residents have chosen to become Israeli citizens.

In a TV interview, Rami Nasrallah, head of the International Peace and Cooperation Centre, surprised the audience when he revealed that only 14,000 residents of the annexed East Jerusalem hold Israeli passports. The majority proudly prefer to go through the great hassle, inconvenience, and expenditures required to renew their five-year courtesy Jordanian passports because they are a sign of their Arab political identity. The alternative practical solution of acquiring Israeli citizenship and thereby transforming the national resistance into a civil rights movement would be our shame. [25]

The fourth Israeli aim has been diplomatic: to secure international recognition for its sovereignty in Jerusalem. In the 1950s this was partly successful: twenty-four countries recognised Jerusalem as Israel's capital and set up their embassies there – although, significantly, the United States and major

European nations refused to recognise Israeli sovereignty in Jerusalem, let alone accept it as the capital.

Israel's annexation of Islamic and Christian holy sites in 1967 and its 1980 Basic Law declaring that 'Jerusalem, complete and united, is the capital of Israel' aroused international anger: twenty-two countries moved their embassies out of the city, finally followed later, in 2006, by the remaining two, Costa Rica and El Salvador.

'Forty years of diplomatic effort on this front have brought Israel nothing but disappointment and failure', says Amirav. Creating 'facts on the ground' has not secured international acceptance.

Promising to recognise Jerusalem as the capital of Israel has been part of the US political scene: Congress has voted that it be done – but gives the president discretion to decide when to implement it. No president, whether Democrat or Republican, has given recognition. In the 2012 presidential election, the Democratic policy platform omitted the usual promise, creating some Jewish angst. The Republican candidate, Mitt Romney, played the game and promised recognition with everyone knowing it was a charade. Jerusalem is too loaded an issue for even the United States to step in where no one else fears to tread.

The fifth objective has been in the religious sphere: to separate the issue of the holy places from the Israeli-Arab conflict. This, says Amirav, has always been the most sensitive and difficult matter to resolve. He argues that Israel had a chance, in 1967, to resolve the issue in accord with the international community and the Muslim world: it could have done so by imposing its sovereignty solely upon the Jewish Quarter of the Old City and the Western Wall and allowing internationalisation of the Christian and Muslim holy sites. But the cabinet rejected it in the 'euphoric and self-assured atmosphere of the time'.

'A most striking illustration', says Amirav, 'of Israel's failure to separate the Temple Mount issue from the Israeli Arab conflict is the significant weight given this issue in the 2000 Camp David summit talks. In essence, contrary to Israel's original policy goal, the holy places became the real core issue of the conflict'.

Of course Jerusalem has, over the centuries, been central to Jewish existence. Throughout exile, the holy city was always the focus of yearning and prayer. It was 'the heart of the Jewish people', as David Ben-Gurion put it, hence the awe and emotion in the conquest of the Old City in 1967. But the political story has been different, and Amirav points out that from the 1880s, when the first Zionist pioneers arrived in Palestine, until 1949, when West Jerusalem, without the Old City, was declared the capital, the city ranked low in Zionist priorities. The crucial goal was to establish a Jewish homeland in Palestine. Zionist policymakers did not view Jerusalem as the political capi-

tal or economic centre of the future state but rather as a spiritual and intellectual centre for the Jewish people.

Amirav notes,

> Jerusalem's marginality was evident in four ways: its lack of political central-
> ity in the Zionist movement in Palestine; the disdain expressed for it in the
> movement's culture and literature; the relatively meager resources allocated to
> the city and to settlement efforts there; and acceptance of the likelihood that it
> would fall outside the framework of the future Jewish state.

In that light, the fervent declarations of Jerusalem as the 'eternal, indivis-
ible capital of the Jewish people' are of relatively recent origin. And they
relate to a city whose boundaries were considerably extended in 1967 in a
man-made political decision which not only had nothing to do with holiness
but contradicted logic and sensible urban planning.

To which can be added that a good amount of cynicism goes with the
declarations of Jerusalem as the 'holy, eternal' city of the Jewish people. The
city is perennially in need of money: two-thirds of its population are ultra-
religious Jews and Arabs who are poor and pay lesser amounts of taxes. The
secular one-third carry much of the burden. The Jerusalem municipality
looks with covetous eyes at the nearby town of Mevasseret Zion: it wants the
tax money of wealthy residents there. If, one day, Jerusalem succeeds in
incorporating the town, it will, overnight, become part of the 'holy, eternal'
city.

* * *

Jerusalem: 'Blessed but also cursed by its holiness'.[26] There was a time, not
long ago, when it seemed that Israelis and Palestinians were on the way to
reaching agreement about the future of the city as part of a wider peace deal.
Although Camp David II failed in 2000, discussions continued, driven by
President Bill Clinton. The 'Clinton Parameters' emerged, and the Israeli
cabinet accepted, with reservations, its plan to divide Jerusalem: Arab neighbourhoods to be assigned to the Palestine state-to-be and Jewish neighbourhoods to remain under Israeli control.

It didn't happen, of course, and if the plan was now to be implemented it
would have to be reexamined in light of the continuing penetration of Arab
neighbourhoods by Jewish settlers. It's become much more complex. But at
the time, agreement appeared to be so close that Palestinians set about con-
structing a parliament building in the ramshackle town of Abu Dis. The
Palestinian leader Yasser Arafat was said to have ensured that the chosen site
was as equidistant, to the east, from the Noble Sanctuary/Temple Mount, as
the Israeli Knesset is to the west from the Western Wall. Abu Dis lies partly

inside the Jerusalem municipal boundary; about ten thousand of its people live inside Jerusalem and fifteen thousand on the Palestinian side. They are separated by the high wall of Israel's security barrier so that what was once a ten-minute drive from the Palestinian side to the centre of Jerusalem is now a roundabout forty-five minutes.

The intention was to move the Abu Dis boundary one hundred or two hundred meters to the east: thus the new Palestinian parliament would fall within the boundaries of Jerusalem, *al-Quds* in Arabic (the holy). A simple, inventive solution.

The building went up, faced in grey stone. But the second intifada was raging. Construction stopped. The windows remained without glass and the interior was not completed. The building stood derelict on the Palestinian side of Abu Dis, until the nearby al-Quds university eventually took it over. It stands as a reminder of what might have been.

Every now and again, as peace hopes surface, any talk about dividing Jerusalem draws emotional rejection from right-wingers and the religious. Thus in 2007 Eli Yishai, then Shas leader and member of the coalition cabinet, said that a division of the Old City and transfer of the Temple Mount to international control was something he was not ready 'even to dream about in [his] worst dreams'.[27] The council of rabbis on the West Bank weighed in: 'The very thought of foreign defilement and control of the Mountain of G-d's Abode and in holy Jerusalem is shocking to every Jew. . . . Those who even mention the possibility of abandoning the Temple Mount and of dividing Jerusalem will be forever remembered in ignominy by the Nation of Israel'.[28] Prime Minister Ehud Olmert's coalition fell apart as he pushed for negotiations with Palestinians and dividing Jerusalem.

More and more, Jerusalem is sanctified as the holy city of the Jews forever, intensely linked with religious and nationalistic emotions, hence the intensity of then deputy prime minister Silvan Shalom:

> Jerusalem will remain Israel's eternal capital forever. This is not a promise, it's a fact. . . . The future of Jerusalem is like the future of the State of Israel, and like that of the entire Jewish nation, Jerusalem will never be divided, and we will never give up Jerusalem.[29]

However, Palestinian insistence on the city as their capital is uncompromising. Their demand for control of the Noble Sanctuary/Temple Mount is strengthened by the worldwide Muslim community which watches Israel's hold over the sacred site with rage and suspicion and with repeated bursts of violent rhetoric, as in Friday mosque sermons. In Cairo in November 2011, in a spin-off from the political protests in Tahir Square, a Muslim Brotherhood rally heard speakers railing against 'treacherous Jews', declaring that '[o]ne day we shall kill all the Jews', and a religious leader, Dr Ahmed al-

Tayeb, on the familiar theme: 'The al-Aqsa Mosque is currently under an offensive by the Jews. . . . We shall not allow the Zionists to Judaise al-Quds'.[30]

Yet, as Amirav notes, Arab states supported internationalisation of the holy places, as proposed by the UN partition decision, from 1947 until 1974. At that time, they changed to supporting the Palestinians' right to Jerusalem'.[31]

Muslim opposition does not stop the Judaising process in East Jerusalem which continues apace with building apartments for Jews on the one hand, and, on the other hand, obstacles are put in the way of Palestinian building and living. Construction is pursued in three ways, all connected. First, neighbourhoods were established from soon after 1967 on land across the pre-war Green Line. Today, they are seen in vistas of neat apartment blocks stretching across the hills, such as Ramot, French Hill and Psagot Zeev. Some are still being expanded on West Bank land, such as Ramat Shlomo.

Second, new neighbourhoods are being established, initiated with massive cash funding from American Jewish billionaires. Har Homa is the best known and fastest growing – an impressive set of apartment blocks off the road to Bethlehem, spacious and clean with well-paved streets and children's play areas. A minute away, up the hill, is an Arab village, neglected and rundown, with broken paving and garbage often overflowing into the street. It's a dramatic transition from first to third world.

Third, again apparently financed by wealthy American Jews, are enclaves inside Arab neighbourhoods, including the Muslim Quarter in the Old City, consisting of one or more houses bought from Arab owners (who are paid large sums and then rapidly leave for abroad; selling to Jews is forbidden and is punishable by death). Land is also obtained by going to court to prove that the house was owned by a Jew pre-1948 and the descendants are merely claiming it back. This legal technique might backfire: what if – or when, because the idea is talked about – Arabs make the same demands in regard to their properties seized by Jews after 1948?

The Jewish enclaves are securely fenced and fly the Israeli flag as a statement of their ultra-nationalistic purpose. They are protected day and night by armed guards hired from a private security company. The cost of $20 million a year is carried by the Ministry of Housing and Construction. Elad, or *Ir David* (City of David), is an NGO the sources of whose clearly considerable funding are kept secret, is in the same mould and is a key player in Judaising. Elad is especially known for an archaeological dig in the Arab neighbourhood of Silwan, two hundred metres from the Old City wall, on a ridge where King David is said to have conquered an existing stronghold to lay the foundations of Jewish Jerusalem perhaps three thousand years ago. Elad works assiduously with government and American private support in Silwan and elsewhere in the city to hunt for archaeological evidence in support of the Jewish presence. Its well-developed 'City of David' site is a major tourist attraction, drawing more than four hundred thousand people a year. Among archaeologists, there is said to be 'keen consternation about Ir David's role because of its strong Jewish focus, which many view as a politicized betrayal of the neutral role of scholarship'.[32] It has also bought dozens of houses in the neighbourhood and about five hundred Jews live there.

Ateret Cohanim is also active. It's a nationalist-religious movement which runs a yeshiva in a prime position in the Old City, overlooking the Western Wall. It also pushes to settle Jews in Jerusalem's Arab neighbourhoods. It enjoys extraordinary influence and money as the saga of its Beit Yonatan venture reveals: it bought a two-story building in Silwan from the Arab owner and in 2002 transformed it into a seven-story apartment block, Beit Yonatan, named after Jonathan Pollard, the American jailed by the United States for spying for Israel and who has become a right-wing cause. It's never been explained how Ateret Kohanim managed to put up the building illegally and without municipal planning permission over many months, even though municipal inspectors were busy in the neighbourhood instigating demolition orders against illegal Palestinian construction.

Protests finally led, on 11 February 2007, to a municipal order to seal the building and expel the seven Jewish families living there. The residents appealed against this seven times, from magistrate's court to district court to Supreme Court. Each time, the court upheld the original decision to seal the building and expel them.

The city did not carry out the court orders, even though its own legal adviser, Yossi Habilio, said it had to do so, as did the country's attorney-general, Menachem Mazuz. Instead, Mayor Nir Barkat was able to get the planning and construction committee to change local zoning laws so that all buildings could be four stories high instead of two. Thus Beit Yonatan would remain, but would be cut down to four stories, and Palestinians would also benefit in that 90 percent of their illegal constructions could be legalised. He was told this was illegal.

Right-wing members of the Knesset defended Beit Yonatan. They accused law adviser Habilio of having a political agenda and accused him and the attorney-general of 'selective enforcement' and discrimination against Jews while ignoring hundreds of transgressions by Arabs. However, a left-wing city council member noted exactly the opposite: since 2000, he said, some eight hundred Palestinian homes had been entirely demolished, and none in the Jewish sector.[33]

At the end of December 2009, Attorney-General Mazuz ordered the police commissioner to take immediate action to evacuate the illegal building. 'This is a grave ongoing case of flouting court orders and cannot be allowed to continue', he said.[34] He was ignored. A new factor was now in the game:

settlers had obtained a court order to evict four Palestinian families – about forty people – from the adjoining Abu Nab house on the grounds that, pre-1948, it had been a Yemenite synagogue and Jewish-owned; they said they would hire private security guards to carry out the evictions. [35]

Mazuz retired and Beit Yonatan still stood. His successor, Yehudah Weinberg, apparently intent on having the rule of law obeyed, ordered the building evacuated and sealed 'as soon as possible'. [36] Two firebombs were thrown at Beit Yonatan by persons unknown; no damage or injury was caused. Mayor Barkat played a new card: he halted the sealing off of Beit Yonatan after Ateret Kohanim withdrew its demand for the eviction of Palestinians from the Abu Nab house. [37] The police stood down: two thousand were said to have been mobilised for the Beit Yonatan evacuation because right-wing counter-action was feared. Legal adviser Habilio resigned because of his disputes with the mayor.

Within days, the attorney-general wrote to Mayor Barkat that a date in the near future must be set to seal Beit Yonatan; he wanted this done at the same time as evicting residents from Abu Nab. [38] Three months later, it was reported that the police had scheduled evictions several times but had called them off at the last moment; riot police had been on standby in case of revenge attacks by right-wing Jews. [39]

In 2014 Beit Yonatan still stood.

There is determined purpose in building housing for Jews in East Jerusalem and intruding into Arab neighbourhoods. It's to create a Jewish ring around Jerusalem, isolating it and its Palestinian residents from the West Bank hinterland and rendering impossible the prospect of Jerusalem as a Palestinian capital. The far-reaching plans include 'E1', which means East 1 – the twelve-kilometre stretch of West Bank land which runs from the Jerusalem boundary to the hilltop Jewish town of Maaleh Adumin, population thirty-five thousand and growing. The intention is to fill the space with housing for thousands of Jews and thus seal off that side of Jerusalem while also cutting the West Bank in two. The talk is that, once this has been achieved, a road tunnel will link the north and south sections of the West Bank. A large, fortified police station has already been built in the area.

* * *

The United States, the European Union, and the Quartet (which brings the United Nations and Russia on board with the United States and European Union in pursuing peace), all totally oppose Israel's actions in Jerusalem. A seventeen-page report by the European Union said with alarm: 'Long-standing Israeli plans for Jerusalem, now being implemented at an accelerated rate, are undermining prospects for a Palestinian capital in East Jerusalem and a sustainable two-state solution. . . . Israel is, by practical means, actively pursuing the illegal annexation of East Jerusalem'.[40] That was in 2008. The buildings keep going up.

The United States has repeatedly rebuked Israel for its building activity. Every time a report appears in the media revealing a new burst of plans for dozens or scores or hundreds of apartments, Washington, whether the president or the secretary of state or both, has made its displeasure known. But it is nothing more than a gentle slap on the wrist and has no effect. For each time Israel has tossed the rebuke aside as of no account and has made the Americans look impotent and foolish. 'Jerusalem is ours and we can do what we like', is the consistent response. The numbers of settlers and settlements keep growing.

The municipality is accused of manipulating statistics to conceal the scale of demolition of Palestinian houses. Official figures show a decrease in demolitions by the municipality and the Ministry of the Interior: in 2008 there were 102 demolitions, going down to 14 in 2011. However, there's a duplicitous side to it: in 2000 the municipality began a policy of 'self-demolitions' whereby homeowners can be made to pay exorbitant fines unless they carry out demolition orders themselves. The municipality does not keep track of self-demolitions, but there were seventy in 2010, according to Meir Margalit, a city councillor.[41]

* * *

The Mughrabi Bridge links the (Jewish) Western Wall and the (Muslim) Noble Sanctuary/Temple Mount and is the only route allowed for non-Muslims for the nineteen-metre (sixty-two-foot) ascent. Tension is never far away from what is described as the most sensitive site in the world. Among Muslims there is acute suspicion about Jewish intentions, which they believe are aimed at destroying *al-Buraq*, the third holiest shrine in Islam, with the Dome of the Rock and the al-Aqsa Mosque atop the mount.

For many years, Jews were forbidden from going onto the mount: this is where the First and Second Temples stood from 960 BCE to 70 CE, and rabbis warned against unwitting desecration of the holy area. However, an increasing number of rabbis have been saying that Jewish law allows it and that has strengthened the resolve of Jewish zealots who insist that Jews have every right of access to the mount. Awareness of the simmering danger means that Israel allows the Mughrabi Bridge to be used for only a few hours a day. Policemen stand guard. Jewish and Christian prayer books must be left with them. On the mount, saying prayers, even moving lips in prayer, is forbidden for Jews and Christians.

The bridge was originally an earthen ramp. It partially collapsed because of a snowstorm in 2004. Three years later, amid international controversy and Muslim opposition, a wooden bridge was put up while a more permanent structure was prepared. Israel consulted Jordan, which administers the site for the Muslim world and apparently secured its agreement for a new structure. Demolition of the wooden bridge was scheduled for Saturday night, 26 November 2011, but the day before, Prime Minister Netanyahu ordered a halt because of the sensitivity of the issue and amid warnings of Muslim repercussions. In Egypt, the Muslim Brotherhood's spiritual leader, Sheikh Yusuf Qaradawi, said Israel wanted the bridge to ease access for settlers and security forces to the al-Aqsa Mosque. Meanwhile, as far as the Jerusalem municipality's engineers were concerned, the wooden bridge was dangerous and a fire hazard and needed to be immediately dismantled.

Muslim emotions about the Noble Sanctuary/Temple Mount are so intense that it doesn't take much for them to overflow. In 2000 Ariel Sharon, then leader of the opposition, went to the mount in an act of electioneering right-wing defiance to demonstrate that he and all Jews could go there if they wanted to; Muslims threw stones, the police responded, people died and that was the trigger that set off what became the second intifada. In another instance, in October 2009, rumours of a 'Jewish takeover' of the mount set off violent clashes between Arab rioters and security forces at the site and in parts of East Jerusalem:

> The rumours were fuelled in part by calls at the time, from a number of Knesset members and prominent national-religious rabbis, that Jews ascend to the Temple Mount with increased vigour. Those calls were portrayed, in turn, by Palestinian clerics as nefarious plans to invade the site or build a synagogue there.[42]

Indeed, that is what Jewish zealots aspire to, and it slots into the messianic drive to ensure that both Jerusalem and the West Bank are under total Jewish control. They try different stratagems. Three of them were found with goats and were arrested on suspicion of planning to sacrifice the animals on the Temple Mount for Passover.[43] The organisation for the renewal of the Temple arranges 'mass pilgrimages' to the mount in honour of Chanukah, the Jewish festival of lights, usually observed in December, to celebrate the rededication of the Second Temple after it was recovered from Hellenist Greeks more than two thousand years ago. A member of the organisation has explained what they are after: 'Little by little, we're going to take back the mount. And it will be done without violence or force'.[44] The words are soft and deceptive, but it's fighting talk.

Both Jewish and Muslim leaders stoke up religious passions. They do so with or without thought about the violent consequences that will inevitably follow.

# Chapter Twelve

# The Way Forward

*Two states, Israel and Palestine, is the only way.*

\* \* \*

The goal is two states, Israeli and Palestinian, side by side. It must be that because nothing else at this time can do as much to meet the fears, hopes and needs of Jews and Arabs and end their conflict. Two states is not easy to achieve. If it were easy, there wouldn't be a problem to solve. It was more attainable after the Oslo Accords were signed in 1993 but both sides messed up. Both Israelis and Palestinians must now be persuaded, pushed and prodded into realising that two states is the only realistic option open to them. In time, the Israeli and Palestinian states could develop into a federation linked with Jordan and ultimately with other neighbours. That is a hope for the future.

Two states is a return to the original United Nations Resolution 181 of 29 November 1947, which determined partition – a Jewish state and a Palestinian state – but negotiated and updated to take account of changes since then. It must be based on the borders of 1948, adjusted by the borders of 1967. There is a limit to the extent that past events can be reversed, the omelette unscrambled.

Two totally opposite forces reject two states. First are Palestinian activists plus their left-wing and anti-Semitic supporters and some Muslim states. They want one state in which Palestinians will be the majority, 'an affirmative, genuinely democratic, secular and multi-cultural state, the only kind that can offer Jewish Israelis and Muslim and Christian Palestinians alike a future free of discrimination, occupation, fear and violence . . . in what was historically a culturally and religiously heterogeneous land'.[1] The aim is wonderful, and, hopefully, one day it can be attained. But to believe that this paradise is remotely possible at this point in time is to live in another world. It puts a gloss on past Jewish-Arab relations: they were only homogeneous in as far as Jews bent the knee and deferred. It looks the other way about the bloodletting of the past one hundred years. How could Jews now possibly agree to go into such a state as a minority? They will not. Nor will Palestinians go into one state if they are to be subservient.

One state means the end of Israel, and this, shorn of all the words about democracy and peace, is what the country's enemies want. They deny Jews the right to self-determination but demand self-determination for Palestinians. They use 'one state' as a propaganda tool. It draws in the gullible and those who have not thought into its real meaning. One state will not happen because Jews will not accept it.

The second rejection comes from right-wing Jews. Their fears and political view are expressed by Naftali Bennett, whose new *Bayit Yehudi* (Jewish Home) Party went into government after the 2013 elections:

> I think forming a Palestinian state west of the Jordan River would condemn Israel to 100 years of unending conflict, millions of refugees flooding our land and overwhelming international isolation following a very short honeymoon. A Palestinian state would be a hostile, failed state like the Palestinian state that formed in the Gaza Strip in 2005–2006 that is still functioning today but much more dangerous, because it would be a 30-second flight from Ben-Gurion airport.[2] And, too, we are not occupiers. You cannot be an occupier in your own home.[3]

Right-wingers want Israel to seize as much of the West Bank as it can get away with. Any further expansionist aims are murky: it is not clear how far to the east some want to go. Apart from wanting Israel to get bigger based on claims from two thousand and more years ago, they argue like Bennett for security and draw their own awful lessons from the Oslo Accords and Israel's withdrawal from the Gaza Strip in 2005. Oslo was a disaster, they say, look at what came from it: a surge in Palestinian violence with the murder of more than one thousand Israelis.

However, this is a simplistic reading of Oslo: for, on the contrary, the accords were a breakthrough of the utmost significance because each side acknowledged the right of the other to exist. Disastrously, both Israelis and Palestinians then made sure it went no further. Israel did so by building settlements on the West Bank and for a time also in Gaza, and Palestinians did their damage by continuing their rejectionist talk and by increasing terror attacks against Israel.

Withdrawal from Gaza was Prime Minister Ariel Sharon at his wiliest. He recognised that the military cost to protect settlers there was too high and unsustainable; at the same time, withdrawal was part of a larger scheme to secure the settlement blocs on the West Bank: the bulk were to be incorporated into Israel while seventy or so settlements with seventy thousand people to the east would be abandoned. Dov Weissglass, the prime minister's chief of staff, was cynically frank in a newspaper interview: 'The significance of the disengagement plan is the freezing of the peace process. . . . The disengagement is actually formaldehyde', he said. 'It supplies the amount of formaldehyde that is necessary so there will not be a political process with the Palestinians'.[4]

In the Gaza Strip, events took a different turn with grave consequences for all. Since the withdrawal, Gaza has been the launch pad for many thousands of missiles fired at southern Israel – and even reaching as far north as Tel Aviv – by Hamas and other rejectionist groups. Look at what withdrawal has done to us, say many Israelis, and yet you want us to allow a Palestinian state on the West Bank which will bring missiles within easy range of our major cities? Binyamin Netanyahu exploited this in campaigning for the general elections in 2009: he took a group of journalists to a hilltop on the West Bank within sight of Ben-Gurion International Airport – to show how missiles from that spot could bring down aircraft taking off or landing.

This, too, is a one-dimensional reading. The fatal flaw in the Gaza withdrawal was that it was unilateral: Israel did not consult, as far as is known, with the Palestinian Authority, which was in charge at the time. No arrangements were made for joint border control, for agricultural and health cooperation (foot-and-mouth disease in cattle does not respect country borders, nor do malaria-carrying mosquitoes), for working together in tourism (Gaza's beaches are glorious and await development), or about water, labour and everything else. Israel walked out, destroying settlement buildings as it went, except, notably, flourishing and profitable greenhouses for fruit and flowers which a group of American Jews bought, for about $12 million, as a gift for Palestinians – who then wantonly and stupidly destroyed them as they also did with the few large buildings which Israel left behind. Israel closed up Gaza and made it into as much of a prison as it could. On its own side, it also mismanaged the withdrawal of Jewish settlers, wrecking lives and creating long-lasting animosities – and at colossal financial cost to the state.

If the right wing rejects two states, their alternatives are clear for the West Bank areas they covet. They can choose (1) to kill all the Palestinians there, (2) evict them at gunpoint, (3) give them the right to vote or (4) continue the current oppression.

Of those offensive options, no doubt number four would be the easiest for them, with some modifications to try to make it look prettier. One of the escapist variations of this comes from Likud's Israel Katz, minister of transportation: 'the right diplomatic situation is an autonomous Palestinian entity, but with Jordanian civilian and political affiliation'.[5] In this and other variations, not only do Palestinian aspirations count for naught, but occupation

and oppression would remain, and Palestinians and the world would therefore dismiss it as much as the current occupation is rejected and pressures
would keep mounting on Israel. Its friends would be embarrassed and less
friendly and less willing to stand by it in international forums. Anyone who
believes that Israel can stand on its own in the world has stopped thinking.
Palestinians will not accept their lot and will strike out at the oppression,
setting off cycles and counter-cycles of protest, suppression and protest. For
Israel, it will mean never-ending war, with its people dying and its soldiers
killing Palestinians.

If this seems a far-fetched scenario, look at those on the Right who actually argue that peace with Palestinians is not possible and all that lies ahead
into the unknown future is ceaseless war. They accept dooming their children
and grandchildren and other generations to come. That cannot and must not
be the way to live.

The settlers are already guilty of colonialism, a crime in international law.
*If* the settlers and the government go on unchecked, they will deserve the
apartheid label: *if* they make discrimination against Palestinians permanent,
*if* they entrench and institutionalise separate laws and separate living and
working areas, they will then stand accused, correctly, of implementing a
new apartheid. The consequences of this will be grave beyond measure because it will lay Israel wide open to international judgment and punitive
action as a pariah state. The settlers and their government supporters are
foolishly and arrogantly blind to the disaster this will bring upon Israel.
Isolation and boycotts could take on real and dangerous meaning.

Until that point, applying the apartheid label to Israel is inaccurate. It also
plays into the hands of real enemies of Israel: they do not seek to have Israel
reform itself internally, and they do not want to see an Israeli and a Palestinian state side by side. They want to destroy Israel. The easy, lazy use of the
apartheid word is naïve and aids them.

This applies to those Jews in Israel and the world who turn to the apartheid tag out of despair, saying that Israel is set on a disastrous course and
anything, but anything, must be tried to change this. They do this without any
real knowledge of the meaning of apartheid and foolishly, and dangerously,
draw analogies with Israel which do not exist. They should instead turn to the
ethos of the US-based New Israel Fund, which works to further democracy in
Israel. The fund opposes boycotts and lawsuits to bring Israelis to trial in
foreign courts, says its chief, Daniel Sokatch: 'Both strategies, to our mind,
assume that Israel cannot change without extreme pressure from outside; we
think that our work strengthening Israeli democracy is the better way to
pursue positive social change'.[6]

Meanwhile, for as long as the settlement enterprise thrives, the greater the
damage done to Israel. You cannot oppress others and impose unjust laws
without suffering your own moral decay. The soldiers who enforce the occu-

pation – ordinary young men and women conscripted from everyday Israeli society – cannot but brutalise the Palestinians whom they control and are brutalised themselves in doing so. They do not leave this behind when they go home and take off their uniforms; they carry it with them, spreading a cancer of inhumanity, indifference and cruelty among their families, friends and work colleagues. Nor can Israel be immune to the cheating, theft, lies and subversion of the Rule of Law spawned by the settlements: these cannot but seep into the soul of society, debasing everyday values and behaviour; cheating and lies and subversion of the law become the norm.

This is one instance where the comparison with apartheid South Africa is relevant and true because the degradation of society happened there, too – and not only South Africa but any society in which one people lords it over others without compunction or compassion.

* * *

The obstacles to achieving two states are so formidable that it is tempting to follow the advice of the Welsh minister who, preaching on a knotty theological issue, said: 'And here my friends, we meet a difficulty. Let us look it firmly in the eye, and pass by'.[7] But that luxury is not available. The obstacles must be overcome. Ending the occupation is the first step. This will not in itself end the conflict or silence enemies who want nothing less than the elimination of Israel. But it is the first, essential step which must be taken for the good of both Israelis and Palestinians. The West Bank, plus the Gaza Strip when and if Palestinians can settle their internal disputes, is the basis of the Palestinian state of UN Resolution 181.

This goes with agreeing on permanent borders, which means agreeing on the Jewish settlements. How many settlers are so solidly in place that removing them is impractical? How many existing settlements can be hooked onto Israel? How many must be withdrawn? Will houses and amenities be handed to Palestinians, as an act of goodwill, rather than repeat the destruction wrought in Gaza? Can Jews, if they want, remain as Palestinian citizens inside the new state? Even though in mid-2013 Palestinian president Mahmoud Abbas ruled it out, putting the boot into Jewish-Arab acceptance of each other while also feeding Israeli right-wingers who want to get rid of Israeli Arabs. What Israeli land will be exchanged 1:1 for excised West Bank land? Will Palestine be demilitarised as Israel insists? What about the Jordan Valley? Missiles no longer make it the vital eastern defence buffer of before, and it is not as imperative for Israel's security.

The usual assessment that seventy thousand settlers would have to be evacuated from the West Bank has been elevated, whether correctly or not, by Gilad Sher, chief of staff to Prime Minister Ehud Barak from 1999 to 2001: he spoke of one hundred thousand for a two-state solution to be executed at a conference to mark the twentieth anniversary of the Oslo Accords. Dov Weissglass, former chief of staff to Prime Minister Ariel Sharon, agreed.[8]

There cannot be unilateral decisions. The inflexible principle must be to resolve every issue through negotiation.

The future of Palestinian refugees must be resolved. Their human need demands it, and their present existence is a festering sore out of which no good comes. The refugees face a nothing future while they remain cat's paws: to Arab states and Israel's enemies, they are a propaganda weapon with which to bludgeon Israel through the right of return mantra. The refugees' caregiver, UNRWA, has become self-perpetuating; for the many thousands who work for it, their livelihoods are at stake and they don't want it to end.

Israel will not budge on refugees. There will be no mass return. To keep pushing the 'right of return' is cynical and a cruel abuse of the refugees. No doubt limited numbers of people will be allowed for family reunification, as per Camp David II and peace deal drafts. Again, this must be decided through negotiation. Meanwhile, Israeli insistence on Palestinian recognition of it as a 'Jewish state' can best be seen as an attempt to preempt reaching agreement on refugees.

The Israeli government's attempt, resuscitated in September 2012 after more than sixty years, to link the Palestinian refugees with the departure and flight of Jews from Arab lands after 1948 is a crude attempt to create confusion about the Palestinian refugees and delay getting to grips with the problem. The issue of Jewish refugees deserves attention, but separately.

Jerusalem must be divided because Palestinians, too, view it as their capital. Israel has to back off from its exclusivist stand. Each side has to persuade itself and the other that it does not covet the holy places of the other, whether the Wall or the Mount/Sanctuary, and that they will cooperate to preserve ancient structures. Do the two sides need an earthquake with damage done to the ancient stones to make them see that they have a joint interest to protect? The growth of Jewish settlement in East Jerusalem makes division much more complex, but agreement has to be reached.

Additionally, agreement must be reached for water, customs, health cooperation, shared border control, imports and the other myriad details of a friendly separation. Much of this work was done earlier by officials from both sides after Oslo.

The obstacles are daunting, but human inventiveness can achieve wonders – as in the Abu Dis capital that nearly was (described in chapter 11), whereby Palestinians came close to establishing their parliament inside Jerusalem.

There is no doubt that any Israeli government, whatever its political outlook, which sets about withdrawing settlements will face grave difficulties.

In money terms, right-wing members of Knesset claimed in 2010 that it would cost more than $100 billion for the government to expel West Bank settlers.[9] That could be an exaggeration for political purposes, but the cost would certainly be immense and Israel would need international help.

The government would need a strong popular base to act. In 2005 soldiers who carried out the eviction of settlers from the Gaza Strip were hand-picked and specially trained; officers quietly excused soldiers uncomfortable with the job. The traumas experienced then would pale in comparison to any West Bank evictions where settler zeal and numbers are far, far higher. That more than 30 percent of the IDF's officer corps are now estimated to be national-religious, overtaking the original high proportion of kibbutzniks, is a warning flag. Many soldiers, both officers and other ranks – exactly how many cannot be said – live on settlements and would have to deal with orders evicting their families, relatives or friends. Spasms of rebellion have already surfaced, as in 2009 when a small number of soldiers mutinied against the partial dismantling of a settler-outpost on the West Bank.[10] Rabbis on the West Bank speak in support of such action.

There are searing emotional dilemmas. Roi Klein was a much-decorated major in the IDF's Golani Brigade. He died in 2006 during the Second Lebanon War: he saved the lives of his men by throwing himself onto an exploding hand-grenade. He was posthumously given the highest award, the Medal of Courage.

Major Klein lived in Hayovel, an illegal settlement outpost on the West Bank. He built a house there the year before he died. That was also the year that the Peace Now movement petitioned the High Court of Justice to halt all construction there, but while the case was underway twelve houses were completed and the owners moved in. As on a host of other West Bank outposts, all or some of the Hayovel houses were apparently built on Palestinian-owned land.

Major Klein left behind his widow and two young sons. They remained in the house.

In 2010, while the case was still dragging on in the courts, another Hayovel resident, Major Eliraz Peretez, died during a firefight with Palestinians on the Gaza border. He, too, was a hero. His widow and children remained in their house.

Whatever the law, can the families be evicted? No government can do that to the families of men who gave their lives for their country. Peace Now responded to the emotions and told the court it would not object to the two families staying in their houses if judgment was given on the other houses.

Leadership is crucial. Once determined on a course, leaders have to persuade the public to follow them. The hazards faced by an Israeli prime minister leading the way towards compromise and agreement are matched by a Palestinian leader persuading his people to compromise on borders, refugees and settlements. Prime Minister Yitzhak Rabin was courageous and visionary in changing direction, which was why an assassin struck him down; Ariel Sharon changed his belligerent course late in life and was taking his people, or most of them, with him until he suffered a stroke. Generally, however, Palestinians and Israelis have not been well served by their leaders: Yasser Arafat balked at taking the next step at Camp David II and never went further; President Mahmoud Abbas and Prime Minister Binyamin Netanyahu have both talked the talk about going forward to two states: both repeatedly called for talks 'without preconditions'; both repeatedly then set out preconditions for holding talks without preconditions. Each blamed the other for the lack of peace progress.

* * *

Israel itself must be a Jewish and democratic state, exactly as pledged in the Declaration of Independence and as buttressed by several Basic Laws. That is Zionism and morality. To keep it secure, Jews must make their peace with their Arab/Palestinian countrymen. It's a Jewish state because that is the will of the majority, and this will not change. But the minority Arab community needs to be embraced as citizens to fully share the benefits – and the burdens in military and community service – of a country of achievements.

Discrimination against Arabs must be rooted out, and the inherited neglect in land, housing and education must be dealt with. The charter of the Jewish National Fund in restricting use of 13 percent of the land to Jews must be the first to go. The argument that the charter is fixed in perpetuity is not sustainable: if, say, a wealthy family in America in the mid-1880s set up a trust fund to provide education for the children of runaway slaves, it would be meaningless 150 years later because there would be no one to educate; the trustees could apply to court to change the charter. This is also the case with the JNF charter. It's out of date and does not belong to the twenty-first century.

The Law of Return needs to be argued over between Jews and non-Jews. It's not God-given. The Jewish majority insists that it is critical to the basis of the Jewish state but, sensibly, needs to heed the resentment it causes among the excluded minority. In any event, it isn't a racist law unique to Israel as some critics claim: many countries provide preferential treatment, notably the right to return, to diaspora descendants. Ireland, Lithuania and Greece are among them.

What else can be changed to foster a greater sense of nationhood among Arabs? The national flag? The Star of David and the two blue lines are specific to the Jewish community. Israel is not unique: the flags of Britain, Scotland, Switzerland and others have the Christian cross and their non-Christian communities live comfortably with it; the same for non-Muslims in many Muslim countries such as Pakistan, which have the crescent. The national anthem? *Hatikvah* (hope) is so strongly and emotionally Zionist that Arabs have difficulty relating to it. The issue was in the open when Supreme Court Justice Salim Joubran, an Arab, stood silently as the anthem was sung during a public ceremony in March 2012. Angry Jewish right-wingers wanted him dismissed but Prime Minister Netanyahu defended him, making it known he understood Joubran could not sing the words such as 'a Jewish soul yearns'.

But the words could be adjusted, just as the new South Africa did in blending the African National Congress' *Nkosi Sikele iAfrika* (God Bless Africa) with apartheid's *Die Stem* (The Call) in Afrikaans and English. *Forward*, the American Jewish newspaper, suggested a few possible changes so that words about the soul of a Jew could become the soul of an Israeli, and the eye that 'looks for Zion' could be altered to 'yearn for our country'.[11]

Jews and Arabs must make the decisions. No one can force them to live alongside each other in peace. They must be willing partners. But the world can help – and not by boycotting, because it hardens Jewish resistance. Instead, the opposite is beneficial: Jewish fears must be soothed; Jews must be persuaded that they are not in danger of being driven into the Mediterranean or of being murdered wholesale. Friendship and contact, used purposefully and intelligently, will yield greater gain than hatred and yelling. The principle covers everything, from art and writing through tourism and sports to students and politics.

The United States under President Ronald Reagan tried this approach in dealing with apartheid South Africa. It was called 'constructive engagement'. The idea was sound and it looked good, but the way that Washington applied it amounted to a cover for supporting the white rulers. Honestly used, it could be a powerful tool for changing attitudes.

As a last resort, one weapon is available which is in a different dimension from boycotting and derives from Israel's dependency on one country above all others for survival: the United States, which provides military aid at $3.1 billion a year with extra millions for developing joint missile defence systems. (In 2012 Afghanistan received a higher amount of US military and other aid.) About 75 percent of the money helps to keep US arms manufacturers in business, but Israel gets the weapons it must have, such as the coming F-35s, the most technologically developed warplane, to keep enemies at bay, and many of the millions go to its own arms industry. The United States does not give Israel economic aid, but it does provide $3.8 billion in loan guarantees, which enable access to low-interest loans; the guarantees have not been used for some years, but their existence boosts the country's international credit rating.

The guarantees can only be used for money to be spent inside the pre-1967 boundaries. In 2003 the United States reduced the then $3 billion loan guarantee because Israel was building settlements and the security barrier. That could be repeated to coerce Israel into backing off on settlements and the occupation. However, for now and in the immediate future no US president could apply such a sanction; given the amount of support for Israel and the particular threats levelled by Iran and Hezbollah, it would not be tolerated by Congress or the American public. But the precedent exists, and no one can be totally certain about future American attitudes, nor its financial ability to remain a benevolent and protective Uncle Sam. The 2013 financial crisis in the United States proved that.

Peace must be sought within the Middle East, and even more, acceptance. A move towards this came in 2002 with the Saudi Arabian Peace Initiative, which was endorsed by the Arab League and repeated in 2007 and again in 2013. It offered to normalise relations between the entire Arab region and Israel in exchange for a complete withdrawal from the occupied territories including East Jerusalem and a 'just settlement' of the Palestinian refugee problem based on UN resolutions. Prime Minister Sharon barely gave it a glance and Israeli governments since then have adopted the same nonstarter stance, except for an occasional muttered show of interest. The formal reason is that the reference to UN resolutions means the Palestinian right of return, and that is unacceptable.

But this is an offer of a deal, to be treated as the start of negotiation. Perhaps rejection of a Jewish state in a Muslim region remains so strong that no wider peace is possible beyond the peace treaties in existence with Egypt and Jordan. Perhaps, on the other hand, as has seemed likely at different times, some Arab states are tired of unceasing conflict and want to concentrate on their economic growth. The turmoil following the Arab Spring revolutions gone wrong offers opportunities of dealing with states wanting stability. The bottom line is that the peace initiative needs to be put to the test. Israel does itself a disservice in not responding with enthusiasm to the hand put out by the Saudis and others. Meanwhile, Arab leaders could help reduce the emotional temperature by not cursing Jews and Zionism and by not threatening to wipe out Israel.

* * *

There is no sentimentality in advocating peace. The South African experience offers a guide – not false, contrived analogies with apartheid but instead drawing on hard-headed self-interest. Both blacks and whites finally reached the conclusion that they could not go on as before and struck a deal, which is what Jews and Arabs must do. A particular South African input is in the wisdom of Robert Mangaliso Sobukwe, who wrote from solitary confinement on Robben Island prison after the 1967 war to urge that Israel 'wash the enemies' wounds'. Make a 'grand gesture' for peace, he said.[12] And, indeed,

Israel holds the power to do that. Despite all the threats, it is secure and thriving. It should have the self-confidence to make a 'grand gesture', as Egypt's president Anwar Sadat bravely did when he visited Jerusalem to address the Knesset in 1977.

\* \* \*

Is it too late for two states? Are the doomsayers correct? Have the settlements spread so far and wide in the West Bank and East Jerusalem that a viable, independent Palestinian state is no longer possible? Has a point of no return been passed? That is a real and huge anxiety. Israel's enemies and even some Israelis claim it to be so, and hence insist on one state. At the other side of the spectrum, the settlers crow that they have won, that the idea of two states is dead, and they are on the way to one state ruled by Jews. 'Our presence in all of Judea and Samaria – not just in the so-called settlement blocs – is an irreversible fact', according to a settler leader, Dani Dayan. 'Trying to stop settlement expansion is futile, and neglecting this fact in diplomatic talks will not change the reality on the ground; it only makes the negotiations more likely to fail'.[13] The settlers offer muddled beyond-reality scenarios for the future in which Palestinians will not have normal rights.

Both enemies and settlers are in dreamland. None of what they have on offer has the slightest chance of bringing peace for the elementary reasons that Jews will not accept the one, and Palestinians will not accept the other. At Israeli government level, whichever party is in charge, policy veers between words pledging two states and actions on the ground which make a mockery of the words.

The future for Jews and Palestinians is two states, and it must be made to work.

# Appendix 1

Jewish history timeline, with approximate dates:

- 1020 BCE: Jewish monarchy established under King Saul
- 1000: King David establishes Jerusalem as the capital of an Israelite king-dom over much of Canaan and parts of Jordan
- 960: His son, King Solomon, builds the First Temple in Jerusalem
- 930: The kingdom splits between Judah in the south and Israel in the north
- 722: Assyrians conquer Israel
- 586: Babylonia conquers Judah, destroys Jerusalem and the Temple and exiles Jews
- 536: Persians conquer Babylonia. Jews return, Temple rebuilt
- 332: Alexander the Great conquers Persian Empire. Hellenic rule insti-tuted
- 167: Maccabean revolt against restrictions on practice of Judaism
- 1 CE: Jesus Christ born in Bethlehem
- 70: Romans destroy Jerusalem and Second Temple and expel Jews
- 73: Last Jewish stand, ending in suicide, at Masada
- 135: Romans name the area Palaestina (Palestine)
- 313–636: Byzantine rule: the Eastern Roman Empire in the Middle Ages
- 636–1099: Muslim Arabs invade from Arabia. Dome of the Rock built on site of Temples
- 1099–1291: Christian Crusaders are dominant
- 1291–1516: Mameluke rule: the military caste originally composed of slaves from Turkey
- 1517: Ottoman (Turkish) rule starts, from the capital of Constantinople (now Istanbul)

- 1537–1541: Sultan Suleiman the Magnificent builds the Old City walls, encompassing one square kilometre (two hundred acres)
- 1860: First Jewish neighbourhood built outside Old City walls
- 1862–1903: First Aliyah (mass immigration), mainly from Russia
- 1897: 1st Zionist Congress, convened by Theodor Herzl, in Basel, Switzerland
- 1904–1914: Second Aliyah, mainly from Russia and Poland
- 1909: First kibbutz, Degania, founded, and first modern all-Jewish city, Tel Aviv
- 1917: British conquest ends Ottoman rule
- 1919–1923: Third Aliyah, mainly from Russia
- 1920: Histadrut (General Federation of Labour) formed, and Haganah (Jewish defence organisation), and Vaad Leumi (National Council)
- 1921: First *moshav* (cooperative village)
- 1922: League of Nations grants Britain mandate over Palestine. Transjordan (today, Jordan) set up on 75 percent of the area
- 1947: United Nations General Assembly votes for partition of Palestine into Jewish and Arab states
- 1948: State of Israel

# Appendix 2

The UN Special Committee on Palestine (UNSCOP) released its Palestine report on 1 September 1947 and a majority said:

1. The basic premise underlying the partition proposal is that the claims to Palestine of the Arabs and Jews, both possessing validity, are irreconcilable, and that among all of the solutions advanced, partition will provide the most realistic and practicable settlement, and is the most likely to afford a workable basis for meeting in part the claims and national aspirations of both parties.
2. It is a fact that both of these peoples have their historic roots in Palestine, and that both make vital contributions to the economic and cultural life of the country. The partition solution takes these considerations fully into account.
3. The basic conflict in Palestine is a clash of two intense nationalisms. Regardless of the historical origins of the conflict, the rights and wrongs of the promises and counter-promises, and the international intervention incident to the Mandate, there are now in Palestine some 650,000 Jews and some 1,200,000 Arabs who are dissimilar in their ways of living and, for the time being, separated by political interests which render difficult full and effective political co-operation among them, whether voluntary or induced by constitutional arrangements.
4. Only by means of partition can these conflicting national aspirations find substantial expression and qualify both peoples to take their places as independent nations in the international community and in the United Nations.
5. The partition solution provides that finality which is a most urgent need in the solution. Every other proposed solution would tend to induce the two parties to seek modification in their favour by means of persistent pressure. The grant of independence to both States, however, would remove the basis for such efforts.

6.  Partition is based on a realistic appraisal of the actual Arab-Jewish rela-
    tions in Palestine. Full political co-operation would be indispensable to the
    effective functioning of any single-State scheme, such as the federal State
    proposal, except in those cases which frankly envisage either an Arab or a
    Jewish-dominated State.
7.  Partition is the only means available by which political and economic
    responsibility can be placed squarely on both Arabs and Jews, with the
    prospective result that, confronted with responsibility for bearing fully the
    consequences of their own actions, a new and important element of politi-
    cal amelioration would be introduced. In the proposed federal-State solu-
    tion, this factor would be lacking.
8.  Jewish immigration is the central issue in Palestine today and is the one
    factor, above all others, that rules out the necessary co-operation between
    the Arab and Jewish communities in a single State. The creation of a
    Jewish State under a partition scheme is the only hope of removing this
    issue from the arena of conflict.
9.  It is recognized that partition has been strongly opposed by Arabs, but it is
    felt that that opposition would be lessened by a solution which definitively
    fixes the extent of territory to be allotted to the Jews with its implicit
    limitation on immigration. The fact that the solution carries the sanction of
    the United Nations involves a finality which should allay Arab fears of
    further expansion of the Jewish State. [1]

# Appendix 3

INTERNATIONAL CONVENTION ON THE SUPPRESSION AND
PUNISHMENT OF THE CRIME OF APARTHEID, UN GENERAL
ASSEMBLY RESOLUTION 3068 ENTERED INTO FORCE
18 JULY 1976[1]

## Article I

1. The States Parties to the present Convention declare that apartheid is a crime against humanity and that inhuman acts resulting from the policies and practices of apartheid and similar policies and practices of racial segregation and discrimination, as defined in article II of the Convention, are crimes violating the principles of international law, in particular the purposes and principles of the Charter of the United Nations, and constituting a serious threat to international peace and security. 2. The States Parties to the present Convention declare criminal those organizations, institutions and individuals committing the crime of apartheid.

## Article II

For the purpose of the present Convention, the term "the crime of apartheid", which shall include similar policies and practices of racial segregation and discrimination as practised in southern Africa, shall apply to the following inhuman acts committed for the purpose of establishing and maintaining domination by one racial group of persons over any other racial group of persons and systematically oppressing them:

a. Denial to a member or members of a racial group or groups of the right to life and liberty of person:

(i) By murder of members of a racial group or groups;

(ii) By the infliction upon the members of a racial group or groups of serious bodily or mental harm, by the infringement of their freedom or dignity, or by subjecting them to torture or to cruel, inhuman or degrading treatment or punishment;

(iii) By arbitrary arrest and illegal imprisonment of the members of a racial group or groups;

b. Deliberate imposition on a racial group or groups of living conditions calculated to cause its or their physical destruction in whole or in part;

c. Any legislative measures and other measures calculated to prevent a racial group or groups from participation in the political, social, economic and cultural life of the country and the deliberate creation of conditions preventing the full development of such a group or groups, in particular by denying to members of a racial group or groups basic human rights and freedoms, including the right to work, the right to form recognized trade unions, the right to education, the right to leave and to return to their country, the right to a nationality, the right to freedom of movement and residence, the right to freedom of opinion and expression, and the right to freedom of peaceful assembly and association;

d. Any measures including legislative measures, designed to divide the population along racial lines by the creation of separate reserves and ghettos for the members of a racial group or groups, the prohibition of mixed marriages among members of various racial groups, the expropriation of landed property belonging to a racial group or groups or to members thereof;

e. Exploitation of the labour of the members of a racial group or groups, in particular by submitting them to forced labour;

f. Persecution of organizations and persons, by depriving them of fundamental rights and freedoms, because they oppose apartheid.

# Appendix 4

## AREA C, ISRAELI CONTROL: BASIC FACTS [1]

- Israel maintains full responsibility for security and civil affairs. The Palestinian Authority has no powers, except those delegated by Israel.
- Comprises about 61 percent of the West Bank (approx. 3,300 square kilometres), excluding East Jerusalem
- Sixty-six percent is 'state land'
- More than 33 percent is closed military zone/firing zones, which include fifty-nine Palestinian communities
- Three percent is Israeli military bases and the security zone along the Jordanian border
- Palestinian population is estimated at 150,000, 5.8 percent of the West Bank Palestinian population, excluding East Jerusalem
- About 350,000–400,000 Israeli settlers live in 124 recognized settlements and approximately 100 outposts
- Municipal area of settlements is 5.5 percent
- Forty percent of land on which settlements are built is privately owned by Palestinians
- Two hundred and seventy-one Palestinian communities have more than 50 percent of their built-up areas in Area C, including many which are entirely in Area C
- Palestinian construction allowed without Israeli permit in approximately 1 percent of Area C
- Palestinian construction is prohibited in 70 percent of Area C (settlements, firing zones, nature reserves, buffer zone around barrier) and is heavily restricted (Israeli permit necessary) in 30 percent of Area C

- Ninety-four percent of Palestinian building permit applications have been rejected in recent years

# Notes

## PREFACE

1. Even compared with developed Western nations, 'it is indeed unusual that Israel has increasingly exposed itself to soul-scarching debate over its actions and policies in the 1948 war, within a generational span of time and despite the continued Palestinian conflict', according to Avraham Sela, professor of Middle East Studies at the Hebrew University, 'Jerusalem: Israeli Historiography of the 1948 War', in *Shared Histories: A Palestinian-Israeli Dialogue*, ed. Paul Scham, Walid Salem and Benjamin Pogrund (Walnut Creek, CA: Left Coast Press, 2005), 205.

## 1. THE BEGINNING

1. For details, see Mark R. Cohen, *Under Crescent and Cross: The Jews in the Middle Ages* (Princeton, NJ: Princeton University Press, 1994).

2. David Bridger, ed., *New Jewish Encyclopedia* (West Orange, NJ: Behrman House, 1976), 101.

3. From the English translation by Shlomo Eidelberg, *The Jews and the Crusaders*, 32, cited in Cohen, *Under Crescent and Cross*, 174.

4. Amos Elon, *The Pity of It All: A Portrait of Jews in Germany, 1743–1933* (London: Allen Lane, 2003).

5. Howard Morley Sachar, *The Course of Modern Jewish History* (New York: Dell Publishing, 1958), 70.

6. Colin Shindler, *A History of Modern Israel* (Cambridge: Cambridge University Press, 2008), 13.

7. Sachar, *Course of Modern Jewish History*, 243.

8. Ibid., 244.

9. Quoted by Sachar, *Course of Modern Jewish History*, 245.

10. From the *Diary of One of the Bilu Members*, Tel Aviv, 1925, quoted in *Encyclopedia Judaica*, vol. 4 (Jerusalem, 1972), 998.

11. Lucy Dawidowicz, ed., *The Golden Treasury: Jewish Life and Thought in Eastern Europe* (Syracuse, NY: Syracuse University Press, 1996), 406.

12. *New York Times*, 28 April 1903.

13. Colin Shindler, *What Do Zionists Believe* (London: Granta, 2007), 21.

14. Sachar, *Course of Modern Jewish History*, 269.

15. *Times*, obituary, 7 July 1904.

16. Sachar, *Course of Modern Jewish History*, 267.

17. Shindler, *What Do Zionists Believe*, 62.

18. David Fromkin, *A Peace to End All Peace* (New York: Owl Books/Henry Holt, 2001), 294.

19. Isaiah Friedman, *The Question of Palestine: 1914–1918: British-Jewish-Arab Relations* (London: Routledge & Kegan Paul, 1973), 22–23.

20. Ran Aaronsohn, 'The Beginnings of Jewish Settlement and Zionism, to World War 1', in *Shared Histories: A Palestinian-Israeli Dialogue*, ed. Paul Scham, Walid Salem, and Benjamin Pogrund (Walnut Creek, CA: Left Coast Creek, 2005), 63.

21. Henry Katzew, conversation with David Ben-Gurion, *Solution for South Africa: A Jewish View* (Cape Town: Simondium, 1955), 37.

22. Saadi Goldberg in *Struggles of a Generation: The Jews under Soviet Rule*, ed. Benjamin West (Tel Aviv: Massadah, 1959), 155.

23. My father, Nathan Pogrund, from Lithuania, was among them: he went on to live in South Africa. He used to tell me about existing in Palestine on 'water and mustard'.

24. *Columbia Encyclopedia Online*.

25. *The First Governor: Sir Ronald Storrs, Governor of Jerusalem , 1918–1926* (Tel Aviv: Eretz Israel Museum, 2010).

26. Nirit Shavel Khalifa, 'Sir Ronald and the Knights of the Stone Order', in *The First Governor*, 22e.

27. Fromkin, *A Peace to End All Peace*, 513; and Benny Morris, *Righteous Victims: A History of the Zionist-Arab Conflict, 1981–1999* (London: John Murray, 2000), 92–104.

28. Ibid., 513.

29. Ibid., 292–93.

30. Friedman, *A Peace to End All Peace*, 290.

31. Ibid., 268.

32. Adel Manna, 'Continuity and Change in Palestine: The Late Ottoman Period, 1856–1918', in *Shared Histories*, 53.

33. Rashid Khalidi, *Palestinian Identity* (New York: Columbia University Press, 1998), 124.

34. Rashid Khalidi, *The Iron Cage: The Story of the Palestinian Struggle for Statehood* (Boston: Beacon Press, 2006), 94.

35. Ibid., 31.

36. Ibid.

37. James Barker, 'Policing Palestine', *History Today*, June 2008.

38. William L. Cleveland, *A History of the Modern Middle East* (Boulder, CO: Westview Press, 1994), 242.

39. Jeffrey Herf, *Nazi Propaganda for the Arab World* (New Haven, CT: Yale University Press, 2009), 76.

40. Ibid., citing transcripts of recordings by the US Embassy in Cairo.

41. Ibid., 77.

42. Ibid., 242, quoting a Muslim Brotherhood newspaper.

43. Shindler, *What Do Zionists Believe*, 10.

44. Menachem Begin, *The Revolt* (Jerusalem: Steimatzky, 1951), 43.

45. Anne Applebaum, *Iron Curtain: The Crushing of Eastern Europe 1944–56* (London: Allen Lane, 2012), 152.

# 2. FREEDOM AND WAR

1. Benny Morris, *1948: A History of the First Arab-Israeli War* (New Haven, CT: Yale University Press, 2008), 76–77.

2. Ibid., 81, quoting a minute of 22 December 1947.

3. UN Special Commission, 16 April 1948, paragraph 11.6.

4. The Irgun website, written by Yehuda Lapidot, www.etzel.org.il.

5. Meron Benvenisti, *Sacred Landscape: The Buried History of the Holy Land since 1948* (Berkeley: University of California Press, 2002), 119.

6. John Setsinger, Truman Papers, OF 204-Misc, quoted in *Truman: The Jewish Vote and the Creation of Israel* (Stanford, CA: Hoover Institution Press, 1974).

7. Morris, *1948*, 118.

8. Ibid., 121.

9. Ibid., 119.

10. Ibid., 109.

11. *New York Times*, 13 April 1948.

12. Uri Milstein, *The War of Independence*, vol. 4, *Out of Crisis Came Decision* (Tel Aviv: Zmora-Bitan, 1991), 268–69; and interview with Mordechai Ra'anan, translated by Ami Isseroff.

13. Milstein, *War of Independence*, 4:274.

14. Bir Zeit Documentation Centre, 'Deir Yassin', Monograph No. 4, 1987, 7–8.

15. Julie Flint, 'The Sharon Files', *Guardian*, 28 November 2001.

16. *New York Times*, 13 April 1948, 7.

17. Morris, *1948*, 95.

18. Walid Khalidi, 'Why Did the Palestinians Leave, Revisited', *Journal of Palestine Studies* 4, no. 2 (Winter 2005): 42–54.

19. Morris, *1948*, 153.

20. Ibid., 397–98.

21. Electronic Intifada, Key Historical Events.

22. Ilan Pappe, *The Ethnic Cleansing of Palestine* (Oxford: One World, 2007), 90.

23. Ilan Pappe writes a great deal about the Middle East; generalisations without substantiation are an unfortunate characteristic of his work. Israeli historian Benny Morris comments on an earlier Pappe book, *A History of Modern Palestine: One Land, Two Peoples*: 'This truly is an appalling book. Anyone interested in the real history of Palestine/Israel and the Palestinian-Israeli conflict would do well to run vigorously in the opposite direction' (*New Republic*, 22 March 2004). Pappe's 'ethnic cleansing' book is described by Milton Shain, professor of history at the University of Cape Town and director of the Kaplan Centre for Jewish Studies, as 'a blatantly tendentious polemic', and that his work is 'riddled with distortions and even untruths' (Milton Shain, 'Attack on Israel Reduces a Very Complex History to a Ragbag of Myths', *Cape Times*, 5 November 2010).

24. *Palestine Post*, 4 June 1948.

25. Ibid., 1 July 1948.

26. Larry Collins and Dominique Lapierre, *O Jerusalem!* (Bnei Barak, Israel: Steimatzky, 1995), 400.

27. Yoav Gelber, *Palestine 1948* (Brighton: Sussex Academic Press, 2001), vii.

28. 'Living with the Contradiction', *Haaretz*, 28 April 2009.

29. Ibid.

30. *Palestine Post*, 14 July 1948.

31. For details, see Colin Shindler, *A History of Modern Israel*, 2nd ed. (Cambridge: Cambridge University Press, 2013).

32. Ibid., 103.

33. Rashid Khalidi, *The Iron Cage: The Story of the Palestinian Struggle for Statehood* (Boston: Beacon Press, 2006), 135.

34. Ibid., 136.

35. Reuven Pedatzur, 'The Occupation and Its Effect on the Israel Defence Forces', in *The Impacts of Lasting Occupation*, ed. Daniel Bar-Tal and Izhak Schnell (Oxford: Oxford University Press, 2013), 209.

36. *Guardian*, 24 June 1967, quoted in Eric Silver, *Dateline Jerusalem* (Brighton: Revel Barker Publishing, 2011).

37. Michael B. Oren, *Six Days of War: June 1967 and the Making of the Modern Middle East* (New York: Presidio Press, 2003), 157.

38. Ibid., 306.

39. Shlomo Gazit, *The Carrot and the Stick: Israel's Policy in Judaea and Samaria, 1967–68* (Washington, DC: B'nai Brith Books, 1995), 37.

40. Ibid., xiii.

# 3. INSIDE THE GREEN LINE

1. 'Inequality Report: The Palestinian Arab Minority in Israel', *Adalah*, December 2010, 4.

2. *Jerusalem Post*, 28 July 2002.

3. *Haaretz*, 2 September 2011.

4. Daniel Pipes, 'Ending the Palestinian "Right of Return"', *National Review Online*, 17 January 2012.

5. Ibid., according to attorney Sawsan Zaher.

6. *Haaretz*, 12 January 2012.

7. Arutz Sheva, 9 January 2007.

8. *Haaretz*, 3 February 2012.

9. Al-Jazeera, 5 June 2010.

10. Arutz Sheva, 28 October 2007.

11. *Haaretz*, 8 April 2008.

12. *Haaretz*, 27 June 2012.

13. Adalah News Update, 19 September 2010.

14. *Haaretz*, 19 January 2012.

15. *Haaretz*, 28 August 2007.

16. An estimated eight hundred thousand people, 10 percent of Israel's population, attended Rabbi Yosef's funeral in Jerusalem on 8 October 2013.

17. *Israel Hayom*, 20 July 2013.

18. Kairos Palestine, 8 April 2011.

19. *Haaretz*, 3 April 2012.

20. David Kretzmer, *The Legal Status of the Arabs in Israel* (Boulder, CO: Westview Press, 1990), chap. 4, p. 1.

21. Ibid.

22. UN Conciliation Commission for Palestine (UNCCP), cited by Kretzmer, chapter 4, footnote 7. There is considerable variation in the descriptions of the amounts of land involved and who owned what; for example, the arable land said to have been owned by Arabs ranges from 1,373,000 to 4,574,000 dunams.

23. Gereny Forman and Alexandre Kedar, 'From Arab Lands to Israel Lands: The Legal Dispossession of the Palestinians Displaced by Israel in the Wake of 1948', *Environmental Planning D: Society and Space* 22 (2004): 815.

24. Ibid., 816.

25. Kretzmer, *Legal Status of the Arabs in Israel*, 12.

26. John Berncastle, UNCCP report, 14 August 1951.

27. Kretzmer, *Legal Status of the Arabs in Israel*, 18.

28. Alaa Mahajna, 'Loyalty to the Values of Zionism as a Condition for Acceptance to Community Settlements in Israel', *Adalah Newsletter* 67 (December 2009).

29. *Haaretz*, 10 September 2007.

30. *Haaretz*, 8 March 2012.

31. *Haaretz*, 12 February 2012.

32. Michael Nelson, 'Gated Communities: Class Walls', *History Today*, November 2011.

33. 'Israel Ditches Historic Land Administration', *Green Prophet*, 20 August 2009.

34. *Haaretz*, 19 January 2012.

35. The Arab Center for Alternative Planning, 18 March 2012.

36. *Haaretz*, 20 February 2012.

37. *Haaretz*, 3 April 2012.

38. *Haaretz*, 7 March 2012.

39. *Jerusalem Post*, 4 June 2013.
40. *Jewish Virtual Library*, 2 September 2003.
41. *New York Times*, 8 February 2007.
42. *Haaretz*, 3 February 2012.
43. Arutz Sheva, 10 December 2010.
44. *Haaretz*, 3 April 2012.
45. *Adalah*, 6 August 2012.
46. *Haaretz*, 21 November 2011.
47. 'Suggested Questions for the UN Human Rights Committee Considering Israel's Compliance with the ICCPR: The Rights of Palestinian Arab Citizens of Israel', *Adalah*, 18 February 2009, 16.
48. Ibid., 18.
49. 'New Discriminatory Laws and Bills in Israel', *Adalah*, June 2011.
50. *YNet*, 1 June 2010.
51. *Cape Argus*, 18 April 2012.
52. *Jerusalem Post*, 24 May 2011.
53. *Haaretz*, 19 January 2012.
54. *Haaretz*, 15 March 2010.
55. *Jerusalem Post*, 4 December 2007.
56. *Jerusalem Post*, 12 December 2012.
57. *YNet*, 10 August 2009.
58. Israel Government Press Office, 22 March 2011.
59. Israel Central Bureau of Statistics, quoted in 'Glaring Arab-Jewish Wage Gaps', *Haaretz*, 19 January 2011.
60. 'The Marker', *Haaretz*, 3 March 2012.
61. *Haaretz*, 18 January 2011.
62. *Haaretz*, 21 June 2012.
63. Arutz Sheva, 25 July 2008.
64. The Association for Civil Rights in Israel, 14 May 2011.
65. *Haaretz*, 4 November 2011.
66. *The World Factbook*, 2013 estimates, Central Intelligence Agency, Washington, DC.
67. J. Tarabei et al., 'Differences in Infant Mortality Rates between Jews and Arabs in Israel, 1975–2000', *Israeli Medical Association Journal* 6 (July 2004): 403–7; and Israel Central Bureau of Statistics, 29 August 2010.
68. Tarabei et al., ' Differences in Infant Mortality Rates'.
69. Taub Center for Social Policy Studies in Israel, Jerusalem, E-Bulletin, 21 September 2010.
70. *Jerusalem Post*, 21 December 2011.
71. *Jerusalem Post*, 4 July 2010.
72. David Harman, 'Developmental Trends in Education in the Jewish Education System of Mandatory Palestine and Israel', qualifying paper, Harvard University, May 1970.
73. Dina Kraft, 'Separate but Not Equal', *Moment*, September/October 2010.
74. *Jerusalem Post*, 5 June 2013.
75. Such as from Israel's Central Bureau of Statistics, 2007, reported in *The Sikkuy Report, 2008: Equality Index of Jewish and Arab Citizens in Israel*, ed. Ali Haider, and The Association for the Advancement of Civic Equality, 2009.
76. David Harman, interview with author, 27 May 2011.
77. 'Inequality Report', *Adalah*, 30.
78. Ibid., 6.
79. Ibid., 30.
80. *The Sikkuy Report, 2008*, 39.
81. *Haaretz*, 23 August 2102.
82. Ibid.
83. *Jerusalem Post*, 4 November 2013.
84. Details are in an insightful report by Meirav Arlosoroff, 'We Are Helping Arabs Town Fail', *Haaretz*, 17 January 2011.

85. *Haaretz*, 20 January 2011.

86. *Jerusalem Post*, 22 February 2011.

87. *Haaretz*, 5 September 2012.

88. Electronic Intifada, 17 October 2011.

89. *Jerusalem Post*, 3 September 2013.

90. Shoshan Brosh-Vaitz, 'On the State of Literacy in Israel, Education for All Global Monitoring', background paper for Education for All Monitoring Report *Literacy for Life*, UNESCO, Paris, 2006/ED/EFA/MRT/PI/17, 42.

91. UN Development Report 2007/2008.

92. Nachum Blass, 'Israel's Education System: A Domestic Perspective', Policy Paper No. 2010 (Jerusalem: Taub Center for Social Policy Studies in Israel), 4.

93. *Haaretz*, 21 October 2012.

94. *International Herald Tribune*, 31 July 2007.

95. *New Age*, 28 June 2011.

96. *Cape Times*, 13 July 2010 and 9 August 2011.

97. *Haaretz*, 1 June 2012.

# 4. THE OCCUPATION

1. The Gaza Strip and the Golan Heights were also seized by Israel in 1967. Egypt had occupied Gaza during the 1948 war but did not annex it. Israel took it over, did not annex it, but built settlements. Palestinians persistently attacked and were so effective that settlers had to travel in convoy with army escorts. In 2005 Prime Minister Ariel Sharon withdrew the settlements and the army. Gaza was taken over by a Hamas government. Israel keeps the territory under siege and is heavily criticised for it; but much overlooked is that Egypt imposes as stringent a blockade along the southern border. Israel annexed the Golan Heights but had discussions with Syria about returning at least part of it; however, this foundered because of Israel's refusal to allow Syria access to its main water source, Lake Kinneret, at the foot of the Golan.

2. Two books tell the story: Idith Zertal and Akiva Eldar, *Lords of the Land: The War over Israel's Settlements in the Occupied Territories, 1967–2007* (New York: Nation Books, 2007), and Gershom Gorenberg, *The Accidental Empire: Israel and the Birth of Settlements* (New York: Holt, 2007).

3. Zertal and Eldar, *Lords of the Land*, 156–58.

4. The Center for Jewish Studies in Israel, Jerusalem, 5 July 2003.

5. Naftali Bennett, economics minister, Arutz Sheva, 17 June 2013.

6. CNN, 27 May 2003.

7. Zertal and Eldar, *Lords of the Land*, 163–64.

8. *Jerusalem Post*, citing Central Bureau of Statistics, 17 September 2012.

9. 'One Offence Begets Another', Peace Now, 14 March 2007.

10. *Haaretz*, 3 September 2012.

11. *Haaretz*, 2 November 2011.

12. *Haaretz*, 25 April 2012.

13. *Haaretz*, reporting Central Bureau of Statistics and Peace Now, 31 July 2012.

14. *Haaretz*, 6 September 2007.

15. Government Press Office, 9 September 2012.

16. Zertal and Eldar, *Lords of the Land*, 5.

17. Early in the 1980s the author interviewed Rabbi Levinger for the *Rand Daily Mail* when he visited Johannesburg. His stock reply to virtually every question was: 'The Bible says so'. When asked the final question: 'Do you ever, for a split second, wonder whether you are wrong about anything?', he drew a cold look and replied, 'No'.

18. *Haaretz*, Association for Civil Rights in Israel and B'Tselem, 14 May 2005.

19. Arutz Sheva, 4 May 2011.

20. *YNet*, 25 June 2012.

21. *Jerusalem Post*, 17 June 2013.
22. *Haaretz*, 19 August 2012.
23. Foundation for Middle East Peace, Settlement Report 15, no. 2 (March–April 2005); 'Lords of the Land: Debating the Impact of the Settlements', Yakar Center for Social Concern, Jerusalem, 13 November 2007; *Wikipedia*; and *Times of Israel*, 16 April 2012.
24. 'Lords of the Land'.
25. *Haaretz*, 19 April 2012.
26. Uri Blau, 'Secret Israeli Database Reveals Full Extent of Illegal Settlement', *Haaretz*, 20 January 2009.
27. *Haaretz*, 7 June 2012.
28. *YNet*, 6 June 2012.
29. Arutz Sheva, 20 June 2012.
30. *Haaretz*, 28 November 2012.
31. Jewish Telegraphic Agency, 11 February 2013.
32. *Haaretz*, 5 June 2012.
33. Israel and the Occupied Territories, *Human Rights Report*, US Department of State, Washington, DC, 8 April 2011.
34. *Haaretz*, 29 November 2012.
35. *Haaretz*, 23 June 2013.
36. *Jerusalem Post*, 4 December 2013.
37. 'Netanyahu Intervenes to Stop Government Backing Annexation of W. Bank', *Haaretz*, 14 May 2012.
38. *Haaretz*, 29 November 2011.
39. *Haaretz*, 9 April 2008.
40. *Jerusalem Post*, 8 July 2013.
41. 'The Economic Cost of the Israeli Occupation for the Occupied Palestinian Territory', Palestinian Ministry of National Economy, Ramallah, in cooperation with Applied Research Institute–Jerusalem, September 2011.
42. *Huffington Post*, 25 July 2012.
43. Information Brief No. 79, Palestine Center, 11 July 2001.
44. B'Tselem, February 2013.
45. B'Tselem, 1 January 2012. However, the World Health Organization, in a report on 11 May 2012, said Palestinian consumption was fifty litres a day, one-fourth the average Israeli consumption from available fresh water. It also said that about two hundred thousand West Bank Palestinians had no access to water network connections.
46. World Health Organization, 11 May 2012.
47. 'Water Deal Irks Lesotho's New Rulers', *Mail&Guardian*, 7 December 2012.
48. *Haaretz*, 3 July 2013, citing the Israel Parks and Nature Authority.
49. Dr Yossi Yakhin, 'Water in the Israeli-Palestinian Conflict', Institute for Public Policy, Rice University, June 2006.
50. B'Tselem, 1 January 2012.
51. Benjamin Pogrund, 'Springs of Hope', *New Statesman*, 16 August 2007.
52. *YNet*, 21 July 2012.
53. *New York Times*, 9 December 2012.
54. *Haaretz*, 17 December 2007.
55. *The World Factbook*, 2013 estimates, Central Intelligence Agency, Washington, DC. The World Health Organization, in 'Health Conditions in the Occupied Palestinian Territory, Statistics for 2010', 11 May 2012, reports different infant mortality rates: West Bank 18.8, Gaza Strip 23.0. So, for Israel, does the Israeli Central Bureau of Statistics.
56. *Haaretz*, 21 March 2011.
57. *Haaretz*, 11 May 2012.
58. 'The Illusion of Rule of Law on Route 443', ACRI, 25 May 2010.
59. ACRI letter to author, 29 May 2012.
60. *Haaretz*, 13 November 2012.
61. *Jerusalem Post*, 18 July 2013.
62. *Haaretz*, 23 June 2013.

# 5. WHAT WAS APARTHEID?

1. Material for this chapter is drawn from Muriel Horrell, *Race Relations as Regulated by Law in South Africa, 1948–1979* (Johannesburg: SA Institute of Race Relations, 1982); Hermann Giliomee and Bernard Mbenga, *New History of South Africa* (Cape Town: Tafelberg Publishers, 2007); T. R. H. Davenport, *South Africa: A Modern History* (Cape Town: Southern Book Publishers, 1988); David Welsh, *The Rise and Fall of Apartheid* (Johannesburg: Jonathan Ball Publishers, 2009); Benjamin Pogrund, *How Can Man Die Better: The Life of Robert Sobukwe* (London: Peter Halban Publishers; Johannesburg: Jonathan Ball Publishers, 2000/2012); Benjamin Pogrund, *War of Words: Memoir of a South African Journalist* (New York: Seven Stories Press, 2000); Benjamin Pogrund, 'The Bitter-enders', *Haaretz*, 29 October 2010; and the author's personal experiences in South Africa.

2. Although I opposed communism, I was prosecuted under the Suppression of Communism Act for possession of banned documents: three copies of a communist newspaper published twenty-five years earlier which I was using to prepare a submission for a PhD thesis. Found guilty, despite challenging the verdict in the country's highest court, I was given a suspended prison sentence and hence became a 'Statutory Communist'. The meaning and consequences of this legal label were never clear. That I had several times been secretly considered for banning under the Suppression of Communism Act was revealed when some of my security files became available after the end of apartheid.

3. As a journalist, I specialised in reporting on the black community, and the Johannesburg Municipality gave me a permit allowing me to enter black townships at any time of the day or night; but the government barred me from entering black rural 'reserves' after I wrote a report mocking the cabinet minister in charge.

# 7. COMPARING ISRAEL AND APARTHEID SOUTH AFRICA

1. The categories are derived from Heribert Adam and Kogila Moodley, *Seeking Mandela: Peacemaking between Israelis and Palestinians* (Philadelphia: Temple University Press, 2005).

2. Moshe Amirav, *Jerusalem Syndrome: The Palestinian-Israeli Battle for the Holy City* (Brighton and Portland: Sussex Academic Press, 2009), 148.

3. *Jerusalem Post*, 30 November 2010.

4. *Jerusalem Post*, 1 December 2010.

5. See the Hamas Charter 1988 on Google.

6. *Jerusalem Post*, 9 September 2013.

7. *Jerusalem Post*, 16 August 2013.

8. B'Tselem, 1 July 2013.

9. 'Walled World', *Guardian*, 19 November 2013.

10. The Basement Geographer, http://basementgeographer.com/.

11. Cited (approvingly) by Henry Norris in Mondoweiss, 30 November 2013.

12. Gideon Shimoni, 'Could There Be Apartheid in Israel?' Van Leer Institute, Jerusalem, 20 February 2013.

13. Benjamin Pogrund, 'Jerusalem', in *Something to Write Home About*, ed. Claude Colart and Sahm Venter (Johannesburg: Jacana, 2004), 251–53.

# 8. THE CRITICS (1)

1. 'Preoccupation with Israel in the British Media', *Just Journalism*, 19 May 2011.

2. Numbers of South Africans visited the West Bank during the second intifada when conflict was at its height, and that is what they remember; since then, the occupation oppression continues, but hundreds of Israeli checkpoints have been removed and the number of Palestinian prisoners in Israeli prisons has decreased from 9,850 in 2007 to 4,998 in 2013.

3. *Independent on Sunday*, 13 June 2010.

4. *Sunday Times*, 17 March 2009.

5. Milton Shain, *Antisemitism* (London: Bowerdean, 1998), 5.

6. *Jewish Week*, 11 May 2013.

7. *Haaretz*, 7 April 2013, citing the Kantor Centre for the Study of Contemporary European Jewry, Tel Aviv University.

8. *Haaretz*, 8 November 2013.

9. Shain, *Antisemitism*, 94.

10. *New York Times*, 10 December 1971.

11. UN Document A/CONF.189/PC2/9.

12. I was a member of the Israeli government delegation, invited because of my knowledge of apartheid.

13. South African Department of Foreign Affairs, 10 March 2002.

14. Roger Cohen, 'Jimmy Carter Attempts to Provoke, and Succeeds', *New York Times*, 7 February 2007.

15. *Democracy Now!* National Public Radio, 30 November 2006.

16. Jewish Telegraph Agency, 30 August 2012.

17. Irwin Cotler, 'UN Poisons Its Human Rights Mission', *Australian*, 4 October 2010.

18. Asher Susser, 'The Prejudice and Double Standards of Israel's Critics', *Mail & Guardian*, 9 June 2010.

19. Benjamin Pogrund, 'How Goldstone Erred', *Haaretz*, 25 September 2009.

20. Benjamin Pogrund, 'Beyond Goldstone', *Jerusalem Report*, 9 November 2009.

21. International law permits the use of white phosphorus shells for illuminating the sky at night but not to harm civilians. On 26 April 2013 the BBC reported that the IDF said it would stop using artillery shells with white phosphorus to create smokescreens on the battlefield.

22. Nahum Barnea, 'Goldstone Aftershocks', *New York Times*, 10 April 2011.

23. *Al-Watan*, 7 April 2013.

24. Michael B. Oren, 'Ambivalent Adversaries: David Ben-Gurion and Israel vs the United Nations and Dag Hammarskjold', *Journal of Contemporary History* 27, no. 1 (January 1992): 89–127.

25. Permanent Mission of Israel to the UN website.

26. *Israel Hayom*, 23 February 2013.

27. *YNet*, 12 November 2007.

28. A/56/440, 4 October 2001.

29. E/CN.4/2000/32, 6 March 2002.

30. E/CN.4/2006/29, 17 January 2006.

31. A/HRC/7/17, 21 January 2008.

32. A/HR/4/17, 29 January 2007.

33. John Dugard, 'Apartheid and Occupation under International Law', Hisham B. Shabari Memorial Lecture, Palestine Center, Washington, DC, 30 March 2009.

34. Ibid.

35. Statement to the Special Session of the UN Human Rights Council, 5 June 2006.

36. 'Occupation, Colonialism, Apartheid: A Re-assessment of Israel's Practices in the Occupied Palestinian Territories under International Laws', executive summary, study by the Middle East Project of the Human Sciences Research Council of South Africa, 2009.

37. 'Palestinian Workers at Salit Quarries Make History', *Solidarity Magazine*, 20 June 2011.

38. Introduction to 'Occupation, Colonialism, Apartheid: A Re-assessment of Israel's Practices in the Occupied Palestinian Territories under International Laws', executive summary, study by the Middle East Project of the Human Sciences Research Council of South Africa, 2009.

39. Sduma Dlamini, president, Congress of South African Trade Unions, 'Call to Arms for a "Living Wage"', *Mail & Guardian*, 8–14 July 2011.

40. *Cape Times*, 13 July 2011.

41. Electronic Intifada, 19 November 2009.

42. *Jerusalem Post*, 11 June 2013.

43. Electronic Intifada, 12 July 2011.

44. *Guardian*, 25 June 2011.

45. *Democracy Now!* 28 September 2012.

46. *Cape Times*, 20 July 2011.

47. The next year, 2012, activists again sought to fly into Ben-Gurion airport, reported IPS on 16 April. Israel again gave airlines names of passengers who would not be allowed to enter. A participant, clearly an innocent about international travel barriers, complained of 'illegal orders from the Israeli government since European regulations state that people have the right to travel'. Inevitably, apartheid was dragged in as a sound bite, not because it made any sense but as a laughable attempt at a slur: 'It's an apartheid state that doesn't want the world to find out that it's an apartheid state', said his colleague Mazin Qumsiyeh.

48. Chris Barron, 'So Many Questions', *Sunday Times* (Johannesburg), 31 July 2011.

49. Zionism and the Peace Settlement in Palestine', Zionist Organisation of America, July 1943, cited in Colin Shindler, *A History of Modern Israel* (Cambridge: Cambridge University Press, 2008), 60.

50. As referred in Palestine Monitors Network, 17 Mark 2009.

51. Ibid.

52. Ibid.

53. *Haaretz*, 24 May 2007.

54. *Middle East Monitor*, 11 March 2010.

55. *Cape Times*, 18 June 2007.

56. Electronic Intifada, 7 April 2008.

57. Al-Jazeera, 20 May 2011.

58. *Al-Hayat al-Jadida*, 4 February 2014.

59. Palestine Media Watch, 21 February 2014.

60. Nora Barrows-Friedman, Electronic Intifada, 26 February 2016.

61. Rod Such, Electronic Intifada, 28 February 2014.

# 9. THE CRITICS (2)

1. *Independent*, 28 April 2008.

2. 'Johann Hari: Left-Wing Commentator in Plagiarism Row', *Telegraph*, 23 July 2011.

3. *Jerusalem Post*, 19 August 2009.

4. *Jerusalem Post*, 14 September 2009.

5. *Guardian*, 20 December 2009.

6. *Jewish Chronicle*, 11 February 2010.

7. *Jewish Chronicle*, 29 February 2012.

8. *Just Journalism*, 26 March 2010.

9. A/HRC/13/NGO/230.

10. *Times of India*, 21 July 2008.

11. Palestinian Media Watch, 9 July 2008.

12. *Memri*, 13 March 2002.

13. *AFP*, 18 September 2009.

14. *AFP*, 8 May 2008.

15. Reuters, 14 May 2008.

16. Reuters, 3 June 2008.

17. www.president.ir.

18. *AFP* and *Times of Israel*, 21 November 2013.

19. *Daily Star* and *al-Akhbar*, Beirut, 3 August 2013.

20. Arutz Sheva, quoting Fox News, 30 January 2013.

21. *Times of Israel*, 24 January 2013.

22. FoxNews.com, 29 January 2013.

23. *Unpetrified Opinion* (blog), February 2011, http://unpetrified-opinion.blogspot.com.

24. *YNet*, 5 April 2012.

25. *Die Welt*, 5 April 2012.

26. *YNet*, 5 April 2012.

27. *Independent*, 26 July 2013.

28. *Mail & Guardian*, 4 April 2007.

29. See the Palestinian website www.palestinehistory.com.

30. *The Daily Life of Kawther Salam* (blog), 1 November 2006, www.kawther.info. Fifteen months later, the missiles were still terrorising southern Israel and that gave scope to Israel's own extremists: *YNet* reported on 21 February 2008 that Safed's Chief Rabbi Shmuel Eliyahu urged action: 'We don't have to kill the people living there, but we must definitely destroy Beit Hanoun'. The government did not follow his advice.

31. *Citizen*, 15 May 2008.

32. Nationmaster.com.

33. As by Omar Barghouti, Electronic Intifada, 8 May 2008.

34. *New York Times*, 22 August 1969.

35. 'Background Briefing', ABC Radio National, Australia, 23 August 2009.

36. UNSC Resolution 271, 15 September 2009.

37. *New York Times*, 17 September 1969.

38. Arab News, 21 August 2002.

39. *Jordan Times*, 21 August 2011.

40. Agence de Presse Senegalaise, 8 March 2008.

41. Cited by International Middle East Media Centre, 22 August 2008.

42. Palestinian Media Watch, 15 March 2010.

43. Cited by Daniel Gordis, *Saving Israel: How the Jewish People Can Win a War That May Never End* (Hoboken, NJ: John Wiley & Sons, 2009), 75.

44. Ibid., 80.

45. Ibid.

46. YouTube, 18 August 2011.

47. *Mail & Guardian*, 14 September 2012.

48. Zochrot, 18 March 2010.

49. *New Statesman*, 8 January 2009.

50. *Independent*, 11 February 2012.

51. Statement to UN General Assembly, 30 November 1973.

52. *The European Journal of International Law* 23, no. 23 (2013): 807–913.

53. Electronic Intifada, 3 April 2009.

54. Karine Mac Allister, 'Applicability of the Crime of Apartheid to South Africa', *BDS and the Global Anti-Apartheid Movement*, Summer 2008.

55. Ibid.

56. As at a conference in Toronto, 26–29 October 2005.

57. The author is also a victim, with a quote from an interview attributed to him about apartheid South Africa that is not only inaccurately reported but doesn't even make sense: 'The media disseminated the establishment's propaganda claiming the virtuous nature of the Apartheid system (e.g., defending Christianity, fighting terrorism, defending their own land and rights, defending the free world and civilization . . . ). According to Benjamin Pogrund, the Whites owned the big newspapers and they addressed the Whites. They showed the Whites in total control and when referring to the Blacks they showed only the "Black riots". However, by the Eighties a few voices of an alternative critical media started to develop'.

58. *Washington Post*, 9 April 2007.

59. Gush Shalom, 20 January 2007.

60. Steven Friedman and Virgina Tilley, 'Taken for a Ride by the Israeli Left', *Counterpunch*, 24 January 2007.

61. *Haaretz*, 15 April 2008.

62. *Haaretz*, 25 April 2008.

63. *Guardian*, 30 November 2012.

64. Electronic Intifada has counterparts on the other side of the line: the Israel-right-or-wrong basis of websites like HonestReporting and Palestinian Media Watch doesn't always ensure fairness or accuracy.

65. Electronic Intifada, 29 March 2012.

66. 'How Detention without Trial Links Israel and Apartheid South Africa', Electronic Intifada, 6 April 2012.

67. Amnesty International, 13 March 2012.

68. As a reporter in apartheid South Africa, the author was twice the target of stone-throwers while driving. These were frightening and life-threatening experiences.

69. IPS, Electronic Intifada, 31 July 2012.

70. *Malaysia Chronicle*, December 2011.

71. *Jerusalem Post*, 23 June 2013.

72. *Haaretz*, 12 July 2013.

73. *Haaretz*, 16 October 2013.

74. *Jerusalem Post*, 31 October 2013.

75. 'The Wall Must Fall', CUPE British Columbia, International Solidarity Committee, June 2005.

76. Arutz Sheva, citing *Memri*, 21 June 2009.

77. *Independent*, 12 June 2012.

78. *Jerusalem Post*, citing Wafa (official Palestinian news agency), 1 December 2012.

79. *Jerusalem Post*, 8 November 2013.

80. *Jerusalem Post* citing *Der Spiegel*, 29 June 2008.

81. Al-Jazeera, 25 January 2011.

82. Amena Saleem, 'BBC Intensifies Its Whitewashing of Israel', Electronic Intifada, 30 November 2013.

83. *Voice of the Cape*, 5 February 2012.

84. *Washington Post*, 12 March 2009.

85. 'Arabs in the Jewish State', Yakar and Ittijah seminar, Jerusalem, 3 June 2003, not published, 71.

86. Palestinian Media Watch, 16 March 2010.

87. JC.com, 21 May 2009.

88. *Guardian*, 6 December 2013.

89. *Haaretz*, 23 October 2013.

90. *The Seventh Eye*, November 2012.

91. *Business Day*, 13 September 2013.

92. See the text of the diary entry: Derek J. Penslar, 'Herzl and the Palestinian Arabs: Myths and Counter-Myths', *Journal of Israeli History* 24, no. 1 (March 2005): 65–77.

93. Hamas Charter 1988.

94. 'Shamir Promises to Crush Rioters', *New York Times*, 1 April 1988.

95. Letter to Hanan Ashrawi, 23 December 2004.

96. Electronic Intifada, 10 May 2009.

97. 'Jenin "Massacre Evidence Growing"', BBC, 18 April 2002.

98. Sabeel website. Sabeel is Arabic for 'the way', also a 'spring' of life-giving water.

99. Statement by Kairos Palestine and others protesting a tourist conference held in Jerusalem, 1 February 2011.

100. Original interview in *Middle East Monitor*, 17 November 2011.

101. Unhappily, Boesak fell from grace. He was found guilty of misappropriating for his own use thousands of dollars donated by a Danish aid group and others for children in need. Sentenced to six years' imprisonment, he was released after one year, and was later given a presidential pardon, leading to accusations of cronyism. Extramarital affairs led to the end of his marriage. He has had a zigzag noncareer in politics.

102. Naim Ateek, Sabeel, 6 April 2001.

103. I am a long-standing friend going back to apartheid days.

104. Alan Dershowitz, the Harvard law professor and unstinting supporter of Israel, has used these intemperate words about Archbishop Tutu: 'Among the world's most respected figures is South Africa's Bishop Desmond. His recognizable face – with its ever present grin – has become a symbol of reconciliation and goodness. But it masks a long history of ugly hatred toward the Jewish people, the Jewish religion and the Jewish state. . . . He has invoked classic anti-Semitic stereotypes and tropes about Jewish "arrogance", "power" and money. He has characterized Jews a "peculiar people", and has accused "the Jews" of causing many of the world's problems. . . . Were he not a Nobel laureate, his long history of bigotry against the Jewish people would have landed him in the dustbin of history' (Alan Dershowtiz, 'Bishop Tutu Is No Saint When It Comes to Jews', Gatestone Institute, 20 December 2010).
105. Conversation with author, Cape Town, 24 August 2011.
106. *Times Live*, 26 September 2010.
107. *Times Live*, 26 October 2010.
108. Washington Report on Middle East Affairs, January–February 2008.
109. Ervin Staub is noted for *The Roots of Evil: The Origins of Genocide and Other Group Violence* (Cambridge: Cambridge University Press, 1989); and *Overcoming Evil: Genocide, Violent Conflict and Terrorism* (Oxford: Oxford University Press, 2011).
110. Correspondence with author, 6 April 2012.

# 10. BOYCOTTS

1. 'Blunt Instrument', *Boston Review*, 6 February 2012.
2. Professor Mats Lundahl is at the Stockholm School of Economics.
3. Much of the information here derives from my work as a journalist in South Africa; at the time, restrictive laws prevented the publication of details.
4. Robin Knight, *A Road Less Travelled* (London: Knightwrite, 2011), 223.
5. *Race Relations Survey* (Johannesburg: South African Institute for Race Relations, 1987/1988), 411–20.
6. Wassi al-Adel, 'How Arab Normalization Is Undermining the Boycott Movement', Electronic Intifada, 29 August 2008.
7. *Guardian*, 6 April 2002.
8. JC.com, 23 April 2004, citing *Maariv*.
9. Omar Barghouti, 'Drum', ABC News, Australia, 19 April 2011.
10. *World Factbook*, 2013 estimates (Washington, DC: Central Intelligence Agency).
11. *Guardian*, 17 September 2009.
12. *Jewish Chronicle*, 13 June 2013.
13. *Al-Ahram*, 14–20 August 2008.
14. Letter to the *British Medical Journal*, 16 October 2004.
15. 'What Is the WMA For? The Case of the Israel Medical Association', *Lancet* 361, no. 9355 (1 February 2003): 424.
16. JC.com, 27 May 2009.
17. Malke Borow and Yoram Blachar, 'Response from the Israel Medical Association to Derek Summerfield in the *British Medical Journal*', Scholars for Peace in the Middle East, 2 October 2007.
18. Yehuda Shoenfeld et al., 'British Medical Journals Play Politics', *Israeli Medical Association Journal* 11 (June 2009): 82–83.
19. 'The Wounds of Gaza', Lancet Global Health, 8 February 2009.
20. JC.com, 30 December 2009.
21. Israelwhat.com, 10 October 2009.
22. Socialist Youth website, quoted in Israelwhat.com/norwaywatch, 30 January 2012.
23. *Haaretz*, 14 June 2102.
24. Israelwhat.com/norwaywatch, 30 January 2012.
25. COSATU, 28 February 2013.
26. Palestine Solidarity Campaign, July 2010.

27. Audrea Lin, ed., *The Case for Sanctions against Israel* (London: Verso, 2012).
28. Ibid., 31–32.
29. Newsclick, 2 August 2011.
30. Robert Wintermute, 'India's Visa Rule Is Unfairly Persecuting Innocent Pakistanis . . . Comment Is Free', *Guardian*, 14 August 2010.
31. CBS News, 17 December 2013.
32. *Inside Higher Ed*, 5 December 2012.
33. CBS News, 17 December 2013.
34. Palestinian Students' Campaign for the Academic Boycott of Israel and the University Teachers' Association in Palestine, 20 July 2010.
35. Compactmusic.com, 20 July 2010.
36. *Haaretz*, 9 April 2012.
37. 'Activism News', Electronic Intifada, 7 July 2010.
38. Electronic Intifada, 16 September 2009.
39. University of Johannesburg, 27 March 2012.
40. BDS media file, 14 March 2013.
41. *Mail & Guardian*, 17 May 2013.
42. *Cape Times*, 12 June 2013.
43. *Nation*, 8 January 2009, cited by Sami Hermez, Electronic Intifada, 1 October 2009.
44. Alternet, 1 September 2009.
45. See further: Ervin Staub in chapter 9 of this book and Benjamin Pogrund, 'Pay Heed to Jewish Fears', Centre for International Political Studies, Pretoria University, No. 54/2005.
46. *Guardian*, 12 August 2013.
47. *Haaretz*, 12 June 2013.
48. Times Books, New York, 2012.
49. Electronic Intifada, 17 July 2013.
50. *Jerusalem Post*, 17 July 2013.
51. Jerusalem Center for Public Affairs, 18 July 2013.
52. *Jerusalem Post*, 18 July 2013.
53. *Jerusalem Post*, 21 July 2013.
54. *Jerusalem Post*, 4 December 2013.
55. *Jerusalem Post*, 26 February 2014.
56. *Star*, 11 December 2013.
57. Electronic Intifada, 12 December 2013.
58. *Haaretz*, 31 January 2014.
59. Central Bureau of Statistics, *Haaretz*, 3 March 2014.

# 11. THE BIG ISSUES

1. Benjamin Pogrund, 'Different Histories, Different Futures', *Palestine-Israel Journal* (Jerusalem) 15, no. 4 (2008) and 16, no. 1 (2009).
2. Alain Gresh, *Le Monde Diplomatique*, February 1999.
3. Electronic Intifada, 2 April 2012.
4. Anne Applebaum, *Iron Curtain: The Crushing of Eastern Europe, 1944–56* (London: Allen Lane, 2012), 132.
5. UNHCR Global Trends, 2012.
6. 'Inside Report', al-Jazeera, 4 September 2013.
7. There is no certainty about the original number because the last general census was in 1931: 726,000 was the UN estimate in December 1949, neighbouring Arab countries estimated 750,000 to 800,000 refugees, and the Israeli estimate was 555,000.
8. Cited by Isabel Kershner, 'Back to Haunt the Peacemakers', *Jerusalem Report*, 2 August 1999.
9. Cited by Isabel Kershner, UN Special Committee of the General Assembly, *Jerusalem Report*, 2 August 1999.

10. Cited by Salim Tamari, *Return, Resettlement, Repatriation: The Future of Palestinians in Peace Negotiations* (Institute for Palestine Studies, 1996).

11. Mark Heller, 'The Right of Return', *Jerusalem Post*, 19 December, 1997.

12. Shlomo Gazit, 'The Palestinian Refugee Problem', in *Final Status Issues: Israel-Palestine* (Tel Aviv: Jaffee Centre for Strategic Studies, Tel Aviv University, 1995), 9.

13. Ibid., 11–12.

14. Electronic Intifada, 5 June 2012.

15. Salman Abu Sitta, 'The Implementation of the Right of Return', *Palestine-Israel Journal* 15, no. 4 (2008) and 16, no. 1 (2009).

16. 'Palestinian Refugees', Palestinian Academic Society for the Study of International Affairs, Passia, Jerusalem, May 2004.

17. 'Fixing UNRWA: Repairing UN's Troubled System of Aid to Palestinian Refugees', Washington Institute for Near East Policy, Policy Focus 91, January 2009.

18. *Haaretz*, 8 February 2009.

19. *Jerusalem Post*, 23 October 2010.

20. *Jerusalem Post*, 31 October 2010.

21. Benny Morris, *Righteous Victims: A History of the Zionist-Arab Conflict, 1981–1999* (London: John Murray, 2000), 225.

22. *Wikipedia*, 'Jewish Quarter (Jerusalem)'.

23. Moshe Amirav, *Jerusalem Syndrome: The Palestinian-Israeli Battle for the Holy City* (Brighton and Portland: Sussex Academic Press, 2009). Material in this section is extracted from a review by Benjamin Pogrund, *Palestine-Israel Journal* (Jerusalem) 17, nos. 1 and 2 (2011).

24. *Jerusalem Post*, 8 May 2013.

25. *This Week in Palestine*, 27 September 2012.

26. Ziad Abuzayyad and Hillel Schenker, editorial, *Palestine-Israel Journal* 17, nos. 1 and 2 (2011): 7.

27. *Haaretz*, 11 September 2007.

28. Arutz Sheva, 18 October 2007.

29. Arutz Sheva, 20 May 2009.

30. *YNet*, 25 November 2011.

31. Amirav, *Jerusalem Syndrome*, 210.

32. *New York Times*, 17 May 2009.

33. *Jerusalem Post*, 14 December 2009.

34. *Haaretz*, 1 January 2010.

35. BBC, 23 October 2010.

36. *YNet*, 17 November 2010.

37. *YNet*, 25 December 2010.

38. *YNet*, 13 January 2010.

39. *Haaretz*, 14 April 2011.

40. EU Heads of Mission Report on East Jerusalem, December 2008.

41. *Jerusalem Post*, 13 July 2012.

42. *Jerusalem Post*, 16 December 2009.

43. *YNet*, 29 March 2010.

44. *Jerusalem Post*, 16 December 2009.

# 12. THE WAY FORWARD

1. This widespread view has been well articulated by Saree Makdisi, professor of English literature at the University of California, in the *Guardian*, 28 July 2008.

2. *Jerusalem Post*, 24 June 2013.

3. Arutz Sheva, 3 September 2013.

4. *Haaretz*, 6 October 2004.

5. *Jerusalem Post*, 11 July 2013.

6. *Haaretz*, 14 July 2013.

7. Quoted by Geoffrey Wheatcroft, 'Zion Story', *The Times Literary Supplement*, 20 February 2008.

8. *Jerusalem Post*, 12 September 2013.

9. Arutz Sheva, 19 March 2010.

10. Reuters, 17 November 2009.

11. *Forward*, editorial, 29 April 2012.

12. Letter to author, 1967.

13. *New York Times*, 25 July 2012.

## APPENDIX 2

1. UNSCOP Report, chap. 6, pt. 1, articles 1–9.

## APPENDIX 3

1. Human Rights Library, University of Minnesota

## APPENDIX 4

1. *Settlement Report*, vol. 22, no. 4, Foundation for Middle East Peace, Washington, DC, July–August 2012.

# Selected Bibliography

Amirav, Moshe. *Jerusalem Syndrome: The Palestinian-Israeli Battle for the Holy City.* Brighton and Portland: Sussex Academic Press, 2009.

Applebaum, Anne. *Iron Curtain: The Crushing of Eastern Europe 1944–56.* London: Allen Lane, 2012.

Bar-Tal, Daniel, and Izhak Schnell, eds. *The Impacts of Lasting Occupation.* Oxford: Oxford University Press, 2013.

Begin, Menachem. *The Revolt.* Jerusalem: Steimatzky, 1951.

Benvenisti, Meron. *Sacred Landscape: The Buried History of the Holy Land since 1948.* Berkeley: University of California Press, 2002.

Bridger, David, ed. *New Jewish Encyclopedia.* West Orange, NJ: Behrman House, 1976.

Cleveland, William L. *A History of the Modern Middle East.* Boulder, CO: Westview Press, 1994).

Cohen, Mark R. *Under Crescent and Cross: The Jews in the Middle Ages.* Princeton, NJ: Princeton University Press, 1994.

Colart, Claude, and Sahm Venter, eds. *Something to Write Home About.* Johannesburg: Jacana, 2004.

Collins, Larry, and Dominique Lapierre. *O Jerusalem!* Bnei Barak, Israel: Steimatzky, 1995.

Davenport, T. R. H. *South Africa: A Modern History.* Cape Town: Southern Book Publishers, 1988.

Dawidowicz, Lucy, ed. *The Golden Treasury: Jewish Life and Thought in Eastern Europe.* Syracuse, NY: Syracuse University Press, 1996.

Elon, Amos. *The Pity of It All: A Portrait of Jews in Germany, 1743–1933.* London: Allen Lane, 2003.

*The First Governor: Sir Ronald Storrs, Governor of Jerusalem, 1918–1926.* Tel Aviv: Eretz Israel Museum, 2010.

Gazit, Shlomo. *The Carrot and the Stick: Israel's Policy in Judaea and Samaria, 1967–68.* Washington, DC: B'nai Brith Books, 1995.

Gelber, Yoav. *Palestine 1948.* Brighton: Sussex Academic Press, 2001.

Giliomee, Hermann, and Bernard Mbenga. *New History of South Africa.* Cape Town: Tafelberg Publishers, 2007.

Gordis, Daniel. *Saving Israel: How the Jewish People Can Win a War That May Never End.* Hoboken, NJ: John Wiley & Sons, 2009.

Gorenberg, Gershom. *The Accidental Empire: Israel and the Birth of Settlements.* New York: Holt, 2007.

Herf, Jeffrey. *Nazi Propaganda for the Arab World.* New Haven, CT: Yale University Press, 2009.

Heribert, Adam, and Kogila Moodley. *Seeking Mandela: Peacemaking between Israelis and Palestinians*. Philadelphia: Temple University Press, 2005.

Horrell, Muriel. *Race Relations as Regulated by Law in South Africa, 1948–1979*. Johannesburg: SA Institute of Race Relations, 1982.

Katzew, Henry. 'Conversation with David Ben-Gurion'. In *Solution for South Africa: A Jewish View*. Cape Town: Simondium, 1955.

Khalidi, Rashid. *The Iron Cage: The Story of the Palestinian Struggle for Statehood*. Boston: Beacon Press, 2006.

———. *Palestinian Identity*. New York: Columbia University Press, 1998.

Knight, Robin. *A Road Less Travelled*. London: Knightwrite, 2011.

Kretzmer, David. *The Legal Status of the Arabs in Israel*. Boulder, CO: Westview Press, 1990.

Lin, Audrea, ed. *The Case for Sanctions against Israel*. London: Verso, 2012.

Ma'oz, Moshe, ed. *Studies on Palestine during the Ottoman Period*. Jerusalem: Magnes Press, Hebrew University, 1975.

Milstein, Uri. *The War of Independence*. Vol. 4, *Out of Crisis Came Decision*. Tel Aviv: Zmora-Bitan, 1991.

Morris, Benny. *1948: A History of the First Arab-Israeli War*. New Haven, CT: Yale University Press, 2008.

———. *Righteous Victims: A History of the Zionist-Arab Conflict, 1981–1999*. London: John Murray, 2000.

Nusseibeh, Sari. *Once Upon a Country: A Palestinian Life*. London: Peter Halban Publishers, 2009.

Oren, Michael B. *Six Days of War: June 1967 and the Making of the Modern Middle East*. New York: Presidio Press, 2003.

Pappe, Ilan. *The Ethnic Cleansing of Palestine*. Oxford: One World, 2007.

Pogrund, Benjamin. *How Can Man Die Better: The Life of Robert Sobukwe*. London: Peter Halban Publishers; Johannesburg: Jonathan Ball Publishers, 2000/2012.

———. *Nelson Mandela*. Watford: Exley, 1991.

———. *War of Words: Memoir of a South African Journalist*. New York: Seven Stories Press, 2000.

Sachar, Howard Morley. *The Course of Modern Jewish History*. New York: Dell Publishing, 1958.

Scham, Paul, Walid Salem, and Benjamin Pogrund, eds. *Shared Histories: A Palestinian-Israeli Dialogue*. Walnut Creek, CA: Left Coast Press, 2005.

Shain, Milton. *Antisemitism*. London: Bowerdean, 1998.

Shimoni, Gideon. *The Zionist Ideology*. Hanover, NH: Brandeis University Press, 1995.

Shindler, Colin. *A History of Modern Israel*. Cambridge: Cambridge University Press, 2008.

———. *A History of Modern Israel*. 2nd ed. Cambridge: Cambridge University Press, 2013.

———. *What Do Zionists Believe*. London: Granta, 2007.

Silver, Eric. *Begin: A Biography*. London: Weidenfeld and Nicolson, 1984.

———. *Dateline Jerusalem*. Brighton: Revel Barker Publishing, 2011.

Staub, Ervin. *Overcoming Evil: Genocide, Violent Conflict and Terrorism*. Oxford: Oxford University Press, 2011.

———. *The Roots of Evil: The Origins of Genocide and Other Group Violence*. Cambridge: Cambridge University Press, 1989.

Welsh, David. *The Rise and Fall of Apartheid*. Johannesburg: Jonathan Ball Publishers, 2009.

West, Benjamin, ed. *Struggles of a Generation: The Jews under Soviet Rule*. Tel Aviv: Massadah, 1959.

Zertal, Idith, and Akiva Eldar. *Lords of the Land: The War over Israel's Settlements in the Occupied Territories, 1967–2007*. New York: Nation Books, 2007.

# Index

Abbas, Mahmoud, 141, 210, 243, 275
Abdulhadi, Rabab, 175
Abdullah, king of Jordan, 40, 41
Abdullah, king of Saudi Arabia, 208
Abu Dis, 262–263, 274
Abu Gosh, 37
Academic Boycott of Israel and the
  University Teachers' Association in
  Palestine, 236
Acre, 181
ACRI. *See* Association for Civil Rights in
  Israel
Adalah (Arab advocacy organisation), 55,
  59, 65, 70, 71
Afghanistan, 191, 235
African National Congress (ANC), 86,
  129, 130–131, 144, 145, 146, 169, 210,
  216, 237, 277; Youth League, 129
African Nationalism, 8
Afrikaner Nationalists, 115, 131
Afrikaners, 115–118, 150; religion, 139
*Aftonbladet* newspaper, 184, 185
Ahmadinejad, Mahmoud, 54, 186–187
AIDS, 73, 125, 173, 206
Ain al-Hilweh refugee camp (Lebanon),
  248
ALA. *See* Arab Liberation Army
*al-Ahram* newspaper, 206
al-Aqsa Mosque, 193–195
al-Assad, Hafez, 161
Alawites, 173

Aleppo, 46
Alexander III, tsar, 6
Alexander II, tsar, 6
Algeria, 46, 240, 250
Algerian National Committee for the
  Development of Health Research, 184
*al-Hayat al-Jadida* newspaper, 181, 186
al-Husseini, Hajj Amin, 20, 24–25
Aliyah, 12–14, 23, 57
al-Jalahma, Umayma Ahmad, 186
al-Jazeera, 195, 207
*al-Karmil* (weekly Arabic-language
  newspaper), 20
Allenby, Edmund, 16
Allister, Karine Mac, 199–200
al-Majdahl, 199
al-Quds Foundation of South Africa, 208
al-Quds University, 236, 263
*al-Riyadh* newspaper, 186
al-Shabati, Hana, 203
*Altalena* (American ship), 43
al-Tayeb, Ahmed, 263
*Altneuland* (Old New Land) (Herzl, 1902),
  11
*al-Watan* newspaper, 165
Amer, Abdul Hakim, 49
American Studies Association (ASA), 234
Amirav, Moshe, 140, 258–262, 264
Amnesty International, 213
ANC. *See* African National Congress
Andoni, Lamis, 181

Ang, Swee, 230
Annan, Kofi, 166
Anti-Defamation League (US), 156
anti-Semitism, 5, 23, 46, 156–157, 241
apartheid: acts as foundation stones of,
    119; apprehensions concerning,
    118–119; background, 54–56; carrying
    of passes, 124–125; Carter's comments
    on, 161–162; communism and,
    122–123; creation of Bantustans, 125;
    definition, 115; detention/torture, 129;
    District Six (Cape Town), 121;
    Dugard's report (2007), 172; ending of,
    131; entry into cities, 128; equated with
    Israel, 157–160, 236–237; hospitals/
    health under, 126; inaccuracy of
    applying to Israel, 272; jobs/
    employment, 127; Kasril's comments
    on, 178–180; laws/regulations imposed,
    119–120; media, 129, 181–182, 198,
    199–200, 201–202, 203; migrant
    labour, 125–126; (mis)statements,
    201–202; not the same as oppression,
    155; origins/history of, 115–118;
    professional business people, 128;
    prohibitions/segregation under,
    123–128; race/population classification,
    120–122, 131–132; resistance to,
    129–131; scale/depth of oppression
    under, 120; social welfare, 127; sports
    facilities, 128; strikes/trade unions, 128;
    UN Convention, 197–198; universities/
    education, 126–127
Applebaum, David, 208
Arab Association of Human Rights, 71
Arab Higher Committee, 23, 29, 30
Arab Lawyers' Union, 158
Arab League, 30, 40, 41, 48, 51, 197, 223,
    254, 278
Arab League General Assembly, 37
Arab Legion, 40, 44, 50
Arab Liberation Army (ALA), 30, 44
Arab News, 194
Arabs. See Israeli Arabs/Palestinians;
    Palestinian Arabs
Arab Spring (2011), 97, 153, 188, 215,
    224, 263
Arafat, Yasser, 161, 188, 254, 262; at
    Camp David talks, 68; becomes Fatah

    chairman, 48
Aref, Abdel Salam, 49
Argentina, 210
Ariel College (formerly College of Judea
    and Samaria), 94
Ariel settlement (West Bank), 235
army, 58–60
Ashkenazi (Western Jews), 2, 3, 34, 46, 54,
    55
Asian Group, 167
Association of Civil Liberties in Israel, 87
Association for Civil Rights in Israel
    (ACRI), 112
Ateek, Naim, 215–216
Ateret Cohanim (nationalist-religious
    movement), 265–266
Attias, Ariel, 67
Aung San Suu Kyi, 203
Australia, 198, 224
Auto-Emancipation, 7–8
Aviner, Shlomo, 90
Avnery, Uri, 41–43, 201–202
Ayalon, Ami, 59
Azzam Pasha, Abdul Pazek, 41

Badil Resource Center for Palestinian
    Residency and Refugee Rights, 199,
    253
Badran, Amneh, 200–201
Bahour, Sam, 105
Bahrain, 203, 205
Bailey, Clinton, 87
Baker, Alan, 242
Baker, Mona, 211
Balad Party MK, 59
Balfour, Arthur. See Balfour, 1st Earl
Balfour, 1st Earl (Arthur Balfour), 18, 19
Balfour Declaration (1926), 17–19, 20, 24
Baltic states, 249
Bangladesh, 163, 235, 248
Ban Ki-moon, 163
Bantu, 116
Bantustans, 125, 142, 155, 174, 192, 199,
    201
Barak, Ehud, 68, 94, 273
Barghouti, Omar, 225–226
Barhoom, Masad, 78
Bar-Ilan University, 94
Barkat, Nir, 265, 266

Basharat, Oudeh, 67
Basic Law, 72
Basotho, 117
Basques, 170
Battle Blood River (1838), 117
Baum, Michael, 230–231
Bayit Yehudi Party, 242, 270
BBC, 153, 191, 207, 213
BBC Caversham Park, 37
BDS. *See* Boycott, Disinvestment and Sanctions (BDS) movement
Bedouin, 54, 55, 59, 77, 85, 86–87
Begin, Menachem, 26, 50, 92, 211
Beilin, Yossi, 89
Beinart, Peter, 240
Beit El settlement, 100, 101
Beit Hanoun, 190–191
Beit Yonatan, 265–266
Belarus, 203, 235
Belgium, 69, 248
Ben-Gurion, David: articulates war-time dilemma, 24; believes in military force to secure borders, 46; comment on refugees, 252; comment on UN, 166; comment on use of Jewish labour, 13; decrees that no settlement should be abandoned, 31; driving force behind Declaration of Independence, 39; frees scholars from military service, 59; Jerusalem as heart of the Jewish people, 261; as leader of coalition, 45; as leader of mainstream Jewish Agency, 26; orders shelling of American ship, 43; as refugee from Russian pogrom, 12; war against Egypt, 50
Ben-Gurion International Airport, 271
Ben-Gurion University, 217
Benizri, Shlomo, 74
Bennett, Naftali, 242, 270
Ben-Yehuda, Eliezer, 14
Bethlehem, 183
Bevin, Ernest, 26
the Bible: Abraham, Isaac, Jacob, 2; Book of Genesis, 2; King David, 264; Moses, 2, 15; Ten Commandments, 2
Biko, Steve Bantu, 8
Birnbaum, Nathan, 10
Bir Zeit University, Research and Documentation Centre, 34

Bishara, Azmi, 71
Blachar, Yoram, 229
Black Consciousness, 8, 148
Black Death, 4
Black Power, 8
Black September (1970), 254
Black Sunday (14 November 1937), 31
Boers, 116–118
Boer wars (1899–1902), 118
Boesak, Alan, 214–215
Border Police, 59
Borow, Malke, 229
Borton, William, 16
Bostrom, Donald, 184
Botha, Stoffel, 132
Botswana, 149
Boycott, Disinvestment and Sanctions (BDS) movement, 196, 224–227, 231–232, 234, 236, 238, 239, 240, 243
boycotts: actors/theatre companies, 235; apartheid label, 226, 232, 233–234; attempts at, 224–226; BDS campaigns, 236–239; calls for, 221–222, 224; COSATU, 232; definition, 221; as denial of human interaction, 236; everyday effects, 224; grounds for, 226–228; immunity from, 239–240; (in)effectiveness of, 222–223, 224; medical profession, 228–231; Norway and France, 231–232; pop singers/bands, 235; settlements as target, 240–244; spread of, 234–235
B'Tselem, 106, 107, 205
Burundi, 203

Cambodia, 203
Camp David talks, 68, 140, 262, 274, 275
Canada, 144, 198, 234, 236, 243, 256
Cape Town, 123, 130; District Six, 121
Cape Town Opera, 217, 218
Cape Town university. *See* University of Cape Town
Carter, Jimmy, 160–162, 226
*The Case for Sanctions against Israel* (2012), 233
Catalans, 170
Catherine the Great, 5, 6
Central African Republic, 248
Central Boycott Office, 223

CERN (European Organisation for Nuclear
  Research), 243
Chechnya, 170, 248
*Chicks* (children's show on Palestinian
  Authority TV), 209
China, 149, 163, 170, 173, 193, 198, 203,
  235, 238, 243, 248, 250
Chinkin, Christine, 164
Chmielnicky, Bogdan, 6
Christians, 61, 62
Chunfang, Duan, 203
Churchill, Winston, 17
Circassians, 55, 59
Civil Administration, 99, 100, 107, 113
Clinton, Bill, 262
Cohen, Leonard, 235
Cohen, Meir, 67
Cohen, Yoram, 58, 69
Colombia, 203
Communist Party of South Africa,
  122–123, 130
comparisons. *See* Israel–South Africa
  comparisons
Congress of South African Trade Unions,
  192
Congress of South African Trade Unions
  (COSATU), 232
Conservative Judaism, 5, 56, 61
Corrie, Rachel, 162
COSATU. *See* Congress of South African
  Trade Unions
Cotler, Irwin, 162
Council of Churches, 192
Council for Higher Education, 85, 94
*The Crisis of Zionism* (Beinart, 1012), 240
Crusades, 3
Cuba, 157, 163, 203
Cunningham, Alan, 40
CUPE British Columbia trade union, 205
Curzon, George. *See* Kedleston, 1st
  Marquess Curzon of
Cyprus, 61, 149
Czechoslovakia, 35, 48, 63, 167, 248, 249

*Daily Mail*, 197
*Daily Telegraph*, 153
Dalal, Marwan, 209
Dalits, 159
Davidson, Eron, 203

Davis, Gaye, 155
Dayan, Danny, 97
Dayan, Moshe: believes in military force to
  secure borders, 46; war with Egypt, 49,
  50
Dead Sea, 105, 108, 202
Declaration of Independence (1948), 39
Deedat, Yousef, 158
Defiance Campaign Against Unjust Laws
  (South Africa, 1952), 130
Deir Yassin massacre (1948), 33–35, 36,
  38, 180–181, 189, 190, 192
Deir Yassin Remembered organisation, 33
Democratic List of Nazareth, 45
Democratic Republic of the Congo, 248,
  250
DGCS. *See* Italian Development
  Corporation
*dhimmi*, 2–3
Diab, Khalid, 210
*Die Judenstaat* ('The Jewish State' or 'The
  State of the Jews') (Herzl, 1896), 10
*Die Welt* newspaper, 189
Dingane (Zulu king), 117
Diskin, Yuval, 97
Division on Palestinian Rights, 167
Dreyfus, Alfred, 9
Druze Arabs, 45, 51, 54, 55, 59, 65, 75
Du Bois, W. E. B., 8
Dugard, John, 168–171, 174, 190, 198, 226
Dugard report (2007), 171–174
Dundee University (Scotland), 213
Durban Forum (2001), 157–160, 168
Dutch East India Company, 116
Dutch Reformed Church, 115, 116, 117,
  125, 214

EAFORD. *See* Elimination of all Forms of
  Racial Discriminations
East Jerusalem, 52, 55, 61, 78, 90, 93, 111,
  241, 246, 258, 259
East Timor, 248
Eban, Abba, 252
Ecumenical Caucus, 158
Ecumenical Theological Liberation Center
  (Jerusalem), 214
Edelstein, Yuli, 56, 73
education, 73, 136; British mandate, 78;
  discrimination/disparities in, 81–82,

83–84; funding of, 82; in Jerusalem, 83–84; Ottoman, 78; types of schooling, 79, 80
Education Ministry, 73, 79, 81
Egypt, 30, 40, 41, 43, 44, 46, 48–51, 53, 58, 104, 153, 167, 188, 203, 204, 205, 208, 212, 238, 240, 254, 263
Eid al-Fitr Muslim holiday, 70
Eidelman, Leonid, 78
Eilat (formerly Umm Rashrash), 44, 49
El Al airline, 147, 224
el-Baradei, Mohammed, 188
Eldar, Akiva, 95, 101
Electronic Intifada, 181–182, 203, 207, 208, 236
El Farrar, Mohammed, 194
Elimination of all Forms of Racial Discriminations (EAFORD), 185
el-Tal, Abdullah, 257
*Emir Farouk* (ship), 44
End Occupation Campaign, 192
Entebbe, 189
Equatorial Guinea, 203
Erdogan, Recep Tayyip, 168
Erekat, Saab, 256
Eritrea, 203
Esack, Farid, 212–213
Eshkol, Levi, 95
Ethiopia, 56, 73, 75, 203
Etkes, Dror, 100
Etzion Bloc, 30
EU Fundamental Rights Agency, 156
*European Journal of International Law*, 198
European Union, 145, 156, 175, 188, 241–243, 245, 250, 266
Exeter University (Britain), 201
*Exodus* (book and film), 25

Falk, Richard, 174–175, 198, 226
Fatah (Palestinian Liberation Movement), 48
Feisal, Emir, 21, 22
Ferguson, Clarence Clyde, Jr, 198
*Filastin* (weekly Arabic-language newspaper), 20
*Financial Times*, 153
Fort Hare University College, Eastern Cape (South Africa), 118, 129

Fourth Geneva Convention (1949), 95, 193
France, 18, 144, 191, 198, 223, 224, 231–232, 243
Freeman, Charles, Jr, 208–209
French Revolution (1789), 4, 7
*The Future Vision of the Palestinian Arabs in Israel* (2006), 69

Gaddafi, Muammar, 163, 185, 238
Galilee, 69
Gallo/Getty agency, 207
Gandhi, Mahatma, 146
gated communities, 66, 72
Gaza Strip, 166; attacks on, 190–191; blockade of, 162; divisions/discrimination in, 55; economy, 104; Goldstone's investigation into, 163–165; infant mortality rate in, 109; Israeli withdrawal from, 51; Jewish settlement in, 52, 91, 96, 226; Law of Return, 57; military bureaucracy in, 50; missiles launched from, 271; number of Palestinians in, 53; occupied by Egypt, 45; seized by Israel, 49; siege of, 154; violence in, 160; withdrawal from, 271
Gazit, Shlomo, 51, 253
Geller, Uri, 189
Geneva Conventions, 38
Georges-Picot, François, 15
Georgia, 235, 243
Germany, 19, 23, 24–25, 58, 122, 144, 191, 198, 223, 243, 249
Gershwin, George, 217
Ghana, 205
ghettos, 4
Gibraltar, 193
Gillerman, Dan, 168
Givati Brigade, 43
Globe Theatre (London), 235
Golan Heights, 50, 51, 52, 59, 96, 166, 197, 241
Golani Brigade, 55, 275
Goldberg, Dennis, 237
Goldstein, Baruch, 95
Goldstein, Shaul, 99
Goldstone, Richard, 163–165
Gordimer, Nadine, 235
Gordon, A. D., 2
Granada, Spain, 3

Grass, Günter, 189
Great Trek (1835), 117
Green Lines (agreed borders), 44, 45, 53, 94, 103, 241, 264
Green Olive Tours, 202
Group Areas Act (South Africa), 119, 120–122, 192
*Guardian* newspaper, 34, 49, 149, 153, 165, 184–185, 189, 202, 224, 239
Guatemala, 243
*Gush Emunim* (Bloc of the Faithful), 96

*Haaretz*, 41–43, 99, 100, 110, 202, 210
Habilio, Yossi, 265, 266
Habimah Theatre (Tel Aviv), 235
Hadrian, Emperor, 2
Haganah, 23, 31, 32–33, 34, 35–36, 37, 41, 45
Haifa, 37, 54, 181
Haifa University, 234
Haiti, 185, 203
*Hakeshet Hademokratit Hamizrahit*, 65
Halacha (Jewish law), 56
Hamas, 54, 104, 163, 164, 190, 191, 206, 208, 211, 271
Hammarskjold, Dag, 166
Haniff, Dato Hussein, 204
Haniya, Ismail, 191
Hari, Johann, 183–184
Harman, David, 80
Harvard University: Divinity School, 212; Palestine Solidarity Committee, 181
Hasson, Nir, 111
Hawking, Stephen, 234
Health Ministry, 73
Hebrew, 14
Hebrew University (Jerusalem), 258
Hebron, 54, 95–96, 106
Hertzog, Chaim, 167–168
Herzl, Theodor, 9–11, 12, 18, 39, 161, 195, 210
Hezbollah, 54, 71, 188
Higher Arab Monitoring Committee, 81
Hilltop Youth, 96, 97
Hindraf Makkal Sakthi (NGO), 204
Hirsch, Baron Maurice de, 10
Hisin, Chaim, 7
Hitler, Adolf, 195
HMS *Euryalus*, 40

Holocaust, 4, 25, 45, 59, 186, 188, 237, 256
Home Front, 59
Hong Kong, 193
Hope-Simpson Commission (1930), 23
Horizon 2020 programme, 241
Horton, Richard, 230
HSRC. *See* Human Sciences Research Council of South Africa
human rights, 154, 154–155, 161, 162–165, 182, 238
human rights reports, 168–171, 171–174
Human Rights Watch, 226
Human Sciences Research Council of South Africa (HSRC), 171–174, 198, 226
Hungary, 249
Hussein, king of Jordan, 50, 254
Husseini family, 20

IAW. *See* Israel Apartheid Week
Ibrahim, Nora, 231
IDF. *See* Israel Defense Forces
IMA. *See* Israeli Medical Association
Immorality Act (South Africa), 123
IMR. *See* infant mortality rate
*Independent* newspaper (London), 183–184, 189, 197, 235
India, 173, 193, 198, 234, 248
Indonesia, 198, 203
infant mortality rate (IMR), 75, 76, 77, 109, 110
Institute for Palestine Studies, Photograph Collection, 206
International Atomic Energy Agency, 188
International Criminal Court, 174, 198
International Geographical Union, 234
International Relations and Cooperation (formerly Foreign Affairs Ministry), 173
Internet, 175, 184, 185
intifadas, 52, 54, 68, 105
Iran, 149, 157, 189, 191, 203, 222
Iraq, 21, 30, 46, 50, 70, 191, 238, 248, 250
Irgun (National Military Organisation), 21, 26, 31, 33–35, 38, 43, 190
Islam, 61, 140
Islamic Conference, 191
Islamic Jihad, 190

Ismail, Hazem Abu, 206
Israel: accused of organ stealing, 184–185;
admitted to UN regional group, 167;
Alice Walker's comments on, 177;
apartheid connected with, 157–160;
apologises for deaths in Hanoun,
190–191; Arab refugees from, 46–48;
attitude towards Palestinian Arab
refugees, 46–47; birth/creation of State
of Israel, 3, 39–41, 53; boycotts (*see*
boycotts); citizenship in, 56–58, 70;
civil liberties in, 54; criticisms of,
154–155; as democratic state, 53–54;
discrimination in, 55, 69–74; education
in, 78–79, 80, 81–82, 83–84, 85; effect
of Durban Forum (2001), 158–160;
effect of Law of Return, 56–58;
elections in, 45; health in, 73, 77, 78;
hostility towards, 157; HSRC report on,
172–174; infant mortality rate (IMR),
75, 76, 77; internal/external problems,
154; Jewish immigrants/refugees in, 44,
46, 56; Jimmy Carter's attitude
towards, 161–162; John Dugard's
reports on, 169–171, 172; land
ownership/appropriation in, 62–67;
media coverage of (*see* media
coverage); migrant problem, 237;
military service in, 58–60; mood/
attitudes in 1948, 41–43; national
insurance in, 77; nation-building,
45–46; poverty rate, 75; prejudice
against, 206; recognized by United
States, Soviet Union and Britain, 40;
relationship with UN, 166–168; religion
in, 97–98; Richard Falk's comments on,
175; Ronnie Kasrils' comments on,
177–178, 179–181; securing of borders,
44; South African interest in, 155–156,
160; status of Arabs/Jews post-1948,
54–56; status of Arabs/Jews pre-1948,
54; threats to, 54; trade in, 224,
243–244; treatment of children,
204–205; UNHRC attacks on, 163–166;
victory in UN General Assembly, 168;
War of Independence (1948), 30–39,
43–45; war with Egypt, 49–51; Women
of Color Feminists comments on, 176;
work/earnings in, 74–75

Israel Apartheid Week (IAW), 181, 185,
236–237
Israel Defense Forces (IDF), 37, 44, 50, 58,
95, 100, 112, 165, 205, 275
Israel-Egypt war (1956), 49–51
Israel Foreign Ministry, 243
Israel Government Tourist Office, 209
Israeli Arabs/Palestinians: achievements,
55; citizenship rights, 67–68;
discrimination against, 53, 54, 55,
69–74, 75, 81–82, 83–84; as diverse
community, 55; education, 77, 78–79,
81–82, 83–84, 85; effect of Law Return
on, 57–58; *Future Vision* document, 69;
health of, 78; illiteracy amongst, 85;
infant mortality rate (IMR), 75, 76, 77;
land/property rights, 64–67, 70;
medical personnel, 78; military service,
59; quality of life, 55; right to vote, 55;
state's relationship with, 68; status
inside the Green Line, 54–56;
subjugation of, 89; uncertainty over
identity, 69; viewed as potential fifth
column, 67; work/earnings, 74–75
Israeli Civil Administration, 92
Israeli Medical Association (IMA), 185,
229, 230
Israel Land Administration, 64, 65, 66
Israel–South Africa comparisons, 155;
army, 137; citizenship, 137;
conclusions concerning similarities,
150–152; curfew, 138; democracy, 133;
economy, 142–144; freedom from
want, 134; freedom of association, 134;
freedom of movement, 134; freedom of
religion, 136, 139–141; freedom of
speech, 134; health, 135; health
insurance, 135; higher education, 136;
identity document, 138; international
position, 144–145; land, 137; language,
138; legal system, 138; marriage, 134;
personal aspects, 148–150; police, 137;
prisons, 135; private facilities, 137;
public facilities, 137; right to work,
136; schools, 136; sex, 134; social
welfare, 135; sport, 138; third-party
intervention, 145–146; trade unions,
136; transport, 138; violence, 146–147;
voting, 133

Isserof, Ami, 212
Italian Development Corporation (DGCS),
    236
Italy, 198, 223
Iyat, Hatam, 58

Jaffa, 9, 13, 20, 29
Jamjoun, Hazem, 199, 253
Japan, 222, 223
Jenin, 213
Jerusalem, 54; Allenby's entrance into, 16;
    Arab education in, 83–84; attacks on,
    35, 50, 51, 257; competing religious
    claims over, 22, 140–141; declared
    capital of Israel, 51; as divided city, 45;
    division of, 245; as focus of Jewish
    existence, 2; history of, 257; immersed
    in myths, propaganda, delusions, 258;
    internationalisation of holy places in,
    264; Israeli aims/objectives, 258–262;
    Israel's occupation of, 257; Jewish
    enclaves/building in, 264–266; known
    as the City of Peace, 257; mass protest
    by Arabs in, 29; Noble Sanctuary/
    Temple Mount, 61, 139–140, 193, 261,
    262, 267–268, 274; opposition to
    Israel's actions in, 266–267;
    Palestinians in, 262–264; proposals for,
    257; Roman colony of Aelia Capitolina,
    2; siege of (70 CE), 2; threatened by
    Arabs, 41; violence in, 20, 22–23
*Jerusalem Post* (formerly *Palestine Post*),
    36, 184
*Jerusalem Syndrome: The Palestinian-
    Israeli Battle for the Holy City*
    (Amirav), 258–262
Jerusalem Writer's Festival (2008), 235
Jewish Agency, 26, 33, 34, 65, 200
Jewish Agency for Palestine, 40
Jewish Caucus of NGOs, 158
Jewish Council for Public Affairs, 140
Jewish National Fund (JNF), 13, 62,
    64–65, 66, 111, 276
Jewish Voices, 192
Jews: attitude of Arabs towards, 21–22,
    22–24; attitude to Zionist dream, 11;
    coexistence with Arabs, 54; definitions
    of, 56–58; Enlightenment and
    Emancipation, 4–5, 7–8; history of,

2–4, 239; intensification of war, 35–38,
    39, 43–45, 47–48; mass emigration, 8,
    10; in Muslim countries, 2–3; myths
    concerning, 3; religious divisions, 54;
    in Russia and Poland, 5–9; and
    settlement in Palestine, 9, 10–14; start
    of civil war with the Arabs, 29–32;
    sustained hatred against, 3–4
Jordan, 17, 30, 44, 45, 49, 53, 108, 159,
    194, 203, 245, 250
Jordan River, 108
*Jordan Times*, 195
*Journal of the Royal College of Medicine*,
    229
Judea and Samaria Council for Higher
    Education, 94

Ka'adan, Adel and Imam, 65
Kadi, Andrew, 241
Kahane, Meir, 72, 97
*Kahane Chai* (Kahane Lives) Party, 72
Kairos Palestine, 214, 215
Kairos Palestinian declaration (2009), 214
Kapeliouk, Amnon, 211
Kashmir, 173, 193
Kasrils, Ronnie, 171, 177–181, 213, 226
Kastel, 33
Kathrada, Ahmed, 237, 238
Katsav, Moshe, 74
Katz, Israel, 271
Kedleston, 1st Marquess Curzon of
    (George Curzon) 18
Keita, Salif, 213
Kellerman, Aharon, 234
Kerry, John, 181, 182, 241
Kfar Etzion, 95
Khalidi, Rashid, 21
Khalidi, Walid, 37
Khameini, Ali, 187
Khayatti, Mustafa, 184
Khoikhoi (formerly known as Hottentots),
    116
Khoisan, 86
Khomeini, Rubollah, 187
Khosravani, Nazanin, 203
kibbutz(im), 12, 13, 30, 31, 66, 95, 200
Kibbutz Elifaz, 65
King Faysal University (Saudi Arabia),
    186

Kiryat Arba settlement, 95
Kiryat Malachi, 73
Klein, Naomi, 238
Klein, Ron, 275
Knesset, 53, 54, 55, 56, 63, 66, 67, 69, 71,
   72, 78, 211, 232, 262, 265, 274, 278
Knesset Public Petitions Committee, 103
Knesset Research and Information Center,
   75
Kochav Hashahar, 99
Kohona, Palitha, 204
Kol, Adi, 103
Kosovo, 248
Kosygin, Alexei, 50
Kovel, Joel, 196
Kretzmer, David, 62
Kron Kalfa, Ofir and Danalee, 66
Kruger, Arnd, 206–207
*Kupai Cholim*, 77
Kurds, 157, 159, 170, 173, 212
Kurtzer, Dan, 99
Kuwait, 46, 254

Lahat, Shlomo, 212
Lancet Global Health website, 230
*Lancet* journal, 229–230
Land (Acquisition for Public Purposes)
   Ordinance (1943), 200
Land Authority, 66
Land Day (30 March 1976), 68, 248
Lanning, Hugh, 228
Laqueur, Walter, 41
Law of Return (1950), 56–58, 71, 176,
   226, 232, 256, 276
Lawrence, T. E., 16, 21
League of Nations, 16, 17, 20
Lebanon, 16, 30, 44, 45, 50, 53, 61, 70,
   108, 160, 166, 181, 182, 188, 206, 250
Lebanon War (2006), 71, 275
Legal Center for Arab Minority Rights in
   Israel, 209
Lehi (Freedom Fighters of Israel), 21, 26,
   31, 33–35, 38, 43
Leigh, Mike, 235
Lembede, Anton, 8
Lesotho, 106
Leveson inquiry (2012), 206
Levinger, Miriam, 95
Levinger, Moshe, 95–96

Levy, Edmund, 91
Levy, Gideon, 93, 210
Libya, 30, 46, 153, 163, 185, 191, 203,
   238, 254
Lie, Trygve, 40
Lieberman, Avigdor, 100
Lifshitz, Zalman, 63
Likud, 271
Likud Party, 66, 67, 103, 259
Lilienblum, Moshe Leib, 10
Lindsay, James G., 255–256
Litzman, Ya'acov, 78
Livni, Tzipi, 243
Lloyd George, David, 18, 19
Lod (formerly Lydda), 44, 54, 181
Lydon, John, 235

Maaleh HaHamisha (the Hill of the Five),
   31
Macau, 193
Macia, Mido, 232
Madonna, 235
Mahane Yehuda outdoor market
   (Jerusalem), 71
Maki (communist party), 45
Malan, D. F., 116
Malaysia, 204
Malik, Yarov A., 157
Mandela, Nelson, 126, 129, 130, 210, 213,
   225, 237, 238, 243
Mandela, Winnie Madikizela, 203
Mandelson, Peter, 197
Mapai (Labour party), 45
Marmari, Hanoch, 210
Marr, Wilhelm, 5
marriage, 61, 119, 134
Massad, Joseph, 202
Maswadeh, Wadeh, 205
*Mavi Marmara* (Turkish ship), 72,
   162–163, 176, 234
May Laws (1882), 6–7
Mazuz, Menachem, 265–266
Mbeki, Thabo, 180
media coverage: al-Aqsa Mosque fire, 192,
   195; anti-Semitism, 156, 175, 197;
   apartheid, 129, 181–182, 198, 199–200,
   201–202, 203; boycotts, 224, 235;
   condemnations on 60th anniversary,
   189, 192; Deir Yassin massacres, 34,

189; Electronic Intifada point of view, 181–182, 203, 207–208, 236; exceptional attention given to Israel, 153–154; existence of Israel, 49, 154–157, 181, 209; Hari's lies, 183–184; horror stories, 184–186, 206; humanitarian actions, 207–208; Kasrils comments, 177–181; major incidents in South Africa, 238; medical personnel, 228, 229–230; misquotes, 210–212; Plan Dalet, 189; police, 207; security barriers, 149; technology, 239; Zionism, 189, 199, 200–201

Meretz Party, 99, 202
Merkel, Angela, 243
Mexico, 149, 243
Michael, Dennis, 195
Middle East Project, 173
Middlesex University (London), 185, 237
Migron outpost, 93
Minhelet Ha'am (People's Administration), 39
Ministry of Defense, 98, 101
Ministry of Finance, 111
Ministry of Foreign Affairs, 107, 194
Ministry of Housing and Construction, 98, 264
Mitzpeh Cramim, 99, 101
Mixed Marriages Act (South Africa), 119
Mizrachim (Eastern Jews), 55, 65
Mizrachi schools, 79
MKs, 71, 72
Modern Orthodox movement, 5, 54
Mohamed, Ismail, 121
Moldova, 203
Monaco, 193
Monita, Shimon, 34
Montagu, Edwin, 11
Moor, Ahmed, 207
Morocco, 46, 50, 149, 240
Morris, Benny, 29, 37, 38
Morsi, Mohammen, 188
moshav(im), 12, 31
Mossad, 237
Mossawa Center, 67
Motlana, Nthato, 118–119
Mount Scopus, 245
Moyne, 1st Baron (Walter Guiness Moyne), 26

Moyne, Walter Guiness. *See* Moyne, 1st Baron
Mozambique, 222
Mughrabi Bridge, 267
Munich Olympic Games (1972), 206–207
Munir, Sully, 227
Muslim Judicial Council, 208
Muslims, 2–3, 54, 55, 58, 61
Muslim Youth Movement, 192
Myanmar, 203, 238

Nabulsi, Mohammed, 111
*Nakba* (catastrophe) (1948), 30, 43, 69, 248
Nashashibi family, 20
Nasrallah, Hassan, 188
Nasser, Gamal Abdel, 49–50, 50, 51
Nats (Nationalist Party members, South Africa), 116, 119, 122, 126, 129, 130
Nazareth, 72
Nazis, 13, 23, 24–25, 56, 116, 122, 189, 231
Ndebele, 117
Negev, 86, 87
Netanyahu, Benyamin, 70, 74, 91, 93, 101, 112, 189, 193, 242, 271, 275, 276
Netherlands, 116, 198
Neturei Karta, 60, 158
New Historians, 37
*New Statesman*, 211
*New York Times*, 35, 116, 161, 194
New Zealand, 198
Ngwala, Sibusiso, 155
Nigeria, 170
Nokdim settlement, 100
Non-Aligned Movement, 159, 167
North Korea, 149, 238
Norway, 231
Norwegian Association of NGOs for Palestine, 231
Novak, Robert D., 201

Obama, Barack, 43, 208
Occupied Palestinian Territories, 168, 170
Offra settlement, 107
OIC. *See* Organisation of the Islamic Conference
O'Keefe, Ken, 237
Olim (new immigrant Jews), 55

Olmert, Ehud, 191
Oman, 149
Operation Defensive Shield (2002), 213
Operation Nachshon, 33
Or, Theodor, 68
Oren, Michael, 52, 62
Organisation of Islamic Cooperation, 167, 195
Organisation of the Islamic Conference (OIC), 163, 167, 195, 223
Orthodox Judaism, 55, 56, 59, 61
Osborne, George, 206
Oslo Accords (1993), 57, 68, 90, 91, 105, 107, 246, 273, 274
Ottoman Empire, 15–16, 20, 21, 54, 61, 78, 92
*Overcoming Zionism* (Kovel), 196

Pahad, Aziz, 159–160
Pakistan, 63, 149, 173, 193, 198, 240, 248, 250
Pale of Settlement, 5, 6
Palestine: British mandate in, 15–19, 20, 21–26, 32, 39, 40, 53, 54, 78, 92; establishment of Jewish homeland in, 9, 10, 10–14, 24; history of, 15; as independent state, 155; land acquisition in, 62–63; nationalist beliefs, 20; partition recommended for, 26–27, 283–284
*Palestine: Peace Not Apartheid* (Carter, 2006), 160–162
Palestine Authority, 108, 174, 188, 206
Palestine Liberation Organization (PLO), 48, 68, 161, 188, 246, 254, 256
*Palestine Post* (later *Jerusalem Post*), 36
Palestine Solidarity Campaign (PSC), 224, 228, 232, 238
Palestine Solidarity Committee, 192
Palestinian Arabs: attitude towards Jews in Palestine, 21–22, 22–24, 31; driven from their homes and land, 36–38, 38–39; effect of British Palestinian Mandate on, 19, 20, 21–22, 22–26; effect of Egyptian interventions, 49–52; effect of Plan Dalet, 32–33, 36, 37; intensification of war, 35–38, 39, 43–45, 47–48; Israeli occupation of

land in the West Bank (*see under* West Bank); loss of land, 63–64; massacre at Deir Yassin, 33–35, 36; reaction to Jewish Declaration of Independence, 40–41; refugees, 46–48, 50; response to partition, 29–30; revival of identity/national movement, 48; start of civil war with the Jews, 29–32; violence by and against, 20, 22, 23, 24
Palestinian Authority, 69, 93, 105, 143, 169, 181, 186, 195, 196, 199, 210, 245
Palestinian Authority Ministry of Information, 140
Palestinian Bureau of Statistics, 143
Palestinian Campaign for the Academic and Cultural Boycott of Israel (PAC-BI), 224
Palestinian National Covenant (1964), 161
Palestinian State, 245–248
Palestinian Students Campaign, 236
Palmach, 45
Pan-Africanist Congress (PAN), 130, 145
Paraguay, 243
Paris Peace Conference (1919), 21–22
partition, 257; agreement with, 206; Arab protests against, 29–32; birth of State of Israel, 39–43; effect of Plan Dalet, 32–39; nation-building, 45–46; problem of refugees, 46–48; UN commitment to, 26–27; war and delineation of borders, 43–45, 48–52
Peduel settlement, 110
Peel, 1st Earl (William Peel), 23
Peel, William. *See* Peel, 1st Earl
Peel Commission (1937), 23, 31
Peled-Elhanan, Nurit, 196
PEPSI, 206
Peres, Shimon, 70, 89, 211
Peretez, Eliraz, 275
Peru, 243
*Pesach* (Passover), 70, 95
PFLP. *See* Popular Front for the Liberation of Palestine
Philippines, 207
Pilger, John, 197
Pillay, Navanethem, 185
Pinsker, Leon, 7
Plan Dalet (*Tochnit Dalet*), 32–39, 189, 190, 197

Planners for Building Rights (Bimkom), 87
PLO. *See* Palestine Liberation
  Organization
Poland, 5, 6
Polasario, 149
Pollak, Jonathan, 196
Pollard, Jonathan, 265
Popular Front for the Liberation of
  Palestine (PFLP), 48
Population Registration Act (South
  Africa), 119, 120
'Porgy and Bess' opera, 217
Pounder, Derek, 213–214
Powell, Colin, 158
PressTV (Iran), 184
Primary Health Care (Palestine Authority),
  206
Prime Minister's Office, 98
Protocols of Zion, 158, 175
PSC. *See* Palestine Solidarity Campaign
Public and Commercial Services Union
  (UK), 228
Purim festival, 186

Qatar, 163
Qleibo, Ali, 260
Quartet (European Union, United States,
  United Nations, Russia), 145, 266
Qumram, 209
Qumsiyeh, Mazim, 211

Ra'anam, Mordechai, 34
rabbis, 34, 39, 56, 60, 70, 90
Rabin, Yitzhak, 50, 68, 89, 275
Radio Islam, 175
Radio Kol Israel, 211
Rafiqui, Asim, 150
Ramallah, 100, 101, 105, 111, 112, 140
Ramlawi, As'ad, 206
Ramle, 44, 54
*Rand Daily Mail*, 178
Reagan, Ronald, 277
Reform Judaism, 5, 56, 61
refugees: Palestinian, 248–249, 250–256;
  solving, 252–253; treatment of, 254;
  UN resolution 194 (1949), 251, 256;
  UNRWA's role, 254–256; worldwide,
  249–250
religion, 61–62

Retief, Piet, 117
Reuters, 104
Reynolds, John, 198
Rhodesia, 222
Rich, Adrienne, 196
right of return. *See* Law of Return (1950)
Rivlin, Reuven, 66, 67, 72
*Roadmap to Apartheid* (film, 2012), 203
Robinson, Mary, 158, 159, 163
Rohan, Dennis Michael, 194
Roma, 159
Roman Catholics, 3
Roman Empire, 2
Romania, 243, 249
Rome Statute (1998), 198
Romney, Mitt, 261
Rose, Hilary, 224
Rose, Jacqueline, 195–196
Rose, Steven, 224
Rothschild, Nathaniel, 197
Rothschild, 2nd Baron (Walter
  Rothschild), 19
Rothschild, Walter. *See* Rothschild, 2nd
  Baron
Russell, Bertrand, 178
Russell Tribunal (2011), 72, 171, 198
Russia, 5–9, 11, 18, 170, 203, 238, 245,
  266
Rwanda, 170

Sabeel, 214–216, 218
Sabra (Israel-born Jews), 55
Sadat, Anwar, 278
Safed, 54, 181
Sahel, 248
Salah, Khayed, 96
Salamah, Salem, 206
Salim (refugee), 248–249
Samia (refugee), 248
Samuel, Herbert, 19
San Bushmen, 116
Saraj, Iyad, 248
Sarid, Yossi, 202
Sasson, Talia, 98–99
Sasson Report (2005), 98–100, 242
Satmar sect, 60
Saudi Arabia, 44, 58, 149, 163, 194, 203,
  205, 254
Schjedt, Thea, 231

Schlomka, Fred, 202
Schoeman, Ben, 116
Scotland, 248
Scott, C. P., 18
Seck, Fod, 204
secular Judaism, 55
Senegal, 163
Sephardi, 2, 3, 34, 46, 54, 74
Sephardic Shas Party, 60, 74
September 11 (2001), 159, 224, 237
Serbia, 203
settlements. *See under* West Bank
Sha'are Hagai (formerly Bab-al-Wad), 31
Shain, Milton, 156–157
Shalit, Gilad, 170–171, 208
Shalit, Tilad, 190
Shalom-Wahat as-Salam (Oasis of Peace) village, 79
Shamir, Yitzhak, 211
Shapira, Joseph, 112
Sharett, Moshe, 46
Sharm el-Sheikh, 149
Sharon, Ariel, 91, 98–99, 211–212, 270, 273, 275, 278
Sharpeville massacre (1960), 130, 192
Sheva, Arutz, 70
Shihab-Eddam, Fathi, 188
Shikaki, Khalil, 251
Shimoni, Gideon, 151
Shinali River Women's Labour Camp, 203
Shin Bet, 58, 97
Shindler, Colin, 47
Shukairy, Ahmed, 41
Sikkuy Report (2008), 81
Silver, Eric, 50
Simeon Bar Kochba revolt (132–135 CE), 2
Simhon, Shalom, 104
Sinai, 49, 51, 167
Singapore, 193
Sittah, Ghassan Abu, 230
Six-Day War (1967), 49–52, 95, 157, 197, 245
Smuts, Jan Christian, 115–116
Sobukwe, Robert Mangaliso, 8, 126, 129, 130, 278
Socialist Youth League, 231
Somalia, 203, 238

South Africa, 106, 234; analogies to/ understanding of Israel, 155; boycotts, 221–223; British interests in, 116–117, 118; communist suppression in, 122–123; concentration camps in, 118; discovery of diamonds/gold in, 118; District Six (Cape Town), 121; Durban Forum and, 157, 159–160; Dutch in, 115–118; education in, 126–127; effect of Nationalist election victory (1948), 115, 116, 118–119; employment/social welfare in, 127–129; everyday life in, 123–128; Great Trek, 117; hatred/ discrimination in, 238; health/poverty in, 125–126; HSRC in, 173–174; laws/ regulations, 119–120; pass system in, 124–126; population registration in, 120; prisons in, 124; Race Classification Boards in, 120; relationship with indigenous peoples, 116–118; residency areas in, 120–122; resistance, violence, torture in, 129–131; slavery in, 116, 117; sports facilities in, 128. *See also* apartheid; Israel–South Africa comparisons
South African Communist Party, 192
South Korea, 149
Soviet Union, 40, 48, 49, 56, 122, 131, 157, 167
Spain, 170, 223, 248
Spanish Inquisition, 4
Sparks, Allister, 210–211
Special Committee to Investigate Israeli Practices affecting the Human Rights of the Palestinian People and Other Arabs of the Occupied Territories, 167
Sri Lanka, 203, 204, 205, 243, 248
*Star* newspaper (Johannesburg), 131
Staub, Ervin, 218, 219
Steenkamp, Anna, 117
Steinitz, Yuval, 112
Stern, Abraham, 21
Stern Gang or Group, 21, 190
Storrs, Ronald, 16
Straits of Tiran, 49–50
Strategic and Intelligence Affairs Ministry, 243
Strydom, Hans, 116
Sudan, 170, 203, 212, 238, 248

Suez Canal, 49, 51
suicide bombings, 58, 108, 169, 180, 208, 234, 260
Summerfield, Derek, 228–229
*Sunday Times* (London), 164
*Sunday Times* (South Africa), 155
Suppression of Communism Act, 119, 122–123
Supreme Court, 57, 65, 70, 74, 83, 100, 101, 103, 105, 107
Susser, Asher, 162
Swaziland, 123
Sweden, 234
*Sydsvenskan* newspaper, 184
Sykes, Mark, 15
Syria, 16, 30, 44, 45, 49, 50, 53, 70, 108, 153, 161, 173, 181, 203, 207, 222, 238, 248, 250, 254

Tacitus, 2
Tafesh, Haza and Nibal, 65
Taha (author), 141
Tajikistan, 203
Tambo, Oliver, 129
Tamnu-Shata, Pnina, 73
Tehran meeting (2001), 157–158
Tel Aviv, 13, 29, 31, 39, 181, 199, 202, 271
Tel Aviv–Jerusalem road, 31, 33, 45
Tel Aviv Museum of Art, 39, 233
Tel Aviv Opera House, 217
Tel Aviv University, 55, 225
Terrorism Act (South Africa), 129
Teva (drugs company), 240
Thatcher, Margaret, 144
Thompson, Emma, 235
Tiberias, 54
Tibet, 170, 173, 193, 238, 248
Tibi, Ahmed, 78
Tilley, Virginia, 171, 174, 186–187, 188–189
Tolouee, Roya, 203
Tonge, Baroness (Jenny Tonge), 185
Tonge, Jenny. *See* Tonge, Baroness
Torah, 2, 59
Trade Union Council (TUC) (UK), 227–228
Trading with the Enemy Act (UK, 1939), 63, 71

Transjordan, 16, 17
Truman, Harry, 27, 32, 206
Tunisia, 50, 153, 205
Turkey, 170, 173, 235, 238, 248
Turkmenistan, 203
Tutu, Desmond, 216–218, 220, 226, 232, 233
Twain, Mark, 62
two states goal: abandonment of discrimination against Arabs, 276; achieving, 269, 279; agreement concerning Jerusalem, 274; emotional dilemmas, 275; fostering of nationhood among Arabs, 276–277; friendship/ contact encourage, 277; Israel as Jewish/democratic state, 276; joint decision making, 277; Law of Return to be negotiated, 276; leadership as crucial, 275; obstacles to, 273–275; offensive options, 271; Palestinian rejection of, 269–270; peace/acceptance in Middle East as a whole, 278; refugee problem, 274; right wing rejection of, 270–272; settler problem, 273, 275, 279; South African experience as guide, 278; UN Resolution on, 269; US loans/ guarantees, 277; world help needed, 277
Tzippori, 2

Uganda, 163
Ukraine, 6, 203, 249
Ulpana outpost, 100–101
ultra-Orthodox Judaism, 54, 55, 56, 59, 60, 61, 93
Um al-Kheir Bedouin village (West Bank), 113
Umar, Abdul Aziz, 208
UN Alliance of Civilisations, 168
UN Annual Day of Solidarity with the Palestinian People, 167
UN Anti-Racism Conference (Durban, 2001), 224
UN Apartheid Convention, 172
UN Committee on the Elimination of Racial Discrimination, 103
UN Committee on the Exercise of the Inalienable Rights of the Palestinian People, 167

UN Committee on the Rights of the Child, 205
UN Conciliation Commission for Palestine (1949), 64
UN Development Programme, 173
UNESCO, 93, 236
UN General Assembly, 163, 166, 167, 197, 198, 245
UN High Commissioner for Human Rights, 158, 163, 185
UN High Commissioner for Refugees (UNHCR), 250, 254, 255
UN Human Rights Commission, 169
UN Human Rights Council, 162–165, 167, 169–171, 175, 185
UNICEF, 205
UN International Convention on the Suppression and Punishment of the Crime of Apartheid, 197–198
UN International Day of Solidarity with the Palestinian People (1997), 210
United Arab Emirates, 149, 240
United Arab List-Ta'al, 78
United Kingdom, 198
United Nations, 17, 26, 29, 32, 40, 41, 43, 47, 145, 146, 157, 191, 202, 222, 266
United States, 8, 19, 25, 32, 40, 50, 131, 144, 146, 149, 156, 159, 163, 166, 188, 191, 198, 203, 245, 250, 267, 277
Universal Declaration of Human Rights, 193
University of Cape Town, 126, 196
University of Johannesburg, 217
University of the Witwatersrand, 126
UN Office for the Coordination of Humanitarian Affairs, 167
UN Relief and Works Agency (UNRWA) for Palestine, 163, 167, 250, 254–256, 274
UN Resolution 181 (1947), 273
UN Resolution 194 (1948), 176, 251, 256
UN Resolution 242 (1967), 51–52
UN Resolution 3379 (1975), 168
UNSCOP. *See* UN Special Committee on Palestine
Un Security Council, 51, 166, 191, 194
UN Special Committee on Palestine (UNSCOP) (1947), 26–27, 32, 283–284

UN Special Committee to Investigate Israeli Practices in the Occupied Territories (1948), 204
UN World Conference Against Racism, Racial Discrimination, Zenophobia and Related Intolerance (Durban, 2001), 157–160
Upper Galilee, 44
Upper Nazareth, 67
US Campaign to End the Israeli Occupation, 193
US Congress Subcommittee on Intelligence Policy, 186
US-initiated Road Map (2003), 90
US National Intelligence Council, 208
Ussarov, governor of Bessarabia, 7
US State Department, 97; human rights report (2010), 101–102
U Thant, 49

Verwoerd, Hendrik, 178–179, 213
Voortrekker Monument, Pretoria, 117

Wafa (Palestinian news agancy), 186
Walker, Alice, 176
*Wall Street Journal*, 62
War of Independence (1948), 30–39, 43–45, 54, 63, 90, 166, 192, 245
War on Want, 227
*Washington Post*, 165, 208
Weinberg, Yehudah, 266
Weissglass, Dov, 270, 273
Weizmann, Chaim, 17, 18, 21, 25, 32
West Bank: Arab settlement of, 45; border with, 53; cars/roads in, 106; Carter's comments on, 161; citizenship in, 70; community matters, 69; cost of occupation, 105–108; different types of settlements, 91; discrimination in, 55, 57, 226; as disputed territory, 91; economic exploitation in, 104, 105; first Israeli settlement in, 95; Goldstone's report on, 164; government deceit/ duplicity concerning, 110–111, 112–113; government spending on, 94; growth of Jewish settlements in, 246; heartlessness/bureaucratic inflexibility concerning, 89, 113; human rights in, 89, 101–102, 154; infant mortality, 109,

110; influence of settlers, 89–90; King
Abdullah's designs upon, 41; lack of
regard for rights/humanity of
Palestinians, 89; land seizure, 92–93,
110–111; law in, 102–104; legal
justification for settlements, 91;
marriage in, 61; messianic outlook in,
90; not apartheid, 151; numbers of
settlers, 90; occupation based on
idealistic beliefs, 89, 90; Palestinian
state envisaged in, 90, 91; reasons/
motivations for continued occupation,
95; religion in, 61; residency permits,
108; Road 443 problems, 111–112;
Sasson report on, 98–100; secret
database on settlements, 100; securing/
maintaining settlements, 93–94;
security issues, 92, 93, 94, 99, 102, 104,
106, 108; seized by Israelis, 51, 52, 53;
settlement as damaging to Israel, 272;
settlement of, 100–101, 160;
settlements as target for boycots,
240–244; split into three areas, 90; state
support for, 98–101; violence/
harassment in, 95–97; visited by
Women of Color Feminists, 175–176;
water/sewage in, 106–108
Western European and Others Group, 167
Western Sahara, 149
West Jerusalem, 71, 245
Whitley, Andrew, 256
Wilson, Woodrow, 19
Witwatersrand university. *See* University
of the Witwatersrand
WMA. *See* World Medical Association
Woodhead, John, 23
Woodhead Commission (1938), 23
World Alliance of Reformed Churches,
214
World Bank, 105, 107
World Council of Churches, 158
World Medical Association (WMA), 229
World War I, 6, 15–16, 16, 19
World War II, 21, 46, 115, 249
World Zionist Organisation, 10, 18, 21, 98,
112

Xhosa, 117

Ya'alon, Moshe, 101
Yadin, Yigael, 32
Yanqiong, Fan, 203
Yemen, 46, 50, 149, 203, 238, 250
Yesha, 97
Yesh Atid Party, 103
yeshiva (religious school), 59
Yiddish, 14
Yishai, Eli, 60, 74, 263
Yishuv, 23, 32, 36
Yisrael Beiteinu Party, 60, 69
Yitzhar West Bank settlement, 71
Yosef, Ovadia, 60
Yugoslavia, 249

Zahalka, Jamal, 59
Zertal, Idith, 95
Zilin, Ding, 203
Zimbabwe, 149, 203, 235, 238
Zionism, 33, 276; Arab reaction to
partition, 30; British politics and
attitudes, 15–19, 20, 21–26; Carter's
comments on, 161; effect of Russian
pogroms, 5–9; effect of war and
Holocaust, 24–25; equated with
Nazism, 189; equated with racism, 157,
167; evolving intelligentsia, 9–10;
foundation stone of, 10; growth of,
12–15, 54; *Hatikvah* as official anthem,
39; ideas of freedom and nationalism,
4–5; land acquisition, 62; language, 14;
linked to apartheid, 188; as mainly
secular, 90; origins and development,
1–5; people and land, 12–14; support
for, 11–12; terminology coined, 10; UN
resolution on partition, 26–27
Zionist Congress, 10, 25
Zionist Federation, 11, 19, 159
*Zionist Israel and Apartheid South Africa*
(Badran), 200–201
Zoabi, Hanin, 72
Zulu, 117
Zvi, Ramit, 110

# About the Author

**Benjamin Pogrund** was born in Cape Town, South Africa, and holds four degrees from the universities of Cape Town and the Witwatersrand. As a student leader at the University of Cape Town, he fought against the government's imposition of apartheid on the university. He was on the Cape and Transvaal provincial committees of the Liberal Party in promoting nonracism.

He was with the *Rand Daily Mail* newspaper in Johannesburg for twenty-six years and pioneered the reporting in the daily press of black politics and black existence under apartheid. He was jailed for refusing to disclose the source of information of a report. He was later prosecuted over a period of four years for exposing abusive conditions in prisons of blacks and political prisoners. He was also prosecuted for possession of 'banned' newspapers. He was denied a passport for more than five years. He was also the Southern African correspondent for the *Sunday Times* (London), the *Boston Globe* and wrote for the *Economist* and the *New Republic*.

He was serving as deputy editor of the *Rand Daily Mail* when it was shut down in 1985 because of its opposition to apartheid. As a result, he emigrated to Britain and was diplomatic editor of *Today* and then chief foreign subeditor of the *Independent*. He lectured on international news in the Graduate School of Journalism at City University, London. He broadcast frequently for BBC TV and radio, ITV and Sky TV during the closing years of apartheid. After a year in Boston as editor of the *WorldPaper*, he emigrated to Israel in 1997 to found the Yakar Center for Social Concern in Jerusalem: it was devoted to dialogue between Jews and Jews, Jews and Muslims, Jews and Christians and Israelis and Palestinians. He was director for twelve years.

He is the author of three books: *How Can Man Die Better: Sobukwe and Apartheid*; *Nelson Mandela*; and *War of Words: Memoir of a South African*

*Journalist.* He is coeditor of *Shared Histories: A Palestinian-Israeli Dialogue* and *Shared Narratives: A Palestinian-Israeli Dialogue* and is on the editorial board of the *Palestine-Israel Journal.* He has written for the *Guardian* (London); *Facta* (Tokyo); *Haaretz* (Tel Aviv); the *Star*, *Cape Times* and *Daily Dispatch* in South Africa, and many others, and he has lectured about the Israeli-Palestinian conflict in the United States, Britain, South Africa, Canada, Jordan, the Netherlands, Poland, Finland and Israel.

His work during the apartheid era in preserving documents of opposition and underground movements has been acknowledged by the US Center for Research Libraries in naming the 'Benjamin Pogrund Collection of Southern African Materials'.

He was an exchange journalist with the *Boston Globe* and an Honorary Nieman Fellow at Harvard University. He is the recipient of the UK United Nations Association's Media Peace Prize, the Global Citizens Circle Award for Justice and Reconciliation and Tufts University's Dr Jean Meyer Global Citizenship Award. In 2007 he was an INSPIRE Fellow at the Institute for Global Leadership at Tufts University. In 2010 and again in 2011 he was visiting fellow at the Kaplan Centre for Jewish Studies and Research at the University of Cape Town. In 2013 he was given a Lifetime Achievement Award by the Next Century Foundation's International Council for Press and Broadcasting (London). In August 2013 the South African Jewish Board of Deputies gave him its Human Rights Award.

He and his wife, Anne Sassoon, an artist, live in Katamon, Jerusalem.

www.ingramcontent.com/pod-product-compliance
Lightning Source LLC
Chambersburg PA
CBHW030637270326

41929CB00007B/106